Tree of Rivers

The Story of the Amazon

JOHN HEMMING

Tree of Rivers

The Story of the Amazon

with 70 illustrations, 20 in color

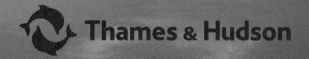

Thames & Hudson

pp. 2–3 *The Amazon, near the Peruvian-Brazilian frontier, some 3,000 kilometres (1,860 miles) from its mouth.*

pp. 4–5 *Pacajá river, Xingu.*

Maps by Martin Lubikowski, ML Design, London

First published in 2008 in hardcover in the United States of America by Thames & Hudson Inc., 500 Fifth Avenue, New York, New York 10110

thamesandhudsonusa.com

First paperback edition 2009

Library of Congress Catalog Card Number 2007906973

ISBN 978-0-500-28820-7

Printed and bound in Slovenia

Contents

MAR   2014

At its mouth, the mighty Amazon river fragments into a labyrinth of islands and channels.

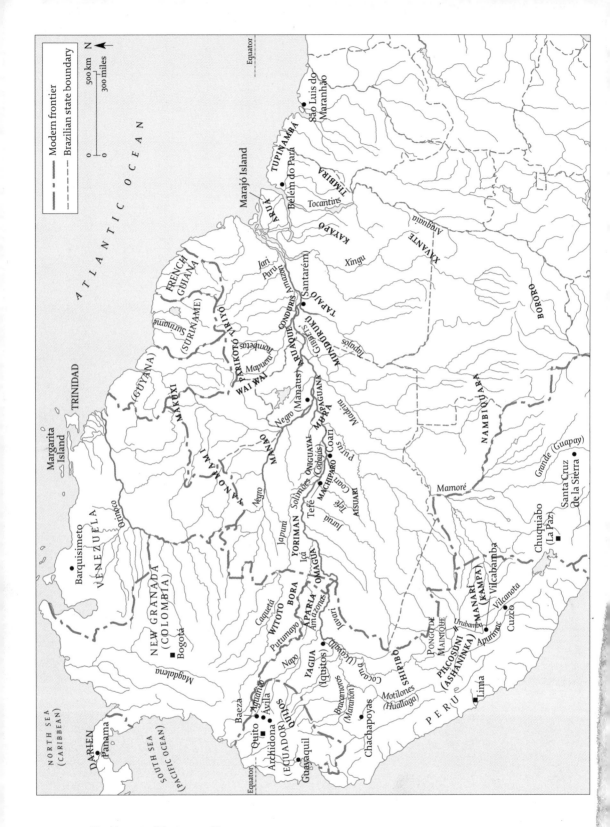

First descents of the Amazon River

Right A black-water river in Venezuelan Amazonia, where the lack of sediment from ancient rocks and the tannin from decaying vegetation make waters as black as coffee. Forests are at their most exuberant on river banks, because of the sun and water.

Left Palm trees are wonderfully useful to man, from the earliest foragers to present-day riverbankers. Graceful *Buriti* palms (*Mauritia flexuosa*) soar to 30 metres (100 feet), and supply nutritious red fruits, fronds for roofing, fibres for baskets and hammocks, and trunks for beams.

Above left This caterpillar of a hawk moth (*Pseudosphinx tetrio*) is an example of 'Batesian mimicry', named after the nineteenth-century naturalist Henry Walter Bates. A predator thinks that such a gaudily coloured insect must be poisonous, so this edible caterpillar's only defence is to mimic such ostentation.

Above right Most creatures in a tropical forest are high in the canopy, or nocturnal, or brilliantly camouflaged, like this long-horned grasshopper (*Tettigoniidae* family) mimicking a leaf and twig.

Opposite A macaw-lick, or *collpa*, such as this one near Manú National Park, Peru, is one of the most thrilling sights of the western Amazon. Every morning in certain months pairs of macaws and smaller parrots crowd onto a riverbank bluff in a blaze of colour to peck at the earth. Scientists are not agreed on why the birds do this, but it occurs when they have nestlings.

Right Amazonia has more species of monkey than any other region in the world – almost a hundred, mostly endemic. Little grey squirrel monkeys (*Saimiri sciureus*) can be playful or mischievous: they pelt or urinate on intruders they dislike.

Opposite below Caymans (*Jacaré*) once teemed on Amazonian lakes and streams, but are easily shot, particularly at night. Because their skins are saleable, caymans are now becoming endangered.

Below Most of Amazonia's hundreds of species of snake are harmless to man, but not these deadly rattlesnakes (*Crotalus terrificus*). They hunt by night, attracted by the warmth of their prey.

Below White-lipped peccary (*Tayassu pecari*) move in large packs, scouring the forest floor for nuts and roots. If threatened, these powerful animals attack fearlessly and are one of the few animals that can hurt humans.

Right The largest indigenous nation, the Yanomami, live in forested hills between Brazil and Venezuela. Here a mother decorates herself with red annatto dye, feathers gummed to her hairline, and palm-spine 'feline whiskers'.

Below Yanomami archers use immensely powerful bows and two-metre-long (6½-foot) arrows, often tipped with curare poison and with different points for different types of game. They carry chewing tobacco in a wad in their lower lips.

Below Kayapó women of central Brazil dye their skin with black genipapo dye, for decoration and as protection against insects, and they ritually shave their own and their children's frontal hair.

CHAPTER ONE

Arrival of Strangers

The ancient certainties, the relative tranquillity and the isolation of the Amazon's indigenous peoples were shattered forever in the year 1500. Strange craft appeared at the mouth of the great river and sailed up it for a few days. These were the ships of the Spaniard Vicente Yáñez Pinzón. This experienced seaman had been the owner and captain of Columbus's caravel *La Niña* in 1492. Now, eight years later, he crossed the Atlantic again and sailed along the coast of Brazil. When he saw fresh and muddy water at the mouth of a huge river, he thought it might be the Ganges in India. He sailed up for a short distance and met natives, 'many painted people who flocked to the ships with as much friendship as if they had conversed with us all their lives'. But he also had a skirmish and seized thirty-six men 'bigger than large Germans' to take home as slaves. This was an ominous portent of misery in store for the native peoples.

Yáñez Pinzón's ships were only several times larger than the dugout canoes of the indigenous people – whom the Spaniards thought to be Indians from India. What must have surprised the few natives who saw the ships was their being covered by decks, having men living on board, with many ropes thicker than the Indians' own cord, and above all their propulsion by canvas sails. In the later mythology of another tribe, the arrival of the first white men in a flotilla of sailing boats was depicted as a swarm of flying ants. Even more curious was the way in which the sailors covered their bodies in a material – cloth. There was ugly hair growing on their faces, and this was sometimes of freakish colours other than black. (Native South Americans have practically no body hair, and most pluck any that does appear on their skins; and their hair is invariably black.)

The most sensational impact was caused by the strangers' metal tools. When the Portuguese landed further south in Brazil a few months after Yáñez Pinzón, they made a cross to celebrate the first mass in this new land. One of them,

Pero Vaz de Caminha, wrote that 'many of them came there to be with the carpenters. I believe that they did this more to see the iron tools with which these were making it, than to see the cross itself.... For they have nothing made of metal. They cut their wood and boards with wedge-shaped stones fixed into pieces of wood and firmly bound between two sticks.' He was absolutely right. This was the intense thrill of people first witnessing the cutting-power of metal tools. It was a technological miracle in a forested world where men's most wearisome task was felling trees to create garden clearings. For the next five centuries, from 1500 to the present day, metal blades – from knives and machetes to axes and saws – have been the currency of contact with every isolated tribe. Such tools are an irresistible lure. Again and again, after contact has been made, it is learned that the indigenous people had seen blades and were desperate to acquire them, either by raiding or coming to terms with whites.

The next adventurer to see the Amazon may have been the Florentine Amerigo Vespucci. As the agent in Seville of the Medici princes, Vespucci in 1499 joined some Spaniards to obtain a royal licence to cross the Atlantic. But when the squadron reached South America it divided and the Italian took two caravels in a southerly direction. He also investigated the mouth of a great muddy river, but its forested banks prevented a landing. Vespucci then sailed southeastwards before being driven back by adverse currents. It is impossible to tell how far south he sailed since Vespucci was a hopeless surveyor: the coordinates he gave for the Atlantic coast of Brazil would have located it far out in the Pacific. His fame stems from a voyage three years later, when he was a passenger on a Portuguese flotilla. He spent three weeks among Brazilian Indians and sent his Medici master an enthusiastic but rather inaccurate account of the wonders he had seen. Most such reports were kept secret by European rulers, but Vespucci's letter was published, rapidly translated into several languages, and became an instant bestseller by the standards of its day. He was the first to write that this was a 'new world' rather than a mere island. Such was the power of the new printing press that a map-maker in Lorraine wrote a version of his first name 'America' on a map showing the 'Mundus Novus' of the new discoveries. The name stuck. So two continents are named after an undistinguished sailor, an inaccurate navigator, and a boastful chronicler. Amerigo Vespucci must be the patron saint of all travel-writers.

For the next forty years, life in Amazonia continued as usual. Europeans traded sporadically along the Atlantic coast of Brazil, largely for logs of the brazil-wood tree (*Caesalpinia echinata*) that contained an attractive though unstable red dye – and that gave its name to the new country. These seamen also brought back parrots and other exotica, and a few slaves. But this 'new world' and its primitive peoples seemed to have no really valuable commodities like precious metals, pearls and jewels, textiles, ivory or spices.

Although the *written* history of Amazonia started in 1500, with Yáñez Pinzón's laconic report, human beings had been flourishing there for thousands of years. We will leave the theories and fierce debates about when man first reached the great river and how early humans developed agriculture, ceramics and sophisticated chiefdoms until a later chapter, when we shall see how modern archaeologists teased the evidence from this (for them) difficult terrain.

By our sixteenth century, there was a kaleidoscope of tribes spread over the Amazon basin. Their villages extended for considerable distances along the banks of the large rivers. But inland, in the drier upland forests (*terra firme*), most lived far from one another, either in temporary villages or totally nomadically as foragers. If such a settlement grew too large it simply fragmented, with part of the tribe migrating to settle in a new site. This was easy for self-sufficient hunter-gatherers who knew every clearing and stream. Most tribes lived in isolation, but some traded with neighbours. There were occasional inter-tribal wars, either to pursue vendettas or to get desirable commodities such as women or children. Some indigenous people were naturally bellicose, with warlike traditions and young warriors who gloried in fighting and collecting trophy heads. An early European exclaimed that 'there are so many of them and the land is so great and they are increasing so much that if they were not continuously at war ... it could not contain them'.

All indigenous peoples adored hunting and fishing. Men were immensely skilled in finding, stalking and killing all types of game, from peccary and tapirs, to birds and monkeys, to alligators and snakes. They killed with bows and arrows, and (generally north of the Amazon river) also with blow-guns and darts tipped with curare poison. The twentieth-century French anthropologist Pierre Clastres was thrilled by the beauty of a hunt. He wrote that a man's weapon was the symbol of his masculinity, and he was judged by his ability and luck. 'The Indians are so agile, so skilled, their gestures so precise and efficient – this was total mastery of the body.' For them, 'hunting is always an adventure, sometimes a risky one, but constantly inspiring.... Tracking animals in the forest, proving that you are more clever than they are, approaching within arrow's range without revealing your presence, hearing the hum of the arrow in the air and then the dull thud as it strikes an animal – all these things are joys that have been experienced countless times, and yet they remain as fresh and exciting as they were on the first hunt. The [Indians] do not grow weary of hunting. Nothing else is asked of them, and they love it more than anything else.' Women, the fertile sex, tended vegetable gardens or gathered edible grubs and insects. They cooked, and of course cared for children. Men, when not hunting, fishing or clearing forests, busied themselves making artefacts and ornaments, but their greatest care went into weapons for hunting, fishing or fighting.

Language is a sure guide to movements of peoples. There are a dozen linguistic 'trunks' among Amazon Indians. When Europeans landed on the Atlantic coasts, the first language they encountered was Tupi (or Tupi-Guarani). This was spoken in a gigantic arc from the plains of Paraguay in the south, along the entire Atlantic seaboard of Brazil, and for thousands of kilometres up the Amazon river and its major tributaries. It survives at either end of this arc: as the second national language of Paraguay, among some tribes in southern Brazil, and by Tupi tribes far up the Amazon's great southern tributaries in Brazil and Peru. Jesuit missionaries adopted Tupi-Guarani as their *lingua geral* ('general language') throughout Brazil.

The heart of Brazil, south of the main river, was home to Je-speaking tribes, notably groups known collectively as Kayapó, Xavante (pronounced Shav-ant-eh), and Timbira. These Je are less aquatic than the Tupi-speakers, so they are found in another huge arc of forests, grassy plains and scrublands of the central Brazilian plateau. Je warriors keep fit by competing in relay races in which they carry immensely heavy logs on their shoulders. They can move so fast that they outrun savannah game, and their favourite weapon is a club. Other Je-related speakers lived outside the Amazon, in the hinterland of northeast Brazil and in the far south.

On the islands of the Caribbean Sea there was ferocious rivalry between Carib- and Arawak-speaking tribes. Arawak (or Aruak) was the most widely spoken of all native South American languages, extending all around the Caribbean from Florida to Central America and the Amazon basin. When Europeans arrived, Arawak peoples were migrating into the Amazon from the northwest, down the great rivers that rise in Colombia; but they were also established along the coast of the Guianas, inland in Roraima, and around the mouth of the Amazon. Highly mobile in their canoes, some settled far up southern tributaries Xingu, Juruá, Purus and Ucayali. Other Arawak pressed on to the southernmost rivers of the Amazon basin. Some settled on the Madre de Dios river system in southern Peru, others on the great plains near the Grande in what is now Bolivia, and a few beyond the Amazon on the upper Paraguay.

Carib-speakers also entered the region from the north. They are now almost extinct on the islands of the sea named after them, but there are populous Carib tribes throughout the Guianas. Notable among these are the Makuxi of Guyana and northernmost Brazil and the Tirió in Suriname and Brazil. Carib-speaking peoples are also found on the Amazon's southern tributaries, far up the Xingu and Tapajós.

Other linguistic families include the Tukanoan, in forests between Brazil and Colombia, and Panoan south of them between Brazil and Peru. But many tribes speak linguistically isolated tongues that do not seem to relate to any major language. The Yanomami (between Venezuela and Brazil), Mura at the mouth of the Madeira, Nambiquara in southwestern Brazil, Bororo in Mato Grosso, Karajá on the Araguaia river, Guaykuru (now Kadiwéu) near the Paraguay river, and many others, have unique languages.

By my calculation lowland Amazonia at the time of European arrival in 1500 contained four or five million people – of whom three million were in Brazil – divided among four hundred peoples. I have derived this estimate from reports of first contacts, probable rates of destruction, and the numbers and locations of those who survive. My figure is the sum of population estimates by area, river valley or nation, rather than by extrapolation from the carrying-capacity of different types of terrain. It is around the middle of the range of guesses by other demographers.

With human ingenuity and centuries of experience, native peoples had adapted to life in each of the Amazon's habitats. They had learned to live well in every type of forest, along the rivers and lakes, in the *várzea* floodplains (see also p. 340), on *cerrado* scrubland, and in the species-rich cloud forests of the Andes. Recent research indicates that Amazonian hunter-gatherers were taller and healthier than dwellers in cities of Peru or Mexico, doubtless because their diets of fish, game and vegetables were better balanced than those of the agriculture-dependent urbanites.

Pero Vaz de Caminha, the first Portuguese to write about Brazilian Indians, in 1500 told his king: 'Truly, these people are good and of pure simplicity.... The Lord has given them fine bodies and good faces, like good men.' Although they had no farm animals or cereal crops, 'they are stronger and better fed than we are with all the wheat and vegetables we eat.... Their bodies are so clean and plump and beautiful that they could not be more so.' Amerigo Vespucci was impressed by the architecture of communal huts as well as the naked beauty of the Indians. He was also dazzled by the bounty of the Amazon environment, listing some of the profusion of strange trees, animals and birds. He concluded: 'I fancied myself to be near the terrestrial paradise.'

Although the hundreds of nations and tribes evolved a rich diversity of cultures, they shared broad similarities of way of life, physique and even temperament. Vespucci felt that indigenous people achieved their idyllic lives without any of the apparatus of European government. 'They have no laws or faith, and live according to nature. They do not recognise the immortality of the soul, and they have among themselves no private property because everything is common. They have no boundaries of kingdoms and provinces, and no king! They obey nobody and each is lord unto himself.... They are a very prolific people, but have no heirs because they hold no property.' Other early chroniclers made these same observations. The institutions of monarchy, nobility, church and judiciary seemed unnecessary to achieve a good life. These radical ideas were seized upon by European philosophers, including Erasmus, More, Montaigne, Rousseau, Voltaire and even Marx, to develop subversive theories against the class system, autocratic government and established religion.

The notion of noble savages living in an uncontrolled paradise was somewhat flawed. In reality, indigenous peoples *did* have a degree of hierarchy, particularly when they developed great chiefdoms. They were deeply conservative, with unwritten codes of conduct governing all activities and every stage of the life-cycle. Living close together in villages with no personal privacy inside their huts, people had to conform. Many activities were communal – hunting, farming, hut-building, forest-clearance, celebrations. The penalty for eccentric or antisocial behaviour, or if someone was deemed to be cursed by malign spirits, could be ritual execution. People were also spiritual, with faith-healing by shamans who were the custodians of botanical knowledge, ceremonies and a rich mythology. Every tribe had different forms of burial, and respect for ancestors was almost universal. While Amazonia's indigenous peoples were not as ruthlessly bellicose as Europeans, they did fight many battles. So they were not the utopian 'noble savages' of some philosophers' imagining, devoid of kings, laws or churches.

In 1494, only two years after Columbus's landfall in the Caribbean, Pope Alexander VI divided the world between the two Iberian kingdoms of Spain and Portugal in the Treaty of Tordesillas. Each received a hemisphere for the purpose of conversion to Christianity and possible colonization. The Pope was a Borgia – a name derived from Borja in Spain – and he thought that he was awarding Marco Polo's China and India to his native country. This was because Columbus and he relied on the calculation of the size of the earth made by Claudius Ptolemy in about

AD 150, but Ptolemy had reckoned our planet to be far too small, leaving no room for the Pacific Ocean. Throughout his life Columbus was convinced that Mexico was the mainland of Asia, Cuba was Marco Polo's offshore island Cipango (Japan), and the inhabitants of his discoveries were Indians. The misnomer 'Indians' has stuck, for indigenous peoples of both American continents.

Contrary to the Pope's intention, the Line of Tordesillas in fact favoured tiny Portugal, whose population was little over a million. The Treaty placed the longitudinal divide between Spain and Portugal 360 leagues (some 2,000 kilometres; 1,250 miles) west of the Cape Verde archipelago, with a corresponding longitude on the far side of the globe. The Portuguese obtained Africa because their navigators had already rounded the Cape of Good Hope, but because the Earth was so much larger than was thought, the divide in the Orient ran between what are now the Philippines and Indonesia. The Portuguese thus also got India and almost all of Asia as their sphere of influence. Spain's share proved to be the not-yet-discovered American continents. Thus, by the absurdly presumptuous 'Papal donation', the entire Amazon basin fell into the Spanish sphere.

When Brazil was discovered six years after Tordesillas, Portugal's hemisphere included only the easternmost bulge of the new land, and did not embrace the future cities of Rio de Janeiro or São Paulo. In later years the Portuguese asserted that their realm ran from the mouth of the Amazon to the mouth of the Plate (in Uruguay). In 1532 the King of Portugal awarded 4,000 kilometres (2,500 miles) of 'his' coast of Brazil to fourteen 'donatories' for the purpose of permanent settlement. Their fledgling colonies of course stopped short of the Amazon. During the remainder of the sixteenth century, the Portuguese gradually conquered this Atlantic seaboard, subduing tribe after tribe – often by the familiar colonialist tactic of divide-and-rule, exploiting vendettas between indigenous peoples. In the 1560s they crushed a French attempt to colonize Rio de Janeiro, and half a century later in 1615 expelled another French colony from Maranhão not far from the mouth of the Amazon. One Frenchman complained that the Portuguese were so warlike and adventurous – their trading posts and colonies by then stretched from Brazil to Japan – that they must have 'drunk the dust of the heart of King Alexander [the Great] to show such exaggerated ambition'.

In 1532, on the Pacific side of the continent, the Spanish adventurer Francisco Pizarro landed in northern Peru with fewer than two hundred men and some horses. By the end of the following year, in one of the most extraordinary conquests in history, he had captured the Inca ruler Atahualpa, deceived and executed him, and marched through the Andes to the Inca capital Cuzco. This sumptuous city lies between two great headwaters of the Amazon, the Vilcanota-Urubamba and the Apurímac, both of which flow into the Ucayali which is the main trunk of the Amazon. During the first two decades after the conquest of Peru, there was sporadic fighting against Inca resistance, a series of civil wars between the gangs of conquerors, and various ill-fated expeditions eastwards into the edges of the Amazon rain forests.

At the end of 1540, Governor Pizarro sent his youngest brother Gonzalo to be lieutenant-governor of the Inca's northern capital Quito, in what is now Ecuador. Gonzalo, aged about thirty, was the most dashing of the four Pizarro brothers – handsome, richly dressed, brave, impetuous and cruel. He was already a seasoned soldier: a good rider, lancer and swordsman who had been in action continuously since he reached the Americas a decade earlier.

When Gonzalo Pizarro arrived in Quito he found the town's Spaniards abuzz about a report of rich lands to the east. An expedition had just returned from nearby headwaters of the Amazon and reported seeing what it took to be cinnamon trees, *canela* in Spanish. Spices were prized in those days before refrigeration, partly because they disguised the taste of rotting meat. Even more excitingly, the expedition heard rumours of a land so rich in gold that its ruler regularly anointed his skin in that precious metal. He became gilded, *dorado*; so his fantastic kingdom was known as La Canela or El Dorado. A contemporary Spaniard heard that 'this great lord or prince goes about continually covered in gold dust ... which he washes away at night and renews each morning. He looks as resplendent as a gold statue worked by the hand of a great artist.' Pondering this, the writer mused: 'I would rather have the sweepings of the chamber of this prince than the great meltings of gold there have been in Peru.'

The hysteria was not unreasonable. During the previous quarter-century, Spaniards had discovered and conquered the hitherto-unknown empires of the Aztecs and Maya in Mexico, Incas in Peru, and Muisca under their chief Bogotá in Colombia. Each of these conquests was fabulously rich, and their conquerors became some of the world's wealthiest men. It seemed quite possible that there was a fourth glittering prize to be won.

Gonzalo Pizarro immediately decided to conquer the kingdom of El Dorado. 'When this news spread in Quito everyone who was there wanted to take part in the expedition.' In a few days he assembled 220 Spaniards – which was more than his older brother Francisco had used to overthrow the entire Inca empire. They were supported by hundreds of Indian porters and great herds of llamas, pigs (already being bred in the New World) and other livestock. This lengthy column marched out of Quito at the end of February 1541. The men were in high spirits. Each carried only his sword and shield, for Indians and llamas bore all the baggage. They started in high grasslands surrounded by beautiful snow-capped volcanoes, then descended through valleys of Andean vegetation, and were soon down in the westernmost rim of the Amazon rain forests.

Pizarro's second-in-command was his thirty-year-old friend Francisco de Orellana, who came from the same Extremadura province of Spain as did most of the conquerors of the Incas. The young Orellana had spent half his life in the Indies, had fought with the Pizarros in the conquest of Peru and its civil wars, and had been sent by them to colonize the coast of Ecuador (he lost an eye while sub-duing the area around Guayaquil). Orellana was a stern but respected governor, hospitable to passing Spaniards, and fairly intellectual by conquistador standards.

These young Spaniards were the finest fighting men in Europe. With their horses and steel swords they were invincible in the Caribbean and open parts of the Andes. But as soon as they descended into the Amazon forests they became help-less incompetents. It was, and still is, extraordinary how Europeans never learned to live sustainably in the world's most diverse ecosystem. By contrast, indigenous people practised hunting and fishing from childhood. They understood the potential of hundreds of plants, as food, medicine or building materials. One race blundered around, torn, bitten and starving, while the other slipped through the vegetation in good health and with a balanced diet. Europeans were lost, fright-ened and frustrated in this alien jungle; natives loved it more than open space, and recognized individual trees as unerringly as an urban dweller knows streets.

It was the rainy season, with tropical downpours and constant lightning strikes on higher ground. Pizarro's expedition was soon depleting its supplies, losing men and animals, and having to fight local people for food. The first disap-pointment was the 'cinnamon' trees of 'La Canela'. The trees looked like large olive trees, with big flowers and pods, and were of the magnolia family, *Nectandra* and *Ocotea*, related to avocadoes. Their nut is the size of an olive, in 'a little husk shaped like a small hat, of the same colour and taste as oriental cinnamon'. But the trees were too scattered and remote to be of commercial value, and they were no substi-tute for the spices brought back from India by Portuguese sailors.

There were few indigenous people, and they were naked hunter-gatherers who seemed primitive compared to the Incas' subjects in the highlands. Gonzalo Pizarro kept asking these Indians how soon he would emerge into open country and the rich realms of El Dorado. The natives replied that they knew only of other forest-dwellers like themselves. Pedro de Cieza de León (a contemporary soldier, but one with a conscience) wrote that 'Gonzalo Pizarro was angry that the Indians had not answered what he wanted to hear'. So the ruthless conquistador ordered cane platforms built 'and the Indians put on them and tortured until they told "the truth". The innocent natives were promptly stretched on those frames or *barbecues* by the cruel Spaniards and some of them were burned alive.... The butcher Gonzalo Pizarro, not content with burning Indians who had committed no fault, further ordered that other Indians should be thrown to the dogs, who tore them to pieces with their teeth and devoured them.'

Short of food, wretched in the rains, and lost in the interminable forests, the expedition hacked forward on foot. Horses were now useless, and in any case there was nothing for them to eat on the forest floor. Pizarro later wrote that 'we endured great hardships and spells of hunger on account of the roughness of the country and dissension among the guides; as a result of which ordeals a few Spaniards died'. This was true exploration: cutting blindly into the forest, never knowing what lay ahead, trying to gauge the slope of the forest floor in order to find streams and water.

Europeans still have to cut trails by hand – in this respect nothing has changed in almost five hundred years since Pizarro and Orellana. The only way to open a path is by slicing laboriously with a machete – or cutlass, or in Portuguese *facão*, 'big knife' – occasionally using a compass to keep the trail straight. The author has been on such expeditions in various Amazon forests. It is a dark world, dank with the smell of rotting leaves. Sometimes high forest opens into the majesty of a cathedral, with fallen tree trunks lying like tombs. In such places the going is easy and the greatest danger is of losing direction, for the sun is visible only filtered through the canopy far overhead and it is impossible to tell its orientation. Occasionally a shaft of sunlight pierces the gloom, illuminating huge blue *morpho* butterflies or rare coloured plants that brighten the prevailing browns and greens. More often, the jungle is low and dense. There are lush fans of spiny palms and ferns, tangled cascades of creepers, mosses and lichens everywhere, and pineapple-like bromeliads and other epiphytes perched on trees. But the beauty is lost on explorers having to hack through such foliage. Thin saplings can be severed easily with a blow from a machete, but creepers dance aside when struck and have to be pinned against a tree and chopped. Cutting gets harder in the afternoon, when it is hotter, arm muscles are tired, and blades need frequent sharpening. The carpet of dead leaves seethes with ants, ticks and jiggers. During the day there can be swarms of biting blackfly (*Simuliidae*) – called *pium* or *borrachudo* in different parts of Amazonia – and at night mosquitoes. Men opening trails wear broad-brimmed hats, for a blow at a creeper might bring down a column of army ants, twigs, scorpions or even tree snakes, or the cutting might disturb a colony of fierce forest hornets. After a few weeks of such toil, non-indigenous men are pale, with clothes torn and boots disintegrating. Their skin is covered in bites, thorns and festering scratches, and the glands that filter insect poison from arms and legs are swollen and sore. Pizarro's men expected to be basking in luxury as conquering heroes. Instead, they scrambled through forest drenched in rain, there was danger from falling trees and branches, and the ground could turn to slimy pink mud, or swamp, or floodwater. Mosquitoes were most active during this rainy season.

Gonzalo Pizarro wasted ten terrible months of 1541 in this futile exploration of headwaters of the Coca and Napo rivers, skirmishes with tribes, and interrogations and torture of captives. One scouting party found a large village and the expedition hurried there to steal food. At another place there was a gorge defended by local Indians: the Spaniards built a log bridge and crept across above a raging waterfall.

One campsite too close to a river was struck by a flash-flood that swept away supplies and equipment. 'Gonzalo Pizarro was greatly distressed at finding that he could not reach any fertile or abundant province beyond such rough country.... He frequently deplored having undertaken this expedition.'

Further north, another proud conquistador was equally thwarted. Gonzalo Jiménez de Quesada, who had just invaded the Muisca of Chief Bogotá, also heard the El Dorado rumour and became obsessed by it. He sent his brother Hernán Pérez de Quesada to try to find it. Hernán wrote to his king, Holy Roman Emperor Charles V: 'I left this New Kingdom [modern Colombia] on 1 September 1541 with 260 Spaniards and almost 200 horses and all the other equipment needed for that expedition.' By another account, that 'other equipment' included 'over six hundred head of free Indians, men, women and children, all tied and imprisoned, removed by force and against their will.... All of them died, without a single one returning.' This ugly expedition pushed into the forested hills of the Amazon's northwestern sources, fighting tribe after tribe, slaughtering Indians to steal their food, and losing men, horses and hapless Andean Indians to starvation and the rigours of the jungle. They were the first Europeans on the upper Caquetá and Putumayo. They discovered great stands of the false 'cinnamon' trees, but 'the lands where that spice grows are unbelievably uninhab-itable, full of swamps, rivers and quaking bogs, and above all sterile of fruits, roots, birds or fish, so that there is scarcely any food to be found throughout them.' A few emaciated survivors of this northern group staggered back to Bogotá, with all their Indians and animals dead, and with no mock-cinnamon – let alone gold of El Dorado.

For Gonzalo Pizarro, the only way forward seemed to be by river. Therefore, 'reflecting that of all the [hundreds of] porters brought from Quito not one remained, and none could be found where they were, the Spaniards decided that the best plan was to build a craft on which their supplies might go down the river, with the [remainder of the men] following by land. They thus hoped to reach some region of plenty, for which they all besought Our Lord.' There was no short-age of timber, lianas for cordage, or resin for pitch. The camp was scoured for metal that could be turned into nails. Charcoal kilns were built to raise heat for smelting. 'In this manner, and with the labour of all, the boat was built.' The vessel was described as a *bergantín*, a brig or large open rowing boat. Loaded with the provisions and some thirty men it sailed downriver, while the rest cut through forests alongside and forded or bridged tributaries. The two groups reunited each night. By Christmas Day 1541 they were desperately hungry, boiling leather from saddles to make thin soup.

Pizarro became convinced from questioning Indians that there was a village with large fields of manioc two days' march downstream at the junction of two broad rivers. The plan was for Orellana and fifty-seven men to sail in the brig accompanied by a score of canoes, and (according to Pizarro's later deposition) *return in twelve days* with the looted food. Everything went wrong. There was no village at the junction of the streams, nor on a larger river beyond. Orellana pressed ahead, always hoping to find habitations he could pillage. His men were very weak, reduced to eating the soles of their shoes cooked with herbs or crawl-ing into the forest in search of anything edible. Seven of them died of starvation. 'They were like madmen, without sense.'

The river led them on enticingly, with the constant hope of finding a settle-ment beyond each forested bend. It rained incessantly, and during the rainy season the current on Amazon rivers is swift and powerful. Drifting with the flow was the only thing the exhausted men could do. 'As the river flowed fast, we pro-ceeded at the rate of from twenty to twenty-five leagues [110–140 kilometres; 70–85 miles] a day, for the river was now high and swollen by many other rivers which emptied into it…. Although we wanted to return to the expedition where the Gov-ernor had remained behind, it was impossible to go back because the currents were too powerful.' So, by the reckoning of those with marine experience, they advanced over a thousand kilometres (620 miles) in eight days. They were by now clearly far beyond the point of no return. Indigenous people can paddle up these rivers in canoes, preferably during the dry season and exploiting eddies or quieter water near the banks, but the Spaniards could not conceivably have manoeuvred their makeshift craft against such a powerful current for such a distance.

It remains a question in the annals of exploration: did Orellana always intend to desert Pizarro or, if not, at what point did he decide that he could not return upriver? Was it treachery, or force of circumstance, or a foreseen eventuality? Orellana tried to protect himself with a written document, signed or marked by all the men. This took the form of a petition, drawn up by the scribe Francisco de Isásaga on 4 January 1542, in which the men begged their leader Orellana not to attempt to return upriver, because it was too dangerous and thus 'contrary to Your Worship's duty to God and the King'.

Pizarro was convinced he had been betrayed. With the remaining 140 men, he pressed down beside the river, opening a trail, fording swamps and *várzea* floodplains, crossing streams on rafts and canoes. 'The heavens poured down water from their clouds so copiously that for many days and nights the rain never ceased.' It was a harrowing journey, with the men kept alive by eating every remaining horse and dog and forest foods they managed to forage.

In March 1542 Pizarro decided to abandon the wait for Orellana's return. He tried to regain Quito by another river that might have more habitations, possibly the Aguarico. The Spaniards found a few manioc plantations that they could loot. But they did not understand about leaching bitter manioc, so some suffered or died from poisoning. Half a year later in September 1542 the wretched survivors, gaunt, wounded, half-naked and devoid of everything but rusty swords (which some used as crutches) staggered into Quito and gave thanks for their survival. Pizarro launched a furious denunciation to the King about his trusted lieutenant's treachery. 'Instead of bringing food, he went down the river without leaving any provisions, leaving only signs and blazes showing where they had landed or stopped at the junctions of rivers.... He thus displayed towards the whole expedition the greatest cruelty that faithless men have ever shown. He was aware that it was left unprovided with food, trapped in a vast uninhabited region and among great rivers. He carried off all the arquebuses and crossbows and munitions and iron materials of the whole expedition.' A major legal enquiry ensued.

What is the manioc that Pizarro's starving men were so desperate to steal from the Indians and that lured Orellana's home-made boat down the river? Manioc is, and always has been, the staple of Amazonian agriculture. It is *Manihot esculenta* or *M. utilissima* to botanists, *mandioca* in Tupi and modern Brazilian, *yuca* in Spanish, and *cassava* (*tapioca* when heated) to Caribs. Manioc is the super-crop that enabled early man to evolve from foraging to farming: it is probably a 'cultigen', a plant evolved by human breeding. The tubers of this splendid plant are rich in carbohydrates and energy-giving calories, though deficient in protein.

Manioc is easy to grow: you simply replant a cut stalk. It can be planted at any time, and when harvested may be stored underground (or under water) for months. Its myrtle-like shrub springs up between the debris of felled forest, yields several harvests of tubers a year, and resists insects and plant diseases because many of its varieties are toxic. There are two main types: 'bitter' which is full of prussic acid or cyanide, and 'sweet' (*aypi* in Tupi) which is less poisonous but also less durable or nutritious. It is not easy to tell them apart. The anthropologist Betty Meggers wrote: 'Subtle morphological traits differentiate the deadly "bitter" from the innocent "sweet" plants, and their recognition is literally a matter of life and death.' Some European explorers, ravenously hungry in forests they did not understand, fell upon native manioc plantations and died in agony from eating the untreated bitter variety.

Manioc is the only major food crop that requires the extraction of a lethal poison before it may be eaten. We will never know how or when early man learned how to rid manioc of its poison. To this day, different tribes use different methods to dig up the tubers, carry them back to the huts, store them if necessary, rinse and slice them. The peeled white manioc flesh is then either pounded or grated. Pounding is usually done by pairs of women, working rhythmically with massive mortars in an upright hollowed tree trunk. This is a familiar sight and sound in native villages – attractive to onlookers but hard work for the women. Some peoples prefer to grate their manioc, using concave boards studded with quartz or hardwood splinters: such handsome graters are a speciality of the upper Rio Negro and some Xingu tribes. These graters can be fastened into ceramic vessels, and archaeologists have found fragments of such pottery in early sites.

The next stage is the crucial leaching-out of prussic acid. The pounded or grated pulp is put into a long, sausage-shaped tube closed at one end and called *tipití* in Tupi. *Tipitís* were a groundbreaking invention of early man. Because they are made of diagonally woven basketwork, they easily expand and contract. A *tipití* of two metres or more (seven feet) is filled with soaked manioc pulp and suspended from wooden frames. A heavy log or stone at the bottom causes the tube to stretch and thus contract, gradually squeezing out the poison-laden water and starch.

After repeated leachings, the manioc is ready to be cooked or processed into a rich menu of foods and drinks, using techniques and implements that differ slightly from tribe to tribe. It can be made into tasty *beijú* cakes like unleavened bread or boiled up as *mingau* porridge. Fermented, it becomes the milky and mildly alcoholic drink *cashiri* or *cauim* that has enlivened countless indigenous festivals. Roasted manioc forms a granular flour (*farinha* in Portuguese, *fariña* in Spanish) that tastes good, like a nutty breakfast cereal. This is insect- and rot-resistant, and therefore became the mainstay of every expedition throughout the history of the Amazon. Manioc has been exported to other equatorial environments and is now, after rice, the world's most important tropical crop.

Francisco de Orellana's home-made boat and canoes sped down the Napo river during January and early February 1542. One of the leader's accomplishments was remarkable aptitude as a linguist. He picked up enough words of native dialects to converse with tribes along the river. (In this part of what is now Ecuador and Peru this was probably a dialect of Tukanoan, as spoken by its present inhabitants the Witoto and Bora; or it might have been related to Peban spoken by Yagua, who now live east of the Napo.) Orellana persuaded Indians to barter their food – manioc, turtles and parrots – for some of the Spaniards' remaining beads and trinkets. Friar Gaspar de Carvajal, a Dominican friar who wrote an invaluable account of the expedition, said that 'his knowledge of the language was, after God, the deciding factor in preventing us from perishing on that river'.

On 11 February Orellana's men sailed out of the Napo and onto the main stream of the Amazon. (This junction is some seventy kilometres – 45 miles – downriver from the modern Peruvian city of Iquitos.) The Spaniards had no idea that they were attempting a descent of the world's largest river; they thought that it debouched into the 'North Sea' by which they meant the Caribbean (north of the Isthmus of Panama as opposed to the 'South Sea' or Pacific Ocean). In any case, they had no option but to hurtle downstream with the all-powerful current.

Villages were quite frequent on this part of the Amazon: rows of thatched huts on bluffs in front of the unbroken wall of rainforest vegetation. This is a monotonous landscape, with the swirling expanse of river, either pale khaki-coloured or blue to reflect the sky, flanked by the dark green line of trees that never ceases for thousands of kilometres from the Andes to the Atlantic. A splash of colour from yellow kapok blossoms is a rarity. The greatest beauty and movement is in the sky, where there is an ever-changing spectacle of clouds, of every shape and configuration, from white to menacing grey, sometimes racing across the sky or reflecting lightning pyrotechnics. For a few minutes at dawn and sunset there is a pageant of fast-changing blazes of orange, crimson and purple, gold and silver, dazzlingly mirrored on the river's broad surface.

Orellana's boats kept to the middle of the river, where the flow was fastest and smoothest. When they turned into villages, their reception was sometimes hesitant or hostile, but they generally managed to obtain good food – a wonderful variety of fresh or dried fish, turtles, and also monkeys and manatees (those gentle great freshwater mammals, whose breast-feeding may have inspired the mermaid legend). The Amazon here has frequent islands and clumps of floating water-weeds. As a result, a dozen Spaniards in two canoes became lost in the labyrinth of channels. After two very anxious days, in Carvajal's words, 'Our Father was pleased to reunite us, amid great rejoicing'. Many days of empty riverbanks followed.

The explorers then entered the lands of a rich nation, whose principal village and paramount chief were called Aparia. This people occupied six hundred kilometres (370 miles) of the Amazon, well into what is now Brazil. They had some twenty villages, each with up to fifty large huts, on either side of the river and separated by extensive farms of maize and manioc.

As the Spaniards approached Aparia's village, they were welcomed by canoes bearing presents of food, including tasty *jaú*, 'like Spanish partridges but bigger', and freshwater turtles 'as large as leather shields'. The bearded strangers were guided up a tributary to meet Chief Aparia, who wore finery of a feather head-dress and ornaments and body paint. Orellana had mastered some words of Tupi, which impressed the chief. (Two native words recorded by Carvajal show that these 'Aparia' spoke a Tupi dialect so they may have been the Omagua, who were living in this region a century later as a subtribe called Ariana.)

The reception by Aparia's people was so good that Orellana decided that this was the place to build a second boat. Among his men he found enough craftsmen to fell and transport trees, cut the wood into a keel, frame and planks, produce nails from scraps of metal smelted with charcoal, caulk the craft (with a gum the Indians showed them, possibly rubber latex), and make rope and sails. The Spaniards were bothered by swarms of black-fly by day and mosquitoes by night, but they were well fed by Aparia's people. It took them thirty-five days to build a 'nineteen-ribbed' vessel larger than their existing *San Pedro*, and they called her *Victoria*.

There was also an episode to fuel the fantasies of El-Dorado-seekers. 'During the boat-building, four Indians came to see us – each taller by a handspan than the tallest Christian, quite pale-skinned and with splendid hair hanging down to their waists. They wore gold ornaments and fine clothes.' These men were generous with food, polite and deferential, and said that they had been sent by their powerful chief to investigate the intruders. The description of these

Indians is plausible, for sixteenth-century Spaniards were quite short; some Panoan-speaking tribes of the Ucayali wore long *cushma* tunics of cotton or bark-cloth; and it was later learned that people of the Amazon-Solimões obtained gold objects from the Muisca of the northern Andes by paddling through flooded forests to the middle Rio Negro and thence upriver.

The expedition still feared repercussions from its failure to return to Gonzalo Pizarro. So the scribe drew up another document, reiterating the hardships, starvation, strength of the current, impossibility of paddling back upstream, and with the men beseeching Orellana to lead them out of 'such wild and heathen country'. The Spaniards remained as Aparia's guests until 24 April, when they set off down the Amazon. They were never again to enjoy such warm hospitality.

As the expedition sailed into what is now Brazil, habitations ceased. 'We endured more hunger and hardships than ever before and found even more uninhabited regions. Forest succeeded forest on the banks, so that we could find no place to camp at night, still less anywhere to fish. We were consequently reduced to our previous diet of herbs varied with a little roasted maize.'

In mid-May the explorers entered the lands of the next indigenous nation, the people of Chief Machiparo. This great tribe did not welcome the strangers. Brightly decorated war canoes, filled with warriors protected by long shields of manatee or tapir hide, attacked the two boats. 'The Indians advanced with a great yell, beating many drums and blowing wooden trumpets, threatening us as if they meant to devour us.' The Spaniards had to fight hard with crossbows and occasional arquebus fire. Onslaughts by disciplined flotillas of canoes continued throughout the next two nights and days. But the explorers survived, and they sailed for days through Machiparo country. When they tried to land to capture a palisaded village – to seize food and find a secure place to rest – they had hours of desperate hand-to-hand fighting, of Toledan-steel swords against *chonta*-palm wooden clubs. When they regained the boats every man was wounded, eighteen of them seriously.

At Machiparo's main village Indians paddled out to inform the expedition that the chief wished to see them, to learn about their tribe, destination and purpose. The Spaniards landed and advanced on the village in battle order, with the fuses of their arquebuses lit and their crossbow strings cranked back ready to fire. 'When the chief saw them to have different dress and aspect from all other people he had seen, and all bearded, he revered them to some extent and was courteous towards them.' He lodged them in part of his village.

Machiparo's nation had plenty of food – maize, manioc, yams, beans, peanuts, turtles which they farmed extensively, and vast stores of dried fish. All this was too much for the hungry Spaniards, who ran amok and started to pillage huts and turtle tanks. The Indians concluded that they were not deities but only uncouth and greedy mortals. So they suddenly attacked, coming at the disorganized looters with clubs and spears and protected by long shields. The invaders rallied and drove off the attack, killing many Indians and capturing some shields, but they suffered two dead and sixteen wounded, and they had to flee down the Amazon.

Machiparo turtle-farming was simple and effective. At the breeding season, females were released to lay eggs in their customary sandbanks. As the baby turtles emerged, they were flipped on their backs, small holes were drilled into their shells and they were towed back to the villages behind canoes. They were kept in their thousands, in tanks enclosed by wooden fencing. Fed on vegetation, they provided an excellent and sustainable source of food. 'Thus these barbarians never know what hunger is, for one turtle suffices to satisfy the largest family.' At that time, Amazon rivers teemed with these great freshwater turtles, *Podocnemis expansa*. Turtles and fish should even now be the main source of protein on the world's most abundant mass of flowing fresh water, but we shall see how profligate modern man has squandered this source of delicious food.

Gaspar de Carvajal wrote that 'the further we went [into Machiparo's territory], the more thickly populated and better did we find the land'. The banks on both sides of the Amazon were settled with a succession of villages never more than two or three kilometres (1 or 2 miles) apart. The greatest had houses continuously for over 25 kilometres (15 miles). (Machiparo's people may have been those later known as Aisuari, who occupied the Amazon-Solimões for some 220 kilometres – 135 miles – between its small southern tributaries, the Tefé and Coari.)

Beyond lay the country of a nation that the explorers confusingly called Omagua. (This was probably the Oniguayal tribe, who were later recorded on the north shore near Codajás 250 kilometres – 155 miles – above the confluence with the Rio Negro, whereas the true Omagua were probably Aparia's people, far upriver.) Orellana's men called this people's main settlement 'Pottery Village' because of its mass of beautiful ceramics, now known to archaeologists as Guarita style. To Carvajal it was 'the finest seen in the world, for Malagá-ware does not equal it. It is all glazed and enamelled in every colour, amazingly vividly. Beside this, the designs and paintings on their pottery are so symmetrical and natural that they work and draw everything like Romans.'

This was a stretch of *várzea* where, at the end of the rainy season in May, the swollen river rises up to the canopies of mighty trees and floods thousands of square kilometres of forests. Another Spaniard wrote two decades later that these Indians had two sets of houses in their great village: one on land for the dry season and the other 'built in the trees like magpie nests, with everything they needed to be able to live there while the river is in flood.... The people were naked. There was much food in this settlement, with abundance of manioc, maize, *guamote* sweet potatoes, yams and other root crops in abundance, and much fruit.'

Downstream, after another uninhabited no-man's-land, came the Curuci-rari nation. The Spaniards admired its 'numerous and very large settlements, very pretty country, and very fruitful land'. But what impressed them most was a different style of fine glazed polychrome pottery. They recorded ornate 'candelabra' and storage jars large enough to hold 450 litres.

The next tribe was ruled by a chief called Paguana. The first of its villages received the strangers hospitably and loaded them with food, including pineapples, avocado pears and *chirimoya* custard-apples. Thereafter, 'there was one day when we passed more than twenty villages', one of which stretched for some ten kilometres (six miles) beside the river. Then came a very large, flourishing village with many landing-stages, each crowded with a horde of warriors. Orellana tried to pass by in midstream, but the Indians came out in canoes to attack the strange boats. The Spaniards were again saved by crossbow and arquebus fire, which Carvajal described as – next to God – the Christians' main salvation. Two successive tribes were so hostile that the Spaniards never learned their names: they simply raced on down the Amazon, occasionally landing to seize food, skirmishing in villages, and often fending off fighting canoes.

On 3 June the boats passed the mouth of a great river whose black waters streaked the muddy brown of theirs for many kilometres: clearly the Rio Negro. Modern visitors to nearby Manaus are taken to see the 'meeting of the waters', where the Negro's tannin-stained black water flows alongside the sediment-laden 'white water' of the Amazon. A week later, Orellana's boats passed the mouth of the great Madeira river entering from the south. After one battle, the Spanish captain ordered some prisoners to be hanged, 'in order that the Indians from here on might become afraid of us and not attack us'. This barbarity had the opposite effect.

Villages of a nation below the Madeira had posts festooned with trophy heads of its enemies. The Spaniards called this the Province of Gibbets. It was possibly the territory of the Munduruku, a warlike people who continued until the nineteenth century to decorate their huts with such grisly trophies. Landing here to steal food, the explorers were furiously ambushed. A lucky crossbow shot killed the native chief, but individual Indians retreated into the village and defended each hut 'like wounded dogs'. Orellana ordered the place to be set on fire and his men escaped in the confusion. They seized some turtles, turkeys and parrots – and a girl prisoner. She was an intelligent young woman, who somehow managed to communicate with her captors. She told them that they were now passing gleaming white villages of 'the excellent land and dominion of the Amazons'.

When native canoes menaced the passing boats and rejected peaceful overtures, the intruders decided to fight. They rowed their brigs against a village defended by masses of warriors. Spanish guns and crossbows took a heavy toll of the defenders, but these fought back with barrages of arrows. They danced and shouted, heedless of their losses. Some Spaniards protected themselves with manatee shields acquired from Machiparo's people, but their boats were hit so often that they looked like porcupines. Five men were wounded, including the chronicler Friar Gaspar de Carvajal. He was struck by an arrow that pierced his ribcage and 'had it not been for the thickness of my habit, that would have been the end of me'.

The attackers jumped into chest-high water and slashed into the warriors. Carvajal was convinced that the defenders' determination resulted from being subjects of the Amazons. 'We ourselves saw ten or twelve of these women, fighting there as female captains in front of all the Indian men. They fought so courageously that the men did not dare to run away. They killed any who did turn back, with their clubs, right there in front of us; which was why the Indians maintained their defence for so long. These women are very pale and tall, with very long braided hair wound about their heads. They are very robust and go naked with their private parts covered, bows and arrows in their hands, fighting as much as ten Indian men.' The Spaniards reckoned that they killed seven or eight of these Amazons before escaping to their boats. They drifted off with the current, too exhausted to row.

An Indian captured in the battle was interrogated about the Amazons. He seemed to say that he had visited their villages, a week's walk to the north of the river. Carvajal then retailed all the preconceived ideas from the classical legend – warrior women who rejected men except for intercourse once a year, who kept only female children, and who cut off one breast to facilitate drawing a bowstring. The native informant described an opulent land that, to his eager interrogators, sounded just like the Peru of the Incas, complete with stone buildings, llamas, and plenty of gold and silver. The chronicler Francisco López de Gómara, who was living in Mexico, was scornful when he heard these tales: 'No such thing has ever been seen along this river, and never will be seen! Because of this imposture many already write and talk of the "River of the Amazons".' He recalled that other Spanish explorers had heard about female tribes in other parts of the Americas. Rumours of Amazons were reported by Gonzalo Jiménez de Quesada on the Magdalena river (in Colombia) in 1537 and by Ulrich Schmidel on the Paraguay a few years later. One of the few printed books in Spain at that time was a compendium of classical legends. Many conquistadors had this as reading for the Atlantic crossing. So it was not surprising that they were on the lookout for such curiosities, in a New World brimming with unknown marvels. The name Amazon stuck. The world's largest river is called after the legendary tribe of sexually liberated women.

One possible explanation for the tall warriors with hair piled on their heads is that they were Parikotó or Wai Wai *men*. These Carib-speaking peoples now live several days' journey up the Mapuera and Trombetas rivers, which flow from the north into this stretch of the Amazon. The American explorer William Curtis Farabee in 1914 described how Wai Wai warriors 'wear their hair like women, but rolled up in a white bark that presses the hair into a spiral.... One fine-looking young fellow was very proud of his physical appearance. Every morning after taking his bath ... he would oil and comb his beautiful long hair, twenty-eight inches [70 cm] in length, and slip on his well-decorated hair tube; then he would paint his face with a variety of designs.' Men and women of this tribe wear small aprons over their genitals, and the men are quite tall.

At the mouth of another southern tributary they passed the greatest of all the riverbank chiefdoms: the Tapajós, after whom that river is now named. The banks were lined by fine villages and in the distance, inland, 'could be seen some very large cities'. War canoes attacked the intruders: Carvajal reckoned that there were two hundred of these, each carrying twenty or thirty men. On the shore were hundreds more, in brilliant feather cloaks and headdresses and waving palm fronds in menacing unison. As a further sign of their social organization, the Tapajós had canoes full of musicians playing what looked like horns, pipes and three-stringed lutes. The Spaniards escaped annihilation thanks to the surprise of their noisy guns.

Orellana's veterans survived many more skirmishes as they descended the seemingly interminable river. In one attempt to raid a village, Friar Gaspar was hit by another arrow. 'I have lost my eye from this wound, and am still not free from suffering or pain.' By late July they were near the mouth of the Amazon, aware of tides and salt water. They spent some weeks refitting their makeshift boats for an ocean voyage. They had no compass, no anchors, no maps, no qualified sailors, and pathetically little food or water. Despite this, and against all odds, the journey went remarkably smoothly. Light winds and currents carried the brigs past the coasts of the three modern Guianas, Trinidad island, and the mouth of the Orinoco, to the Spanish island of Margarita off Venezuela – an amazing ocean voyage of 2,200 kilometres (almost 1,400 miles). The two boats arrived on 9 and 11 September 1542. They had inadvertently completed one of the greatest explorations of all time.

Spaniards descended, reported on, and named the world's largest river three centuries before other Europeans discovered the sources of Africa's rivers. Of the original fifty-nine men, they had lost only three in battle and a similar number from disease or starvation. The contemporary historian Gonzalo Fernández de Oviedo described it as 'far more than accidental, more a miraculous event'.

Three messages emerge clearly from Carvajal's wonderful account of the descent. One is that stretches of the Amazon were densely populated by well organized chiefdoms, although other parts of the river and most of the forested hinterland were empty. Another is that indigenous peoples had learned to feed themselves amply, whereas European interlopers could do nothing but starve in the forests or try to steal natives' provisions. The third is that many tribes were at war with one another.

The aftermath for Francisco de Orellana was a tragic anticlimax. Most of his men returned to Peru, but Orellana and some officers sailed to Europe where he faced a furious denunciation by Gonzalo Pizarro. He survived the legal onslaught, thanks to the two documents his men had signed, the magnitude of his achievement, a pile of affidavits by the explorers, and the eclipse of the Pizarros. (Governor Francisco Pizarro was assassinated by a rival in Lima in 1541. The handsome hothead Gonzalo later rebelled in protest against pro-Indian legislation, and was eventually defeated and executed outside Cuzco in 1548.)

Orellana obtained a licence to return to colonize the Amazon. This enterprise was a disaster. During the Atlantic crossing, some two hundred men were lost, from an epidemic in the Cape Verde Islands, the sinking of a ship, and massive desertions at each port of call. Orellana entered a lesser mouth of the Amazon at the end of 1545, with only two ships and perhaps 150 men and women. He never found the main river. One ship was wrecked; an exploring party was lost; Orellana went in search of them, but he too disappeared in the labyrinth of swampy islands. Others sought him in a boat they had taken three months to make, but a third of the expedition perished from disease, starvation or Indian arrows. Finally in 1546 a shipload of only twenty-five would-be settlers, including Orellana's young wife Ana, put to sea from the Amazon and were swept by currents to the island of Margarita – just as the Spaniard had been four years earlier. Orellana's widow said that he had died from grief over his lost men and from illness.

The Spanish and Portuguese colonies in the Americas were the world's first maritime empires, the first conquests separated from their mother countries by oceans. There was considerable doubt and debate about the morality of such invasions. The chief critic was Bartolomé de Las Casas, a colonist who in 1514 saw the error of his ways, joined the church, and became Bishop of Chiapas in southern

Mexico. Throughout a long life, Las Casas wrote powerful books deploring the destruction, oppression and enslavement of the indigenous peoples conquered by his countrymen. To the Spaniards' credit, they published all the Bishop's writings and listened to his polemics against the immorality of torturing and killing native Americans – arguments that Protestant enemies seized upon to fuel the *leyenda negra*, the 'black legend' of Spanish cruelty. The devout King-Emperor Charles V became concerned that his soul was in jeopardy because of the atrocities being committed in his name. In 1549 he therefore organized a panel of theologians and jurists in Valladolid, to hear a debate between Las Casas and Ginés de Sepúlveda – a patriot who justified the colonial conquests because Spaniards were a master race spreading the true religion. Both theorists used the Bible and Aristotle as the sources for their arguments. They spoke for days on end, in Latin, in the heat of summer, so that the sleepy panel never reached a firm conclusion. However, the effect of this debate was an absolute ban on further conquests until the threat to the King's salvation was resolved. If anyone found and conquered a people without a royal licence, he would lose not only his conquests but probably also his head. This embargo was finally lifted in 1560, but during the eleven years before then there was no exploration activity on the Amazon or anywhere else in Spanish America.

In 1556 Spanish settlers in Chachapoyas, on an Amazon headwater in northeastern Peru, were amazed by the arrival of a flotilla of indigenous canoes. These were 'some three hundred Indians who said they were from Brazil and had left it in far greater numbers, led by two [Europeans] who died on the journey'. They said that they were fleeing from oppression by the Portuguese, who were by then establishing colonies along the Atlantic seaboard. They had migrated overland and then paddled *up* thousands of kilometres of the main Amazon, the Marañón (then called Bracamoros) and the Huallaga (Motilones) to reach Chachapoyas. Their chief Uiraraçu ('Big Bow') and some of his warriors were taken to Lima to meet the Viceroy. 'They told great news of their journey continually upriver, in which they had spent ten years. They emphasized the variety and multitude of tribes they had encountered, and particularly the wealth of a province they called Omagua.' This epic migration, its detailed reports of great tribes and villages along the way, and the hardships these Indians had overcome, all caused a sensation. It seemed to confirm the El Dorado legend and the hints of richer civilizations glimpsed by Orellana's expedition.

Peru was by now full of Spanish adventurers, young men who had crossed the Atlantic to make a fortune in the fabulous Indies. They had arrived too late. Peru had long since been parcelled out to the first wave of conquistadors in *encomiendas* of tribute-paying Indians. So the newcomers were destitute, but too arrogant and idle to work. The number of such unemployed was swollen by hundreds of Spaniards who had been on the losing sides in a series of civil wars that wracked Peru's conquerors. The authorities were at a loss as to what to do with all these 'vagabonds'. They were an unruly rabble who contributed nothing to society, terrorizing any Indians they could catch, and drunken, licentious, quarrelsome and always liable to sedition. The Viceroy was therefore delighted when in 1558 El Dorado fever swept these adventurers – and this coincided with the lifting of the royal embargo on expeditions and conquests.

Peru was cleansed of several hundred of these desperadoes on a grandiose failure known to history as the Ursúa-Aguirre expedition. This became a best-selling story throughout Europe because of its irresistible mix of violence, treason, sex, extreme adventure and spectacular failure. Modern audiences know a condensed and garbled version of the expedition from Werner Herzog's film *Aguirre, The Wrath of God*.

The Viceroy chose a young officer called Pedro de Ursúa to lead the attempt to conquer and colonize the lands of the Omagua, now thought to be the kingdom of El Dorado. Ursúa had no difficulty in recruiting ruffians and raising finance for his venture. During his fundraising travels he fell in love with a beautiful mestiza widow, Doña Inés de Atienza, a lady who had already caused a scandal by cuckolding her husband with a relative of the Viceroy. Ursúa returned to a camp on the Huallaga where his boats were being built, with the lovely Inés, her lady companion and other servants. There was immediate murmuring among his men, who envied and resented their leader's female company.

The movie *Aguirre, The Wrath of God* opens with an unforgettable sequence. A long column of armour-clad, bearded Spaniards, Indian porters straining under gigantic loads, horses, mules, fighting dogs, pigs, sheep and llamas threads its way down a steep descent into the Amazonian cloud forest. This was the most accurate part of that powerful but fanciful film. For Ursúa's expedition *was* very big. It had over three hundred Spanish soldiers – twice the number with which Francisco Pizarro had originally conquered Peru – including 120 arquebusiers since firearms were by now in common use. There were three priests, and twelve women. The Europeans were served by 'six hundred head of Indians, male and female', some black slaves, thirty horses and plenty of livestock. The modern road from Chachapoyas down to Tarapoto on the Huallaga is not unlike the dramatic descent with which Herzog introduced his film. It drops from the open farms and heathland of the high Andes, through mossy bromeliad-laden trees of the cloud forest, and down to the typical lowland forests that flank the brown waters of the Huallaga.

The expedition to conquer 'the land of Omagua or El Dorado' finally departed in September 1560. It sailed in a fleet of canoes and three broad-beamed transports. The leader Pedro de Ursúa made the mistake of preferring to remain on his comfortable boat with Inés to camping on shore with his men. After seven weeks and twelve hundred kilometres (745 miles) of river, they had passed the mouths of the mighty southern tributary the Ucayali (then called Cocama) and then Orellana's Napo entering from the north. They reached the fertile territory of a Chief Pappa, whose people wore cotton tunics like nearby modern Shipibo.

The expedition sailed on, demoralized by weeks of seeing nothing but almost-uninhabited forested banks and the onset of the rainy season. Morale should have improved when Ursúa's men reached the lands of Machiparo. These were the people who had so impressed Orellana with their numbers, good order and plentiful food – particularly the tanks teeming with turtles. They proved fairly hospitable to this second invasion by bearded strangers, lodging them in village huts and providing a small amount of food. A party of Spaniards went south to search for richer lands, but returned empty-handed. The men were plagued by swarms of mosquitoes and black-flies. Even more demoralizing was the growing realization that the empire of El Dorado might be a chimera.

This discontent was fertile territory for the expedition's canker and eventual nemesis – the Basque soldier Lope de Aguirre. By now aged about forty-five, Lope had spent most of his life in the Americas, first in Venezuela but mostly in Peru. Lope was always unlucky. He was sometimes on the wrong side in civil wars, and even when he helped against Gonzalo Pizarro's rebellion he got no reward for loyalty to the King. He got two bullet wounds in his leg and, in another skirmish with forest Indians, lost a hand. In Cuzco his Indian concubine bore a mestiza daughter, Elvira, whom he adored (he took her on the Amazon expedition and protected her honour as jealously as Rigoletto guarded his Gilda in Verdi's opera). So he joined Ursúa as a junior officer – a veteran soldier, but maimed in body and twisted in mind. He had nothing to show for a lifetime's fighting but self-pity and paranoid fury at the powers that he felt had cheated him.

During the early months of the Amazon expedition, Lope de Aguirre gained the support of many of the ordinary men. A persuasive talker, he addressed old soldiers as one of them. Tormented by grievances, he knew exactly how to spread rumour and discontent. Governor Ursúa made mistakes. When he tried to punish those who stole food from Indians, he appeared dictatorial; when he made every man surrender any metal in his possession (the only trade good desired by Machiparo's people) he seemed greedy; and his more comfortable quarters, better food and beautiful mistress aroused bitter envy.

The expedition sailed on to a lesser village of Machiparo called Mocomoco. There, on New Year's Day 1561, Lope de Aguirre and twelve other conspirators decided that the time had come to destroy their royal Governor. After dinner, Pedro de Ursúa was in his hammock attended by servants. The assassins ran in and silently stabbed to death the Governor and an officer who came to his aid. In the confusion after the murders, the conspirators named an ineffectual young gentleman, Hernando de Guzmán, as the expedition's general, with Lope as camp-master – the virtual leader, since he controlled the boats, supplies and men. Inés de Atienza overcame her grief and transferred her affections to one Juan de la Bandera who had always desired her. The new leaders then drew up an extraordinary *Información*, which has survived in the Archive of the Indies in Seville. This listed all Ursúa's alleged crimes, particularly stealing money due to the Crown. It was notarized by the expedition's lawyer 'at Mocomoco in the province of Machiparo, 2 January 1561'. Guzmán signed first and put 'General' beside his name. But when Lope de Aguirre signed, he defiantly wrote 'Traitor'. Some onlookers laughed nervously; others argued that the murder had been done in the royal interest. But Lope told them the stark reality: by killing their official leader they had rebelled. Even if they discovered a land of fabulous wealth, they would be hounded down. The legal authorities 'will accuse us of all the crimes in Hell, and we shall all lose our heads'. The self-confessed traitor urged them to return to attack Peru to regain that country from the King and clergy, all of whom he resented and hated.

The new Governor Guzmán still hoped for a conquest, and the expedition proceeded downstream. The original boats were made of the wrong wood and leaked, so that only one remained. Most of the men had to travel in canoes or hack laboriously through the riverside forest. Reaching an abandoned village, the expedition set about building more boats. Lope ordered that the surviving thirty horses and the dogs be slaughtered, for their meat and hides. It took ten weeks to build two boats, and morale deteriorated. Many Indian porters managed, despite night-time shackles, to escape with most of the canoes. The ruthless Lope ordered the murder of officers thought to be plotting against the rebels, including Inés's paramour Bandera.

Hernando de Guzmán repeated Ursúa's mistakes of leaving the management of the men to Lope, treating himself to better food (some of which he hunted in the forest), and performing no labour. Despite this, on 23 March the scribe drew up another weird document, signed or marked by all 180 expeditioners. This has also survived. It proclaimed Don Hernando as 'Prince of Peru, *Tierra Firme* [the Spanish Main] and Chile'. Lope flamboyantly kissed the hand of the new prince, and the others followed his example. The new royal ruler started to act out the fantasy, lying in his hammock fanned by a page while he appointed court officials, whom he rewarded with fictitious salaries, estates and even unsuspecting Spanish ladies then living in Peru. Lope's daughter Elvira was betrothed to Prince Hernando's brother Martín, *in absentia* since he was not on the expedition. Any idea of discovering and conquering new lands was abandoned, in favour of Lope's obsession of returning to claim Peru. He planned to do this by continuing down the Amazon and then marching back overland along the Andes. By early April the two boats were ready, each of 360 tons and between them large enough to carry the expedition and its depleted supplies.

The camp was riddled with intrigue. Lope became increasingly paranoid. One officer was heard talking Latin: Lope's henchmen promptly sentenced and hanged him, with a sign round his neck saying '*Por hablador*' (for talking too much). The next victim was Lorenzo de Zalduendo, the besotted new lover of Inés de Atienza – stabbed to death as he begged for mercy in Don Hernando's tent. The Prince tried to organize resistance to the murderous Basque, but Lope completely outmanoeuvred him. 'He formed for himself a company of forty men, the best and most heavily armed in the camp, all friends of his … who would follow him blindly and die for him.' Prince Hernando capitulated and told Lope: 'Kill whomever you want. You are an experienced soldier and I rely on your judgment.' The first victim was Doña Inés herself, cut down in a pool of blood and robbed of her jewels and finery as she lay dying. 'Thus ended the poor lady who was the most tragic figure in all the world, the most beautiful in Peru according to all who knew her.' Other deaths followed, of officers against whom Lope bore a grudge. A few days later, in a dawn attack, his fanatics murdered a cleric and rushed into Prince Hernando's quarters. They cut down or shot with their arquebuses three of his captains as they awoke, and finally shot and killed the young Don Hernando 'without confession and showing no respect for his spurious and absurd princely title'. Justifying the murders in a speech to the assembled expeditionaries, Lope de Aguirre called them the Marañones ('Men of the Amazon') and himself 'The Wrath of God, Prince of Freedom', and lord of Peru and Chile.

The boats continued down the lower Amazon, raiding or trading for food from native villages. Lope drove his men downstream as fast as the current and their oars would carry them. The greatest danger came from the leader's bloodlust, fuelled by class conflict. The Elizabethan chronicler Richard Hakluyt (translating a report by the eye-witness López Vaz) appalled his readers: Lope 'determined not to carry with him any gentleman or persons of qualitie, and therefore slew all such persons; and then departing only with the common souldiers.... If I should rehearse all the cruell murthers of this wicked man one by one, I should be over tedious unto you.... Had he seene at any time but two souldiers talking together, he would streight suspect that they were conspiring of his death.' During those months on the Amazon, the Spaniards were reduced by almost forty per cent, from 370 to 230. Lope was even crueller to his Andean Indians. The surviving 170 men and women were callously marooned on the banks of the Amazon, simply to lighten the vessels for the ocean voyage. They wept and complained at the injustice. And when some Spaniards tried to intercede for them, they were immediately garrotted for insubordination.

After weeks of manoeuvring through the labyrinth of channels around Marajó Island, the adventurers embarked on the Atlantic Ocean in July 1561. Favourable currents swept them northwestwards to the Spanish colony of Margarita Island, just as they had Orellana nineteen years previously. The island's unsuspecting authorities welcomed the explorers, unaware that they were led by a psychopathic traitor. Lope soon seized Margarita, gradually killed many of its few settlers, and then led his terrorized band onto the mainland of Venezuela. He was still obsessed by the fantasy of leading his force for thousands of kilometres along the Andes to establish himself as Prince of Peru. The authorities of New Granada (Colombia) scraped together a force and confronted the rebels near Barquisimeto on 27 October. The battle never took place, for Lope's men deserted as fast as they could escape from his clutches. Their leader ran into his tent to kill his daughter Elvira, so that she could not be raped by royalist troops or live as the offspring of a traitor. Lope was then gunned down by his enemies. His body was quartered, and pieces of him were exhibited outside towns as a warning to any who dared to defy the King of Spain.

Shortly before he died, Lope wrote an extraordinary letter to that monarch, Philip II. It was a mixture of obsequiousness and rebellious defiance, megalomania and self-pity. He told the King of his twenty-four years' service and two wounds, and then accused him of being cruel and faithless to the conquistadors. It was *they*, not the King, who deserved the spoils of the lands they had taken. Lope inveighed against corrupt friars and venal lawyers, and he boasted of having killed Ursúa, Guzmán and all the others whom he suspected of plotting against him. He then warned about the horrors of the Amazon river that he had just descended. 'God knows how we escaped from such a fearful lake! I advise you, Lord and King, do not organize or permit any fleet to attempt this ill-fated river. For I swear to you, King, on my word as a Christian, that even if a hundred thousand men came, none would escape. For the reports are false: there is nothing on that river but despair, especially for novices from Spain.'

King Philip doubtless never saw this wild rant, but it was preserved in the archives. The Amazon had acquired a bad reputation. Half a century elapsed before its inhabitants were again disturbed by bearded intruders. And Lope was right about inexperienced Europeans being unable to thrive in that tropical environment.

Spaniards performed amazing feats of exploration in their frenzy to see whether the interior of South America contained riches. Far away at the southernmost tip of the Amazon basin, Spanish adventurers penetrated the plains of what is now eastern Bolivia. Starting from the Plate and Paraguay rivers, conquistadors got Indians to guide them onto broad savannahs around the Grande river, which flows northwards for thousands of kilometres, changing its name to Mamoré and then Madeira before it joins the main Amazon.

Guarani warriors used to ascend rivers from what is now Paraguay, across the forbidding Chaco, to attack the southeastern fringes of the Inca empire. They raided the Chiriguano who lived in the foothills of the Andes, and returned with metal stolen from the Incas; and some later settled in that southern part of the Amazon basin. One Guarani invasion, in the early 1520s, was accompanied by some shipwrecked white men. Their leader, a Portuguese called Aleixo Garcia, was the first European to see the edge of the Inca empire. He probably returned to the newly founded Asunción, but was killed in about 1525, either by the Guarani or by other Europeans intent on stealing his pieces of Inca treasure.

Thousands of these Guarani in the 1540s guided the governor of Asunción, Domingo Martínez de Irala, up the Paraguay and westwards across the Pantanal swamplands to the savannahs of the Llanos de Chiquitos. Irala was hoping to find gold mines or other wealth. He reached the edge of Spanish-occupied Peru. Its governor Pedro de la Gasca (who had just, in 1548, defeated the rebellion of Gonzalo Pizarro) advised Irala to return to Paraguay – which he did, taking thousands of illegally acquired Indian slaves as the only profit from his expedition.

In 1561 Irala despatched a captain called Ñuflo de Chaves and a force of Guarani and settlers from Asunción to found a settlement in the grasslands he had seen: it looked like potential cattle country. Ñuflo de Chaves was intent on creating his own governorship. He and his Guarani settled among the Arawak-speaking Chané and the Tupi-speaking Chiriguano. There was a drought, so Ñuflo made a wooden cross and processed with it in a form of Christian rain-dance. 'God sent them heavy rain, which was the means of conversion of those Indians. From that time onwards, they held the Holy Cross in great veneration and had recourse to it for all their necessities and tribulations.' So the Spaniards named their settlement, near the Grande (or Guapay) river, Santa Cruz. The region did prove to be excellent for cattle-ranching. In the following century the Jesuits congregated the indigenous peoples of these plains into mission reductions at this edge of their Paraguayan theocracy. (In recent times, Santa Cruz de la Sierra has become Bolivia's boom city, wealthy from cattle, agriculture, natural gas – and drugs.)

In 1572, a decade after the lurid Ursúa-Aguirre adventure, the last remnant of the Inca empire was extinguished on the upper Amazon. Peru's conqueror Francisco Pizarro had in 1534 tried to elevate a prince called Manco to be his puppet Inca. After a few months, Manco Inca realized the enormity of the Spanish conquest and organized a massive resistance to the odious invaders. Cuzco was besieged for a year in 1536–37 and many Spaniards were killed. But ultimately, Spanish reinforcements, fighting skills, horses and swords triumphed. Manco was forced to flee to the forested Vilcabamba hills northwest of the old capital. Gonzalo Pizarro led an expedition to try to capture Manco, in 1539 – just before he went to Quito and the ill-fated El Dorado venture. Manco survived, and built himself a small capital, also called Vilcabamba, down where the Andean foothills give way to the forested lowlands of Amazonia. Manco Inca was eventually murdered in 1545 by some Spanish fugitives to whom he had given sanctuary. Three of his sons succeeded him as rulers of this tiny fragment of the once-mighty Inca empire. For almost three decades, there were embassies to Vilcabamba: missionaries and diplomatic envoys tried to lure these young Incas out of their forested retreat. Although Vilcabamba town was down almost in lowland forests – far below the altitude that the highland Incas preferred – 'the Incas enjoyed scarcely less of the luxuries, greatness and splendour of Cuzco in that distant or, rather, exiled land. For the Indians brought whatever they could get from outside for their contentment and pleasure. And they enjoyed life there.'

In 1572 a dynamic Viceroy of Peru, Francisco de Toledo, decided that the Vilcabamba enclave must cease. Peru's native peoples would never become loyal subjects of the King of Spain and genuine Christian converts as long as there was an independent Inca at large. So Viceroy Toledo organized a gigantic expedition of heavily armed Spaniards and native auxiliaries. There were attempts at resistance, notably with a repeat of rolling boulders down at a place where Gonzalo Pizarro's column had been ambushed in 1539. (I myself walked along this trail, the only way down into Vilcabamba, knowing that some of the boulders are still poised on the steep hillside far above. They were discovered by the American scholar-explorer Vince Lee in the 1980s.) But the Spaniards swept past all obstacles. On 24 June 1572 they 'marched into the city of Vilcabamba, all on foot, for it is in the most wild and rugged country in no way suitable for horses'. Vilcabamba's several thousand inhabitants set fire to the thatched roofs and wooden walls of their 400 houses, shrines and palaces, and fled into the surrounding forests. The Inca's own lodging was built on different levels, of stone and cedar-wood, lavishly painted outside, and roofed in imitation curved Spanish roofing-tiles instead of the usual thatch. (Fragments of those tiles can still be seen, buried among the roots of trees that have choked the site during the past four centuries.)

The Inca remnant hoped that its scorched-earth policy would force the attackers to depart for lack of food and accommodation. The nobility had escaped to different Amazonian forest tribes. But the Spaniards were determined to capture all the Incas and put an end to Vilcabamba. Groups of them chased off along each trail out of the burning jungle city. Their commander knew that these forests were alien to the Incas, a mountain people who went 'at risk of their lives, for they cannot survive there and it is no country for them'. One contingent hurried northwards towards the Pilcosuni people (now called Asháninka), scaling a steep forested mountain 'with incredible difficulty ... for that jungle contained a great number of extremely dangerous rattlesnakes'. After six days this group caught a young prince and his pregnant wife. Another squadron marched for some sixty kilometres (35 miles), crossed a broad river on a log raft, and took native officials and 'a golden idol of the sun, much silver, gold and precious stones and emeralds, and much ancient cloth – all said to be worth over a million [pesos de oro]'.

The most important fugitive, Manco's thirty-five-year-old son the Inca Tupac Amaru, was still at large. An ambitious captain of the Viceroy's guard, Martín García de Loyola, volunteered to pursue him. With forty hand-picked soldiers, he descended the Cosireni river from Vilcabamba for forty leagues (some 225 kilometres; 140 miles) towards its junction with the Urubamba-Ucayali. They spotted warriors on a riverbank and crossed the broad river on a balsa raft. Plunging into the forest, they came across a long hut with twenty doorways. The bravest Spaniards charged in and managed to capture eight warriors of the Manarí (a sub-tribe of the Chuncho, Arawak-speakers now known as Machiguenga). To their amazement, they found that this hut was an Inca storehouse full of thirty loads of Inca and Spanish cloth, plumage, and above all quantities of gold and silver tableware.

The posse learned that Tupac Amaru was downstream in Manarí country, confident that he was protected by 'the density of the country and the difficulty of descending the river full of cataracts, currents and rapids'. This torrent was doubtless the Urubamba, with the famous whirlpools and races of the Pongo de Mainique. García de Loyola did not hesitate. He boasted that 'I made five rafts and sailed down the river with [twenty] soldiers. [We were] in great personal danger and on several occasions saved our lives by swimming. [Our rafts] were very crude, so that some ran aground and others foundered.' They covered fifty leagues in three days.

At a rapids in the turbulent river, the Manarí chief Ispaca led many Indians out to do battle. But using all their powers of oratory the Spaniards persuaded him to desist. They offered him some of the looted Inca treasure, which he indignantly refused. But he did reveal that Tupac Amaru was planning to flee downriver to the Pilcosuni. García de Loyola also learned that 'Tupac Amaru's wife was frightened and depressed because she was about to give birth. Because he loved her so much he was ... travelling in short stages. Tupac Amaru ... begged his wife to enter the canoe so that they could travel by water. But she was too terrified to trust herself on that open water [and refused].'

The Spaniards plunged into the forests, guided by Manarí warriors. They marched by night, by the light of flaming torches. They captured the Inca's commander-in-chief 'in a jungle so dense and wild that it would have been impossible to have found him without the [Indians'] advice'. The pursuers then pressed on down forest trails, 'on foot and unshod, with little food or provisions because we had lost these on the river'. After what seemed like eighty kilometres, in the pitch darkness of night, their advanced scouts saw a camp-fire in the distance. They approached cautiously, and then saw the Inca and his wife warming themselves by the fire. García de Loyola arrested Tupac Amaru, and started the journey back to Vilcabamba with him next morning. The Spanish captain was elated by his success – but admitted that his quarry had been close to rescue by Guambo tribal allies and would never have been caught had he sailed further down the Urubamba. His downfall was due to concern for his pregnant wife.

The triumphant Vilcabamba expedition marched back into Cuzco in September 1572. Captain García de Loyola led his captive by a golden chain, with the Inca wearing a tunic of crimson velvet and the royal Inca headdress and fringe. Tupac Amaru was entrusted to a battery of the most persuasive ecclesiastics in Cuzco, and they achieved rapid success. The Inca showed 'remarkable intelligence in understanding [Christianity]. In three days he knew all that was necessary to enable him to be baptised.' However, the Viceroy was determined to crush the

Incas, to eliminate any possibility of their resurgence. So he ordered the summary trials and execution of Vilcabamba's five native commanders and of Tupac Amaru. The Inca was charged with every killing that had occurred in or near Vilcabamba during the previous decade, which was patently unjust since for most of that period his older brother had been Inca. Every churchman begged Toledo to spare the innocent young man, but in vain. So Tupac Amaru was taken to the main square of Cuzco, wearing black, his hands and neck tied, and riding a black-draped mule. The streets, walls and roofs were packed by silent Peruvians – so densely that one observer said that had you dropped an orange it would not have reached the ground. Spanish men and women (some weeping) crowded at windows and balconies, and the prisoner was guarded by hundreds of armed men. The last reigning Inca made a speech from the scaffold, received extreme unction, and was beheaded by the machete of an Indian of the Cañari tribe (bitter enemies of the Incas). A heartrending lamentation went up from thousands of Peruvians, and every church bell in Cuzco was tolled.

The name Tupac Amaru lived on in Peruvian history. It was adopted in the late eighteenth century by an Inca descendant who rebelled against Spanish rule and was also executed. That later Tupac Amaru was honoured as a precursor of the independence of Peru. His iconic image appeared on twentieth-century coinage, and his name inspired both the Tupamaro of distant Uruguay and Marxist guerrillas in Peru.

When Francisco Pizarro conquered the Inca empire, he rewarded his conquistadors with quotas of tribute-paying Indians. The area whose people were condemned to forced labour was called an *encomienda*, and the Spaniard who received the tribute was an *encomendero*. He and his family were required to live in a Spanish town – for security and because colonists preferred this village life among a few compatriots – but this meant that the Indians had to carry their tribute to their master's town house. The quantity of tribute was intolerably heavy, so that the system was little better than slavery. One ecclesiastic wrote: 'The tributes and taxes they pay ... are endured only with great difficulty and hardship.... They live in poverty and lack the necessities of life, and never finish paying debts or the balance of their tributes.' Another pitied these Indians who 'live the most wretched and miserable lives of any people on earth. As long as they are healthy they are fully occupied in working for tribute. Even when they are sick they have no respite, and few survive their first illness, however slight, because of the appalling existence they lead.... They are deeply depressed by their misery and servitude ... and have come to believe that they must continue to work for Spaniards for as long as they or their descendants live, with nothing to enjoy themselves. Because of this they despair; for they ask only for their daily bread and cannot have even that.... These people climb with their loads up slopes that a horse could not climb. They go sweating up the hillside with their loads, and it is heart-rending to see them.'

Nowhere were Indians overworked as savagely as in the northern province of Quito, modern Ecuador. This region had already suffered conquest by the Incas themselves, who imposed their tax system of labour known as *mita*; the oppression intensified with the Spanish conquest. Imported diseases raged; forced labour destroyed family life, and *mitayo* workers could not feed their families. The result was a demographic catastrophe, with the population of Ecuador declining from an estimated 1.5 million to some 200,000 by the end of the sixteenth century.

Quito had almost no mines or obvious riches (apart from some emeralds), so its colonists made money from cloth – woven by the Indians from llama or sheep wool in the Andes, and from cotton grown on the Amazonian foothills. Below Quito the Spaniards founded three small towns, Baeza, Ávila and Archidona, to grow this cotton. This was in the forests of the Quechua-speaking Quijos people, at the headwaters of the Napo, where in 1542 Gonzalo Pizarro's destitute survivors had staggered back after the failure of the El Dorado expedition.

Spanish settlers in the three new towns demanded excessive tribute from their Quijos Indians. The Spaniards' behaviour was so outrageous that a royal judge was sent to investigate. He demanded that fierce dogs used to terrorize the Indians be destroyed, and he fined the guilty colonists. But, in a cruel irony, the cost of this royal visitation and the fines it imposed were piled onto the same natives that it was supposed to help. They had to grow more cotton, weave quantities of additional cloth, and carry it all up to Quito.

It was too much. In 1579 two shaman/chiefs, Beto and Guami, rose up in rebellion. These shamans (called *pendes* by the Quijos) preached a messianic vision whereby the natives would regain control of their forests from the conquerors. They declared that the Christians' god had told them that the oppressors and their towns must be destroyed. Pende Beto said that 'they must kill all the Christians in those two towns because of the many abuses and vexations they received from them every day, and which were getting steadily worse. For during the seventeen years since the founding of that town, their labours had multiplied: they were forced to sow crops for [the settlers] to eat, to spin and weave for them to clothe themselves and their wives and daughters, and they were made to carry much of what they had woven on their backs to Quito for sale, and they returned with other loads.' The Spaniards were increasing in numbers, as was the work they demanded, and there was no end in sight.

The rebellion was carefully planned. Warriors assembled in secret. Five Spaniards who happened to be visiting indigenous villages were killed so that they could not alert the townspeople. Beto took his men against Archidona, and Guami against Ávila. Both attacked simultaneously, at midday when Spaniards were eating or enjoying a siesta. Most Indians wore fighting paint and feather ornaments, and carried their bows, arrows, slingshots and war clubs. Some warriors seized the towns' squares, others blocked escape roads, but most charged into each colonist's house and killed all the inhabitants. They achieved total surprise. The contemporary chronicler Toribio de Ortiguera said that every Spaniard fought desperately with steel swords, arquebuses and horses, but they were destroyed one by one. 'Those barbarous Indians ... killed all Spaniards they found, with their wives, children and servants (if these were not natives of that land) leaving none alive.' When it was all over, the victors sacked and burned the entire town of Ávila, toppled its walls, and cut down European trees in its orchards. The colonists in Archidona had been forewarned, so they defended a makeshift redoubt, but after three days they ran out of food and ammunition and were overpowered and killed. That town was also razed.

The victorious Quijos, under their paramount Chief Jumandi, marched against the larger town of Baeza. But Baeza is a mere two days' walk from Quito, on the main road down into the Amazon forests. So three hundred Spanish cavalry and footsoldiers had been hurried into the town, armed with plenty of gunpowder and shot. The forest Indians advanced towards the central plaza, but they were decimated by volleys of gunfire and then slaughtered by horsemen. In the ensuing campaign, the tribesmen fought valiantly, with repeated attacks on the Spaniards, but they were overwhelmed by superior weaponry and fighting skills.

A punitive force reached the two destroyed towns and buried the rotting corpses of their settlers. Indians who surrendered were forced to rebuild Ávila and Archidona, before resuming their *mita* labour. The leaders, the *pendes* Beto and Guami and Chief Jumandi, were hunted down in the forests, taken to Quito for trial, condemned, carried through the streets held by red-hot irons in a tumbrel, and hanged on the pillory. Chiefs from their tribe and from all over the highlands were brought to watch the executions, and the victims' heads and quartered bodies were exposed for many months – just as Lope de Aguirre's had been eighteen years earlier. The defeated Quijos reverted to grinding labour. They worked from dawn to dusk, in the cotton fields, or chained to looms in sweatshops called *obrajes*, or heaving great loads to and from Quito.

CHAPTER TWO

Anarchy on the Amazon

By the early seventeenth century, fifty years after Lope de Aguirre's descent of the Amazon, Europeans had forgotten the mad Basque's advice to avoid the 'fearful lake' of that cursed river. Dutch, English, Irish and Portuguese all tried to colonize the Amazon. It is difficult to see what attracted them. It may have been a lingering fantasy that El Dorado was in the realm of the Amazons. Sir Walter Raleigh published the enticing *The Discoverie of the Large, Rich and Bewtiful Empyre of Guiana*, in which he promised that its forests hid such wealth that soldiers who conquered it would be paid in slabs of gold. 'Guiana is a country that hath yet her maidenhead, never sacked, turned, nor wrought ... the graves have not been opened for gold, the mines not broken with sledges, nor their images pulled down out of their temples.' Perhaps these fabled lands might be reached from the south, up the Amazon's northern tributaries rather than from the Caribbean? Another attraction may have been the notion that exuberant tropical vegetation represented fertility and would be easy to farm. It should yield lucrative crops of tobacco, cotton or even sugar. We now know that weak soils, pounding rains, blazing sun, destructive blights and insects make this very difficult. But it is easy to understand why the idea of a tropical Eden persisted until the twentieth century.

The aggressive Portuguese had gradually occupied the entire Atlantic seaboard of Brazil. In 1615 they annihilated a determined French attempt to settle in Maranhão, southeast of the river's mouth. Immediately after expelling the French, the Portuguese sent Francisco Caldeira de Castelo Branco with 150 men in three ships to establish an outpost on the Amazon. In January 1616 they founded a wooden fort on an island where the Guamá river joins the Pará. (The broad Pará river is the southern shore of Marajó Island and is thus arguably the southern mouth of the great river. The word *pará* is the Tupi for a large river, which is why the map of Brazil is littered with variations of this name.) The indigenous peoples were welcoming, descending in great numbers to take the trade goods offered by the newcomers. The fort developed, and is now the city of Belém do Pará (Bethlehem of the Pará River).

Good relations with the Indians did not last long. At the end of 1617 the settlers at Belém had a month of 'very hotly contested' fighting against warriors from Marajó Island. Then in 1618 there was a serious 'revolt' by their Tupinamba friends. These Tupi-speakers lost their awe of the newcomers and were outraged by the 'extortions and injuries received from some men who went "ransoming" [the euphemism for slave-raiding] in their villages. They killed these [slavers], remained in rebellion, and immediately placed the new settlement of Pará under close siege.' Tupinamba all along the coast of Maranhão joined the struggle. They destroyed thirty defenders of a fort on Cumã bay near São Luís as well as a boatload of fourteen Portuguese on the Pará river. But their attack on another stockade failed after 'the most desperate opposition', with the loss of many Indian lives.

The Portuguese besieged in Belém begged for help from compatriots to the south, and Jerónimo de Albuquerque – the victor over the French – arrived with soldiers from Pernambuco. 'He found our men still besieged and suffering great hunger. After relieving them, he pursued the heathen for almost two hundred leagues [1,100 kilometres; 690 miles] up the banks of the Pará. He himself died there, after performing many heroic deeds on this campaign.' The tide of battle turned in favour of the firearms, fighting skills and ruthless determination of the Portuguese. 'Captain Bento Maciel Parente went by land from Maranhão with eighty [Portuguese] men and six hundred bowmen from the Maranhão villages. He greatly ravaged these heathen. Most of them, having abandoned their villages, fled to the forests and fell into the hands of *tapuias* – another nation who were their enemies – who took this opportunity to kill, eat or enslave any that they found. It is understood that the dead and prisoners exceeded five hundred thousand souls.' Hordes of indigenous captives were forced to labour as slaves for the rest of their lives. A bishop wrote that 'within a hundred leagues [550 kilometres; 345 miles] of Pará every Indian is at peace and subdued by the Portuguese, whom they fear more than slaves fear their masters.… In Pará, there were once so many Indians and villages along the banks of its great rivers that visitors marvelled. Now few remain unscathed. The rest have perished, from the injustices to which slave-raiders subjected them.'

English and Dutch seamen had been nosing along the northeastern shores of South America for several decades. One Sir Thomas Roe obtained a royal commission to 'make a foothold and settlement on the great river of the Amazons … which was not yet settled by white people'. Roe's Guiana expedition of 1610–11 sent an experienced seaman called Matthew Morton to reconnoitre the lower Amazon. A map of 1615 by Gabriel Tatton (now owned by the Duke of Northumberland) indicated that Morton surveyed far upriver to the mouth of the Xingu. One of Morton's companions may have been an Irishman called Philip Purcell, who then traded on the Amazon for many years. This Purcell created a tobacco plantation at a river called Tauregue, possibly the Maracapuru that flows into the Amazon's northern mouth west of Marajó Island. Nearby was an English stockade established by Thomas King in about 1612.

The Dutch, who already had prosperous tobacco plantations on the Guiana coast, built two stockaded forts called Orange and Nassau on the lower Xingu. In 1616 the burghers of Flushing sent Pieter Adriaenszoon Ita in the ship *Golden Cock* to plant a colony on the Amazon. He took 130 men, fourteen of whom had their families with them, and settled on the north shore between rivers they called Coropatube and Genipape (possibly the modern Jari and Paru). These colonists made friends with Supane Indians who helped them create a plantation, so that they were soon sending shiploads of tobacco and red *urucum* (anatto) dye back to Holland.

In 1620 the English were back. One of Raleigh's captains called Roger North launched the English Amazon Company. He took 120 English and Irish colonists upstream for a hundred leagues and settled 'where the sight of the country and people so contented them that never men thought themselves so happy'. Local Indians helped them clear another tobacco plantation. They sent a small boat under William White exploring for a further two hundred leagues up the Amazon. He described a thriving land, unspoiled since Orellana's voyage almost eighty years earlier. 'In this discoverie, they saw many townes well inhabited, some with three hundred people, some with five, six or seven hundred; and of some they understood to be of so many thousands, most differing verie much, especially in their languages.... Most of them [are] starke naked, both men women and children, but they saw not any such giant-like [Amazon] woman as the rivers name importeth.'

Among North's Irish colonists was a young man who became the most delightful of the many adventurers trying their luck on the great river. Bernard O'Brien was a son of the Earl of Thomond, who had had his castles confiscated because of his Catholicism. King James, however, encouraged Irish Catholics to plant colonies for him in remote places. O'Brien landed on the north bank of the Amazon's mouth at a place called Pataví ('Coconut Grove') with twelve Irishmen and their four English servants. They had quantities of trade goods – 'beads, bracelets, knives, mirrors, boy's whistles, combs, axes and other different small things' – so got on well with the local Arawak-speaking Aruã Indians. O'Brien built an earth-and-wood fort with a ditch, and he delighted the Indians by using his muskets to help them defeat their enemies. They fed his men and worked in the plantation; he in return taught two thousand of them about the Catholic faith, God, Heaven and Hell – and modern fighting skills.

The young Irishman went on a voyage of exploration with five musketeers and fifty of his Indian friends in four canoes. They paddled far up a river (doubtless one of the Amazon's northern tributaries) past tribe after tribe until they reached the land of the Amazons. O'Brien claimed, with a dose of blarney, to have visited the Amazon queen Cuña Machu (the Inca for 'Great Lady') and to have 'dressed her in a Holland shirt, with which she was very haughty. At the end of a week I took my leave, promising to return, and she and her vassals signified that they were sad at my departure.' He tantalizingly gave no details of this legendary land, beyond repeating the classical legend that it contained many women but no men and that the Amazon warriors had 'their right breasts small like men's, artificially stunted in order to shoot arrows; but their left breasts are broad like other women's'. Back at Pataví after more adventures, O'Brien sailed to Europe in 1624 on a Dutch ship, with a cargo of tobacco and cotton and leaving his compatriot Philip Purcell in charge of the tiny fort.

Having crushed Indians near Belém do Pará, the Portuguese turned against the other European intruders – most of whom were hated Protestants. In 1623 an expedition of seventy soldiers under a captain from Portugal and the notorious Indian-fighter Bento Maciel Parente was despatched to the main Amazon river. It contained the Friar Cristóvão de São José (a Franciscan of St Anthony, who had volunteered to go to Brazil as an Inquisitor), who was so well liked and trusted that a thousand friendly Indian bowmen in forty canoes joined as volunteers. These also brought plenty of food, and were rewarded with tools, beads, combs, mirrors, fish-hooks and other trade goods. The English and Dutch who were settled near the northern mouth of the river could do nothing against this powerful force. Their indigenous allies harassed the Portuguese and killed some as they paddled through the *furos* (forested channels to the west of the island that are just wide and deep enough to take modern ocean-going ships) but, when the expedition landed, the outnumbered English could only flee inland to the safety of friendly tribes.

The tough Portuguese moved up the river, defeating Aruã Indians who liked the northern Europeans. In one battle, musketeers fired so many shots that they burned their hands on their gun barrels. Beyond, on the lower Xingu, was Fort Orange defended by fourteen Dutchmen and some Africans and Indians: it was burned. Seventy kilometres (45 miles) up the Xingu was the larger Fort

Nassau. This surrendered and was also demolished. Back on the Amazon, a large Dutch ship appeared, but it was run aground, holed and, after a fierce struggle, its 125 crew and passengers were massacred. Inter-colonial scrapping during the next two years saw a Dutch ship destroy a Portuguese fort on the south shore near Gurupá, but the Iberians swiftly counterattacked under the experienced Pedro Teixeira and wiped out another Dutch stockade, English plantations and the Irish fort. In one lengthy battle against some eighty northerners, sixty were killed including Philip Purcell.

The irrepressible Bernard O'Brien appeared in Holland, and its West India Company sent him back to the region he claimed to know so well. He arrived in April 1629, with 18,000 escudos worth of trade goods, and was soon helping his Indian friends to defeat their enemies. But the Portuguese were never slow to react. A force of white soldiers and hundreds of Indians attacked the natives near the new Dutch/Irish fort. O'Brien hurried back with 42 whites and many Indians, fought a fierce battle during which he suffered three gunshot and arrow wounds, and won the day. The Irish rapidly strengthened their Fort Tauregue, which was up a northern tributary near Macapá (later a fortresss, and now capital of the State of Amapá). The bastion was square, surrounded by a deep moat and a broad rampart surmounted by a parapet almost a metre (3 ft) high and equally thick – all of stout logs and earth, and defended by some cannon.

Pedro Teixeira reappeared in September 1629 with a great expedition of 120 Portuguese and 1,600 Indians in 98 canoes, but he could do nothing except lay siege to Tauregue. After a month some English ships sailed up and offered to help the besieged. But sectarian rivalry intervened. Some Irish on the ships wrote to O'Brien, in Irish, warning that the English planned to remove him and other Catholics. So, by his account, the gallant and devout O'Brien decided to surrender to Teixeira's fellow Catholics rather than see his fort and Indians fall to hated Protestants. The Jesuit Luís Figueira, who was with the attackers, said that the envoy who emerged from the stockade was a cavalier, booted and spurred and speaking excellent Latin. A solemn treaty was drawn up, in Portuguese and Irish, on the authority of King Philip of Spain and Portugal and his local Governor-General, 'in the name of the Holy Evangels, with a missal, on our knees in front of a crucifix'. Eighty men of the garrison marched out with the honours of war, and entrusted their fort and weapons to the Portuguese. It was a cruel deception. The treaty and symbols of Catholic faith proved meaningless. No sooner were the Irish back in Portuguese settlements than Governor Coelho de Carvalho and the expedition's commanders robbed them of money, possessions and clothes, tied them up, killed some, and mistreated all. Their native allies were mercilessly massacred or enslaved. O'Brien complained bitterly that 'they forced us to work and do farm labour for the Portuguese, which we have been doing to the present day, without keeping their word or oath'. When eighteen Irish managed to escape to the West Indies, the angry Governor held O'Brien in chains for many months and then exiled him to live among the supposedly man-eating Cururi Indians. He misjudged his prisoner, for the Irishman wrote that 'in my exile I gained the friendship of the cannibals and learned their language. I went inland for over 200 leagues [1,100 kilometres; 690 miles] discovering the rivers, forests, and medicines and secrets of the Indians. I reduced a province of them to my devotion, and also taught them a better way to live.' All the Irish were finally released, thanks to protests on their behalf by Franciscan friars.

O'Brien sailed away at the end of 1634; had adventures among Caribbean pirates; was captured by the Dutch; back in Amsterdam was sentenced to death for surrendering Fort Tauregue; but was pardoned and offered a burgher's daughter as a wife if he would convert to Protestantism and lead another attempt on the Amazon. Either the bride or religious conversion was too much for O'Brien. He escaped to London and was about to lead a venture for the English Guiana Company, when his faith again proved too strong: he fled to Spain and offered his services to its King, via a splendid Petition in which he told his amazing adventures. His story then goes cold. Spain never accepted his offer, and he may have died in prison there.

Back on the Amazon, bitter fighting continued between the rival colonists. Having duped, betrayed and robbed O'Brien, Pedro Teixeira went on to defeat other English and Dutch settlements. He was greatly assisted by Potiguar Indian allies from the coast of Brazil. These fought with reckless bravery, swimming to overturn Dutch canoes, storming into stockades, and matching European gunfire with their arrows. The English were back in 1630, with two hundred men under an Amazon veteran called Thomas Hixson who had a fort on a river near Macapá. These were attacked by Jacomé Raimundo de Noronha, with only a few white soldiers but 36 canoe-loads of indigenous warriors from around Cametá on the lower Tocantins. The Jesuit Father Luís Figueira told the King that 'Your Majesty is under an obligation to the Indians ... who help the Portuguese with their arms, by supplying them with roast manioc *farinha*, meat and fish, and always paddling the war canoes.' The English were defeated and surrendered in March 1631. When some tried to escape in a launch by night, the Indians allied to the Portuguese overtook them and splashed so much water onto them that they were unable to use their firearms. 'Our Indians then entered [their boat] and slaughtered them all. If we lacked Indians we would have to abandon this land.'

The northern powers returned with boatloads of desirable trade goods. But these were no match for the Portuguese aura of invincibility. The Portuguese had been established in Brazil for a century, spoke Tupi, knew the ways of the indigenous peoples, and were skilled in warfare in this tropical land. Tribes who sided with the English or Dutch came to realize that they faced defeat and, when vanquished, would be killed or enslaved. Father Figueira commented: 'All these heathen are subjected by fear – and the high opinion they have formed of the valour of the Portuguese.' The Iberians cleared the Amazon of foreign competitors just in time – for in 1630 they lost to the Dutch the far richer colony of Pernambuco on the northeastern bulge of Brazil. That was the world's greatest producer of the wonder-crop sugar. It took over twenty years of savage fighting for Portuguese settlers and their Indian allies to drive the Netherlanders from that part of South America. This was Holland's golden age, when its fleets were dislodging the Portuguese from trading posts and colonies all over the world. But the Amazon, devoid of lucrative sugar, precious metals or oriental spices, was too unimportant for them to return to it. Since 1631 there has never been an international conflict in Amazonia.

The Portuguese now had a free hand to exploit and pillage the Amazon. In 1621 they separated Maranhão and Greater Pará (the Amazon) politically from the rest of Brazil. Because trade winds and currents made it easier to sail across the Atlantic than up the coast from Bahia, Brazilian Amazonia was ruled directly from Portugal until 1777. The only remaining competitor was Spain, Portugal's nominal partner under the same King Philip. (This dual monarchy occurred because in 1578 the young Portuguese King Sebastião literally *disappeared* during a disastrous defeat by the Moors in Morocco. His celibate great-uncle Cardinal Henrique succeeded as King; when he died in 1580 the heir to the throne was King Philip II of Spain.) Many Portuguese were unhappy about having a Spanish monarch. A group that included Pedro Teixeira and Governor Coelho de Carvalho plotted to restore a true Portuguese to that country's ancient throne. These nationalists were determined to make the great river a Portuguese rather than Spanish preserve. They were aided by geography. The Spaniards in Peru had to cross the great barrier of the Andes to reach the Amazon's headwaters; and with the wealth of the Incas at their disposal they had no inducement to colonize dreary rain forests. They also had bitter memories of attempts to find El Dorado there.

The two Iberian kingdoms were still operating under the Papal donation of Tordesillas of 1494, and even the most pro-Portuguese interpretation of this division of the world put the entire Amazon basin within the Spanish sphere. The anti-Spanish plotters in 1637 persuaded the King to award a captaincy that was west of the Line to the *Portuguese* Captain (and Indian-slayer) Bento Maciel Parente. Parente and his sons duly enslaved all the indigenous people they could catch in their new fiefdom, which corresponded to Brazil's modern state of Amapá, north of the Amazon's mouth.

In that same year the local Portuguese launched another master-stroke that was to lead eventually to Brazil acquiring the majority of the Amazon. Early in 1637 the settlers of Belém were surprised by the arrival of a canoe that had come all the way down the river from Quito. This contained two Spanish Franciscan friars and six soldiers, who had been trying to convert Indians of the Napo river; but when these resisted the friars decided to make the great descent in a single canoe on a voyage of discovery. The brave travellers were welcomed. But the governor of Maranhão, Jacomé Raimundo de Noronha (another Portuguese patriot), kept them under gentle house arrest so that they could not reveal their findings to any Spanish authorities. He then organized a huge expedition to force its way *up* the Amazon against the formidable current. In October 1637 this set off, with 70 Portuguese soldiers and 1,100 Indians in 47 canoes, commanded by Pedro Teixeira. On the lower river some of the motive power came from sails, but for most of the immense journey it was the Indians who had to paddle for week after week against the force of the river. It took eight months to reach the first Spanish settlements. The long-suffering Indians longed to return to their families. 'The *tapuia* [non-Tupi] paddlers were in despair at their sufferings and determined to desert. But [Teixeira] persuaded them that they had almost conquered the river – when they were in fact only half way.' They had to be constantly urged onwards. 'They were all exhausted by efforts of this magnitude and congratulated themselves each day because it would be the last of their great exertions.'

Noronha was an interim governor whom the settlers had installed in Maranhão. He gave Captain Teixeira sealed orders, to be opened only after he had passed the territory of the Omagua and was entering the Spanish province of Quito. When, after months of paddling, the expedition finally left the Omagua, Teixeira opened his instructions. These told him to found a Portuguese settlement and to erect boundary markers bearing only the *Portuguese* coat-of-arms. This was a move of breathtaking audacity. On 16 August 1639 Teixeira obeyed the order by planting stones a staggering 2,400 kilometres (1,500 miles) beyond the Line of Tordesillas. The markers have never been located (although some modern Brazilians tried to find them far up the Napo river at its junction with the Aguarico). The modern frontier between Brazil and Spanish-speaking Peru and Colombia is two-thirds of the way across South America – almost as far as Noronha and Teixeira tried to fix it.

Pedro Teixeira left most of his men in a camp near this location and proceeded in a dozen canoes up the swift Quijos river and mountain road to Quito. The Portuguese were given a tremendous welcome, with civic receptions, bullfights, fireworks, speeches and parties. The only reward for the gallant indigenous paddlers was to be allowed to kill some bulls with their arrows. However, we know from official correspondence that the Spanish authorities were suspicious about the entire venture and unsure what to do about the explorers. It was finally decided that they must return to Belém, but accompanied by Spanish observers. One of the latter, the Jesuit Cristóbal de Acuña, wrote a brilliant report on the state of the river in 1539 – but this was kept unpublished as a Spanish state secret.

Governor Noronha was arrested and sent back to Portugal, but he was acquitted by a court full of Portuguese patriots. And in 1640 these plotters ended the sixty years of rule by Spanish monarchs, by proclaiming the Portuguese Duke of Bragança as King João IV. (Spain fought back sporadically, but this was a time when its armies were heavily engaged against the French and Dutch in Flanders and Germany. The Portuguese were helped by French forces and English ships of Oliver Cromwell's navy. They finally defeated the Spanish at Villaviçosa in 1665, and Portugal's independence was formally recognized three years later.) The greatest legacy of the six decades of Portugal's subservience to Spain was on the Amazon. A handful of Portuguese frontiersmen defeated first the Indians, then other Europeans, and then cleverly exploited the Spanish dual monarchy to Brazil's lasting gain.

Father Acuña and his fellow expeditioner Maurício de Heriarte were most impressed by the Omagua. Highly intelligent, dextrous and well governed, some Omagua had already adopted ideas learned from Spaniards higher up the river. Both sexes wore cotton robes, from cotton that they grew, spun, wove, and decorated with dyed threads and painting. They also, however, practised deformation of infants' skulls, pressing them so that adults' heads were flattened in front and behind and bulged to the sides. The head 'becomes deformed in such a way that it looks more like an ill-shaped bishop's mitre than the head of a human being.... This causes ugliness in the men, but women conceal it better with their abundant tresses.' As a result, this people were known as Cambebas (from the Tupi for 'flat heads' – also the word for hammerhead sharks). It is strange that there was no mention of this curious custom by anyone who descended the Amazon in the sixteenth century: it must have evolved in the intervening years.

Acuña painted an idyllic picture of the life of the peoples of the middle Amazon. The annual rise of the river produced a fertile layer of mud on its islands and *várzea* floodplain – in contrast to the impoverished soils under *terra firme* upland rain forests. The Omagua planted huge quantities of manioc and maize, sweet potatoes, gourds and broad beans on this flooded land; but, since they otherwise ate only fish and manatees, they rarely ventured away from the river and its islands. They knew how to bury manioc roots so that they survived flooding. They also loved *cauim*, a mild spirit made from fermented manioc. 'With the help of this wine they celebrate their feasts, mourn their dead, receive their visitors, sow and reap their crops. Indeed, on any occasion on which they meet, this liquor is the mercury that attracts them and the riband that detains them.' But the greatest bounty of the Amazon was fish, and the Omagua were brilliant fishermen. They rigged traps across streams, stunned fish in creeks with *timbó* poison, and shot fish from their canoes using arrows attached to floats. Acuña described the electric 'eel' long before the discovery of electricity. 'It has the peculiarity that, when alive, whoever touches it trembles all over his body, while closer contact produces a feeling like the cold shivers of ague – which ceases the moment he withdraws his hand.'

The Jesuit Acuña also told how the Omagua towed thousands of baby turtles back to stock the tanks that surrounded their villages. Here, penned by palisades, the freshwater turtles were fattened on foliage until the largest weighed as much as a human being, 70 kilograms (150 pounds). Sadly for these magnificent animals, their meat is delicious and each female produces hundreds of eggs 'almost as good as hen's eggs though harder to digest' that contain oil that is excellent for cooking or lighting in lamps. Turtle shells had many uses, and their jawbones could be sharpened into hatchets. This was sustainable aquaculture on a grand scale. Each Omagua had a couple of dugout canoes, and these people moved everywhere by water 'like Venetians or Mexicans'.

The Omagua 'are governed by chiefs in their villages, and in the midst of this very extensive province is their chief or king, whom all obey with the greatest subjection. They call him Tururucari, which means their God, and he considers himself as such.' He told Heriarte that he was born in heaven and knew its secrets. 'They have a house of idols to which they sacrifice those they capture in battle. They anoint their idols with blood, and keep the heads of those they sacrifice in separate houses that are used only as a treasury for these religious trophies. They bury their dead.' They keep 'an infinite number of slaves whom they treat with great imperiousness and who ... obey with great humility.' These tended riverside farms, using tools of stone or tortoiseshell.

There was considerable trade between indigenous nations, with each having a speciality such as growing cotton or making canoes, stools or throwing-sticks. Some even wore gold nose pendants traded from the Muisca and Tairona in the northern Andes beyond the headwaters of the Rio Negro. In general 'they were meek and gentle.... They conversed confidently with us, and ate and drank with us without ever suspecting anything. They gave us their houses to lodge in, while they all lived together in one or two of the largest in the village. And though they suffered much mischief from our Indian allies ... they never returned it by evil acts.'

There seemed to be only one blemish on this idyllic vision. When not trading, these nations were constantly fighting one another. Each tribe had scores of warriors ready for battle and they fought savagely on land and water. The last villages of each nation were fortified outposts, and there was generally a no-man's-land between it and the next people. The killings in these wars seemed to Acuña 'the drain provided for so great a multitude, without which the entire land would not be large enough to contain them'. In this respect, little had changed in the century since Orellana's first descent.

The Spaniard Acuña had been ordered to keep an eye on Teixeira's Portuguese. He duly reported that he often heard them discussing plans to occupy the Amazon as a route to Spanish Peru. He urged the King to colonize the area with Spaniards. For 'if the Portuguese who are at the mouth of the river should attempt, with the aid of warlike tribes that are subject to them, to penetrate by the river as far as Peru or the kingdom of New Granada [modern Colombia] – which is likely, given their small degree of Christianity and less of loyalty – these disloyal vassals of Your Majesty would pillage those lands and cause very great damage.' The Jesuit could not have been more right. Rid of rivals, the Portuguese embarked on centuries of merciless exploitation of the Amazon's inhabitants. To paraphrase Churchill, rarely in human history has so much damage been done to so many by so few. A few thousand colonists gradually destroyed almost every human being along thousands of kilometres of the main river and its tributaries.

There were various reasons for this oppression. One was that Europeans who reached the tropics were determined to renounce all manual labour – even if they had been farm workers in the mother country. Another was that reproducing European life in Amazonia was very labour-intensive. The few plantation crops – tobacco, cotton and (later) rice – demanded back-breaking toil, and none of them grew well amid rain forests. Colonists also needed Indians to feed them (with manioc and other crops, fish and game), to build their towns and houses, and to paddle them on endless journeys. As the years went by, the Portuguese government made Indians construct forts to protect this colony, public buildings in its towns, and shipyards to utilize forest trees and rope-making lianas. All these tasks fell to the indigenous people, for the region was too poor to afford the African slaves who were imported to work in the lucrative sugar plantations of northeast Brazil.

Enslavement of Indians was technically illegal. The royal government in Lisbon issued successive laws on the subject. But whenever it tried to protect the indigenous people there was an aggrieved outcry from the colonists. The King desperately wanted income from his colonies and he had to persuade white Portuguese to settle overseas. So he invariably capitulated to their clamour and either revoked humanitarian laws forbidding slavery or sanctioned glaring loopholes in them.

There were two ways in which Indians were made to work for colonists. Either 'free' indigenous people were brought downriver to live near towns, in missions or official native communities known as *aldeias* (villages). These people's 'freedom' was a sham, for both sexes were obliged to work for the settlers or the authorities for a given number of months a year – initially six months, but this was steadily increased until they enjoyed very little time to work for their own sustenance. They were theoretically paid for this forced labour. But, since there was no monetary economy in the Amazon backwater, their remuneration was in derisory lengths of cotton cloth – which they themselves had to grow, harvest, spin and weave. To add to the grotesque irony of this system, the Indians did not even need the cloth: they naturally went naked in the constant equatorial heat. The clothing with which they were paid was a requirement of warped Christian morality.

The other form of native labour was 'lawful' slavery. Tribes who resisted Portuguese rule or conversion to Christianity could be condemned by royal decree, and those captured in the resulting 'just war' could be legally enslaved. Other innocent indigenous peoples could be 'ransomed' into slavery. 'Ransoming' was a euphemism that sprang from the practice among coastal Tupi-speaking peoples of capturing warriors in inter-tribal feuds and then executing and ritually eating these prisoners. Any Portuguese who rescued such a captive was said to have ransomed him – in the way that Christian Europeans ransomed those who fell into the hands of pirates or North African Muslims. A ransomed prisoner became a slave for life of his liberator. This strange system was open to such widespread abuse that the words 'slaving' and 'ransoming' became synonymous. No-one bothered that almost no Amazon tribe was cannibalistic, so prisoners could not be saved from such a fate.

Ransoming (slaving) expeditions plied the Amazon and its tributaries every year from the 1620s onwards. They were of course paddled by Indians, and their military muscle was a mixture of Portuguese and indigenous fighters. Their success depended on firearms, for guns had a tremendous psychological impact on even the most warlike tribes. Their victims were seized either by brute force, or by persuasion with fraudulent promises of a better life, or purchased by trade goods. When Bento Maciel Parente was governor of Pará in 1626 he sent his son on an expedition, nominally to expel rival European colonists from the Amazon. 'He entirely fulfilled his father's purpose, for he occupied himself only with ransoming many *tapuia* and thus for a time silenced most of the clamours of the people [colonists]' for more slaves. When the next governor briefly tried to crack down on 'the atrocious crimes being committed in the wilds' and forbade all forms of slavery, the colonists howled with outrage. The town council of Belém accused the governor of causing 'irreparable damage to the public utility' and tried to equate slavery with conversion to Christianity. It demanded to know whether 'he wished to bear on his shoulders the formidable burden of answering before both the Divine and Human Majesties for having impeded the reduction of so many souls, the unhappy slaves of paganism!' Governor Coelho de Carvalho immediately caved in. He increased the number of official ransom expeditions and himself profited as much as possible from the traffic. His successor accused him of exploiting the Indians so voraciously that by 1636 the captaincy seemed denuded of people. Dozens of once-teeming villages had gone or were reduced to a handful of overworked survivors.

Some indigenous nations resisted. These were conquered in fierce fighting, with the Portuguese employing the tactic of all colonial powers at all times: divide and rule. Native warriors fought alongside Europeans against traditional enemies, myopically unaware that their true opponents were their white friends. After the Portuguese had annihilated the Tupinamba in the approaches to Belém, they moved against neighbouring tribes. One jingoistic chronicler boasted that 'the blades of their conquering swords were not blunted by too much cutting, their spirits were not satiated with conquest, nor their arms sluggish or tired from wounding.... Instead, they continued to defeat the Indian confederates of the vanquished, who had killed over a hundred Portuguese. They conquered fifteen provinces with over two thousand inhabited villages.' A gallant resistance was mounted by the very numerous Pacajá people, who lived on a small river of that name between the Tocantins and Xingu. The survivors of the Tupinamba were now fighting alongside the Portuguese. One of the latter recalled that 'it was so cruel that the river was dyed with blood. For the Pacajá Indians not only put themselves in battle order to await the fight, but even came out in over five hundred canoes to confront the Tupinamba and their other enemies. Almost all were killed, both the defeated and the victors.' The survivors were concentrated in four *aldeias*, so that the colonists could use their labour.

The few ecclesiastics in Amazonia at this time were in an ambiguous situation. They were there to convert indigenous peoples to Christianity. They wanted to create well-ordered mission villages, in which the converts could receive religious instruction, lead pious lives, and die and go to Heaven as good Christians. In their reports home, they boasted of the numbers of baptisms and of Indians who received the sacraments at death. But this evangelical vision rarely worked in practice. Tribes generally accepted baptism and instruction with enthusiasm, fascinated by the new rituals, the material goods offered by the strangers, and the charismatic missionaries who taught so fervently. But they rapidly tired of the discipline and changes to traditional custom demanded by the Fathers. A more serious threat to the task of conversion came from the colonial settlers. The missionaries saw themselves as champions of the Indians, partly because they wanted them as inhabitants of their missions and to uphold royal laws which their fellow ecclesiastics had influenced. So missionaries and colonists were soon on a collision course. The Capuchin Friar Cristóvão de Lisboa was appalled to see how his compatriots 'razed and burned entire villages, which are generally made of dry palm thatch, roasting alive any in them who refused to surrender as slaves. They overcame others, or subjected them peacefully through execrable deceit. They would promise them alliance and friendship in the name and good faith of the King; but once they had them off-guard and unarmed, they seized and bound them all, dividing them among themselves as slaves or selling them with the greatest cruelty.'

When the Spanish Jesuit Acuña descended the Amazon with Pedro Teixeira in 1639 he tried to stop the Portuguese from seizing slaves. He even refused to erect crosses in riverine villages. He knew that it was a slavers' trick to accuse Indians of neglecting such symbols of Christianity and use this as a pretext for enslaving them. At the mouth of the Tapajós river, the expedition was welcomed by the large nation of that name – one of the last pre-conquest chiefdoms. So Father Acuña was appalled to find the son of Governor Maciel Parente preparing an attack on them. 'Scarcely had I turned my back when [he sailed] in a launch mounting a piece of artillery and other smaller vessels with as many troops as he could get. They fell upon the Indians with a harsh war, when they desired peace.' Maciel Parente persuaded the friendly Tapajó to surrender their arrows tipped with curare poison. He then herded their warriors into a heavily guarded enclosure. He encouraged his own Indians to sack and loot the village, raping its women in front of their men. 'Such acts were committed that my informant, who is a veteran of these conquests, declared that he would ... have given the value of the slaves he possessed in order not to have beheld them.' A decade later, when the Spanish Franciscan Laureano de la Cruz descended the Amazon, he watched slavers still harassing the pathetic remnants of the Tapajó and inciting them to raid other tribes for captives. 'For each "piece" (which is how they refer to a [slave] person) they give three tools, a shirt and two knives, more or less.' By bribing or forcing tribes to attack others, 'every single troop that goes to raid for captives returns laden with people, whom they sell as slaves and call Negroes. Governors and captains-general of those places take the greater part of this traffic.'

The result of such atrocities was demographic catastrophe. Cametá had been a lovely and fertile place, famous for the number of its inhabitants. But when Acuña arrived it was destitute, 'with no one to cultivate the land and nothing apart from the ancient site and a few natives'. Friar Cristóvão de Lisboa lamented: 'Everyone used to be amazed by how many Indians lived in Pará and on the great rivers in that region and how their villages were almost continuous. But today [1647] very few villages survive, for the rest have all perished from the injustices of the slave raiders. When the Indians saw that they were gradually all being enslaved, contrary to all justice and reason, in despair they set fire to their villages and fled into the depths of the forest.' Canon Manoel Teixeira, brother of the conqueror and explorer Pedro, was Vicar-General of Maranhão and Pará. He reckoned that in the decades after their arrival at the mouth of the Amazon his compatriots had destroyed two million Indians through 'their violent labour, exhausting discoveries, and unjust wars'. The figure of two million was too high, but the deaths and suffering were tragically real.

Nominally free Indians fared little better than slaves. The Jesuit Luís Figueira in 1637 accused settlers of 'oppressing these wretches with great violence, forcing them to do very heavy labour such as growing tobacco in which they work seven or eight months on end by day and night. For this they pay them four *varas* [4.5 metres] of cloth, or three varas, or two. And if they fail in this work, the Portuguese put them in the stocks and beat them many times. Because of this they flee into the forests and depopulate their villages. Others die of despair in this labour without remedy.' Another Jesuit condemned 'the injustices, cruelties and tyrannies perpetrated through the greed and ungodliness of the so-called "Conquerors of Maranhão" on the goods, sweat, blood, liberty, women, children, lives and, above all, souls of the wretched Indians'. Unauthorized slaving expeditions pretended that they went upriver in search of gold mines that would swell the royal treasury. In one sermon, Father Antonio Vieira thundered that their 'main and true purpose was to capture Indians, to draw from their veins the red gold which has always been the only mine of that province!'

No-one wanted the indigenous peoples to die out. The Crown hoped that they would become loyal subjects; missionaries needed them to fulfil their soul-counts and swell mission villages; and settlers depended on their labour. Some died in battle, others succumbed to privation and overwork, and the lucky ones escaped to remote forests. But the vast majority were killed by imported diseases against which they had no inherited genetic immunity. There were epidemics of smallpox and measles (which were often confused with one another), possibly plague, cholera, and pulmonary afflictions from influenza to pleurisy and tuberculosis. Yellow fever sometimes struck, but it may have been of American origin since it killed both Europeans and indigenous people. Malarial fevers were scarcely mentioned in Amazonia until the seventeenth century, after which they became the scourge of both travellers and natives.

The early missionaries left heartrending accounts of the devastation caused by these epidemics. They told of entire villages reduced to piles of corpses, of survivors too weak to bury their dead, and of diseases raging in the forests beyond Portuguese colonization. The trouble was that no-one had the slightest idea about diseases – their nature, causes, vectors or treatment. The medical profession had no answers beyond blood-letting and strange potions. Jesuits watched helplessly as their congregations succumbed. One told how, when a measles epidemic was approaching his village, he forced all its inhabitants to sit outside their huts and be purged in torrents of blood.

One description of the misery of pox came from the Friar Laureano de la Cruz, who in 1648 found the Omagua shattered and decimated by disease. This was the populous, proud and productive nation that had so impressed Orellana, Ursúa and Acuña – the latter only a decade before Cruz saw them. The horrified missionary watched an epidemic strike a village and spread rapidly from hut to hut. 'In little over a month every one in that small place, old and young, had fallen miserably. I alone was spared by God. I went among those wretches ravaged by such a contagious and loathsome disease. Just to see their miserable state and dreadful smell was enough to kill one.... Afflicted by the pestilence ... they all died. The howling of the sick and the lamentations they raised for the dead were so great that they seemed to me like the torments of their souls.' They bound the dead and cast them into the midst of the Amazon.

A few years later the German Jesuit João Felippe Betendorf watched smallpox ravage Maranhão and then Pará. Stricken Indians changed from reddish to black in colour; they smelled terribly; and some 'were struck with such force that pieces of flesh fell off them'. Some villages had only one or two Indians still standing – too few to bury the dead. 'The smallpox, being contagious, spread through the town [Belém] and captaincies, devastating Indians so terribly that it finished the greater part of them.' Terrified chiefs came to beg the Jesuits – as potent shamans – to come to help their people. Father Betendorf went to Cametá on the lower Tocantins. Three dying Indians who had fled into the forest were brought to him. 'They were so covered in pox and putridity that they horrified even their own families. When they saw that a Father wanted to hear their confessions, they told me not to approach for the rotten stench they were giving off was intolerable.... But their rotten smell seemed to me like that of white bread when it is removed from the oven. To confess them I was forced to put my mouth close to their ears, which were full of nauseating matter from the pox with which they were entirely covered.' At a mission near Gurupi on the lower Amazon, other Jesuits found that 'the pestilential sickness struck all the *aldeia*'s Indians so thoroughly that there was none but [the two missionaries] who could bury the dead. With repugnance, they nursed them, laid them out for burial, dug their graves and interred them ... having before all else confessed and administered the sacraments to them.' This extreme unction was all-important to the missionaries, and it was the only consolation they could give to frightened, dying Indians.

Settlers complained bitterly about losses of slaves. The slaving expeditions herded their victims into corrals on the riverbanks. 'When the time came to send them back [down the Amazon] half were dead or had fled. Of the remainder, less than half arrived downriver, for they were embarked already infected, hostile and exposed like sardines for a month to the rigours of any weather. Anyone who purchased a slave who arrived like this suffered as a result: he was left with a violent thing, badly acquired.' Another Jesuit who was the priest attached to a 'ransom' expedition reported that 'many died on the journey – more from starvation and lack of manioc flour, and by oppression from the stocks in which they were held, than from disease. Many who were still alive but despaired of life, jumped into the water so that those still living ... could eat the flour they would have consumed. This was tyranny, impiety and unheard-of cruelty. I can affirm in all honesty as a priest that similar things happen every year in almost all the canoes that go to ransom Indians.'

The slaves were worked mercilessly, because European settlers depended on them for *everything*. 'For a man to obtain manioc flour he has to have a small clearing; to eat meat he needs a hunter; to eat fish a fisherman; to wear clean clothes a washerwoman; and to go to mass or anywhere else a canoe and paddlers.' 'All the labour of the settlers is done by the ... native Indians. Because of [indigenous people's] natural weakness, and the idleness, repose and freedom in which they were reared, they are incapable of enduring for long the labour in which the Portuguese make them work – especially that in the cane fields, sugar mills and tobacco plantations. For this reason many are continually dying. Since the entire wealth and support of those settlers consists of [slaves'] lives, it is very common for people who were considered to be the richest... to fall rapidly into poverty. For property does not consist of land, which is plentiful, but of the produce that each settler derives from it. And for this the only instruments are the arms of the Indians.' Another Jesuit almost blamed Indians for dying too readily. 'This State is miserably poor, with nothing worthwhile of its own. Those who have a hundred slaves one day will not have six left a short while later. The Indians, who are anything but robust, have an incredibly high death rate. Any attack of dysentery kills them; and for any small annoyance they take to eating earth or salt and die.' As well as committing suicide, despairing indigenous mothers tried to abort foetuses or kill their infants rather than see them live as slaves. A settler complained: 'If you have ten slaves in a house, ten years later there would not be one left. Yet if a married couple flee into the forest, they will be found in ten years with ten children.'

Europeans completely failed to understand the Amazon or to find a profitable way to exploit it. The most lucrative crops of the Americas – first sugar and cotton, then tobacco, cacao and coffee – grew better in the drier and more temperate climates of the Caribbean, northeastern Brazil, or southeastern North America. Colonists tried to grow tobacco at the mouth of the Amazon, but this plant also thrived better on islands like Cuba and Jamaica or in Virginia. The trouble with the Amazon was that, being on the Equator, it could be too hot; its rainy seasons were too long and torrential; its soils too weak; its vegetation and weeds too aggressive and exuberant; and its insect population, fungi and plant blights all-consuming. Long stretches of the main river were seasonally flooded *várzea*. Some indigenous peoples had learned to adapt their crops to being submerged for months on end, and these natives of course used only local plants and fished or hunted endemic animals. Europeans always made the mistake of trying to rear imported livestock or grow crops with which they were familiar in temperate lands.

Ever since the mid-sixteenth century, Jesuits and other missionary orders had been in charge of indigenous affairs throughout Portuguese Brazil. Spanish Jesuits were creating a theocratic empire among the Guarani of Paraguay. So it seemed logical for these intellectual shock-troops of the Counter-Reformation to move into the Captaincy of Maranhão and Greater Pará (the Amazon basin). Father Luís Figueira led the way. He visited the lower Xingu in 1636 and was impressed by its many Indians ripe for conversion. He returned to Portugal to recruit more Jesuits and sailed back with eleven of them. But as their ship was about to sail into Belém in June 1643 it foundered and sank. Most passengers reached safety, but the twelve Jesuits clung to a raft and were swept northwards to the shore of Marajó

Island. They were captured by Aruã Indians, bitter enemies of the Portuguese, and were all killed. This disaster set back Jesuit aspirations for a decade, during which there was no-one to curb the excesses of the settlers.

The Jesuits' return to Amazonia came in the towering person of Father António Vieira, who was to become the most influential European on the river during that century. Vieira had been educated in the Jesuit school in Bahia, where he took vows to enter the Society of Jesus in 1625 and was fully ordained nine years later. He rose rapidly, thanks to his academic brilliance but particularly to his magnificent oratory. This was an age when the pulpit was the most powerful medium. Vieira's sermons ranged from fiery aggression to mystical emotion, and were always intensely patriotic. He was a master of the beautiful Portuguese language. When in 1640 Portugal shook off the Spanish dual monarchy, Father Vieira was in the delegation sent from Brazil to congratulate the new King João IV. He soon gained great influence in Lisbon society through his oratory, and became confessor to the King. The English consul in Lisbon described Vieira as 'a Jesuit eminent for his preaching, his sermons being bought up as fast as they are printed and ordered from all parts of Spain, Italy and France'. Vieira was sent on secret diplomatic missions to other European countries.

In 1647 Vieira persuaded the King to issue pro-Indian legislation that reiterated the nominal freedom of those who were not 'justly' enslaved. This law said that only missionaries, not rapacious laymen, might administer indigenous villages. Vieira often declared that he wished he were a humble missionary, and he suddenly decided to go to the Amazon to work as one. The mighty preacher's enemies at court were delighted to see the back of him.

Father Antonio Vieira appeared in Belém do Pará in 1653, aged forty-five. He was appalled by what he saw. Belém was a tiny town of 300 whites and their families – officials, soldiers in the fort, a handful of ecclesiastics, and other settlers. The colony's second village, Curupá on the Tocantins, had fifty European residents. Their only export was tobacco, for which a few ships came from Portugal; and they grew sugar for domestic consumption. These few impoverished settlers, in a backwater that was muddy in the rainy season and dusty in the dry, were destroying the indigenous peoples of the Amazon. Legislation controlling slavery was flouted outrageously. Vieira tried impassioned sermons. In one he challenged his sullen congregation: 'I know what you are going to tell me. "Our people, our country, our government cannot be sustained without Indians. Who will fetch a pail of water for us, or carry a load of wood? Who will grind our manioc? Will our wives have to do it, or our sons?".... I answer "yes" and repeat "yes".' He urged the Portuguese to work for themselves rather than from the sweat of others, to free their ill-gotten slaves, to stop seizing innocent people at gunpoint. The reward would be 'a clear conscience ... and the removal of this curse from your homes'. Vieira's eloquence achieved nothing. When he visited villages of supposedly free Indians he found that the men were all away on forced labour. He wrote to the king about conditions in tobacco plantations – which were the region's only fairly successful enterprise. 'None of these Indians goes except by violence and force. The work is excessive, one in which many die every year since tobacco smoke is very poisonous. They are treated with more harshness than slaves; they are called the most ugly names which they greatly resent; their food is almost non-existent; and their pay is [derisory].' They had to travel long distances, for months on end, unable to plant crops to feed their starving families. And they received no religious instruction.

Soon after Father Vieira's return to the Amazon a band of wild explorers appeared in Belém. This was the *bandeira* of António Rapôso Tavares, the toughest of all the slavers operating out of the distant southern town of São Paulo. *Bandeirantes* were ruthless slave-hunters who spent years exploring the heartland of Brazil in search of their indigenous prey. Many of them were '*mameluco*' mixed-blood sons of Indian mothers and Portuguese fathers. Although their motives were despicable, they were unquestionably among the hardiest and most experienced backwoodsmen in the history of South America.

The fifty-year-old Rapôso Tavares left São Paulo in 1649 on what became a four-year expedition covering a staggering 11,000 kilometres (7,000 miles) on foot and by canoe. It has rightly been called the greatest bandeira by the greatest bandeirante. After crossing some of the most forbidding parts of South America to the foothills of the Andes in modern Bolivia, these bandeirantes were the first Europeans to sail down the Amazon's largest southern tributary, the Madeira river. They were amazed by the numbers living on its banks. 'Fifteen days after embarking on the river they began to see settlements, and from then on there was not a day on which they did not see some, and they generally saw many every day. They saw towns with three hundred huts ... with many families living in each.... They reckoned that [one nation] contained 150,000 souls.' This was probably the Tora tribe. It took the explorers eight days to sail through its territory, with villages almost contiguous along the riverbanks. The Indians were startled by their first sight of clothed and bearded strangers. Most were hospitable, but any who tried to defend their villages were given a 'close volley' of musketry and had their huts sacked and canoes stolen. Father Vieira was appalled by the callous brutality of these slavers. It was 'as if they were describing the sport of a hunting party, with the lives of Indians mattering no more than those of boar or deer. All such killings

have for the past sixty years been tolerated in a kingdom as Catholic as Portugal....
[The murderers] continue as before, with no enquiry or trial or punishment and
not even mildly shunned by public disfavour.'

The Jesuits hated Rapôso Tavares because he had killed one of their Fathers
while enslaving mission Indians in Paraguay. But Vieira marvelled at the magnitude of his exploit, 'like the legends told about the Argonauts, a truly great
example of endurance and valour.... It was certainly one of the most notable
[explorations] ever made in the world up to now!' When Rapôso Tavares and his
gang finally returned to São Paulo, he was so ravaged by the ordeal that his family
did not at first recognize him.

In 1655 Vieira's Jesuits were put in charge of 54 *aldeias* in Maranhão and Pará,
and his biographer boasted that these contained 200,000 souls. The next five years
were ones of glorious, euphoric activity by the black-robed Fathers. They paddled
up Amazon tributaries every year, proclaiming the new pro-Indian law and seduc-
ing entire tribes to come to the promised land of their missions. In 1655 a
thousand Tupinamba descended from the Tocantins in seventy canoes, with
three hundred warriors landing at Belém in their gaudy plumage and body-paint.
More would have come, but one shrewd shaman dissuaded them. In the words of
a Jesuit, 'This minister of Lucifer abhorred the precipitate decision by his people
and the ease with which they were going to place themselves among [the Portuguese,] of whose cruelty infinite tribes complained.' Some Indians 'went to
Heaven' on the journey downriver, but on arrival the rest were baptised, cate-
chised – and then put to work for settlers.

Another Tupi-speaking people, the Cátinga, were persuaded to migrate to
Jesuit missions near Cametá. The Jê-speaking Grajaú had to wait for their descent
because there were not enough canoes or manioc for them. A missionary exulted
that 'in this fishing for men, the nets were starting to break from the multitude'.
Some Guajajara descended from the Pindaré river between Pará and Maranhão to
nearby Jesuit missions. But when a greedy governor started to force them to
labour in his tobacco plantations, they were 'so scandalized' that they wisely fled
back to their forests – and they have survived as a tribe to the present day. Other
Jesuits converted some Juruna at the mouth of the Xingu. For a time these
embraced Christianity with fervour, revelling in the processions and mortifica-
tions of Holy Week. But they later tired of the cheerless aspects of the new religion,
and started to migrate up the Xingu.

In 1656 a Jesuit 'reduced to the Faith and obedience to Your Majesty' 500
Pacajá (from the river of that name west of Belém) and many Tapirapé (some of
whom still survive, far up the Araguaia). Other missionaries were active among

the Arawak on the north shore of the Amazon and on the lower Rio Negro. Two Fathers, including the Irish Jesuit Richard Carew, in 1658 brought a thousand Poquiguara from forests near the middle Tocantins: 'Entire villages had to be descended, with their women, children, infants, sick and all the other impedimenta that are found in a transmigration.' It took two months of 'continuous and excessive work and vigilance' to get these Poquiguara to the river. They were then descended to fill 'aldeias closest to the city [of Belém] for the better service of the republic, which in that year was increased by over 2000 Indians, slave and free. But the settlers were not even satisfied by this. For although the rivers of these lands are the greatest in the world, [settler] greed is greater than their waters.'

While they were migrating, the Poquiguara were attacked by the warlike Inheiguara. This was just what the colonists wanted. The governor immediately declared war on the Inheiguara. In 1659 a punitive campaign of 45 Portuguese soldiers, 450 Indian warriors and the Jesuit superior of Pará sailed up the Tocantins and plunged into that tribe's forests. 'They were sought out there, found, surrounded, forced to surrender and ... 240 were taken prisoner. These were judged to be slaves ... for having impeded the preaching of the evangel, and they were distributed among the soldiers'. Jesuit fathers accompanied official ransom troops, and Vieira told them to be liberal (to the settlers) in deciding which captives were 'legitimate' slaves.

There remained the embarrassment that the island of Marajó, so close to Belém, remained hostile to Portuguese expansion. Its Aruã, Mapuá, Anajá, Camboca and other peoples repulsed all campaigns, by determined fighting and by escaping to a nomadic existence in their labyrinth of streams, swamps and forests. They were considered almost invincible 'because of their daring, caution, cunning and determination, and above all their impregnable location'. The colonial governor wanted to launch yet another 'just war' against them; but Vieira asked for one last chance to pacify them by persuasion. He sent native emissaries with flowery assurances that the new royal laws promised Indians a good life under Portuguese rule and Jesuit care. In his heart, Vieira must have known that this was wicked deception: royal legislation was constantly changing, Indians died in droves from disease, and (as he constantly proclaimed from the pulpit) they were either enslaved or subjected to relentless forced labour. To everyone's surprise, the embassy succeeded. The peoples of Marajó were exhausted by fighting and put their trust in the 'great father' Vieira. The Jesuit was invited to visit them, and he went in 1659 with a dozen canoes filled with chiefs of converted tribes but very few soldiers. The Marajó peoples had already built a mission, complete with church and quarters for the missionaries, and they received Vieira with a great ceremony of submission to Portuguese rule. In later years, Marajó became a Jesuit stronghold, with vast cattle ranches and salt pans that made the Company wealthy. But none of its tribal peoples has survived.

Angry settlers, meanwhile, waged a relentless campaign against the black-robed busybodies. They obtained from French pirates a captured letter from Father Vieira to his sovereign, in which he lambasted leading colonists by name. This was read out in the town council. Even the authorities turned against the Jesuits. In 1661 these missionaries were seized throughout the lower Amazon and in their college in Belém. Vieira himself was held under such close arrest 'that he was not even free for a necessity'. He and his fellow missionaries were then packed off to Portugal, with an officer pushing the canoe taking them to their ship and shouting 'Out! Out! Out!'. Back in Lisbon, Father Vieira preached a powerful 'Sermon of the Missions' that moved the Queen-Regent. But before she could act, a palace revolution changed the monarchy and again eclipsed Vieira's influence. A reactionary law in 1663 put 'free' Indians at the mercy of settlers' town councils which were given open-season to launch slaving expeditions. Vieira tried to persuade the new king that this traffic must stop. 'Under the injustice and tyranny cloaked with the name "ransoms" ... many thousands of innocent Indians have been enslaved, killed and extinguished. It is the primary cause of all the ruin of that state.' But it was not until 1680 – after seventeen years of near-anarchy and oppression – that another law returned the *aldeias* to Jesuit control, and tried to outlaw slavery and liberate slaves.

Vieira survived a trial for heresy (for his unduly patriotic and messianic sermons); spent six years as a sought-after preacher in Rome; and returned to his beloved Brazil in 1681, aged seventy-three. He lived for a further sixteen years in the Jesuit college in Bahia, writing lucid letters and championing Indians. His answer to the labour shortage was to urge settlers to import African slaves. It did not trouble him that slavery of blacks was as evil as that of copper-coloured Indians; nor that the colonists on the Amazon were in any case too poor to afford African slaves.

The pro-missionary law of 1680 provoked the usual backlash. In 1684 another settlers' revolt, led by prominent officials called Beckman and Sampaio, again evicted the Jesuits from Maranhão. The rebellion was rapidly crushed and its leaders hanged. But the Court in Lisbon was alarmed, and a law of September 1684 revived private slaveholdings and again authorized governors to send slaving expeditions up the Amazon. The Jesuits felt that they had been too rigid. In 1686 they issued new Regulations for their mission villages, which they controlled absolutely. But they compromised in three serious respects: they permitted their 'free' mission Indians, between the ages of thirteen and fifty, to work for settlers for six months a year; they themselves continued to accompany ransom expeditions to legitimize enslavement of Indians; and they ceded most of the Amazon to other missionary orders, retaining only the south bank as far upriver as the Madeira.

Although the Jesuits generally championed indigenous people against colonialist excesses, they were not disinterested. They wanted their mission villages to be replicas of the theocratic empire that Spanish Jesuits were creating far to the south in Paraguay. Unfortunately, the indigenous peoples of the Amazon forests did not respond to Jesuit discipline and cradle-to-grave tutelage as readily as the Guarani of Paraguay. The Guarani were naturally spiritual, disciplined farmers who lived in large communities and on open savannahs where imported cattle thrived. Amazon Indians were self-sufficient hunter-gatherers and fishermen, accustomed to individual freedom, and able to move rapidly through their forests and rivers. The Jesuits had absolutely nothing to teach them about farming or medicine. So the Jesuits often failed in Amazonia, even more than less-authoritarian Franciscans, Carmelites and Mercedarians who controlled other stretches of the Amazon and Negro.

The Jesuits admitted that their conversion of Amazon Indians was superficial. Almost none of their converts seemed to understand the meaning of Christianity or to believe fully in it. These recited anything to please the missionary who was giving them confession, and their responses about the creed were perfunctory or frivolous. 'Although they generally hear mass, it is from fear of punishment rather than from a desire for spiritual good.... They greatly value veronicas, medallions and images of the saints. But this is for their prettiness rather than from the respect and devotion they inspire. They often decorate their monkeys or puppies with them, hanging them around their necks.' Father João Daniel admired his Indians' lack of greed for material possessions. 'If they have enough to eat – game from the forests or fish from the rivers – they are as content as potentates.... They live lightly and without ceremony, clad only in the fine skins their mothers gave them ... totally naked like Adam in his state of innocence.' Daniel also liked his charges' habit of bathing frequently and their family lives and marital fidelity. But he and his colleagues deplored the Indians' occasional heavy drinking, largely because they became insolent when drunk and no longer respected white men or ecclesiastics. Some Jesuits tried to ban festivities. When one suspected that a party was planned, he went around his village breaking vessels full of alcoholic drink. 'This, however, dampens the festivities and makes them melancholy.'

Father Daniel was a savage disciplinarian. He noted that his Indians 'took advantage' of newly arrived missionaries by bringing them less fish to eat. 'In this way they often make newcomers fast, for these do not know that a thrashing and beating are the cure for [such laziness]. The result of a good thrashing ... was great abundance of fish from then on.' This Jesuit, however, was also aware that the Indians knew far more than he did about the medicinal properties of the cornucopia of forest plants. But native shamans were not prepared to divulge their lore. 'They are extremely tenacious and mysterious about their secrets.... No matter how many gifts, enticements or promises one makes ... it can be extracted from them only with the cane; and even this generally fails, even if you kill them.' The Fathers suspected that the low birth-rate in their missions was because women had herbal methods of contraception or abortion. This was of course anathema to the missionaries, who used every form of violence to discover such potions. Daniel believed that 'fear achieves more with them than respect, a rod than rhetoric, punishment than dissimulation. They generally do no good or any work, except out of fear.... Thrashing is the most convenient and appropriate punishment for Indians.... Only forty strokes is recommended, which is what missionaries customarily give. If the crimes are more atrocious this can be repeated for more days, together with a sentence of imprisonment. They mind this very much, for they find themselves deprived of their hunting, roaming and other entertainments, and especially of their daily bathing, etc. In truth there is no punishment that tames them better than a long spell in prison, with some good shackles on their feet.' He also knew that desperate Indians could commit suicide, by eating earth, sucking their tongues in to choke to death, or simply 'giving up the ghost', and he told his readers ways in which to stop such release.

This same ferocious Father Daniel was appalled by the cruelty of the settlers along the Amazon. 'They kill Indians as one kills mosquitoes. In labour they treat them as if they were wild animals or beasts of the forest.... And they use – or abuse – the feminine sex brutally and lasciviously, monstrously and indecently, without fear of God or shame before [their fellow] men.... Some white men ... kill some [of their Indians] with the violence of their blows and place others at the gates of death. If they themselves had felt how agonising are the pains of a good thrashing, they might perhaps be less inhuman to the poor [Indians].' One settler was accidentally hit on the back by a whip. The pain was so excruciating that he vowed never again to beat his slaves. But he was the exception. Most Portuguese had no qualms about overworking and abusing the few thousand Indians who had survived decimation by disease or had failed to escape into the forests.

CHAPTER THREE
The Empty River

A French scientist, Charles-Marie de La Condamine, went down the Amazon in 1743 and was appalled to sail for day after day past totally uninhabited banks. In the 800 kilometres (500 miles) between Pebas in Spanish Peru and São Paulo de Olivença in Brazil, 'there is no warrior nation hostile to Europeans on the banks of the Amazon: all have submitted or retreated far away'. On the next long stretch of river, he saw only six Carmelite mission villages. But these were 'formed of the debris of ancient [Jesuit] missions and composed from a great number of diverse tribes, most of them transplanted'.

La Condamine was a European *savant*, so he judged indigenous people by the standards of the European Enlightenment. He was impressed by the tidiness of the missions, with their whitewashed brick and stone houses. The Indians wore white cotton clothes and had locked chests full of manufactured possessions – sewing kit, combs, knives and other trinkets – that they bought by selling cacao downriver in Belém. La Condamine did not share the first observers' rapture at the lack of greed or organized government among these 'noble savages'. To him, the docile and devout mission Indians were insensitive, from either apathy or stupidity. They seemed to have few ideas beyond their daily needs. 'Enemies of work, indifferent to all motives of glory, honour or gratitude; solely concerned with the immediate object...; with no care for the future; and incapable of foresight or reflection ... they spend their lives without thinking, and grow old without emerging from childhood, of which they retain all the defects.' It did not occur to the scientist that he was seeing people brainwashed by missionaries, the few survivors of 120 years of depopulation from disease, warfare and enslavement.

Other observers also commented that great stretches of the Amazon were denuded of the once-teeming villages that had so impressed the first explorers. By the eighteenth century, life on the great river had settled into a dismal rhythm:

a handful of regimented mission villages; missionaries 'descending' tribes to restock their settlements; slaving expeditions scouring the forests for human prey; and determined resistance by a few indigenous peoples. It was all punctuated by lethal epidemics.

The division of the Amazon and its tributaries between the missionary orders was by now well established. The Jesuits ran the southern shore as far upstream as the Madeira. They were particularly active on this river (where Rapôso Tavares's bandeirantes had in 1653 seen so many Indians) as well as the Xingu and smaller tributaries between them. Annual reports by each missionary recorded the descents he had made, with long lists of tribes that were still to be contacted. Almost all of these are now extinct, victims of some long-forgotten disease, descent, slave-raid, or colonial or inter-tribal wars. A Mercedarian praised the energy of the black-robed Jesuits. 'I saw the descents they made for their missions from the heart of the jungle, at a cost of much effort and very heavy expenditure.... They spent much wealth on all this: canoes, cotton cloth, tools, knives, crockery, beads, clothing, and grandiose presents – without which one cannot convince Indians to leave their lands for the bosom of the Church. And after these people are descended, they feed and clothe them for two years.' This ecclesiastic failed to note that the canoes, manpower and cloth of the contact expeditions were all supplied by mission Indians; nor that after two years' grace descended tribes had to join the labour pool and work for the Jesuits, settlers and government. One Jesuit justified his exertions: 'The effort one suffers in these descents is greatly eased by the consolation ... of the many souls being gained for Heaven who would otherwise doubtless be lost.'

Less zealous Franciscans had the northern bank of the lower Amazon – an area largely denuded of indigenous inhabitants. Upriver on that shore, a Mercedarian missionary called Theodozio da Veiga converted the Arauakí of the Uatumã and its Urubú tributary. These people had in 1664 resisted a notorious slaver called Antonio Arnau. One of Arnau's gang recalled that 'these heathen prepared a trap for us. They said that they had a village full of bound captives whom they wanted to give us, but that they needed the help of our guns.' Fifteen whites and a hundred Indians of the slaving troop hurried off to gather the booty. They fell into a night ambush and were destroyed. Meanwhile other Arauakí brought some bound women to Arnau's camp early one morning. 'They brought them tied with rotten ropes – and by their treatment it was obvious that these were their wives, but we did not realize this.... Arnau was delighted.... He was in a hurry to get out of bed to see the slave girls. As he emerged from his door the Arauakí chief struck him with a wooden club, of the sort that they use to execute people.'

Arnau's skull was split and his mouth shattered, so that he died in pain 'in the sight of all, without sacraments'. Other slavers were killed in fighting that day. But this noble resistance became the pretext for a 'just war' of reprisal. The governor sent four companies of infantry and five hundred Indian warriors in thirty-four war canoes. There was a series of fierce battles, but firearms prevailed over arrows – even though these were coated in curare poison. The punitive force 'multiplied its devastations so greatly that the last proud member of those heathen wept at the fatal burning of three hundred villages. [This followed] the slaughter of seven hundred of the most valiant men of that nation, and the captivity of four hundred who are now dragging chains in the city of Belém do Pará as the spoils of victory.' In fact, many Arauakí survived: they killed some forty Portuguese and their Indians in skirmishes and ambushes during the next two decades. A six-month campaign against them in 1684 destroyed a further five hundred warriors and old people, and brought back a similar number as slaves.

The surviving Arauakí were the converts of the Mercedarian Friar Theodozio. He succeeded thanks to a warm personality, generosity with trade goods, and a relaxed attitude to native customs that would have infuriated the harsher Jesuits. Friar Theodozio died in 1701, but his successors ruined his missions by being too venal: they constantly sent their charges off on slaving or collecting expeditions, leaving them no time to tend their own plots. The Indians rebelled, killing one friar and expelling others.

Upstream, the Solimões stretch of the Amazon and the Rio Negro was the domain of the Carmelites. In the final years of the seventeenth century, Portuguese Carmelites clashed with Spanish Jesuits moving down from Peru and Quito. Those Jesuits were led by the saintly, intelligent, but morally inflexible Father Samuel Fritz. In the 1680s the Bohemian-born Fritz descended the upper Amazon to continue the conversion of the Omagua that had been started by the Spanish Franciscan Laureano de la Cruz thirty years previously. The Omagua were by now a shattered remnant of the nation that had so impressed Orellana, Carvajal and Acuña: reduced to some four thousand people in thirty-eight small villages on Amazon islands. They still prided themselves on being superior to forest tribes, with their coloured clothing, ceramics, flattened 'hammer-head' skulls, and farming skills. They readily accepted Fritz's Christian teaching. They even encouraged him to convert the Yurimagua downriver of them, another once-great nation that was also 'much intimidated and wasted' by disease, slavery, forced labour, and inter-tribal warfare. The Yurimagua accepted baptism from the foreign shaman Fritz, who offered spiritual solace and protection. The Aysuare and Ibanoma further down the Amazon were also interested in Christianity.

Then in 1689 Father Fritz's mission was shattered by his ill-health. Years on the Amazon and his pious asceticism had taken their toll. He wrote: 'I fell sick of most violent attacks of fever, dropsy [accumulation of liquid] that began in my feet, and other complaints chiefly caused by worms. For almost three months, I was obliged to remain shut day and night in this [bark-roofed] shelter without being able to stir. I felt somewhat easier during daytime, but spent the nights in unutterable burnings.' It was during the months when the river rises and floods huge areas of forests. So, 'although the river passed only a hand's breadth from my bed, it was out of reach of my mouth'. Alligator-like caymans kept the Jesuit awake with their grunts, and one crawled up a moored canoe close to the fever-stricken patient and his boy attendant.

Father Fritz was probably suffering from malaria, an affliction newly arrived on the main Amazon. Malaria was an ancient disease in Europe and Africa: the Greek physician Hippocratus described the symptoms of what he called tertian and quartan fevers (from the number of days between attacks); and the Romans coined the name mal-aria, thinking that it was caused by bad air. Malaria soon crossed the Atlantic. Conquistadors plunging into the heart of Venezuela in the 1540s were prostrated by fevers; it had reached Peru by 1586; and Sir Walter Raleigh often suffered from 'ague' (burning, shivering fever, from the French word for acute). No-one knew how to treat the horrible disease, until Indians in Loja (on the Amazon slopes of the Andes in what is now Ecuador) cured a Jesuit by giving him a bitter powder – from the bark of a tree they called quina. In 1638 the Jesuits heard that the Countess of Chinchón, wife of the Spanish Viceroy of Peru, was dying of fever, so they rushed quinine powder to Lima, and the fevers vanished. (Actually, it was the Viceroy himself who was cured, but the romantic story has always been associated with his beautiful young wife.) The Jesuits were good scientists and smart businessmen, so they started propagating the tree and selling the miraculous quinine. In Europe it was known as 'Jesuits bark' or 'Jesuits powder'. Two rulers of England, Oliver Cromwell and Charles II, both had their ague relieved by quinine – although they concealed the fact that they had consumed a medicine from the hated Jesuits. Someone brought the plant to Europe: the diarist Sir John Evelyn saw the quinine tree growing in the Chelsea Physic Garden as early as 1685.

One of the first scientists to study this magical tree, in Ecuador, was the same Charles-Marie de La Condamine who wrote about his descent of the Amazon. And its botanical name *Cinchona* was given in honour of the Viceroy's lady by none other than the father of taxonomy, the Swedish Carl von Linné. From Fritz's time onwards malaria occurred with increasing frequency. By the nineteenth century, every native and traveller on the great river was plagued by that devastating disease. As with all maladies, no-one had any inkling of the fever's origin or vector.

Father Samuel Fritz went down the Amazon to seek medical help from Portuguese Jesuits. These did their best, but it was worse than useless. Curiously, they did not know about quinine, so they let his blood 'to ease the fevers', fumigated him for dropsy, and fed him other violent remedies. 'But instead of being benefited I was made worse than before. Up until then I was able to stand on my feet; but henceforth I had to allow myself to be carried in a hammock.' He eventually recovered in the Jesuit college in Belém, before returning up the river to Peru in 1692.

On his journeys, Fritz visited the few mission villages remaining on the banks of the Amazon and two Portuguese forts near its mouth. But for six days below Tupinambaranas Island at the mouth of the Madeira he did not see a single settlement. For fourteen days, in which he covered some 600 kilometres (375 miles) from the Tapajós to the Urubu, there was 'neither settlement nor people' apart from one Jesuit mission. Above the confluence of the Rio Negro, where there had once been 'infinite nations' of Carabuyana, Caripuna and Zurina, he travelled for 'nine days without any settlements'. There on the Solimões were burned and abandoned villages – a sad legacy of inter-tribal warfare and slave raids. The Jesuit was then paddled for weeks on end up the swirling brown river, empty of human habitation. From observations on these journeys, Father Fritz drew the first passably accurate map of the Amazon and its tributaries.

During the next decade, the Spanish Jesuit Fritz singlehandedly tried to convert what was left of the Solimões tribes. He was asked to leave by Portuguese Carmelites, who claimed that this stretch of the Amazon was theirs by right of occupation and because of Pedro Teixeira's marker of sixty years earlier. The lone missionary countered that the only treaty between the Iberian empires was still the Line of Tordesillas of 1494, that *he* had been peacefully converting those tribes for many years, and that so-called Portuguese occupation was just 'murders and enslavements by the men of Pará'. But it was Portugal who triumphed. Its Carmelites won over the tribes with lavish presents – and a force of soldiers sent up from Pará.

The stern Jesuit father had antagonized even the Omagua by his austerity. Aggrieved Omagua persuaded uncontacted forest tribes to join them in destroying one Jesuit mission. Fritz got Spanish troops to help him crush this rebellion; he had two chiefs flogged and exiled to prison far upriver in Borja; and he destroyed all the Indians' body-paint scrapers, shamanic regalia and beloved hallucinogenic *curupá* powder. This repression was a mistake. Chief Payoreva of the Omagua escaped from jail, entered Fritz's mission of San Joaquín (now Pebas in Peru, 250 kilometres – 155 miles – below Iquitos) and persuaded almost all its Indians to flee with him deep into the forest and then downstream to their former homes on the Solimões.

Throughout the first decade of the eighteenth century, there was an unseemly tug-of-war between the Iberian kingdoms for possession of what remained of the Omagua and Yurimagua nations. It ended with most of the Yurimagua fleeing far up the Amazon, to Pebas and beyond to La Laguna on the Huallaga (where a few remain to this day). The Omagua were divided, with some on the Ucayali in Spanish Peru and others far away on the Solimões at Fritz's short-lived mission of San Pablo – now São Paulo de Olivença in Portuguese Brazil. As usual, it was the indigenous people who suffered. Hundreds of kilometres of river-banks became a no-man's-land between the colonial powers, denuded of people. Many from both tribes died of disease, or were transported to the slave market in Belém.

Slave-raiding continued unabated throughout these centuries. A Jesuit wrote to the King in 1719 that each year official licences were granted to between 50 and 350 'ransoming' canoes. Apart from the misery inflicted on the people they enslaved, the crews of these expeditions suffered horribly. Each canoe was paddled by some twenty-five Indians. Thus, in a year like 1736 when 320 canoes were licensed, some 8,000 rowers must have been involved. Many of these were press-ganged from mission villages, tied up and dragged to the boats. 'They would be gone for eight to nine months, rowing night and day, sleeping on the hard benches of the canoes, overexposed to the hot river sun, very badly fed, and completely untended when they fell ill. They frequently died from overwork, or were killed in battle against other Indians.' As the main rivers were emptied of inhabitants, the slavers had to push further and further up the Amazon's tributaries. If one of these heavily armed expeditions encountered a missionary descending a tribe to replenish his mission, they often had no compunction about seizing the human cargo. There were plenty of complaints from missionaries about such kidnaps, but no recorded punishment of the aggressors.

The law stipulated that a missionary should accompany each ransom troop to judge which of its victims were 'legitimate' slaves. Modern Brazilian historians have criticized Father Antonio Vieira and his successors for their complicity in this traffic – although the missionaries were required to do this monitoring, and their relations with their compatriot colonists were too precarious for them to refuse. It was almost impossible for a missionary to decide which frightened Indian captives could 'legitimately' be enslaved. Many had been purchased from tribal chiefs who had been incited to seize them. They were thus deemed to be 'ransomed' from alleged execution by their captors. Others came from tribes who had resisted in some way: they were therefore taken in a 'just war'. Those who were considered to be 'free' or 'conditional slaves' (theoretically subject to five years' rather than perpetual servitude) were sent to replenish mission villages – a missionary's reward for his role in the wretched business. It never occurred to anyone to return 'free' Indians to their forest homes.

Slavers would browbeat their captives into mouthing self-incriminating answers, in Portuguese that they could not understand. Many records of slaving judgements have survived. One will suffice to illustrate these heartrending charades: 'On 8th May this year [1726] the Manoa chief Guarunamá sold a girl called Coeminao of the Moveno-minao tribe, approximately seven years old and with a black spot above her right breast. The seller said she was his slave, captured in a just war against his enemies. The girl confessed that this was true. The Reverend Father Missionary and the Troop Leader therefore certified her to be a slave. She was purchased by the troop's treasurer, José Ferreira Sampaio, for one satin skirt and one spade.... She is solemnly baptised Custodia.'

João V of Portugal in 1721 sent an inspector to report on the Amazon slave traffic. He confirmed that virtually every settler, from the governor down, was embroiled in this ugly business and held illegal slaves. The slavers were brutal and inefficient. Captured Indians were held for months in riverside corrals. They were then tightly tied to poles and packed into canoes. 'The greater part died on the journey downriver, and those who survived arrived moribund. Most perished soon after. Thus the work and cost of the enterprise were in vain.'

As the ransom canoes depopulated the main Amazon, slavers wanted to get at indigenous peoples living up the main tributaries – particularly on the Madeira and Negro rivers. For a time, the large Tora tribe defended the lower Madeira and harassed canoes going up it. They were so numerous that other Indians called them an anthill. The Tora were said to have hindered the Jesuits' attempts to descend other tribes. 'They have done us great damage, preventing missionaries from doing the work of God by their hostilities.' So a heavily armed campaign was launched against the Tora in 1719, and this was deemed to be a 'just war' whose victims could be enslaved. It was a bloody affair; and it 'left them extinct'.

The mighty Rio Negro, which drained the entire northwestern segment of the Amazon basin, was home to the Manau nation. These were great travellers and traders. They paddled far up their river, through the Casiquiare canal that links it with the Orinoco, and thence to the Muisca and other gold-mining tribes of modern Colombia. The Manau also ascended the Rio Branco and crossed a flooded plain to the Essequibo in modern Guyana. When Walter Raleigh and his lieutenants were at the mouth of that river in the 1590s, they heard about gold and riches near its seasonally flooded source. This inspired a great mythical lake that appeared on maps for two centuries, with the glittering cities of El Dorado and Manoa (Manau) on its banks. The two Jesuits, Acuña in 1639 and Fritz in 1689, noted that the Manau paddled through *várzea* forests between the middle Negro and Solimões to trade 'small bars of gold, vermilion, and manioc graters' – to this day the speciality of the Desana of a tributary of the upper Negro – with its tribes.

The Manau co-operated with Portuguese slavers by selling prisoners they had captured from other tribes. However, by the early eighteenth century, hundreds of kilometres of the lower Negro were empty of Indians. The Manau controlled the thundering rapids of the middle river and prevented access to the peoples of the upper tributaries. Worse, Manau traders were also dealing with the Dutch colony of Guiana (modern Guyana). The powerful and Protestant Dutch were enemies of the Portuguese throughout the world, and between 1625 and 1650 had almost wrenched Brazil from them. So when something went wrong in barter between the Manau and the ransom troop of 1723, belligerent colonists started a propaganda campaign against the Manau. The King of Portugal was persuaded to authorize a 'just war' because tribes of the Rio Negro 'impede the propagation of the Faith, continually rob and assault my vassals, eat human flesh, and live like brutes defying the laws of nature.... These barbarians are full of arms and munitions, some of which they were given by the Dutch.' No ransom troop had dared to attack the Manau, because they had guns and 'have also entrenched themselves with wood-and-mud stockades, watch-towers and defences.... They have thus become proud and emboldened to commit excesses and killings.'

The Manau produced a heroic leader called Ajuricaba. A Jesuit sent to negotiate with him found that Ajuricaba was flying a Dutch flag from his canoe. 'The infidel Ajuricaba is a proud, insolent man.... All the other chiefs respect him and obey his precepts with fear and respect. All insults done to us were on his orders or suggestion.' A later Portuguese official was more flattering: 'Nature endowed him with a brave, intrepid and warlike spirit.... The greater part of his nation showed him the most faithful love and devotion.... Throughout the course of his life, Ajuricaba was certainly a hero among the Indians.'

The inevitable punitive expedition went up the Rio Negro in 1728. Ajuricaba's stockaded village was attacked by soldiers with cannon and hundreds of Indians recruited from missions. The Manau chief escaped, but he was eventually hunted down in a village of his allies. He and other chiefs were taken downriver chained and shackled, for slavery or execution. When the captives were almost at Belém, Ajuricaba performed the act of bravery that earned him a place in the pantheon of Brazilian heroes. He and his men 'rose up in the canoe in which they were coming in chains and tried to kill the soldiers'. There was a hard but hopeless struggle, of shackled Indians against armed captors. When all was lost, 'with some of his friends bleeding and others dead', 'Ajuricaba leapt into the river with another chief, and never reappeared dead or alive'. He is honoured as the gallant Indian who preferred death to slavery.

Ajuricaba's allies, the Mayapena tribe, continued the resistance from a fortified village near the rapids. But, after a twelve-day siege, they too were overcome. A new governor was jubilant that the barrier of the middle Rio Negro was now breached. Intent on enriching himself to the utmost, he sent a notorious old Indian-hunter called Belchior de Moraes to lead the mopping-up campaign. In two years, Moraes claimed to have attacked and enslaved no fewer than forty-five tribes and killed 20,800 people – unconcerned whether they had been allies or enemies of the Portuguese. Perhaps surprisingly, some Manau survived by continuing to help Portuguese slavers. They were settled in a series of Carmelite missions on the middle Negro, particularly at São Gabriel da Cachoeira (Saint Gabriel of the Rapids).

After a century on the Amazon, Europeans were finally starting to adapt to its luxuriant but alien environment. They found a few places on which to graze their beloved cattle. In 1680 a Portuguese carpenter started to raise beef on natural savannahs on Marajó Island, opposite Belém. Missionaries came to dominate ranching on this island. The animals multiplied, thanks to some husbandry and expanses of well-watered pasture. By 1750 a governor reckoned that the Jesuits had 30,000 head of cattle on Marajó (but when their herds were confiscated nine years later, they were found to have 135,000); the Mercedarians 60–100,000 head; and the Carmelites 8–10,000. After Father Vieira's death, the Jesuit Company had become aggressively mercantile. Using mission and slave labour, it developed six rural estates in Pará. These produced profitable surpluses of hides, tallow fat and meat from the animals, and plantation crops of cotton, tobacco, and sugar to make rum.

The Europeans were also learning to exploit some native plants. Their Indians grew quantities of manioc, since manioc flour was the staple for everyone living in the region. They tried to create plantations of cacao (the Mexican name of the *Theobroma mariae* tree) to satisfy the European craze for chocolate. But the tree's main enemy, the fungal pathogen 'witch's broom', is endemic to the Amazon, so most Brazilian cacao came from further south in Bahia.

Indians were also sent off into the forests to collect plants that had commercially value to the foreigners. These were known collectively as *drogas do sertão* ('drugs of the wilds'). They included: bark of trees such as *Dicypellium caryophyllatum* or *Ambrosia polystachya* (ragweed), which tasted sufficiently like cloves (*cravo*) to conceal the taste of rotting meat; *sarsaparilha*, the dried root of the *Smilax* climber of the lily family, widely in demand for medicinal teas, as a restorative, or a palliative for syphilis; *ipecac* or *ipecacuanha*, another root found at the southern edge of Amazonia and used as an emetic to cause vomiting and reduce fevers; *copaíba* oil, a balsam from the *Copaifera* palm; and saps from *andiroba* (*Carapa guianensis*) and *sumaúma* kapoks (*Ceiba pentandra*), trees whose timber also had a multitude of uses in ship-building. Indians preferred expeditions to gather *drogas do sertão* to soul-destroying drudgery in plantations or public works. But most of the desired trees and shrubs had to be uprooted and killed. So their extraction involved ever-longer forays into the forests and absences from men's families and gardens. Other exports were oil extracted from thousands of eggs of the Amazon turtles (*Podocnemis*) that the Omagua had once farmed so successfully, and dried fish. But Portugal's Amazon colony remained a poor relation to the rest of Brazil.

The wretched Indians in missions along the Amazon rivers were decimated by regular epidemics throughout the eighteenth century. The worst smallpox and measles attacks struck in 1748, 1749 and 1750. A contemporary account said that 'this dire and dangerous illness lasted for two months, but after that time it degenerated into malignant fevers, stupors and mumps. For these diseases they applied ridiculous, almost useless remedies; but these did however bring solace to many. By the end there was no *tapuia* or anyone with [Indian] blood who did not suffer the force of this contagion.... The tears of the settlers were frequent for some ... were reduced to lamentable ruin, since all wealth in this land consists of the multitude of slaves and subjects. There were not enough blacks to wash the corpses.... Their masters themselves had to carry [dead indigenous] slaves, taking them to be thrown to wild animals in forests near the city.' The colonists also complained of lack of meat and mullet fish, because there were no Indians left to bring these from Marajó. The governor reckoned that 40,000 people died near Belém alone. This was 'without reckoning those in the *sertão* of whom, because they live unknown in the impenetrable forests, it seems impossible to give an accurate assessment'. His successor 'was very distressed by the damage, since the number of servants [labourers] was greatly diminished and the epidemic struck that class with greatest rigour'. On a positive note, a royal decree in 1748 finally put a stop to ransom expeditions and official enslavement of Indians.

La Condamine's three-month descent of the Amazon five years earlier in 1743 had lifted the veil of secrecy imposed by the river's Spanish and Portuguese colonial masters. He had spent the previous eight years near Quito on a mission to calculate the shape and size of planet Earth. A splendid team from the French Académie des Sciences laboured across tough mountain terrain to measure, by chains and triangulation, three degrees of latitude (345 kilometres; 215 miles) south from the Equator. They then made celestial observations of the zenith at the ends of their meridian. This proved that Isaac Newton was right to postulate that the Earth bulges slightly at its middle, whereas René Descartes had argued that our planet is elongated at the poles.

La Condamine decided to return to France by the river Amazon. His journey from Quito started with the arduous descent of the eastern slopes of the Andes, stumbling down through cloud forest to turbulent headwater rivers. Once on the main river, he raced through a notorious 10-kilometre (6-mile) gorge with whirlpools known as the Pongo de Manseriche. 'The waters seem to hurl them-selves as they dash against the rocks, deafening the ear with a tremendous noise.... In the course of the different bends I was two or three times flung violently against the rocks.' A canoe would have been smashed to pieces, but La Condamine was on a raft whose liana bindings absorbed all the buffeting. Below the Pongo, the great river pours for thousands of kilometres towards the ocean without further impediment. The scientist marvelled at this 'fresh-water sea' enclosed by the gloom of an immense forest stretching to far horizons. He described the animals, reptiles and fish of this strange world – including vampire bats and electric eels (actually a long fish) whose shock could 'lay one prostrate'. He gave early accounts of curare poisons that Indians used on their blow-gun darts, and of *barbasco* or *timbó* creeper (*Derris* sp.) with which they stunned fish. In addition to describing the quinine tree, La Condamine was the first to tell Europeans about the remarkable latex *cautchouc*, that Indians drew from trees and used to make balls and syringes. The English later called this extraordinary elastic 'rubber'.

We have seen how La Condamine approved of tidy missions, noted the human void along most of the river, and deplored apathetic mission Indians. He also pondered whether there had ever been Amazons on the river named after them. On balance, he felt that there probably *had* been such a tribe, but that these warrior women were not as rich as chroniclers imagined, nor had they cut off a breast for easier archery. As a romantic Frenchman, La Condamine worried about tension among women deprived of the male sex. He reasoned that because of this they would have died out, leaving no trace.

The French scientific expedition also spawned the first non-Indian heroine of Amazon exploration. Its youngest member, Jean Godin des Odonnais, in 1741 married Isabel, the daughter of a prosperous Spanish-colonial family. Eight years and four children later, Jean Godin decided to return to France by descending the Amazon as his colleague La Condamine had done. Amiable but muddle-headed, Godin hatched a crazy plan to descend the river to prepare lodgings for his beloved wife, and then return all the way up it, to fetch her and their children by the same daunting route. He got down the Amazon all right. But once in French Guyane (Cayenne) he ran into an interminable succession of delays – political (permissions refused by the Portuguese), financial (he was broke, and begging letters took two years to reach France and return with a refusal), physical (illnesses, loss of nerve), business failure (he tried hunting manatees), poor communications (ships were often caught by pirates, wars and storms), and personal (he fell out with the governor). All this meant that he was stuck in the steamy colony for *twenty* years.

Isabel Godin had married him when she was thirteen and just out of a convent school. Her married life was typical for creole society – cloistered by her family and constantly waited on by Indian servants. The Godins' children all died, and the middle-aged Isabel finally decided to go to join her husband on the other side of South America. She made the best preparations she could, sold her house, and set off in 1769 with her two brothers, several hangers-on, maids, servants, and native porters carrying most of her worldly goods. Isabel herself wore full skirts and satin slippers. No colonial matron had ever attempted such a journey.

The group descended from the Andes to the Amazon forests, but when it embarked on the Bobonaza river everything went wrong. None of the whites knew anything about canoes or jungles, and a combination of their grotesque incompetence and bad luck turned the journey into tragedy. A village of indigenous people had been destroyed by smallpox, so their paddlers all deserted from fear of this epidemic; a sick Indian built them a dugout canoe, but he drowned when trying to save someone's hat; the totally inexperienced whites rapidly overturned the canoe; and the half-drowned survivors camped on a sandbank. A dubious Frenchman in the party offered to take the canoe and a couple of men downriver to seek help and a crew of paddlers. It was ominously reminiscent of Orellana leaving Gonzalo Pizarro on a nearby river two centuries earlier. Like Orellana, the Frenchman never returned.

Almost four weeks elapsed, and the group marooned on the sandbank suffered from exposure and hunger. In desperation, Isabel Godin and her brothers cut some saplings and made a makeshift raft. This lasted for only a few minutes

Right A Carib-speaking Tiriyó. This indigenous people live north of the lower Amazon, where the first European explorers located Amazons of legend – after whom the world's greatest river was named. Handsomely decorated Carib men might have been mistaken for these female warriors.

Below Native peoples of the Americas were decimated by imported diseases against which they had no inherited immunity. Many of these Tupi-speaking Parakanã died of measles and influenza shortly after first contact.

Left Indigenous Amazonians in canoes welcomed – and marvelled at – the first European sailing ships.

Below A fanciful vision of the legendary female Amazon warriors destroying male intruders, by Theodor De Bry, a Flemish artist who never visited the Americas.

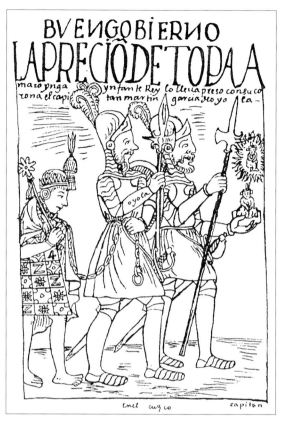

BVENGOBIERNO
LAPRECIÕDETOPAA

maco ynga   ynfante Rey   lo lleua preso con su co
rona el capi   tan martin   garcia oyo la —

oyo la

enel   cuzco   capitan

Left Francisco Pizarro's conquistadors overthrew the Inca empire in the 1530s, but a few descendants of the last Inca survived in the forested Vilcabamba hills until they were crushed in 1572. Tupac Amaru, the young leader of this neo-Inca enclave, was captured deep in Amazonian forests, taken to Cuzco, and executed.

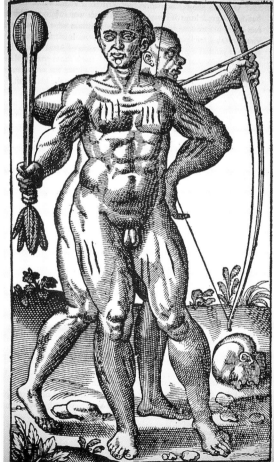

Right The Tupinamba resisted the first Portuguese settlement, at Belém at the mouth of the Amazon, in 1616. Clubs and bows and arrows were favourite weapons of Tupinamba warriors, whose tattoos recorded the number of enemy they had killed.

Above The Brazilian-born Jesuit Father Antonio Vieira
was a powerful figure at the Portuguese court before
going in 1653 to be a missionary on the Amazon. He
was appalled by the destruction of native peoples by
Portuguese settlers through their slaving and diseases.

Above Throughout the seventeenth and early eighteenth centuries, Portuguese colonists captured thousands of indigenous people, whose arrows were no match for firearms. Captives were taken down the Amazon as slaves, but most succumbed to disease or overwork.

Opposite The Jesuits and other missionary orders tried to protect Indians from the excesses of slavers. The exasperated settlers, who were totally dependent on native labour, twice rebelled and expelled the Jesuits from the Brazilian Amazon.

Opposite Europeans have always floundered in tropical forests where indigenous people learned to hunt, fish, farm and forage sustainably. Here, a European traveller has to be carried to a canoe by Indians.

C. M. DE LA CONDAMINE
l'un des Quarante de l'Académie Françoise
Mort à Paris le 16 Février 1774 âgé de 74 Ans

Left Charles-Marie de La Condamine was a French savant who in the 1730s led a measurement of the Equator at Quito but returned down the Amazon. His unauthorized descent in 1743 was the first glimpse of the river (which the Portuguese and Spanish jealously guarded) by an Enlightenment scientist.

Below A Franciscan missionary and his Indians, early nineteenth century. Missionaries brought stability and some degree of protection to their flocks, but at the expense of indigenous culture, beliefs, heritage and identity.

The fort and village of São Gabriel da Cachoeira, at a rapids on the middle Rio Negro.
São Gabriel changed hands during the bloody Cabanagem rebellion of 1836–39,
and was a base for the naturalists Alfred Wallace and Richard Spruce in the 1850s.
The boat is a *batalão*, the workhorse of Amazonian travel, with a crew of tireless
Indian paddlers and a thatched shelter for European passengers.

before smashing into a log, disintegrating, dumping their supplies, and again almost drowning them. They now decided to try to walk through the forest. Isabel, her brothers and a nephew set off, with Isabel finally abandoning her skirt and wearing men's trousers. The party had no map and no compass. So they planned to stay near the river – another error, since the Bobonaza meanders giddily, and the vegetation beside it is far denser and swampier than the *terra firme* forest a short distance inland. The pathetic group suffered terribly from insects (mosquitoes, black-fly, hornets, sweat bees, botflies, ticks and ubiquitous ants), humidity, hunger and often thirst. Their clothes were reduced to rags by tearing, spiny plants. They were soon seized by one of the greatest dangers in high forest where the sun is invisible above the canopy: they became hopelessly lost. They staggered on for almost a month, increasingly weak, wounded and frightened. Then, one by one, the boy, his father and his uncle died horrible deaths from starvation, cradled by the emaciated and dying Isabel. For two days she lay 'stretched on the ground beside the corpses of her brothers, semi-conscious, delirious, and tormented with choking thirst'.

Isabel prayed, and summoned a final shred of energy. She set off again, alone, for eight more days, sustained only by finding a stream of good water, a nest of bird's eggs (a very rare find in rain forest), and some berries. She came upon a river and, although hallucinating from hunger, heard noises. It was a canoe of Indians, and they proved to be friendly – not the warlike Shuar (then called Jívaro) of this part of what is now Ecuador. Isabel Godin was saved, and the kind Indians gradually nursed her back to life. They then took her to a mission, where the priest was amazed by the apparition of a woman who had been given up for dead two months previously. She rewarded her saviours with two gold chains she still had round her neck, but the missionary promptly stole these from the Indians.

People advised Isabel to return to Quito, but she insisted on continuing down the Amazon and up the coast to Cayenne. Her husband came out to meet her ship, and wrote: 'On board this vessel, after twenty years' absence, I again met with a cherished wife, whom I had almost given over every hope of seeing again. In her embraces I forgot the loss of the fruits of our union [their dead children].' The couple reached France in 1773, and lived for a further nineteen years in his family's village in the Auvergne. Isabel Godin des Odonnais' story was a bestseller in its day, and her survival remains unique in the annals of Amazon exploration. But it was caused by staggering naivety and incompetence – another example of the helplessness of Europeans in that alien environment.

Large parts of Amazonia were still unpenetrated by European colonists, and in at least one region the indigenous people managed to regain their independence. This was in eastern Peru, across the Andes from Lima. As the mountains drop towards Amazon forests, there is a plateau that the Spaniards knew as the Gran Pajonal because of its tough, spiky *ichu* grasses (a *pajonal* is a field of stubble in Spanish). It lies above the Perené river, which flows out of the Andes into the Tambo just before it becomes the great Ucayali river.

The Gran Pajonal and the forests below it are home to Aruak-speaking Asháninka (part of the Campa nation, related to the Machiguenga to whom Tupac Amaru was fleeing when he was captured in 1572). These Asháninka did not always take kindly to attempts at conversion to Christianity. In the 1630s a chief (who resented enforced monogamy) massacred an expedition of Dominicans and burned a Franciscan mission. Other missionaries persevered, but in 1694 they were driven out by another general rebellion. There followed the usual cycle of armed reprisals.

The Franciscans tried again, and claimed in their heyday that their missions held over 8,300 Campa converts. But when in 1737 these were hit by epidemics of dysentery and other diseases, Chief Ignacio Torote led another rising that destroyed two missions. Lay Spaniards were starting to establish cattle ranches on the grassy Gran Pajonal. The Franciscans got the colonial government to send a contingent of soldiers, who captured four revered Asháninka chiefs, executed them, and displayed their heads and hands on poles. For a time the missionaries thought that they were gaining a welcome among the Asháninka with presents of metal tools and alcohol, but this was a delusion. In 1742 there was a great gathering of over a thousand Asháninka and other peoples. The assembly declared that the missionaries were not wanted and vowed to resist oppression by Peru's Spanish rulers. Another punitive force, of seventy soldiers assisted by archers from tribes opposed to the Asháninka, invaded the Gran Pajonal. There was a fierce battle against the men of Chief Mateo Santobangori, in which most Spaniards were wounded. Chief Mateo was killed, but other leaders of this 'rebellion' were never found. One of them emerged as the hero of native independence in the Gran Pajonal. This was a mission-educated messiah who claimed descent from the Incas and from God. To his Christian name Juan Santos he added Atahualpa (the Inca executed by Francisco Pizarro in 1533), and he assumed titles from both cultures: Apo [Lord] Capac Huayna Jesús Sacramento. This charismatic figure preached a potent mixture of native myth and Christian doctrine, and he promised a utopian future in which the Campa would rule over Spaniards. Later in 1742 his Asháninka massacred all colonists in the region.

From a fortified base at the former mission Metraro on the upper Perené, Juan Santos Atahualpa mobilized indigenous peoples throughout the Central Selva of Peru. For eleven years he co-ordinated armed resistance by a tribal alliance and he led a permanent indigenous militia. There were risings against Spanish rule in neighbouring areas, and for the next century – the remainder of the colonial period and early independence – the Peruvian authorities lost control of these eastern slopes of the Andes and the Amazonian forests and rivers below them.

In the middle of the eighteenth century the political geography of South America – and of the Amazon in particular – changed forever. Portuguese diplomats scored a diplomatic triumph in the Treaty of Madrid of 1750. The Line of Tordesillas was scrapped after more than 250 years. Instead, the two Iberian kingdoms divided South America according to two remarkably intelligent principles: 'The first and principal one is that the Boundaries ... shall be defined taking as landmarks the best known features ... such as the sources and courses of rivers and the most remarkable mountains; the second that each party shall remain in possession of what it holds at the present time.'

The hardest negotiating concerned the extreme south of Brazil, modern Uruguay; so the Portuguese had little difficulty in acquiring most of the seemingly useless Amazon basin. They claimed prior occupation because their slaving expeditions had been denuding the main Amazon and its accessible tributaries for the past 130 years, and because their missionary orders had villages on the banks of those rivers. After their separation from Spain in 1640, the Portuguese had aggressively built more small forts on the lower Amazon: Barra (future Manaus) in 1670; Santarém in 1697; and Óbidos in 1698. By contrast, Spanish colonists had no incentive to make the difficult crossing of the Andes into the western Amazon forests. They had plenty of highland Indian workers in Peru (partly because imported diseases were less lethal at high altitude); lowland forest Indians would have been useless in the Andes; and no Amazonian produce was worth transporting across the mountains.

The Spaniards were more interested in the open country at the extreme south of the Amazon basin. As we have seen, Ñuflo de Chaves had conquered the Chané, Chiriguano and nearby Chiquitos and in 1561 founded in their midst Santa Cruz de la Sierra, near the Grande headwater of the Madeira (see pp. 41–42). These peoples resisted colonization, but were subdued again in 1690. After that, Spanish Jesuits assembled the Chiquitos and the Mojos to the northwest of them into a series of mission 'reductions'. They called the region Charcas. The Chiquitos and Mojos took readily to horses and cattle-ranching, and by the time of the Jesuits' expulsion in 1767 there were some thirty thousand people in their Charcas missions.

The Treaty of Madrid fixed the frontier between Brazil and Peru at the Javari river, over 5,000 kilometres (3,100 miles) west of the Atlantic Ocean – not far from where the Portuguese patriots of 1639 had so audaciously planted their markers. To the south, the frontier followed the Guaporé and Mamoré headwaters of the Madeira. This was roughly the biogeographical boundary between the mass of Amazon rain forests and the more open plains of the Llanos de Mojos and Llanos de Chiquitos. When the Portuguese discovered gold in Mato Grosso in the early eighteenth century, they tried to establish an outlet for it along these rivers. Wretched Indians had to paddle for months on end up and down the 3,000-kilometre (1,865-mile) Guaporé-Mamoré-Madeira route to the main Amazon.

To the north, Brazil's frontier from the Rio Negro to the Atlantic was defined as the watershed. All rivers flowing south into the Amazon basin were considered Portuguese, while those flowing north towards the Caribbean went to Spain (and, although this was not mentioned in this treaty, to the Dutch, French and later British Guiana colonies). There were subsequent adjustments to these frontiers, but essentially the Treaty of Madrid gave Brazil its modern size, occupying half the continent of South America and two-thirds of the Amazon basin. Indigenous inhabitants were totally ignored in this carve-up. The new borders split the territories of then-unknown tribes like the Yanomami, Makuxi, Ticuna, Tirió and all the peoples of the upper Rio Negro. But because the frontiers followed geographical features that were unambiguous and logical they prevented colonial conflicts. There has never been a shot fired in anger across them. They are the oldest and longest colonial boundary in the world.

CHAPTER FOUR

Directorate to Cabanagem

1750, the year in which the Treaty of Madrid gave Brazil the lion's share of the Amazon basin, also saw the accession of a new King of Portugal, José I. Throughout his twenty-seven-year reign, Portugal was run by a strong-man, his Secretary of State José de Carvalho e Mello, known to history by his later title Marquis of Pombal. Pombal was very tall, handsome and powerfully built, and he was equally forceful as a politician. When in 1755 most of Lisbon was destroyed by an earthquake and subsequent tidal-wave and fire, many wanted to move the capital north to Coimbra. But Pombal insisted on rebuilding the city. This helped confirm him as an effective ruler, and he became a virtual dictator.

This was a period of great wealth for Portugal thanks to an inflow of gold discovered in Brazil. Pombal determined to reform the administration of Brazil, in the gold-mining region of Minas Gerais ('General Mines'), the old sugar areas of the northeast, and newly legalized Brazilian Amazonia. Pombal sent his brother Francisco Xavier de Mendonça Furtado (members of grand Portuguese families often chose to use different surnames) to govern the northern captaincies of Maranhão and Greater Pará. He hoped for a trade bonanza from this vast and apparently fertile region, and created a trading company to stimulate its industry.

If Pará was to become an economic success, it needed a suitably elegant capital. When La Condamine had reached Belém in 1743 after his descent of the Amazon, he'd felt himself transported to Europe. 'We found a city with well-aligned streets, delightful houses, most of which were built during the past thirty years of stone and aggregate, and magnificent churches.' But Pombal wanted more. After the Treaty of Madrid, Portugal sent to Italy to engage engineers to survey Brazil's new frontiers and embellish its towns. One recruit was the distinguished architect Giuseppe Landi from Bologna, who sailed to Belém do Pará in 1753 with Governor Mendonça Furtado. Maestro Landi immediately started

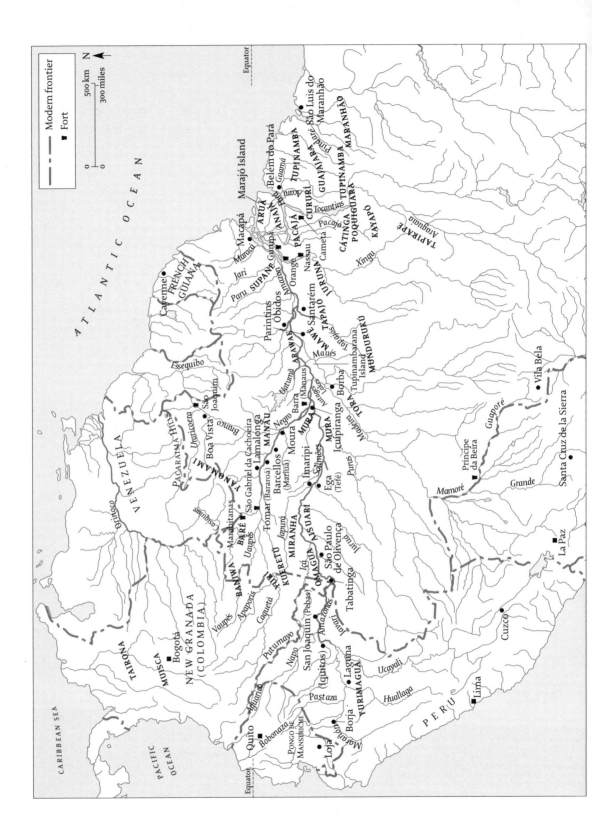

designing baroque churches and stylish houses, and fell in love with the place – and also with a local lady whom he married. He lived there for thirty-eight years until his death in 1791. Antonio José Landi (as he was known in Portuguese) is revered in Belém as the man who transformed the town into the most handsome city in all Amazonia. Among his achievements were the sumptuous Governor's Palace (built 1762–1771), deemed at the time to be the most comfortable in Brazil, and the completion (also in 1771) of the Cathedral in high-baroque, almost neo-classical style. The genial Landi was also interested in natural sciences. He organized the importation from Asia of mango trees, whose dark green foliage and deep shade help make Belém so attractive. He wrote the first study of Pará's flora and fauna, in a 187-page treatise that sadly was never published in his lifetime. He also established a tile-making ceramic factory. Landi is now praised as one of Brazil's greatest architects, as well as being a father-figure and visionary in his adopted city. Tropical Belém was in addition made less squalid by a drainage system and canal, designed by the German engineer Gaspar Gronfeld. Landi's masterpieces and Gronfeld's public works were of course built by indigenous labour.

Governor Mendonça Furtado wrote regular letters to his brother Pombal. A dedicated administrator but a pious, priggish man, he was shocked by the moral laxity of settlers and clergy. In one mission he saw naked girls washing in full view of the Fathers and others wandering around 'in scandalous indecency', while a young missionary arrived in a canoe paddled entirely by women. He accused missionaries of filling their villages with slaves, inflicting harsh punishments, sending men off to labour and keeping them ignorant, quarrelling with one another, being disloyal to the King, and losing their religious vocation. In his eyes, the Jesuits were the worst offenders and the greediest. He reckoned that, in total, missionaries of the various orders had 12,000 people in 63 missions. Of these, the Jesuits ran 19 mission villages but also owned extensive ranches on Marajó and the mainland. Mendonça Furtado reminded his brother that the only real wealth in Amazonia was native labourers, and 'since all Indians in the mission villages, of either sex and of all ages, are the absolute slaves of the monastic orders it follows logically that these will be masters of all the riches of this state unless control of the aldeias is removed from them'. All this fuelled a growing anti-Jesuit paranoia in the dictator Pombal.

The Governor's observations were reinforced when in 1754 he went upriver to visit Portugal's new Amazonian dominions. His four-year tour of inspection sailed off in fourteen boats and twenty-three large canoes, with Mendonça

Opposite *Amazon Basin map relating to the Colonial Era and Cabanagem.*

Furtado himself in a damask-lined vessel 'equipped like a yacht'. Hundreds of Indians were forced to build and paddle this flotilla. Jesuit missionaries were reluctant to assign their men to the Governor so they hid them in the forests, and they treated him with insufficient deference. By contrast, Carmelites on the Rio Negro welcomed him with garlands and choirs. Mendonça Furtado was so impressed that he decided to create a Captaincy of the Rio Negro. The mission village of Mariuá (450 kilometres – 280 miles – northwest of Manaus) was renamed Barcellos and elevated to be the capital of this new authority. The architect Landi travelled in the Governor's entourage and spent six years embellishing the riverbank of Barcellos with a row of Portuguese-style buildings. But the experiment did not last.

Perhaps because he never went to Brazil, the Marquis of Pombal hoped that its indigenous peoples could be persuaded to become ordinary labourers and peasant farmers, with no need for slavery or coercion. He imagined the Portuguese empire embracing subject peoples in the way that the ancient Romans had done to its Lusitanians. So he instructed his brother Mendonça Furtado to treat the Indians humanely rather than with 'injustice and violent and barbarous rigour as has been done hitherto'. In 1755 Pombal also got his King to issue a remarkable 'Law of Liberties', which proclaimed nothing less than the freedom and self-government of the indigenous peoples of Greater Pará and Maranhão. They were to have 'liberty of their persons, goods and commerce', to enjoy all the rights and privileges of ordinary citizens, to work for anyone they chose, and to trade freely. The abolition of indigenous (but not African) slavery and emancipation of slaves were repeated. The Indians themselves were to control their mission villages, which were to get secular Portuguese names. To effect this, missionaries were stripped of any temporal power, although they could continue to preach. A parallel law tried to end racial discrimination against indigenous people: all stigma was to be removed from them and from people of mixed race. Indians should even 'be preferred for posts and occupations ... and capable of any employment, honour and dignity'.

The reader will not be surprised to learn that this amazing legislation – centuries ahead of its time – was never implemented. When he sent it to his brother, Pombal admitted that Indians' natural 'laziness' (their wish to hunt, fish and farm to feed their families, rather than toil for Portuguese masters) might be a problem. Pombal's solution was to suggest that someone (a white man, of course) should preach the virtues of industry and punish the lazy in workhouses. His brother Mendonça Furtado compromised further: he never published the explosive Law of Liberties. When he removed temporal power from the missionaries, he balked at allowing indigenous people their promised autonomy. He described Indians as 'miserable rustic ignoramuses' and was sure that 'it is impossible for them to pass from one extreme to the other.... It [therefore] occurred to me ... to place a [white] man in each settlement with the title of director'. These laymen were to have no coercive power, but were to teach the Indians how to govern themselves and trade successfully. Without doubt the 'hitherto wretched' Indians would become 'Christians, rich and civilised ... if the directors do their duty'.

Even a governor as wrongheaded as Mendonça Furtado cannot seriously have believed this. His earlier letters showed his disgust at the rapaciousness of the settlers. He must have known that none of them was going to endure the discomfort and boredom of living in an indigenous village solely to give disinterested education to its inhabitants. So, when in 1757 he issued instructions for his new Directorate, he urged directors to be kind and helpful – but he rewarded them with full control of all commercial activity by the Indians, plus a commission of 17 per cent of everything that these 'free' people grew or gathered (with the Crown taking a further 10 per cent, and a share to the church). Furthermore, directors and Indian chiefs were to make half the 'eligible' Indians (all males between thirteen and sixty) available at all times to work for settlers and the government. To remove any doubt about this forced labour, the edict stressed that it was obligatory 'even to the detriment of the best interests of the Indians themselves'!

In 1755 Pombal had launched a General Company of Commerce of Greater Pará and Maranhão, and had given it monopolies and privileges. Because of the theoretical emancipation of indigenous people, this trading company was to rely increasingly on African slaves whom the region had previously been too poor to import. The Portuguese government therefore sent several thousand slaves each year from a depot at Bissau in Guinea, but most of these were put to work on rice and cotton plantations in Maranhão and few reached the Amazon.

Pombal then unleashed his fury on the Jesuits. The black-robed Fathers were an easily identifiable minority, with distinct dress and secretive rules, intelligent but arrogant, obnoxious to colonists whose greed they condemned, and perceived to be very rich. They were obvious targets for persecution fuelled by envy. The King of Portugal in 1758 got the Pope to issue a Bull to reform Jesuits in the Portuguese empire, forbidding them to preach or trade. Someone fired a shot at King José. Pombal blamed this on a mad old Jesuit and a ducal family who supported the order: all the alleged culprits were executed, often under torture. We now know that commissioners had already embarked for Brazil to seize Jesuit assets *before* the assassination attempt. A series of laws in 1759 expelled the Fathers and confiscated their property. The wording of this legislation was as hysterical as propaganda from a modern totalitarian regime. Jesuits were denounced as 'corrupted, deplorably alienated from their saintly vocation, and manifestly unsuitable because of their many, abominable, inveterate and incorrigible vices.... They have clandestinely attempted the usurpation of the entire state of Brazil.... Notorious rebels, traitors, adversaries and aggressors ... by this present Law they are denaturalised, proscribed and exterminated.... They are to be effectively expelled from all my Kingdom and Dominions, never to return.'

Six hundred Jesuit Fathers (mostly from Brazil, to the south) were exiled in prison ships. But their wealth proved to be less than Pombal had hoped: 135,000 head of cattle and 1,500 horses on 22 ranches, plus cacao and other plantations, and buildings in the cities. All were sold off. Eight years later in 1767 the King of Spain was persuaded to banish the Company of Jesus from *his* empire; and in 1773 a Pope ordered its extinction. (The Jesuits were revived in the nineteenth century, and their missionaries are now active again with some Amazonian tribes.)

The plight of the Indians under the Directorate can be summed up by three metaphors. They went from the frying-pan of the missionaries into the fire of the directors, who were given open season to exploit them. Far from being the altruistic paragons in Mendonça Furtado's fantasy, the directors behaved like King Herod in charge of a kindergarten. Immediately after the Directorate was announced, one official warned that it would never work. He asked whether the authorities really imagined that directors, most of whom were soldiers, would now defend Indian rights against the needs of other settlers? After the system had been operating for thirty years, a new king sent a judge called Antonio José Pestana da Silva to investigate it. His report was a terrible indictment. He noted that any director who had 'free' Indians working for him under temporary licence was determined to extract the maximum labour from them. 'He gives them cruel beatings and even throws pepper into their eyes to prevent them from falling asleep.' Soldiers were appalling directors: 'for the Indians there could be none more odious than the military'. But colonists were deemed too ignorant for such a sensitive task, and newly arrived Portuguese were 'worse than bloodthirsty leeches ... more like jaguars or ferocious tigers!'

Those who controlled indigenous labour sent their charges off to collect *drogas do sertão*, the forest products that had some commercial value. The armed bosses of these extractive gangs flogged Indians who 'bring back too little produce, for they hate to disappoint their hopes and greed'. Another official asked the Governor to 'consider the great and dangerous work' involved in these expeditions. Canoe-loads of Indians left on them in January and returned only in June. They then had to paddle the cargoes down to market in Belém, which took a further four months. For this the Indians were paid almost nothing – for their director, the state, the gang leader, the church, and commercial middlemen all took a cut before the 'emancipated' indigenous workers received their shares.

A few documents survive about work in directorate villages. These show that the male workforce spent 28 per cent of its time collecting in the forests, 21 per cent on royal service, 15 per cent working for settlers, and 4 per cent for village officials; so they had only 26 per cent for their own communal agriculture and 6 per cent for fishing. A village plantation measured from five to twenty hectares, and it grew manioc, rice, corn and cotton. But most of its harvest went to feed the director and men on expeditions or public works, or for sale in colonial towns. Local people survived on a near-starvation diet of about one *alqueire* (eight litres) of manioc flour to feed a household for a month. The German scientists Spix and Martius, the first non-Portuguese allowed to visit Amazonia, wrote that 'the directors are tyrants, absolute masters of the villages and of the native population of every age and sex. Far from having them taught or instructed, they carefully prevent any contact between them and other whites ... [so that they can] employ the greatest possible number of them solely for their private ends.' Official reports and travellers' accounts are full of indictments of directors. Most were brutes who worked their charges, men and women, incessantly and punished them mercilessly if they failed to produce enough. Some were drunken bullies, others licentious despots who kept harems of native women. One director raped a girl while Bishop João de São José was staying at his village. 'She emerged from his door covered in tears and blood, crying and lamenting injuries that were evident from her pain and innocence.' The bishop vowed to bring this 'wolf among my sheep' to justice; but there is no record of punishment of him or any other director.

Labour for the provincial government was almost worse than for the directors. A large shipyard was established in Belém, and Indians had to provide its timbers, masts, sails, caulking and other materials. In fifty years this yard built 26 ocean-going vessels (including six frigates) and many river-boats. There were other factories to make tiles, bricks and other manufactures. Then the authorities established an immensely long canoe route to link Pará with southern Brazil by river. Native rowers paddled these boats – for fourteen hours a day without pausing – and hauled them up and down rapids. Indians had to build a chain of stone forts to defend the colony, but stone is hard to come by in Amazonia. Native paddlers then had to transport cannon, balls and garrisons to these strongholds. Vauban-style forts survive, at Belém, Macapá, Gurupá and Cametá defending the mouths of the Amazon, at the Óbidos narrows, and at Barra (Manaus) at the mouth of the Rio Negro. Forts confronted Spanish colonies hundreds of miles up tributary rivers – at Tabatinga on the Solimões, São Gabriel and Marabitanas on the upper Negro, and São Joaquim far up the Branco in what is now Roraima. On the middle Guaporé headwater of the Madeira, directorate Indians were forced to build a huge white elephant called Fort Príncipe da Beira. It was completely isolated in forests (as it is to this day), but it may have deterred Spaniards from advancing from the Charcas into what is now Rondônia.

With such crushing workloads and regular epidemics, the number of Indians under colonial control in Pará and the Amazon fell dramatically. There were reckoned to be 30,000 at the start of the Directorate in 1757, but this had fallen to 19,000 forty years later. The main reason for the decline was – as always – disease. One of the boundary commissioners reported that during Mendonça Furtado's governorship there were two outbreaks of smallpox and measles – which greatly concerned the Governor 'because the number of workers was already very diminished, and the greatest rigour of the epidemic fell on that class'. Diseases were so severe in 1762 that four hospitals were crammed with sick Indians – many of whom had been building the warship *Belém* whose construction was seriously delayed. The authorities resorted to mass graves. An official who went up the river in 1775 noted sadly that the town of Tomar (the former mission Bararoá) on the lower Negro had had 1,200 working men but was reduced by almost 90 per cent to 140. He wrote that the rate of depopulation in other riverside villages was equally terrible. The naturalist Alexandre Rodrigues Ferreira reported in the 1780s that 'one sees places on that river that were once inhabited by innumerable heathen but that now show no signs of life beyond the bones of bodies of the dead. And those who escaped contagions did not escape captivity [as forced labourers]'. Once-prosperous missions decayed. With the expulsion of the Jesuits, other monastic orders lost interest in the Amazon, and eventually their missionaries were also removed.

A lesser explanation for depopulation was flight: some desperate Indians escaped into the forests with their families. There were also some revolts. When Governor Mendonça Furtado was trying to establish Barcellos as the capital of Rio Negro, he brought chiefs of the Arawak-speaking Warekena and Baré to the town to be dazzled by its elegance. They were loaded with presents. But when a military expedition went up the Negro and tried to claim those tribes' territories, its native auxiliaries were massacred during a festival by Chief Manacaçari of the Warekena. The white soldiers fled, and all the chiefs of the upper Negro rose against the would-be invaders. Then, in 1757, unpaid and wretched soldiers of the Barcellos garrison mutinied, looted the town, and escaped to Spanish-occupied lands. In that same year there was a genuine rebellion by oppressed Manau, Baré and

Baniwa of the middle Rio Negro, led by one Domingos. They took the directorate villages of Lama-longa, Moreira and Tomar, killing some missionaries and native chiefs who were collaborating too closely with the authorities. However, their attack on Barcellos was repelled in a bloody battle by troops who had just arrived from downriver. So the rebels were defeated: their leaders were executed and their heads left on the gallows as a grisly warning. Another Mercedarian missionary advised the Manau to flee to the forest, because the monastic orders were being expelled and their villages would be administered by secular directors 'under whose rule they would suffer infinite injustice and violence and would ultimately be slaves to the whites'. He was of course right.

During the 'Pombaline era' the most successful export from Pará was cacao, to satisfy the European craze for drinking chocolate. Cacao exports averaged some 600 tons a year during the twenty-three years of Pombal's General Company – which was slightly less than before the Company was created. The other plantation crops were sugar, tobacco and coffee, but none grew as well near the equator in Amazonia as in more temperate northeastern and southern Brazil. Despite all the work that went into gathering 'forest drugs', they were not worth much as exports. Nor was the 'butter' oil from millions of turtle eggs.

Pombal fell from power in 1777 with the death of his royal patron King José I. The failing General Company was wound up. Twenty years later, a new governor recommended the end of the Directorate. He showed how every one of its articles had been flagrantly and continuously violated. The system was doomed, because it depended on lay directors with 'a voracious hunger for gold, who respected nothing to satisfy their greed'. The odious Directorate was abolished in 1798.

The first glimmers of scientific interest in Amazonia's natural environment came at this time. Having fought off incursions by other European powers, the Portuguese were understandably paranoid about excluding foreigners from their Brazilian colony (La Condamine's descent of the Amazon in 1743 was unauthorized). When Captain James Cook called at Rio de Janeiro to water his ship *Endeavour*, in 1768 on his first voyage of circumnavigation, his officers were forbidden to set foot on shore – even though England was Portugal's oldest ally. The young naturalist Joseph Banks did land, disguised as a sailor, but declared in disgust that 'no one even tolerably curious has been here since [Dutch scientists during their invasion] in about the year 1640, so it is easy to guess the state in which the nat. hist. of such a country must be'.

The Jesuits had shown an interest in God's exuberant creations in this rich ecosystem, but their observations were generally revealed only in internal reports. The first inventory of Pará's flora and fauna by the Italian architect Landi was never published (see p. 99). This lack of intellectual curiosity started to change at the end of the eighteenth century – the 'Age of Enlightenment' in northern Europe if not in conservative Portugal. White interlopers gradually lost their fear of tropical rain forests. They never learned to live in them as successfully as indigenous peoples did, but they began to appreciate that this mass of luxuriant vegetation was a treasure-house of natural history.

The catalyst for change was the Treaty of Madrid that in 1750 divided South America between the two Iberian kingdoms. The Treaty lapsed for a time but was renewed, definitively, in the Treaty of San Ildefonso in 1777. As we have seen, the new frontiers in Amazonia were far up tributary rivers or on the watersheds at their sources. They were thus in forests and hills completely unknown to Europeans at that time – and many are still scarcely penetrated. So the two colonial powers had to survey and fix their new boundaries. In the 1780s both kingdoms sent teams of splendid explorers, in the greatest burst of geographical discovery ever seen in Amazonia. These 'boundary commissioners' based themselves at Barcellos on the Negro and Ega (now called Tefé) on the Solimões, and they had their Indians paddle them far up each of the Amazon's northwestern and northern tributaries.

One team pushed up the Japurá-Caquetá and then the Apaporis (which is now the boundary beween Brazil and Colombia). Charming watercolours survive of their two pigtailed, frock-coated and tricorne-hatted leaders, Colonels Francisco Requena y Herrera for the Spanish and Teodósio Constantino de Chermont for the Portuguese. They are shown visiting Indian villages and watching boats being hauled through rapids. This expedition was terribly struck by malarial fevers: both sides sent over a hundred sick men back downriver. But when the few survivors were devastated by another disease, the elegant officers had to roll up their sleeves. Colonel Requena wrote that 'In this labour of mercy the Portuguese commissioner treated his sick; and I, since necessity is the mother of invention, brought myself to prescribe remedies of emetics and bloodletting for those most in need of them, to the best of my ability, and quinine for those with fever. With good luck, I did not lose a single patient.'

Other surveyors mapped the fan of rivers that feed the upper Rio Negro. The Portuguese infantry officer Captain Ricardo Franco de Almeida Serra went up the Negro and then the Branco to explore the rivers of what is now the state of Roraima. He and his fellow surveyors were the first Europeans to visit – and map –

the rapid-infested rivers of the homeland of the Yanomami people. Their journal of the ascent of the Uraricoera headwater of the Branco is typical of years of extremely tough travel. Passing the large riverine island Maracá (most of which is still unexplored), they spent a day struggling up the Tipurema rapids, then the following day passing three more 'with much danger. My canoe sank three times and on one occasion I was left hanging from a tree.' After manoeuvring through fourteen more rapids in a few kilometres, their passage was blocked by 'a horrific waterfall, so frightening that I judge navigation up such a river to be extremely difficult'. This was the remote Purumame falls (which this author has seen). A mighty roar of water crashes down in three gigantic steps, with spray-drenched forests clinging to the sides of its gorge. Almeida Serra also visited the savannahs towards the table-mountain Roraima. He later mapped the wild sources of the Guaporé and Jauru at the southern edge of Amazonia – a land of swampy lakes and dense forests on ancient precambrian geology, that is now the frontier between Bolivia and Brazil – before going on to fix the boundaries along the Paraguay. This unassuming officer must rank as one of Brazil's greatest explorers. He later gallantly defended a fort near the Pantanal swamps against Spanish attack; then settled down with a Terena Indian woman; and died of malaria at Vila Bela (now Mato Grosso City) on the Guaporé.

Another officer (and future governor) with the sonorous name Manuel da Gama Lobo d'Almada followed Almeida Serra up the Uraricoera and on across the Pacaraima hills into what is now Venezuela. One night, his camp was swept away in a flash flood. (This is still a hazard for anyone camping near an Amazonian headwater. Travellers may not know that it has rained upriver, so that a sudden surge of floodwater comes without warning.) Lobo d'Almada struggled onto higher ground through knee-high water, in pitch darkness. The explorers feared that their 'mathematical doctor' Ribeiros had lost his precious sextant, so that he could no longer record latitude, but the instrument was providentially found next day lodged in a tree. On the return down the Uraricoera, Lobo d'Almada reports: 'I was shipwrecked with my canoe ... in a rapid with seven big drops besides many other smaller ones. I was lost in the first of these, so that the canoe went on smashing into the other falls and disintegrated.' The future governor could not swim. One soldier 'started to rescue me but was almost drowned. [Another] brave soldier ... without hesitation jumped into the midst of that raging water. He luckily caught me and disentangled me from [the other soldier]. He seized me by a wrist and held onto the wrecked canoe with his other hand. He continued to support me as the current swept us down, until I was saved on a rock in the middle of the river, far below the rapids.' Horrified watchers said that Lobo d'Almada's ordeal lasted for half an hour and that he vanished beneath the swirling brown waters on four occasions. (I can sympathize. I once lost my footing in one of these rapids and was instantly swept far down the Uraricoera before fetching up in a side eddy.)

One team from Portugal contained the then-27-year-old botanist named Alexandre Rodrigues Ferreira. When he landed in Belém in 1783 he wrote excitedly to the Portuguese colonial minister: 'Your Excellency, this land is a paradise. Right here at the edge of the city, the products of nature are so abundant that I know not where to turn.' Ferreira left Belém with a gardener and two untalented artists, Freire and Codina, a couple of mission Indians, and a field kitchen, medicine chest and eleven-book library. Ferreira followed the boundary commissioners up to the headwaters of the Rio Negro and then to those of the Rio Branco and to the foothills of the table-mountain Roraima. He described his four-year adventure in the famous *Diary of a Philosophical Journey through the Captaincy of the Rio Negro*, as well as writing studies of several tribes and essays on native pottery, masks and huts. Ferreira was interested in the few Portuguese settlements along these empty rivers and their meagre commercial activities. He occasionally gave the lovely indigenous names of the 'abundance of trees that border the river banks: true *molongo*, *macaca* chestnut, *macacú-guaçu*, *mongúba*, *ingapiranga*, *imbirarema*, *apecúitai-hua*, *arapari*, *mututirana*, *paracutaca*, a fair quantity of *uambê* liana, and palm trees – *assaí*, *ibacaba*, *patauá*, *paxiuba*, *iará*, *iaxitara*, *muruti*, *caraná*, etc.' Far from revelling in this tropical paradise, Ferreira urged his King to exploit this wealth of timber for the royal shipyards by sending plenty of African slaves to fell and transport the trees. He sent boxes of samples back to botanical gardens in Portugal, with descriptions and paintings of orchids, fruits and other exotic plants, animals and geology.

After five years of arduous travel and research, Ferreira asked permission to return to Portugal, but the reply that reached him months later was negative. He was told that he had sent too few specimens so must continue his expedition – but south of the Amazon up the Madeira and Guaporé rivers to Mato Grosso and then on to the upper Paraguay. This thirteen-month journey up mighty rivers exhausted the paddlers and their passengers. The gardener Cabo died. His belongings were curious: in addition to the obvious hammock and camping equipment, he had carried into the Amazon forests velvet breeches, lace shirts, silver cutlery, and a hefty dictionary.

Alexandre Rodrigues Ferreira finally returned to Portugal in 1792. Denied a post at Coimbra University and with his great collections dispersed and neglected, he worked on in the royal botanical gardens, but as a disappointed man.

When Napoleon's General Junot invaded Portugal at the end of 1807, the Musée d'Histoire Naturelle sent Étienne Geoffroy de Saint-Hilaire to inspect Lisbon's natural-history holdings. Junot's army looted everything movable in the city, and Ferreira's collections were not spared. Many objects were still wrapped in cloth and boxed, some rotted and disintegrating. The French scientist excused his thefts by noting that 'all are untouched: nobody has taken the trouble to work on them'. So stuffed monkeys, manatees, macaws and other animals and birds, quantities of herbarium plants, and many of Ferreira's notes and journals were shipped off to France. Some of the looted paintings of plants had been given to him by the generous Landi.

During the Directorate years, Brazilian Amazonia was disturbed by two powerful indigenous nations: the Mura and Mundurukú. Portuguese slavers and missionaries had denuded the large southern tributaries of their original inhabitants, so these new peoples contested the vacuum left by vanished tribes. They were very different to one another. The Mura's homeland was a labyrinth of lakes and channels in the *várzea* flooded forest at the mouth of the Madeira and along the lower Solimões. Consummate boatmen, almost nomadic as they camped on sandbanks or islands in their watery world, the Mura were invisible and invincible. They lived very simply, with few villages or possessions beyond their canoes and weapons; and although they wore cloth aprons and tiara-like straw visors, they were otherwise unkempt and unadorned.

Early in the eighteenth century a Portuguese trader treacherously seized some Mura and sold them into slavery. They never forgave this. When the Jesuits tried to establish missions on the Madeira, these were constantly harassed by Mura attacks. One missionary admitted that their 'continuous war against the whites [was] a war of revenge and undying hatred, for which they had good reason'. Frustrated Jesuits appealed to the government to put a stop to the tribe's attacks. A strong contingent in 1749 used guns to inflict heavy casualties on the Mura. The tribe learned from this to avoid pitched battles, and instead became brilliant guerrilla fighters. They used large bows and long arrows, and by holding one end of the bow to the ground with their toes could fire missiles with enough velocity to pass clean through a man. They posted lookouts in the tallest trees, and used these as hides for snipers. The Muras' favourite tactic was to ambush canoes when they were struggling through rapids. The English poet Robert Southey wrote a history of Brazil (based on Portuguese sources and published in

1810) in which he described 'their ambuscades ... usually where the current was strongest and boats had most difficulty in passing: there they were ready with grappling hooks, and a shower of arrows, which often times proved fatal before resistance could be offered.... No other nation impeded the progress of the Pará-men so much, nor inflicted such losses upon them.' Their attacks on Indians in forest gardens or those gathering turtle eggs or labouring in cacao plantations, and any canoe traffic, threatened to bring commercial activity in the middle Amazon to a standstill. 'They would kill our best Indian fishermen and white labourers with great skill and lightning speed.' Successive governors sent expeditions to try to find Mura villages and exterminate them. 'They suffered unheard-of slaughter and all other forms of hostility; but they did not desist from their animosity.' They were too elusive, mobile and cunning, as well as being brave and pitiless. The town of Borba, a former mission on the lower Madeira, had an armed garrison but 'the Mura were nevertheless so bold and so dreadful that they kept the place in perpetual alarm and deterred people from settling there'.

The Mundurukú were the other warrior nation that dominated the southern tributaries at this time. In the 1770s hordes of Mundurukú suddenly swept down onto settlements on the Tapajós. Directors complained that their profits were threatened because Indians could no longer gather forest products or tend their manioc farms. Unlike the wiry Mura, the Mundurukú were handsome men who kept very fit by running and eschewing hallucinogens and starchy foods. Their muscular bodies were covered in tattoos of fine geometric lines and they wore sumptuous ornaments – great headdresses that tumbled down their backs, cloaks of red and blue feathers, and even long tassels of bright fluffy featherwork.

Contemporaries compared the Mundurukú to Spartans, because their warriors lived and fought in austere male fraternities. Very brave, they would attack in daylight in long lines, drilled by reed trumpets. They calmly awaited their enemies' arrows, ducking to avoid them, and their women tried to catch these missiles and hand them to their men. They terrorized weaker tribes. A bishop described the Mundurukú as 'supremely pitiless and cruel heathen who kill everyone, sparing neither sex nor age'. The heads of conquered enemies were mummified with the orifices stuffed with cotton and resin, embalmed in red urucum oil, and then worn as trophies on warriors' belts or adorning the doorposts of their huts. Starting from a homeland on the middle Tapajós, the Mundurukú covered huge distances in their raids. They attacked eastwards towards Maranhão, north to rivers near Belém, and northwestwards to the Madeira where they fought the Mura more effectively than Portuguese soldiers could.

In 1778, João Pereira Caldas (one of the architects of the Treaty of Madrid, and now an effective governor of Greater Pará) organized a defensive war against both the Mura and Mundurukú. But he ordered his commanders to go gently, avoiding 'the inhumanities that are usually perpetrated on similar occasions, with our men killing these barbarians with as much cruelty as *they* do His Majesty's subjects'. The naturalist Alexandre Rodrigues Ferreira, a political hawk, thought that these instructions were too mild: the only way to get men to risk their lives fighting these fierce tribes was to reward them with any captives as slaves. But the Governor was right. In 1785 his gentle policy yielded a minor miracle for the colonial authorities. A horde of Mura suddenly paddled into the settlement of Imaripi at the mouth of the Japurá, a northern tributary of the Solimões. Within a few days other Mura appeared peacefully, at Ega, Alvarães, and far away at Borba on the Madeira and Moura on the Negro. The architects of this unexpected 'surrender' were a Mura chief known as Ambrózio and the enlightened commander of Imaripi, Mathias Fernandes. Chief Ambózio had persuaded his compatriots that they would be better off reaching accommodation with the Portuguese than continuing to fight both them and the ferocious Mundurukú. They trusted promises of friendship from Mathias Fernandes. A historian noted that 'there was surprise at the speed with which their canoes appeared on different rivers, which seemed too far for them to have had time to take the news and give the agreed password "Comrade Mathias"'. The naturalist Ferreira happened to be at Moura when twenty-five Mura appeared in four canoes 'having lost their fear of being punished for past insults, and because of the reciprocal friendship that has been promised to them in our settlements'. He was amazed by 'this so useful and so unexpected reduction'.

Settlers were alarmed by the arrival of the Mura, particularly at Borba which they had terrorized, so garrisons were strengthened in case of treachery. But Governor Caldas insisted that there should be no attempt to congregate the four thousand Mura into villages or to exile them from their watery homeland. Caldas asked Lisbon for special aid for the tribe, but this was never authorized. In later years the Mura were decimated by disease, and seemed to travellers little better than squalid vagrants living in sandbank hovels. However, they escaped the Directorate labour regime, kept their freedom, remained in their flooded forests, and have survived as an entity.

The peace with the Mura inspired Amazonia's first literary work – an epic poem called *The Muhraida, or The Conversion and Reconciliation of the Mura Heathen*, by an officer called Henrique João Wilkens. The poem started: 'The wild, indomitable and formidable heathen Mura have always been lethal to those navigating the

Madeira river' and it described their reign of terror on both white settlers and other indigenous tribes. The 'reconciliation, conversion and settlement' of these feared warriors was an act of God, but the instrument was a 'rustic, common man named Mathias Fernandes' who had won their confidence. Credit was also given to Colonel João Baptista Mardel at Ega, who showered them with gifts after the peace, and to the poem's author Wilkens. The *Muhraida* is not great poetry, but it gives an insight into colonial attitudes. It portrayed Indians as savages living in 'the dense darkness of heathenism', and justified forced labour because of their infuriating indifference to material 'progress'. But it also admitted the settlers' frustration at seeing indigenous people living so well in a forest environment where they themselves floundered and failed.

The warlike Mundurukú seemed even more formidable than the Mura. A strong punitive expedition sent to crush them found a Mundurukú village and was about to attack, but the Portuguese discovered that it was *they* who were surrounded by tribal warriors, and they had difficulty escaping from the trap. Another intelligent governor, the former explorer Manoel da Gama Lobo d'Almada, told his men to try to capture some Mundurukú. During a battle, two young Indians were wounded by gunshot and taken. The Governor ordered that they be healed, shown the advantages of Portuguese civilization, and then returned to their village loaded with presents. The tactic worked. An aged Mundurukú later recalled that in 1795 his people's warriors were moving against another white expedition when 'our two men who had been captured stood up in the canoe and told us not to do anything because these people were our friends. They then advanced and showed us clothes, knives, axes, and many other good things that the whites had given them.' Tribal elders decided to come to terms with the colonists. After this 'miraculous pacification' several thousand Mundurukú were moved to former missions on the lower Tapajós and the rivers between it and the Madeira. They remained remarkably loyal friends to the Portuguese, even helping them fight other tribes. Most of those who migrated downriver disappeared, but those who continued to live near the upper Tapajós survive as a coherent and prosperous people.

On the opposite side of the Amazon basin, where the Branco rises from the slopes of Mount Roraima, there is a vast plain of natural grasslands. Modern scientists do not quite understand why rain forests give way abruptly to savannah, each with totally different vegetation. It seems to result from a combination of altitude, water-table, soil chemistry and micro-organisms, seasonal flooding and micro-climate. The grasslands of Roraima are home to indigenous peoples who prefer open country, unlike most Indians who find more sustenance in forests.

When the boundary commissioners came to these plains in the 1780s, they built a small fort to keep Spaniards from Venezuela at bay, introduced cattle, and tried to settle Indians into six villages along the upper Branco. The villages, one of which was on the site of the modern state capital Boa Vista, functioned for four years. But in 1780 when the tools and food lavished on newly settled Indians dried up, and directors started trying to make them work, the indigenous people understandably objected. They killed some soldiers who oppressed them, and migrated away across the open plain. Some were lured back to different villages, largely by half-Indian trackers. There was another attempt at forced labour, particularly in a fish-salting factory. So there were two more 'rebellions' by these people resisting the monstrous imposition of forced labour in their own homelands – one in 1790 when they killed an overseer in the fish plant and burned their villages, and another in 1798. The first of these was quelled harshly by Lobo d'Almada, who was now Governor of the Rio Negro; and the second was smashed in a massacre at a place that became known ominously as Sandbank of Blood. The only lasting legacies of these decades were Fort São Joaquim, symbol of Brazil's presence in this far-northern territory, and the cattle. The nine cows and bulls taken upriver by Governor Lobo d'Almada roamed freely over the plains. During the next century they multiplied to tens of thousands of head of cattle.

The decree that in 1798 abolished the Directorate was full of fine words. But once again these were a sham. Far from liberating indigenous peoples, the law disbanded their villages and sold off communal land. Any Indian without a house or 'fixed occupation' could be forced to labour for colonists or their government. Outsiders were free to exploit natural resources on indigenous land. And, worst of all, Indians had to serve in a militia corps commanded by their own chiefs or local settlers. A great historian of the Jesuits commented: 'This military regime, by its very nature tyrannical, facilitated oppression – against which the primitiveness, timidity, and habit of humble obedience of the natives made it impossible for them to react.' As always, the new system was intended to maintain the labour supply. Governor Sousa Coutinho ordered the outgoing directors to compile lists of all Indians of working age. Gangs of these were to be removed from their villages and put into camps near the region's four towns, so that they could work for the state or for individuals.

Exports from Maranhão and the Amazon enjoyed a brief boom at the end of the eighteenth century. This was because the American War of Independence interrupted rice and cotton from the Carolinas, and European demand for cocoa remained high. But at the start of the nineteenth century prices for these products fell, and the region went into a long economic decline. This should have been good news for the indigenous peoples and the Africans imported during Pombal's directorate. The iniquitous system of forced labour through 'militias' soon ceased, but conditions for the Indians and black slaves improved very little. Many Indians had drifted into the towns and formed an urban proletariat, an underclass that received no education or even religious attention. A contemporary observer noted the hypocrisy towards these people: 'They are accused of being lazy; and yet … they are the only ones who work. They are accused of being insincere; yet an Indian is lucky if among ten employers he finds one who pays him…. Throughout the province there is still an excessive tendency, if not for slavery, then for a system of using indigenous labour that differs from slavery in name only.'

Conditions on the Rio Negro were even worse than on the main Amazon. What had once been a prosperous domain of Carmelite missionaries was ruined by a succession of greedy governors. These introduced 'the hateful system of shackling *aldeia* Indians for government service…. It is an appalling and insufferable burden to press-gang a married Indian from the bosom of his family for various public works, without wages or pay, for many months or a year of work. His poor hut is surrounded by soldiers, who tie him up and shackle him to carry him off for this labour. What inhumanity!' The man's family was left to starve without him. In the future town of Manaus at the mouth of the Negro, natives worked in chains like convicts. 'There was excessive depopulation of Indians at this time, as a result of such oppression and from interminable work in the fisheries of the Rio Branco…, in rope-making, cloth mills, etc.' Any who resisted or slacked were imprisoned and savagely punished. A 'dishonest and avaricious' governor encouraged 'terrible and infamous raiding parties to enslave' uncontacted tribes for sale to any buyer – a flagrant violation of the laws prohibiting slavery of indigenous peoples. 'The result is and will continue to be the desolation in which [the province] currently languishes.'

Canon André Fernandes de Sousa accused successive governors of Rio Negro captaincy of illegal trafficking in slaves. 'Anyone who can obtain a roll of coarse cloth, some knives and a flask of gunpowder goes up the Japurá river. He engages Indians in one of its settlements and takes them inland to surround the huts of the heathen by night, to tie them up. His men fire guns to terrify them and kill most in this way, for [the slavers'] opinion of them is nil…. Born free and independent, [the victims] are reduced to slavery in their own country! What cruelty! What injustice! I have observed that … in these so-called "peaceful descents" only a third or a quarter survive. This is because they are torn violently from their homes and are despoiled of their children and wives after having their few possessions sacked. Young and old die constantly, either from eating earth [to commit suicide] or struck down by disease.' The raiding party was rewarded by spoils from their victims – blow-guns, bows and arrows, curare poisons, feather ornaments and so forth. The captives were either sold as slaves in Barra (Manaus) or put to work in government factories – a standard excuse: 'Whatever the nature of the labour, it was always "public service".' Men worked constantly, hauling carts of clay and firing bricks, or as fishermen, paddlers or turtle-egg collectors. Their wives grew cotton, picked it, combed it in the mills, and then wove it into cloth – and by a cruel irony, this cloth was still being used as payment for Indians. This was decades after the law of 1748 that abolished slavery and freed Indians to be subjects of the King. Canon Sousa lamented that 'I must report with regret that none of this has been observed, particularly not in the Rio Negro. The remoteness of that captaincy, and the lack of literate people to protest about the oppressions, both combine to allow the abuses to continue unheard.'

A new governor in 1818 was even worse. He ordered that village Indians must pay a third of their manioc harvest to the state. 'The miserable, wretched Indians ... are oppressed not only by these manioc levies ... but also in continual labour: victims are condemned to work throughout their lives until they are carried off on the wings of eternity. In the Rio Negro, Europeans regard Indians as animals of another species.... It was as if the government wanted to give the final blow to this province, already almost inanimate.'

The pious canon was appalled by the white settlers. 'Devoid of education or the fear of God, they are monsters of evil who infect everything with their pestiferous and poisonous breath.' However humble their origins in Portugal, 'on landing here they assume all manner of airs. They are immediately seized by the general contagion of this country: a spirit of dissolution, laziness and negligence that ruins everything.' At first they might run a tavern or ribbon shop, or work as itinerant traders. 'From this they sink into an abyss of sin – vices that undermine their health and render them odious in the eyes of God and men ... scandalous in both their business dealings and their base obscenities. They spend their lives contentedly laughing, enjoying themselves, or in deep slumber.' A British naval officer, Henry Lister Maw, went down the Amazon in 1828 and confirmed all this. He saw slavers with canoe-loads of Indians chained to logs. The settlers and convicts who infested the Amazon loathed Indians, out of 'anger, ignorance or selfishness, or perhaps all three combined.... The fact is that in the remote parts of the province of Pará, "might makes right", and power and interest rather than justice form the practical administration of the law. The Emperor may send forth edicts and the [provincial] President orders, but the isolated branco is himself an emperor, and much more absolute than Dom Pedro at Rio de Janeiro.'

In 1818 the two Bavarian scientists Johann Baptist von Spix and Carl von Martius were the first non-Portuguese permitted to visit the Amazon. They were no romantics – often dismayed by the 'backwardness' and even 'brutishness' of some tribes. But they were equally appalled by the wickedness of some administrators. Martius was taken to the Japurá, a northern tributary of the Solimões. Far up this remote river he saw a settlement run by a white 'magistrate'. Martius wrote that 'these poor people feared the approach of any white man because of the forced labour to which they were subjected, ostensibly for "public works" but exclusively for the benefit of the magistrate. They begged me to expose to the government their helpless condition and the oppression by their enemy. There had already been complaints against this man, both for stealing tithes and for his cruel and lustful behaviour towards his charges.' The German visitor also met Chief Pachicu of the Kueretú, who wore a blue frock coat and cotton breeches as symbols of his rank. This shrewd chief kept his own people well hidden in the forests. (Related to the Tukano, the Kueretú survive to this day, well within Colombia.) But the chief pleased his Portuguese allies by raiding other tribes to capture slaves for sale to settlers – seventy years after the abolition of indigenous slavery. The victims of these 'descents' had pallid colour, swollen bellies and hardened spleens from malaria. 'Because of this and their idleness, white settlers would not buy them.'

To Martius, this degradation contrasted with the atmosphere in a village of free Yurí (part of the Ticuna, who are now the largest indigenous nation on the main Amazon river). He was enchanted by the spacious huts, tidy village, abundance of fish and game, extensive plantations, and peaceful daily round of the Yurí. The day began with everyone bathing in the river; they then rested and conversed, with the naked women painting their children or playing with pets; men then went to hunt and fish and women did domestic chores; everyone bathed frequently; and in the evening there was a moonlit celebration with the men in extravagant masks (a hallmark of the Ticuna) and brandishing tapir-hide shields. Even further up the Japurá lived the Miranya (also related to the Ticuna), who gave the stranger a vivacious welcome. 'We rightly ascribed this innocence – this warm interest in everything about us – to their freedom and natural condition. Far removed from the whites, they were free of the fear of forced labour that is such a horror for all other Indians.' Miranya women were particularly impressive in their cleanliness, dignity and hard work. So the German glimpsed the harmony of indigenous life, still practised by many peoples throughout Amazonia but destroyed wherever colonists had penetrated. He also saw the downside. These tribes were naturally bellicose, with their warriors constantly fighting enemy groups; and their aggression was now channelled into seizing captives for sale to the whites.

Napoleon's invasion of Spain and Portugal had a profound impact on South America. For the Spanish-speaking colonies of the Amazon's headwaters, it was the final impulse towards independence. All the viceroyalties had been shaken by the independence in 1776 of Britain's North American colonies, then by the radical upheavals of the French Revolution in the 1790s. When Napoleon made his brother Joseph King of Spain, the powerful loyalties of Spain's American subjects to their ancient monarchy were severed. The result was the independence movements of Francisco de Miranda and Simón Bolívar in Venezuela and of José de San Martín starting from Buenos Aires. Their military campaigns were fought in the Andes, converging on Lima from the north and the south. The fighting thus skirted the edges of the Amazon basin. It was many years before the newly independent nations Venezuela, Colombia, Ecuador, Peru and Bolivia took any interest in their Amazonian forests.

In Brazil, Napoleon's Peninsular campaign also led to independence, but for different reasons. When a French army was advancing on Lisbon in 1807, the Portuguese royal family escaped to Brazil in a fleet escorted by Portuguese and British warships. This was the first (and almost the last) time that any European monarch visited an overseas colony. For thirteen years Rio de Janeiro became the capital of the Portuguese empire, and the Bragança royals enjoyed life there.

The Napoleonic wars also made a slight impact on the Brazilian Amazon. In January 1809 Portuguese and British warships ferried a contingent from the garrison of Belém up the coast to attack Cayenne (French Guiana). These soldiers captured the town's forts after a few hours of bloody fighting, and the colony surrendered to the Portuguese. Cayenne was handed back eight years later, at the Peace of Paris. But the French outpost contained a virus that alarmed the Portuguese authorities: it was full of subversive ideas. Soon after the French Revolution, propagandists there had published a Portuguese translation of the Declaration of the Rights of Man. The rulers of Belém decreed that anyone caught in possession of such radical literature would suffer life imprisonment, but they could not prevent troops who occupied the colony from learning the thrilling new doctrines. Back on the Amazon, the liberal infection spread through secret societies and intellectual gatherings. One cleric, the vicar of Cametá Friar Luis Zagalo, was so taken with these scandalous teachings that he questioned the immortality of the soul and the perpetual virginity of the Virgin Mary; he was thought to be a freemason; and, worst of all, he incited slaves to demand their freedom.

After the Napoleonic wars were over, Portugal wanted its King João VI back. The King finally returned to Lisbon in 1821, but he left his son and heir Pedro behind as Prince-Regent. Brazilian patriots in Rio de Janeiro had been lobbying for greater autonomy. In 1822 they persuaded this prince to proclaim himself Emperor of a breakaway new nation of Brazil, and independence was achieved in an almost bloodless revolution. All this happened in São Paulo and Rio de Janeiro.

It took a while for news of independence to reach remote Amazonia. As we have seen, the government in Lisbon had for many years kept the region separated as the Captaincy of Maranhão and Greater Pará. It was later reunited with the Viceroyalty in Rio de Janeiro, but settlers in its equatorial forests had little affection for their rich compatriots far to the south. Brazilian nationalists therefore feared that this conservative northern backwater might remain loyal to Portugal, in the way that Canada had stayed loyal to the British Empire after the American War of Independence. The Cortes in Lisbon debated whether to try to get Amazonia to separate from Brazil and remain their colony.

During 1822 forces of the newly independent Empire of Brazil defeated those loyal to Portugal, first in Bahia, then in the provinces of the North-East, and then in Maranhão. The intervention of Brazil's first Admiral, the Scottish Lord Cochrane, was decisive in repelling Portuguese warships and blockading Salvador da Bahia. Having taken Salvador, Cochrane sent the brig *Maranhão* under the English captain John Pascoe Grenfell to quell the pro-Portuguese authorities in Belém. Grenfell succeeded, by pretending that he had a fleet of ships. He blockaded the town and threatening to bombard it, while a pro-independence crowd stormed the government buildings. The town council capitulated and declared for the Emperor Dom Pedro.

The new masters of Belém rounded up Portuguese sympathizers and packed them into the brig *Diligente* as a temporary prison: 253 men were crammed into the airless hull. It was suffocatingly hot; the prisoners had no water; any who tried to escape were fired on through the hatches; and others 'fell to attacking and tearing one another' in their desperation. By next morning all but four were dead, most from asphyxiation. This was Brazil's equivalent of the Black Hole of Calcutta. The American geologist Herbert Smith, who was there, partly blamed Captain Grenfell for the massacre; and Grenfell's Brazilian marines were brutal in suppressing another revolt in 1823. There were further cruelties, with thousands of prisoners dying in the dungeons of forts and in another odious prison-hulk. Many of the victims were blacks and Indians who had been pressed into military service.

Brazilian Amazonia seethed with discontent during the decade after independence. The region was in economic decline, and the new nation Brazil suffered from inflation. Regional separatism simmered, and provincial presidents sent from Rio de Janeiro were inept or unduly harsh. Local politics were polarized between liberals, who focused their hatred on newly arrived Portuguese, and conservatives who opposed reform. By the 1830s there were sporadic disturbances and mutinies in settlements and forts on different Amazon rivers. A revolt in 1831 was savagely repressed; there was heavy fighting at Cametá on the lower Tocantins; and in 1832 soldiers at Manaus (then called Barra [Bar] of the Rio Negro) mutinied, ran amok, and proclaimed independence from Pará. In 1833 Mawé and Mundurukú Indians attacked Parintins town on the island of Tupinambaranas downstream of Manaus. The local magistrate sent a frantic appeal for help: 'A terrible and fearful anarchic volcano erupted ... of local Indians led by Chief Crispim de Leão. He attacked our property, decorum and political existence.... He is, Sir, a turbulent individual who never ceases to seek ways to hurl us into a deep and bottomless abyss of revolts!' These tumults were quelled, with difficulty, by imperial forces sent upriver.

Then in 1835 the oppressed underclass rose in a full-scale rebellion. This was the Cabanagem, named after the *cabanos*, homeless migrants who lived in temporary huts or cabins on the mudflats. It was a spontaneous revolt. One of the final sparks that caused it was the publication of a pastoral letter from the Bishop of Belém condemning freemasonry, which common people and liberals hated. But this spontaneity denied the Cabanagem any unified purpose or leadership.

The Cabano leaders were all white men, but very different from one another. One was Canon João Baptista Gonçalves Campos, a crusading priest and editor of the newspaper *O Liberal*, a brave but moderate man; however, while on the run, hiding at friends' farms south of Belém, he cut a sore when shaving and this became infected and he died, thus depriving the Cabanagem of its best potential president. Another leader, Felix Malcher, was a former infantry officer, sombre, irascible, an astute politician, and an able but impetuous military commander. More attractive were three brothers called Vinagre, tough backwoodsmen from Maranhão with little education. The eldest of the three young Vinagres, Francisco, became a dashing guerrilla leader in the forests and wetlands near Belém, but he was accused of inciting the masses into extreme violence. Lastly there was the ardent young Eduardo Nogueira, a revolutionary with an agenda of radical reform.

Nogueira was also a good military commander, who adopted the nom-de-guerre Angelim after one of the strongest hardwoods in the Amazon forests.

These conspirators operated from Felix Malcher's fazenda south of Belém. They issued a proclamation against the provincial government. Military expeditions sent to suppress the revolt had only limited success. So in January 1835 rebel forces charged into the city of Belém. One column attacked the barracks, and many soldiers and officers changed sides to join them. The other column stormed the government palace, and the President was shot and killed by an Indian. The jail was captured. The American consul Charles Jenks Smith wrote that 'about fifty prisoners were set at liberty, who, in a body, proceeded to a part of the city called Porto do Sol and commenced the indiscriminate massacre of all the Portuguese they could find in the neighbourhood. In this manner about twenty respectable shopkeepers and others lost their lives.' Then, and during the coming months, the mob took vengeance on its oppressors – the provincial élite and anyone from the mother country. A Portuguese officer who was in Belém said that any Portuguese who could escape did so. 'The armed populace, that is the *tapuios* [detribalized Indians], proposed a general blood-letting but the rebel President [Malcher] would never agree to it.... The rabble appeared ever more unbridled ... [wanting] to perpetrate the promised sack and to murder all whites, including even women.... The history of Pará is rich in crimes and atrocities. The Portuguese were filled with horror, recalling that from 1823 to now [1835] over 800 of their compatriots had been killed by Brazilians and coloured people.'

As so often happens in revolutions, the leaders fell out with one another. Felix Malcher proclaimed himself President, but said that he remained loyal to the Empire of Brazil. A few weeks later he tried to arrest Francisco Vinagre. There was fierce fighting in the streets and a bombardment by ships loyal to Malcher, but it was the woodsman who won. Malcher was killed and Vinagre became the Cabanos' second President. In mid-May 1835 an imperial warship bombarded Belém and its marines tried to storm the city. They were repelled and fled to the ship, but a few were taken prisoner and killed by unspeakably cruel tortures. An Englishman wrote to his brother: 'The most horrible barbarities were practised ... the fellows all the time dancing, singing, and shouting the most horrid language, in this manner or worse were served all that fell into their hands.... There are at present two thousand men under arms – all people of colour – all the Portuguese's slaves have joined the soldiers.'

The imperial government sent a new president, Field-Marshal Manoel Rodrigues, and Vinagre handed the province over to him. Rodrigues tried to assert his authority by arresting revolutionaries. He treacherously included Vinagre among these and repeatedly refused to release the Cabano president. So in August, 'a vast host of half-savage coloured people assembled in the retired creeks behind Pará [Belém], and on a day fixed … poured into the city through the gloomy pathways of the forest which encircles it. A cruel battle, lasting nine days, was fought in the streets.' The insurgents won. 'The city and province were given up to anarchy; the coloured people, elated with victory, proclaimed the slaughter of all whites, except the English, French, and American residents. The mistaken principals, who had first aroused all this hatred of races, were obliged now to make their escape.' Marshal Rodrigues fled to some English and French warships, taking the captive Vinagre with him; and the radical young Eduardo 'Angelim' was elected as the third Cabano president. Angelim has been idealized as the most charismatic rebel leader, and his surviving letters to English naval officers reveal him as an able administrator and astute diplomat.

In November a British captain described the terrible plight of some 1,400 refugees from the city, who were living in palm-thatch shelters near the mouth of the river. Almost half had died of smallpox and malaria. 'On board the prison ship *Defensora* out of 280 prisoners 196 have died, and now that the rainy season has set in the numbers will fast increase. Vinagre continues [amid 660 prisoners] in the *Campista*'s hold in irons, his only food is rice.' The second Cabano president died some months later.

The Cabanos held the city of Belém until May 1836, sixteen months after its first capture. This popular uprising never had a united leadership, a political creed or attainable objectives. The rebels hated the rich, Portuguese, and freemasons. They professed to favour Catholicism, Pará, liberty, Brazil and its young emperor Dom Pedro; but even liberals in Rio de Janeiro despised the Cabano leaders as brutish rabble. The Cabanagem was remarkable among revolutions in Brazil's history in four ways: it was a genuine rising of the oppressed masses; its leaders, although white, came from the lower classes; it covered a vast area, spreading throughout Brazilian Amazonia; and it was horribly violent.

Foreigners who were in Pará at that time were appalled and frightened. The German botanist Professor Eduard Poeppig escaped from Belém and sheltered for three months in a nearby village. To him, the rebels were 'hordes of robbing and bloodthirsty mestizos, mulattos and negroes…. They pushed on from place to place … killing whites with indescribable cruelty and plundering and burning set-tlements or passing ships.' Two British naval officers sailed down the Amazon as the rebellion was starting, despite being warned that in Pará 'the Indians are mur-dering all the Europeans'. On Marajó they were welcomed by a creole (a white born in the Americas) called Jacco, 'who infested the lower part of the river and who had murdered great numbers of Portuguese'. The English botanist Richard Spruce, who was there in the following decade, heard that 'to be unable to speak the *lingua geral* [the Jesuits' Tupi-based language spoken by mission Indians and ordinary people throughout Amazonia] and to have any beard were crimes punished with death by the Cabanos, who carefully extirpated any vestiges of hair from their own faces'. (This was because indigenous people naturally grow little or no body hair.)

Daniel Kidder, a young American Methodist missionary, described the Cabanagem as 'a reign of terror. But it was not long a quiet reign. Disorders broke out among the rebels, and mutual assassinations became common. Business was effectively broken up, and the city was as fast as possible reverting back to a wilderness. Tall grass grew up in the streets, and the houses rapidly decayed. The state of the entire province became similar. Anarchy prevailed throughout its vast domains. Lawlessness and violence became the order of the day.' An old lady who lived through it all in Óbidos on the middle Amazon recalled bitterly: 'How we suffered, because of men who wanted something, but none knew what, not even they themselves! The Cabanagem was a scourge sent by God to punish us. It was a plague that ravaged the land where I was born. Everyone suffered from it.' The American geologist Herbert Smith wrote long afterwards: 'A more frightful civil war has never been recorded.... It was a struggle of parties, neighbour against neighbour, a massacre in the streets, a chasing through the forests and swamps.... Men were shot down by scores because they would not renounce their partisan tenets.... The people are hot-headed; in the excitement of political strife they were carried to deeds they would never have dreamed of in sober moments; as for the Indians and blacks, they followed in the wake of their leaders and, being ignorant, often went beyond them in cruelty.'

Prince Adalbert of Prussia, who explored far up the Xingu river in 1842 (with the future 'Iron Chancellor' Count Otto von Bismarck as one of his aides-de-camp), condemned the Cabanagem as 'a reign of horror and anarchy'. But he understood its cause. 'These disturbances were the fruits of the ceaseless oppression which the white population had, from the very first, exercised on the poor natives, and in no part of Brazil more than here.' Almost all Brazilian historians agree with this verdict.

The imperial government in 1836 dispatched a powerful force of 2,500 troops under a new provincial president and military commander, Francisco José de Sousa Soares de Andrea (or Andréia). He was ruthlessly efficient. Cabano units on islands near Belém were destroyed and the city blockaded. President Angelim asked for an amnesty and permission for the rebels to retire to the upper Amazon. Andrea refused. The Cabanos tried to fight their way out of Belém but they had no gunpowder, and by mid-May 1836 the shattered and filthy city was back in government control. An English naval captain wrote that 'The rebels being entirely destitute of provisions and ammunition left the town on the evening of the 12th [May] and ... the legal authorities took possession without firing a shot. The Indians destroyed everything previous to leaving the city and then attempted to burn it, but fortunately from the nature of the buildings they failed in the attempt.'

The new imperial President Andrea gave a lurid report of the situation that confronted him. The Cabanagem was 'a ghastly revolution in which barbarism seemed about to devour all existing civilisation in one single gulp'. Apart from the town of Cametá, fort of Macapá, and a few villages on the Xingu, 'no other part of this vast province escaped the fury of the ruffians. Most sugar mills and fazendas were destroyed and their slaves killed or dispersed.... There were districts in which they left no single white man alive.' Cattle had been slaughtered and food stores consumed. 'Wherever there was a white or rich man who could be killed or something to be robbed, someone would immediately appear to undertake this service.... In some they kept the owners' wives and sons, many of whom were forced to laugh and dance around the corpses of their relatives.' To compound the province's misery, President Andrea reported that 'we have stubborn and repeating malarial fevers, and an epidemic of smallpox that is devouring everything'. This was probably measles, since Andrea said that it seemed resistant to vaccination.

Andrea divided his men into nine forces and sent them to destroy rebels throughout Amazonia. One force pursued President Eduardo Angelim to his base on the Acará river some 500 kilometres (310 miles) south of Belém. An English officer wrote in July 1836: 'All accounts agree that the Indians are separated and their strength is quite broken – that is in consequence of their total want of gunpowder. Bodies of Belgian and Brazilian troops are dispersed all over the country, who bring in few prisoners, shooting the greater number that they take.'

General Andrea admitted chillingly that 'it was necessary to suspend the formalities by which the law shields criminals.... Any revolutionaries ... were imprisoned, despite existing laws and against all rules of individual liberty.' He organized a militia, but enlisting only 'well-educated people of noble sentiments'. He decreed that any 'coloured man who appears in any district without valid motive will immediately be arrested and sent to the authorities to dispose of him'. Anyone 'not regularly employed in useful work will be sent to government factories or hired out to any private individual who needs him'. Those who were lazy or 'deserved it' went to unpaid labour in the naval arsenal or clearing wasteland under armed guard. It was a return to the worst days of slavery and forced labour. Criminals, real or suspected, were locked up. President Andrea wrote that '340 prisoners were confined in irons on the corvette *Defensora*, living in a veritable hell.... They will perish there, asphyxiated from lack of sufficient air to breathe, or they will catch some disease from which they will end their miserable days in the hospital.' The missionary Daniel Kidder generally approved. He wrote that Andrea 'proclaimed martial law, and by means of great firmness and severity succeeded in restoring order to the province. It was, however, at the cost of much blood and many lives. He was accused of tyranny and inhumanity in his course towards the rebels and prisoners, but the exigencies of the case were great, and furnished apologies.' But, like Prince Adalbert, Kidder knew where the blame for the Cabanagem lay. 'We see nothing but the fruits of that violence and injury which, from the first colonisation of Pará by the Portuguese, had been practised against the despised Indians.'

Far away up the Rio Negro and its tributary the Rio Branco, a government officer called Ambrosio Pedro Ayres defeated the Cabanos at Tomar. This village was formerly a mission called Bararoá, so the victor adopted Bararoá as his *nom de guerre*. Bararoá led his force to clear those rivers of rebels. He recaptured Barra (Manaus) in late 1836 and held it against a counter-attack led by the Cabano Apolinário Maparajuba. He went on to storm Maparajuba's stronghold Icuipiranga on the main Amazon and tried to retake towns on the Madeira. Bararoá was a successful commander, but a psychopath who 'practised with impunity, in the name of legality, the most barbarous, inhuman and cannibalistic crimes for the mere satisfaction of his bestial instincts'. He systematically massacred prisoners and ravaged recaptured towns. He particularly loathed Indians, and was brutal towards the Mura, Mawé and other tribes whose warriors assisted the Cabanos.

The suppression of isolated pockets of resistance continued in the vastnesses of Amazonia throughout 1837 and much of 1838. In August 1838 Bararoá led his force of 130 fighters and many able-bodied citizens of Manaus into the Autazes lakes. This is a labyrinth of seasonally flooded lagoons and swamps in the tongue of forests where the Madeira joins the Amazon. It was the homeland of the Mura, the once-fierce people who had made peace fifty years previously, and it was a perfect stronghold and sanctuary for the rebels. For some reason Bararoá suddenly abandoned his force in this watery maze and tried to return to Manaus. As his boat passed through a forested channel, he was attacked by seven canoes manned mostly by Mura. He fought hard, but was overpowered and killed. It was said that the Mura tortured to death their savage opponent. President Andrea's comment was: 'It will be difficult to find another man with the valour, skill and intelligence of this victim.' But the men of Manaus were less charitable about the leader who had deserted them, and the Cabanos were jubilant.

The first great historian of the Cabanagem was Domingos Raiol, whose father had been killed by the Cabanos. But Raiol was appalled by the cruelty of General Andrea's repression. 'No-one could imagine the martyrdoms suffered by those who fell into the power of the so-called expeditions! People speak only of the savagery of the cabanos and forget the brutality of the self-proclaimed legalists.' Raiol told of commanders wearing 'rosaries' of Cabanos' ears, and boasting of drowning canoe-loads, mass shootings of prisoners, and other 'ostentatious' atrocities. 'I calculate that over thirty thousand men were sacrificed to the fury of demagoguery and the reaction of government emissaries. The repression degenerated into racial hatred.... The slaughter was general, and for the most part unrecorded.'

Matters improved with the arrival in 1839 of a new President, Bernardo de Souza Franco. He put a stop to his predecessor's three years of 'obedience inspired by terror'. He understood the grievances of 'the underprivileged and wronged.... The reasons for these are easy to find – in the forced labour, exigencies, constraint and oppression that always accompany such dissents and civil wars.' Souza Franco decided that 'it would be difficult to conclude this war without also using gentle and conciliatory methods, given the vastness of the territories that have to be covered'. He therefore issued an amnesty and general pardon to the remaining Cabanos. In March 1840 hundreds of these surrendered, with their guns and bows-and-arrows, on the Maués River and other forested hideouts.

President Souza Franco tried to calculate the population of the huge area under his control. He reckoned 100,000 to 120,000 for the district of Pará, of whom roughly 30,000 were Indian and black slaves, half were minors under twenty-one, and 13,000 lived in the city of Belém. His rough guesses were 30–40,000 in Lower Amazonas and at least 27,000 in Upper Amazonas (the Solimões and Rio Negro basins). To these should be added uncontacted 'nomadic' Indians, who might be between 100 and 200 thousand people. But he reminded his audience of the havoc wrought by the rebellion. 'Cast your eyes, Gentlemen, on the columns of adult men and women and the excess in numbers of females over males, and you will see one more proof of the immense loss of men that this Province has suffered.' Brazilian Amazonia was left shattered, with a fifth of its meagre population dead from the Cabanagem – in roughly equal numbers from both the privileged and working sides of the ugly conflict.

The shortage of manpower had two effects. On the one hand, white managers were desperate for workers. The young American traveller William Edwards complained that near Santarém in the 1840s 'the scarcity of laborers is most severely felt; slaves being few, and Indians difficult to catch.... Desertion is so common, and so annoying, that it receives no mercy from the authorities.' As late as 1854 the American naval Lieutenant William Herndon reported that 'all the christianized Indians of the province of Pará ... are registered and compelled to serve the State, either as soldiers of the Guarda Policial or as a member of "Bodies of Laborers".' Traders, travellers or bosses of collecting expeditions in the forests all sought workers from these *Corpo de Trabalhadores* press gangs. There was no proper control of the system, so that 'a majority of them ... have become, in fact, the slaves of individuals'. In that same year, the English naturalist Henry Walter Bates said that slave-raiding continued against tribes of the Solimões tributaries. 'This species of slave dealing, although forbidden by the laws of Brazil, is winked at by the authorities, because without it there would be no means of obtaining servants.'

However, the acute labour shortage gave individuals some bargaining clout and freedom. Years of intermarriage between the three races – indigenous, white and black – had produced the hardy breed known as caboclos. The word caboclo was initially pejorative but came to acquire a certain prestige. Caboclos were frontiersmen who had learned how to survive in the Amazonian forests and rivers. They had *jeito* – a splendid Brazilian word meaning being smart, savvy and resourceful. They were the equivalent to the wise and wily 'old-timers' of the American west. Caboclos had been the footsoldiers of the Cabanagem revolt. When it was over, they tended to escape from towns and villages where they could be pressed into service or victimized by the successors to Pombal's directors. They took their families to isolated homesteads on the banks of the rivers, where they could fish, hunt and farm a clearing without molestation. They became *ribeirinhos*, riverbank people who used native skills to live sustainably from endemic flora and fauna.

The first 250 years after Europeans settled on the Amazon were ones of man's inhumanity to man. Europeans and their diseases destroyed the nations that once flourished along the mighty river and its accessible tributaries. There was little to show for this colonial invasion – the town of Belém do Pará (whose population shrank from 24,000 in 1820 to 15,000 three decades later), a few stone forts, and a score of villages where there had once been missions. These remote settlements were little more than a line of low, whitewashed, red-tiled or thatched buildings overlooking the swirling brown waters, with a twin-towered church and a few streets of huts for the indigenous people. Between the towns were thousands of kilometres of uninhabited forests.

The best that could be said for the colonists is that they had done little damage to the forests and rivers. Their farm clearings and cacao plantations were infinitesimal scratches on the expanses of Amazon rain forests. The only lasting environmental catastrophe was the destruction of freshwater turtles. These used to teem in Amazon rivers. As late as the 1870s the railway engineer Edward Mathews watched the great reptiles mating. 'As far as the eye can see, which here-abouts runs straight for some six or seven miles, were continuous rows of turtle at the water's edge: the rows being eight or ten deep, many thousands must have col-lected together' and the clashing of their shells could be heard for miles. The slaughter of these fine animals was relentless and profligate. Throughout the nineteenth century between one and five million eggs were destroyed every year. Their rich oil was used for cooking and to light rich families' chandeliers or caboc-los' lamps. By the twentieth century the Podocnemis had become an endangered species.

Surprisingly, industrialized nations became interested in this difficult terrain. They wrongly equated luxuriant tropical vegetation with temperate agri-culture. They thought that vigorous European pioneers could transform the Amazon in the way that they were opening North America. Humboldt in 1800 had imagined a modern civilization on the banks of the Amazon. Twenty years later, his compatriots Spix and Martius fantasized: 'What marvellous perspectives are opened, when the banks of the majestic stream will one day be occupied by popu-lous cities … and highways link … the Pacific Ocean to the Atlantic, when the empty melancholy forests of the Casiquiare echo to the cries of sailors travelling from the Orinoco to the Amazon … [to] emerge safely on the busy Plate!' A few years later, the British naval Lieutenant Henry Lister Maw predicted that once steam navigation was introduced to the Amazon 'the country will be no more recognisable'.

In the mid-nineteenth century the United States became more ambitious. Its leading hydrographer and oceanographer Lieutenant Matthew Fontaine Maury in 1853 published a study of Brazil's Amazonian and Atlantic waters. He noted that winds and currents made it easier to sail to the Amazon from Florida than from Rio de Janeiro, so that the Amazon 'is but a continuation of the Missis-sippi valley'. He was convinced that the region had the potential to be a second Eden – provided that it was not occupied 'by an imbecile and indolent people [but by] a go-ahead race that has energy and enterprise equal to subdue the forest and to develop … the vast resources that lie hidden there'. Maury prompted his govern-ment to send 'The Amazon Exploration Expedition'. Naval Lieutenants William Lewis Herndon and Lardner Gibbon descended the Amazon, with secret instruc-tions to report on its potential. They were wildly enthusiastic. 'We have here a continent whose shores produce, or may be made to produce, all that the earth gives for the maintenance of more people than the earth now holds.... Let us now suppose the banks of these streams settled by an active and industrious population...; let us suppose introduced into such a country the railroad and the steamboat, the plough, the axe, and the hoe; let us suppose the land divided into large estates and cultivated by slave labour so as to produce all that they are capable of producing; and ... we shall conclude that no territory on the face of the globe is so favourably situated, and that, if trade there is once awakened, the power, wealth and grandeur of ancient Babylon and modern London must yield to that of the ... Orinoco, Amazon and La Plata.' The book by Herndon and Gibbon was a bestseller. One enthusiastic reader was Samuel Clemens ('Mark Twain'), who was 'fired with a longing to ascend the Amazon ... to make a fortune'.

Naval officers were not the only observers to be misled by the Amazon's fertility. The British naturalist Alfred Russel Wallace was also beguiled by 'a country where there is no stoppage of agricultural operations during winter.... I fearlessly assert that here the primeval forest can be converted into rich pasture, into cultivated fields, gardens, and orchards containing every variety of produce.' Wallace's friend Henry Bates was more cautious: he appreciated that Amazonian vegetation could be daunting. But he blamed local people for failing to make the most of their environment. 'It is a case of want of fitness; other races of men ... would have been better fitted to enjoy and make use of the rich unappropriated domain.'

Lieutenant Maury urged his American government to get the Amazon opened to foreign shipping, 'peacefully if we can, by force if we must'. There was a decade of intense diplomatic duelling. But the mercantile imperialists finally got what they wanted. The Empire of Brazil in 1867 decided that open ports were in its interest, and made the Amazon the only river in the world freely open to international merchant shipping.

There was a sad footnote to this hysteria about the region's potential. An adventurer called Lansford Warren Hastings got a huge concession near Santarém from the government of Pará. With the ending of the American Civil War, Hastings persuaded three hundred eager Confederates to try to settle there. Some Brazilians feared that this would lead to the United States annexing thinly populated Amazonia, in the way that it had taken California from Mexico. But, once again, the problems of a tropical rain forest were too much for these pioneers from 'a go-ahead race'. The colony was an abysmal failure, and the surviving Americans limped home. It is ironic that the chiefdom of the Tapajó had once flourished on the site of this doomed settlement, and seventy years later Henry Ford was to suffer his worst financial disaster in that same area.

CHAPTER FIVE

A Naturalist's Paradise

In 1800 the young German Baron Alexander von Humboldt and his French friend Aimé Bonpland made their way from the Caribbean to the northern edge of the Amazon basin. Humboldt is revered as the first great scientist to describe the wonders of South American nature. He was said to be the last true polymath, the last person to know most of the sum of human knowledge. As the two savants sailed and paddled up the Orinoco, they marvelled at the geology, flora and fauna. They were particularly delighted by the toucans, macaws and many other birds. They noted the few hazards. They drove horses and mules into a pond seething with electric 'eels' (*Gymnotus electricus*, a long, slimy, green, carp-like fish), and watched in horror as the creatures rubbed against the horses and discharged 650-volt shocks into their organs, so that the frenzied animals' eyes bulged, their manes stood up, and they were stunned and risked drowning. But the scientists played down the danger of poisonous snakes (which could slide up to sleeping people to enjoy their warmth) and jaguars (which they often heard but never saw). They frequently complained of plagues of mosquitoes and black-flies.

At one beach on which turtles laid their eggs, Humboldt watched in fascinated horror as hundreds of Indians, directed by Franciscan missionaries, plundered every single nest. When the Jesuits had been in charge, they imposed rudimentary conservation by protecting the eggs on half of each such beach. But after the expulsion of those missionary fathers there was profligate looting of every last egg. Humboldt was told that these sandbanks on the lower Orinoco yielded five thousand massive jars of turtle oil each year. He calculated that this had involved the destruction of 33 million eggs laid by some 330,000 female turtles. That was roughly a third of the turtle population of that river. Extrapolated to all the rivers of Amazonia, the quantity of turtle oil was horrendous – as we know from records of tens of thousands of jars of oil exported annually.

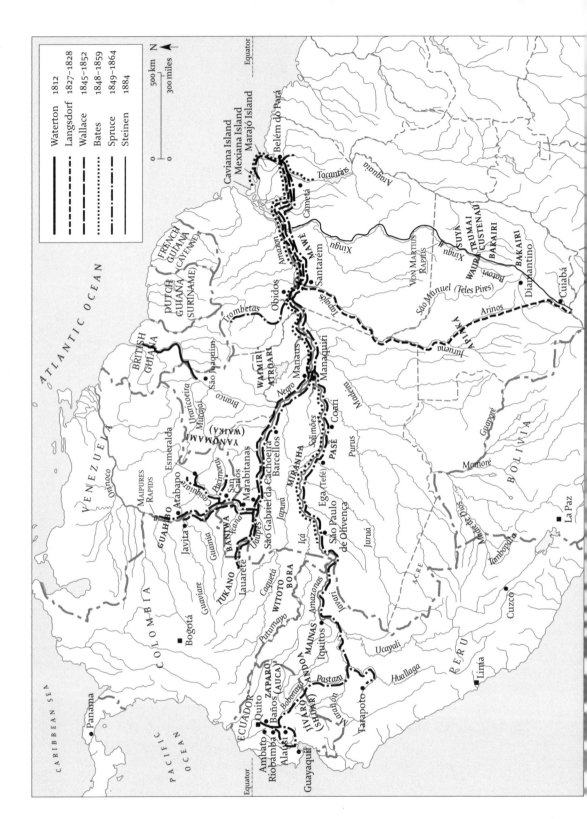

One of Humboldt's goals was the Casiquiare Canal, a remarkable river that links the upper Orinoco and Amazon systems. The land here is so flat that part of the Orinoco's waters flow southwestwards and never rejoin the mother river. Instead, after 300 meandering kilometres (almost 200 miles), they flow into a headwater of the Negro and hence the Amazon. This link had always been known to Indians, and to Europeans for seventy years.

In a month of travel near the Casiquiare, Humboldt saw no human beings except near two Franciscan missions. He was awed by the majesty of nature and insignificance of his race. On 'the uninhabited banks of the Casiquiare, covered with forests, without memorials of times past ... one may almost ... regard men as not being essential to the order of nature. The earth is loaded with plants, and nothing impedes their free development.... Alligators and boas are masters of the river; the jaguar, the peccary, the tapir, and the monkeys traverse the forest without fear and without danger ... as in an ancient inheritance.... Here, in a fertile country, adorned with eternal verdure, we seek in vain traces of the power of man.' At one place, 'we slept in a forest of palm trees. It rained violently, but the pothoses, arums, and lianas furnished so thick a natural trellis that we were sheltered as under a vault of foliage. The Indians, whose hammocks were placed on the edge of the river, interwove the heliconias and other musaceae so as to form a kind of roof over them. Our fires lighted up, to the height of fifty or sixty feet, the palm trees, the lianas loaded with flowers, and the columns of white smoke which ascended in a straight line toward the sky. The whole exhibited a magnificent spectacle; but' – Humboldt shattered the vision – 'to have enjoyed it fully, we should have breathed an air clear of insects.'

Apart from a short stretch of the upper Rio Negro, Humboldt never entered the Amazon basin. At the Spanish border fort San Carlos de Río Negro he was warned that for political reasons it was difficult to pass the frontier into Portuguese Brazil. Humboldt wrote: 'It was known in Brazil ... that I was going to visit the missions of the Rio Negro and examine the natural canal which unites two great systems of rivers. In those deserted forests ... agents of the Portuguese government could not conceive how a man of sense could expose himself to the fatigues of a long journey "to measure lands that did not belong to him". Orders had been issued to seize my person, my instruments, and above all those registers of astronomical observations so dangerous to the safety of states.' We now know that the Portuguese authorities also suspected Humboldt of being a political subversive. So the colonial government issued an order to refuse entry to the German

Opposite Map showing routes of celebrated naturalists' expeditions in the Amazon Basin.

scientist, as 'a foreigner who might possibly conceal plans for the spread of new ideas and dangerous principles among the loyal subjects of this realm, at a time when the temper of this nation is in a condition so dangerous and difficult to deal with'. It is amazing that this paranoid edict was paddled for 3,000 kilometres (almost 2,000 miles) from Belém to a tiny garrison on the distant banks of the upper Rio Negro. To this day, that frontier outpost of Marabitanas is just a speck in the endless lines of riverine vegetation. Humboldt and Bonpland were forced to retrace their arduous route down the Orinoco; they then continued their journey in Spanish colonies, along the Andes to Peru and then north to Mexico.

As we have seen, Napoleon's invasion of the Iberian peninsula provoked independence movements throughout South America. It also led to the continent's opening to European intellectuals. The Prince Regent Dom João fled to Brazil with the rest of the Portuguese royal family in 1807, as a bedraggled French army was marching unopposed into Lisbon. The Portuguese court settled in Rio de Janeiro for what proved to be a thirteen-year sojourn. In 1816 the post-Napoleonic French ambassador, the Duc de Luxembourg, brought a 'French Artistic Mission' of painters, writers and scientists. This was the first chink in the blanket of secrecy about Brazil. Two years later, the King's heir Dom Pedro married the Austrian Archduchess Leopoldina and she also brought an entourage of savants. These included two Bavarians: the zoologist Johann Baptist von Spix and the botanist Carl Friedrich Philip von Martius. Spix and Martius were the first foreign scientists permitted to visit the Amazon, apart from the unauthorized descent by La Condamine in 1743. In ten months in 1819–20 the Bavarians travelled far up the Amazon, Solimões and lower Japurá, Negro and Madeira rivers. They brought back magnificent collections that embraced 85 different species of mammals, 350 of birds, 130 of amphibians, 116 of fish, 2,700 of insects, and 6,500 of plants. Martius was as fascinated as Humboldt by the beauty of palms: he produced a natural history of these trees as well as the first treatise on *Flora Brasiliae*. Spix voraciously collected hundreds of species of fish from Amazon waters. Most of this material was new to Europeans. It was their first taste of the stupendous biodiversity of the earth's richest ecosystem.

Spix and Martius were instructed by their government to observe the peoples of Brazil, their farming methods and medicinal plants. Although sometimes critical of the 'backwardness' of indigenous peoples judged against European 'civilization', the Germans admired tribes that had had least exposure to colonial abuse. As we have seen, they deplored rampant illegal slaving and forced labour – cruelties that were to explode in the Cabanagem rebellion in the following decade. They also noted various medicines used by indigenous people. The Mawé of the middle Amazon had a monopoly of guaraná (*Paullinia cupana*), a plant whose fruit was dried and ground to form a bitter but delicious drink that was, and still is, prized throughout Amazonia. Guaraná was a stimulant that enabled Amazon Indians to hunt for a day without feeling hunger, and they also used it to treat fevers, headaches and cramps. Years later, Martius won a prize from a Brazilian learned society for an essay arguing that the mingling of the indigenous, white and black races could produce a nation in the tropics as vigorous as England with its blend of Anglo-Saxon, Norman, Scandinavian and Celtic peoples. This racial hokum appealed to Brazilian intellectuals striving for a national identity that was different but not inferior to that of their Portuguese mother-country.

The first Englishman to write in praise of tropical forests was Charles Waterton – and he was also his country's first environmental activist. The squire of an estate near Wakefield in Yorkshire, Waterton went as a young man to manage his family's sugar plantations in British Guiana. He made four journeys up-country between 1812 and 1826 and described these in *Wanderings in South America*, a bestseller that introduced the British reading public to the natural glories of Amazonia. Waterton delighted in 'noble trees, whose foliage displays a charming variety of every shade, from the lightest to the darkest green and purple. The tops of some are crowned with bloom of the loveliest hue; while the boughs of others bend with a profusion of seeds and fruits.' He vividly described wild fig trees, particularly the stranglers that gradually suffocate the host tree that supports their greedy push towards the sunlight and rains of the canopy. He also told about lianas. 'A vine called the bush-rope by the wood-cutters, on account of its use in hauling out the heaviest timber, has a singular appearance in the forests. Sometimes you see it nearly as thick as a man's body, twisted like a corkscrew round the tallest trees, and rearing its head high above their tops. At other times, three or four of them, like strands in a cable, join tree and tree, and branch and branch together. Others, descending from on high, take root as soon as their extremity touches the ground; and appear like shrouds and stays supporting the mainmast of a line of battle ship.'

On one journey, Waterton crossed into northern Brazil. He was wracked with malaria, and 'the nights were cold and stormy, the rain fell in torrents, the days cloudy, and there was no sun to dry the wet hammocks. Exposed thus, day and night, to the chilling blast and pelting shower, strength of constitution at last failed, and a severe fever came on.' The Brazilian fort São Joaquim on the upper Rio Branco was intended to exclude all foreigners. But when its commander saw Waterton's condition, he said that 'the orders I have received forbidding the admission of strangers were never intended to be put in force against a sick English gentleman'. So he invited the traveller to his fort and nursed him to recovery.

Charles Waterton adored birds. He wrote pages about them, from snow-white egrets to iridescent humming birds. He adored the macaw. 'His commanding strength, the flaming scarlet of his body, the lovely variety of red, yellow, blue, and green in his wings, the extraordinary length of his scarlet and blue tail, seem all to join and demand for him the title of emperor of all the parrots.' He watched macaws noisily eat palm fruits and then 'rise up in bodies towards sunset, and fly two by two to their places of rest. It is a grand sight in ornithology to see thousands of Araras [macaws] flying over your head, low enough to let you have a full view of their flaming mantles.' He was proud of a new method of preserving birds that he had invented, and he brought specimens of two hundred species back for the British Museum of Natural History.

Waterton was the first to debunk the idea that a rain forest was a hostile environment. He praised the climate of Amazonia – rarely too hot or humid – and said how exhilarated one felt there: 'Every morning ... thou wilt spring from thy hammock fresh as the April lark.' Above all, he wanted to assure readers that the dangers and hardships were 'not half so numerous as they are commonly thought to be'.

Waterton's adventure with a Black Cayman showed him at his eccentric best. His Makuxi Indians baited a rope with wooden hooks and a small rodent, dangled this in the water, and then banged a tortoise-shell to show that something interesting was happening. 'In fact the Indian meant it as the cayman's dinner bell.' They were soon pulling a thrashing saurian onto a sandbank. When the animal was close to Waterton, 'I instantly sprung up, and jumped on his back, turning half-round as I vaulted so that I gained my seat with my face in a right position. I immediately seized his fore legs, and, by main force, twisted them on his back; thus they served me for a bridle. He now seemed to have recovered from his surprise, and probably fancying himself in hostile company, he began to plunge furiously, and lashed the sand with his long and powerful tail.... He continued to plunge and strike, and made my seat very uncomfortable.... The people roared out in triumph.' Waterton was afraid that the cayman might get back into the water and drown him. So he shouted to his men to drag it further onto the sand; which they did for some 40 metres (130 feet). 'It was the first and last time I was ever on a cayman's back. Should it be asked, how I managed to keep my seat, I would answer, — I hunted some years with Lord Darlington's fox hounds.'

Charles Waterton had brushes with other Amazonian fauna. He loved sloths, keeping one as a pet for many months. He was the first to record sloths' behaviour in the wild and begged his readers not to kill 'this harmless, unoffending animal'. He watched vampire bats draw blood without awaking their victim. He played with a highly poisonous fer-de-lance snake, confident that it would not strike if he 'took care to move very softly and gently without moving my arms'. When he unexpectedly came upon a young anaconda, he immediately grabbed its tail and punched its nose. 'I allowed him to coil himself around my body, and marched off with him as my lawful prize. He pressed me hard, but not alarmingly so.'

Another great interest was the curare poison used by indigenous hunters. Waterton brought some back to England and used it to stun several animals in The Royal Society in London, watched by its scientific Fellows. These experiments were important in the history of anaesthetics. The poison apparently killed a cat but, after hours of artificial respiration, it regained a state of profound sleep and then 'awoke and walked away'. A she-ass belonging to the Duke of Northumberland (president of the Veterinary College) died from a massive injection of curare. But a pipe was inserted into the animal's windpipe and, after two hours of air pumped by a bellows worked by a Professor Sewell, 'she rose up and walked about; she seemed neither agitated nor in pain'. The Duke later gave the ass to Waterton, who called her Wouralia (curare) and kept her for a further twenty-four years.

Squire Waterton became increasingly eccentric. He turned his estate into a wildlife sanctuary full of artificial burrows and nests; and he himself liked to dress as a scarecrow and sit in trees. He launched the world's first successful legal action over environmental pollution, against the owner of a nearby soap-works whose chimneys released noxious chemicals. He quarrelled with many scientists of his day. But when Charles Darwin called on the elderly Waterton he wrote: 'He is an amusing strange fellow; at our early dinner our party consisted of two Catholic priests and two Mulatresses!' Charles Waterton was Britain's first eco-warrior and its first genuine lover of tropical forests.

The next two scientific expeditions in Amazonia were by a German and an Austrian. Georg Langsdorff trained in medicine, but gained a place as a naturalist on a

Russian circumnavigation of the world and went on to join the St Petersburg Academy of Sciences as a zoologist and botanist. The Tsar appointed Langsdorff as his first Consul-General in Rio de Janeiro, when it was the residence of the exiled Portuguese royal family. The genial German scholar made the most of this posting: between 1813 and 1820 he was host to all visiting European intellectuals. Langsdorff then persuaded the Tsar to finance a scientific expedition to the interior. After many delays in 1825 the team moved inland, but it did not enter Amazonian waters until 1828. By this time, Langsdorff was in his mid-fifties and had become increasingly unconventional. He had recruited a good team that included two brilliant young French artists, Hércules Florence and Adrien Taunay, but the young men on the expedition came to despise their elderly leader. They accused him of choosing a ludicrous route of rapid-infested rivers for the journey westwards, and of being obsessed by a young German girl he took as a companion. At Cuiabá, a free-wheeling mining town in Mato Grosso, Langsdorff dallied for a year in debauches that his frustrated companions said aggravated his incipient madness.

The expedition split: one team descended to the Amazon by the Guaporé-Madeira route, the other containing the leader by the Arinos-Tapajós rivers. When the main party reached a village of naked Apiaká Indians, Langsdorff decided to 'flatter the chief's self-esteem' by hoisting the Russian state flag, and wearing his full diplomatic uniform, complete with plumed hat, sword and decorations. The young expeditioners mocked the absurdity of this. An Apiaká girl borrowed Langsdorff's gold-braided consular coat and ran into the forest with it. 'The victim began to run like a desperado after his dress-coat, in the utmost and grotesque fury.' The artist Florence made lovely – and ethnographically accurate – paintings of the Apiaká. He was enchanted by their innocence and goodness, just as Vespucci and others had been three centuries earlier. 'Everything about them is simple; but nothing is repellent. They are naked; but they never wear frills or dirty or ragged clothing. Their bodies are always clean.... They do not know the great principle of property. There are no robbers or murderers among them, no poisoners, or cheats, or pilferers – none of the moral evils that afflict civilized men.' But the gentle Apiaká were too kind to white Brazilians. They guided their boats through nearby rapids, they collected masses of sarsaparilla for them, and their beautiful women were all too readily available. 'Since these women have no clothes or artifices they leave visible to all the tragic presence of syphilis with which strangers have infected them.'

Malaria was by now raging throughout Amazonia. This disease struck the expedition as it battled down the formidable rapids – almost waterfalls – on the

Arinos. Langsdorff suffered terribly. He wrote pathetic entries in his journal: 'As to what happened on the 18th, I know nothing. I fell into a delirium'; or 'I was without memory and did not know what took place'; or 'Weak in body and soul, I sit here and the only thing that can be said is that I am alive'. Four days after this last entry, the German diplomat-scientist became completely deranged and ceased to lead the venture. He had made his men agree to publish nothing before he did. Consequently, the findings and paintings of the Russian Imperial Expedition to South America languished in St Petersburg, and were not published until the late twentieth century.

The Austrian Johann Natterer accompanied Archduchess Leopoldina to Brazil in 1817 as a zoologist and artist. After twelve years of travel and collecting in southern Brazil, Natterer in 1829 pushed into the Amazon basin. He descended the Guaporé and Madeira rivers – a year after one of Langsdorff's teams had entered the Amazon by this route. During the next six years, Natterer, alone and in his forties, made one of the most formidable ethnographic and natural-history expeditions ever in the history of Amazonia. He went right up the Rio Negro to the Casiquiare Canal, investigated its main headwaters, then up the Branco and its almost-unexplored Mucajaí tributary, then down to Manaus and up the Solimões, before returning to Vienna in 1835. He had amassed a vast collection of flora and fauna, and almost two thousand artefacts from seventy-two tribes he had visited throughout Brazil. Natterer married a Brazilian girl at Barcellos on the Rio Negro. But he also fathered a daughter by a Baniwa woman on the Içana headwater of that river: Alfred Russel Wallace met this beautiful mestiza there in 1854. Natterer compiled vocabularies of sixty indigenous languages, but sadly never published an account of his extraordinary travels. Back in Vienna, his papers were burned in a house fire during the revolution of 1848, five years after his death from a lung disease. So Natterer's only legacy is his magnificent collections, now in the Ethnographic and Natural History Museums of Vienna.

It was in that year 1848 that two young Englishmen – Henry Walter Bates and Alfred Russel Wallace – first glimpsed the mouth of the Amazon. A third, Richard Spruce, came in the following year. Each of the three was destined to make himself a legend in the world of Amazonian natural history. Wallace, aged twenty-five, was excited by his first sight of the city of Belém 'surrounded by the dense forest.... The general aspect of the trees was not different from those of Europe, except where the "feathery palm-trees" raised their graceful forms.' Bates, two years younger, admired 'a long line of forest, rising apparently out of the water; a densely packed mass of tall trees, broken into groups and finally into single trees, as it dwindled away in the distance. This was the frontier of the great primaeval forest … which contains so many wonders in its recesses, and clothes the whole surface of the country for two thousand miles from this point to the foot of the Andes.' Bates never lost his awe of that stupendous environment. Eight years later, when far up the mighty river, he wrote to his brother in a cascade of enthusiasm. 'The charm and glory of the country are its animal and vegetable productions. How inexhaustible is their study!… It is one dense jungle: the lofty forest trees, of vast variety of species, all lashed and connected by climbers, their trunks covered with a museum of ferns, Tillandrias, Arums, Orchids, &c. The underwood consists mostly of younger trees – great variety of small palms, mimosas, tree-ferns, &c., and the ground is laden with fallen branches – vast trunks covered with parasites, &c.'

When Bates set foot in Pará, he was almost disappointed by how agreeable it was. He wrote to a friend: 'Where are the dangers and horrors of the tropics? I find none of them.' Like Charles Waterton, he wanted to dispel fantasies about fearsome jungles. When he left the Amazon eleven years later, 'I took a last view of the glorious forest for which I had so much love, and to explore which I had devoted so many years…. [It is] a region which may be fittingly called a Naturalist's Paradise…. I was quitting a country of perpetual summer, where my life had been spent … in gypsy fashion, on the endless streams or in the boundless forests.'

Both Bates and Wallace contrasted the exuberance of Amazonian nature with the limitations of its inhabitants. Wallace was struck that the town of Belém, with only fifteen thousand inhabitants, was the largest in a province the size of all western Europe. The people were generally friendly to the young foreigners. But none of them seemed curious about the natural treasure-house in which they lived. Back in England, he found its intellectual life 'incomparably superior … to the sterility of half-savage existence, even though it be passed in the garden of Eden … in equatorial South America, where three distinct races of man live together.'

Henry Bates had left school at thirteen. His family wanted him to go into their hosiery business in Leicester, so he became an apprentice working a thirteen-hour day for six days a week. What saved him, and raised him to scientific immortality, was that his parents were strict Unitarians, dissenters who believed in a rational approach to science and in the virtues of self-improvement. Young Bates taught himself natural history by reading at nights – and he met the young schoolmaster Alfred Wallace in 1844 in the Leicester public library. Wallace had also had only rudimentary education – so little that he felt unqualified to teach at a primary school for more than a year; his only training was work as a land surveyor with his older brother. Wallace became a staunch supporter of Robert Owen, the paternalistic socialist who was a founding father of the cooperative movement, which in turn led to trade unionism. More important than religion or politics was the young men's membership of the local Mechanics' Institute. These splendid clubs, open to men and women, spread popular science to Britain's new middle class, through their collecting excursions, popular meetings, lectures, and affordable guides to flora and fauna. Bates combed the local woods with a home-made butterfly net, and he became a passionate entomologist. This hobby sealed his friendship with Wallace. In 1847 they read a new book about the Amazon by William Edwards, a young American lawyer and enthusiastic naturalist. It was not a great book, but it fired the imaginations of these amateurs. They decided that they *had* to get to the world's largest river and tropical forest; somehow scraped together the transatlantic fares; and left within a few months.

The Yorkshireman Richard Spruce, meanwhile, had become equally ardent about botany. He started collecting plants (particularly his 'beloved mosses') as he walked across the moors on his way to Latin lessons. The son of a respected schoolmaster, Spruce was largely self-taught and of as modest means as Bates and Wallace. His parents had many other children, so Spruce had to fend for himself: he taught mathematics in a school in York to scrape a living, but did not enjoy it. His inspiration was Charles Darwin's journal of his voyage on the *Beagle*, but travel to South America seemed unattainable. However, Spruce had started writing about his plant collecting in the journal *The Phytologist* and this brought him to the attention of keepers at the Royal Botanic Gardens, Kew. He went to London, and Kew's director Sir William Hooker got him a job gathering plants in the Spanish Pyrenees, largely for the keen collector George Bentham. Back in London, it was Bentham who suggested that Spruce might take his tremendous botanical skills to the Amazon: he offered to advance him funds, and helped him find ten other collectors to buy his specimens. At the British Museum Spruce saw animals and insects sent back by Bates and Wallace, and he read their letters published in *Zoologist* magazine. So he needed little persuading to follow them.

Spruce sailed to Pará in June 1849. After three months' botanizing he took a riverboat up the Amazon and caught up with Wallace at Santarém and again at Óbidos (small towns with populations of under three thousand). Spruce was tall and thin with a black beard, quiet and amiable. His notebooks and collections show him to have been exceptionally diligent, meticulous and scholarly. He was seven years older than Wallace, but the two became lifelong friends: sixty years later, it was Wallace who posthumously edited Spruce's journals and thus established his reputation for posterity.

Wallace and Bates had spent the previous year collecting near Belém and on the lower Tocantins river and Marajó Island. At times they travelled together, then on separate excursions. Bates finally sailed up the main Amazon in October 1849, a few weeks after Wallace and then Spruce. Each of them kept stopping to pursue his collecting. In January 1850 Bates and Wallace met again at Manaus. This town was as small as Santarém and Wallace thought that it had no pure Europeans. Its citizens combined a licentious way of life with formality: on Sundays they dressed in dark suits and top hats. The Englishmen spent a few weeks collecting together. They then parted again: Wallace went northwestwards, far up the Rio Negro; Bates sailed westwards up the Amazon-Solimões. Spruce, meanwhile, returned to spend most of 1850 at Santarém; in October he moved to Manaus, where he worked for another year before travelling up the Rio Negro and its headwaters from late 1851 to 1853.

As a passionate and experienced botanist, Richard Spruce was even more dazzled by Amazon flora than his companions had been. He later started to write a book of his travels, which began with his first impressions of primeval forest. 'There were enormous trees, crowned with magnificent foliage, decked with fantastic parasites, hung over with lianas which varied in thickness from slender threads to huge, python-like masses, rounded, flattened, twisted with the regularity of a cable.' Spruce, like Humboldt and Martius, adored palms – he later wrote a fine book on them. He continued: 'Intermixed with the trees, and often equal to them in altitude, grew noble palms; while other and far lovelier species of the same family, their ringed stems sometimes scarcely exceeding a finger's thickness, but bearing plume-like fronds and pendulous bunches of black or red berries … formed a bushy undergrowth.' This thirty-five-page essay, intended for the general reader but written by a professional botanist, goes on to describe everything from lianas, triangular buttress roots that support some trees, strangler figs with their aerial roots, variations of trunks, barks and leaves, forest flowers and fruits, epiphytes (perched plants), and other marvels. No later author wrote a better introduction for a layman entering the towering gloom of a tropical rain forest.

Spruce was staggered by the size and exuberance of everything. 'The largest river in the world flows through the largest forest. Fancy if you can *two millions of square miles of forest* [Spruce's italics], uninterrupted save by the streams that traverse it…. You will hence be prepared to learn that nearly every natural order of plants has here *trees* among its representatives. Here are grasses (bamboos) of sixty or more feet in height, sometimes growing erect, sometimes tangled in thorny thickets through which an elephant could not penetrate. Vervains forming spreading trees with digitate leaves like the Horse-chestnut. Milkworts, stout woody twiners ascending to the tops of the highest trees, and ornamenting them with festoons of flowers not their own. Instead of your Periwinkles we have here handsome trees exuding … a most deadly poison. Violets of the size of apple trees. Daisies … borne on trees like Alders.'

Walking in a mighty Amazon forest, no botanist – however skilled – can identify every tree from the base of its trunk and roots. He has to get at blossoms, leaves and fruit. Trees are so tall and their trunks so straight and smooth that it is extremely difficult and dangerous to climb into the canopy. The easiest way to obtain the identifying trophies is to cut down the entire tree. Spruce was naturally loathe 'to destroy a magnificent tree, perhaps centuries old, merely for the sake of gathering flowers'. Local people brushed aside his scruples – to them, trees grew in such millions that a single one was no more important than a weed in an English field. And when Spruce did fell a great tree, he was rewarded by a mass of lianas, epiphytes, bryophytes, orchids and other flowers that lived on it.

Bates and Wallace had met on bug-hunting walks near Leicester, so insects were a primary aim for both of them. Bates wrote pages about leaf-cutter *saúba* ants. Every visitor to Amazonia is enthralled by columns of these ants, scurrying along lugging sail-like slices of leaf back to their underground ant-hill. The piece of greenery can weigh a hundred times as much as its porter. One column attacked Bates's store of manioc and was carrying off each grain. 'We tried to exterminate them by killing them with our wooden clogs. It was impossible, however, to prevent fresh hosts coming in as fast as we killed their companions. They returned the next night; and I was then obliged to lay trains of gunpowder along their line, and blow them up. This, repeated many times, at last seemed to intimidate them, for we were free from their visits during the remainder of my residence at the place.' It is now known that saúba ants do not eat the leaves they carry back. Instead, they chew them to produce a mulch on which they rear edible fungi – and it is these that break down the cellulose and poisons in the leaves. Ant larvae feed on the fungi.

Bates also described one of the most daunting sights in the forest: a column of *Eciton* army ants in action. The first sign of a column's approach 'is a twittering and restless movement of small flocks of plain-coloured birds (ant-thrushes)'. Indians shout the alarm '*tauóca!*' and race away from the head of the column. If someone is too slow, 'the tenacious insects who have secured themselves to his legs have to be plucked off one by one…. The main column moves forward in a given direction, clearing the ground of all animal matter dead or alive.... It is curious to see them attack wasps' nests ... to get at the larvae and the pupae.' (This author once watched hundreds of army ants sweep up a tree trunk to get at a wasps' nest the size of a medicine ball. However, the wasps had developed a symbiotic relationship with Azteca ants, and these marched down the tree to defend their friends. There was a sharp battle between the two species, at my eye level, with dead ants tumbling to the ground. Then, after a few moments of struggle, the army ants decided that it was not worth the bother. As if on the orders of some commander, they plunged down that trunk and moved on to attack the next.)

On the Tocantins, Bates and Wallace collected animals and birds, including monkeys and agoutis (the only rodent with jaws strong enough to crack Brazil-nut pods), and of course hundreds of new species of insect. When Wallace moved to Marajó Island, he was dazzled by 'the beauty of the vegetation, which surpassed anything I had seen before: at every bend of the stream some new object presented itself – now a huge "cedar" hanging over the water, or a great silk cotton-tree [kapok, *Ceiba pentandra*] standing like a giant above the rest of the forest. The graceful assaí palms occurred continually, in clumps of various sizes, sometimes raising their stems a hundred feet into the air, or bending in graceful curves till they almost met from the opposite banks. The majestic murutí palm [also called *buriti, Mauritia flexuosa*] was also abundant, its straight and cylindrical stems like Grecian columns, and with its immense fan-shaped leaves and gigantic bunches of fruit, produced an imposing spectacle.... These palms were often clothed with creepers, which ran up to the summits, and there put forth their blossoms. Lower down, on the water's edge, were numerous flowering shrubs, often completely covered with convolvuluses, passion-flowers, or bignonias. Every dead or half-rotten tree was clothed with parasites of singular forms, or bearing beautiful flowers, while smaller palms, curiously-shaped stems, and twisting climbers, formed a background in the interior of the forest.' (Richard Spruce later explained how Amazonian 'cedars' [*Cedrela odorata*] acquired their misleading name. Abundant and easily worked, these hardwoods were for local carpenters the equivalent of English deal. 'They are widely removed from the Conifers, to which the Cedars of the Old World belong; yet the colour of the wood, its grain, and particularly its scent, are so like those of true Cedars, that it is no wonder the Spanish and Portuguese settlers called them Cedros.')

Bates, Wallace and Spruce were poor young men who depended on the income from selling their natural-history collections. They were the first professional collectors in the world's richest ecosystem; and mid-nineteenth-century Britain had plenty of museums and rich enthusiasts eager to buy their specimens. It was a century since the Swedish scholar Carl Linné or Linnaeus started to classify nature in his famous *Systema Naturae*. Intellectuals were still eagerly applying his rules of taxonomy to species and genera of plants, animals and insects. Bates somewhat despised the armchair collectors who classified his finds. After his return from the Amazon, he wrote to Darwin disparaging his old friend Edwin Brown because he was 'amassing material at a very great expense' but could never fully understand the ecological context of plants and animals without having travelled and personally observed biodiversity. In another letter he called such naturalists 'species grubbers' on a par with collectors of stamps or crockery. This was unfair, since Bates and his friends depended entirely on selling their specimens and since he himself was making a fine personal collection. He loved classifying his finds and revelled in the thousands of species new to science that he had discovered.

To a modern traveller on the Amazon the financial affairs of the Victorian collectors are amazing, for until very recently it has been impossible to change money, or pay in anything other than cash or barter in towns up-country. The British naturalists lived very frugally but were almost never robbed. During Wallace's four years in the region, Bates's eleven, and Spruce's fourteen, they all survived from the proceeds of their collecting. Riverboat captains took their precious specimens downriver and carefully transferred them to transatlantic ships so that they reached Europe in perfect condition and in huge quantities. Payments, letters of credit and other remittances got to Belém, and cash somehow went up the Amazon to the solitary travellers. Spruce relied on James and Archibald Campbell, 'colonists of long standing' in Belém, to trans-ship his collections and supply him with the necessary funds. In Santarém, all three naturalists enjoyed the hospitality and help of one Captain Hislop, a trader whom Spruce described as 'a sturdy, rosy Scotsman ... an amusing companion and a valuable friend'.

Back in England, their agents really earned their commissions. Bates and Wallace used Samuel Stevens, the brother of an auctioneer of natural-history material and himself a keen entomologist. Stevens not only found buyers for everything that the young men sent, but he also promoted his clients with flair. He persuaded the *Zoologist* to publish extracts from Bates's letters, which he skilfully edited to whet buyers' appetites. He reminded readers that these collections had been gathered in fascinating circumstances and were of unrivalled importance. Introducing the first letters, Stevens wrote that he thought that readers would wish to know how Mr Bates was faring 'on his rambles of South America': despite many hardships, his health was good and the climate benign. Then a sales pitch: 'Among the many charming things now received are several specimens of the remarkable and lovely Hectera Esmeralda, and an extraordinary number of beautiful species of Erycinidae, many quite new.' Stevens wrote to Bates about customers' preferences in both rarity and aesthetics of plants. In return, when Bates sent some 'beautiful Sapphira, which you wished for more particularly', he added: 'Do not think it an abundant species because I now send you so many; it is because I devoted myself *one month* to them, working six days a week with a youth hired to assist me, both of us with net-poles 12 feet long.'

Spruce's botanical collections were accompanied by meticulous notes giving vernacular and scientific names and interesting properties of each plant. If he learned that one had medicinal use, Spruce made a concoction from the bark, leaves or fruit and tested this on himself. He then sent such material to chemists at Kew for further study. He once gave an inkling of his logistical problems, in a letter to George Bentham that accompanied ten thousand specimens. This described buying a six-ton boat and hiring a crew for a journey from Manaus up the Rio Negro. Then: 'I am hard at work packing up my collections for you and purchasing trade goods for the voyage. It is no use taking money up the Amazon.... I am laying out my whole fortune in prints and other fabrics of cotton, axes, cutlasses, fishhooks, beads.... The trafficking of these involves a serious loss of time, but there is no alternative.' His working conditions were gruesome. In his house up the Rio Negro, 'the thatch is stocked with rats, vampires, scorpions, cockroaches and other pests to society; the floor (being simply mother earth) is undermined by [leaf-cutter] ants, with whom I have had some terrible contests. In one night, they carried off as much farinha as I could eat in a month; then they found my dried plants and began to cut them up and carry them off.' Termites were also a nuisance. But the worst problem was that many of the local soldiery were convicted criminals: half of the fourteen stationed at São Gabriel were murderers, and they often entered Spruce's house and stole his spirits, molasses, vinegar and other things.

As well as going up the Rio Negro and Orinoco into Venezuela, Spruce also made a detour westwards up the Uaupés, a long river that flows from Colombia to join the middle Negro. Spruce got as far as the great waterfall of Iauaretê, where the Vaupés in Colombia tumbles into Brazil and becomes the Uaupés. He spent two weeks there, but was frustrated that heavy rains prevented forest trees from opening their blossoms. The weather cleared as he started to return. 'As we shot down ... the river, on a sunny morning I well recollect how the banks of the river had become clad with flowers, as it were by some sudden magic, and how I said to myself, as I scanned the lofty trees with wistful and disappointed eyes, "There goes a new *Dipteryx* – there goes a new *Qualea* – there goes a new the Lord knows what!" until I could no longer bear the sight and covering up my face with my hands, I resigned myself to the sorrowful reflection that I must leave all these fine things "to waste their sweetness on the jungle air".'

Spruce guessed, rightly, that the forests of southern Colombia that stretched endlessly westwards 'offer as rich a field for a botanist as any in South America'. He wrote to Bentham: 'I have lately been calculating the number of species that yet remain to be discovered in the great Amazonian forest.... By moving away a degree of latitude or longitude, I found about half the plants different.... [So] there should remain some 50,000 or 80,000 species undiscovered!'

The three English naturalists roamed the main rivers of the Amazon basin, sometimes together or meeting briefly, but generally on their own. After a few weeks collecting with Bates near Manaus in 1850, Wallace went right up the Rio Negro to the same portage to the Orinoco that Humboldt had used fifty years earlier. He then returned over a thousand kilometres to Manaus, to ship his collection; and then went up the Negro again to its Uaupés tributary that was rich in bird species. Henry Bates meanwhile had gone westwards up the main Solimões. He took a liking to the village of Ega (one of Father Fritz's Omagua missions; now called Tefé) on the south shore some 550 kilometres (340 miles) above Manaus. Its 1,200 people were of mixed blood and seemingly devoid of racial prejudice, and the surrounding rain forests and lagoon were a collector's paradise. Bates spent a year at Ega; then in late 1851 he sailed down the Amazon to spend three-and-a-half years at the town of Santarém and adjacent Tapajós river, before in 1857 returning to Ega where he remained (with two long excursions up the Solimões) until his return to England in 1859.

Malaria had become the scourge of the Amazon, and all three collectors suffered from it. They had frequent fevers and were occasionally prostrated by this wicked plasmodium. On Alfred Wallace's second Negro expedition, when he was on the lower Uaupés, his malaria grew steadily worse. 'The weakness and fever increased, till I was again confined to my rede [hammock] – could eat nothing, and was so torpid and helpless that Senhor L[ima], who attended me, did not expect me to live. I could not speak intelligibly, and had not strength to write, or even turn over in my hammock.' Wallace took quinine and the fevers lessened for a few weeks before returning at daily intervals. 'Their visits, thus frequent, were by no means agreeable; as, what with the succeeding fever and perspiration, which lasted from before noon till night, I had little quiet repose. In this state I remained till the beginning of February [1852], the ague continuing but with diminished force; and though with an increasing appetite and eating heartily, yet gaining so little strength that I could with difficulty stand alone, or walk across the room with the assistance of two sticks.' Wallace managed to get down to São Gabriel on the Negro, where he had arranged to meet Spruce. The latter was appalled by the sight of his emaciated and incapacitated friend.

Two years later, it was Spruce's turn. He had entered Venezuela by the Casiquiare channel and was at Maipures on the upper Orinoco when malaria struck. For six weeks he was 'nearly helpless with continued fever', unable to stir from his hammock and on the verge of death. His Indians sold some of his ox-beef to buy rum, and 'were all so completely stupefied that not one of them was able to help me'. A friend found him a nurse. She proved to be a malevolent harpy, a Venezuelan mestiza 'Carmen Reja by name – I shall not easily forget this woman'. When angry, 'her face put on a scowl which was almost demoniacal'. Through his hallucinations and vomiting Spruce could hear Reja and others discussing how to divide his belongings. 'Among other things she would call out: "Die, you English dog, that we may have a merry watch-night with your dollars".' But Spruce did not die. A Portuguese trader took him back to the Rio Negro, still in a stretcher and pitifully weak.

Back in his own boat, in November 1854, Spruce started downriver with four Indian paddlers. He had by now learned enough of the *lingua geral* – the Tupi-based 'general language' of Amazon caboclos – to overhear his own men in a riverside camp plotting to kill him. They reasoned that he was so weak that no-one would be surprised if he died. Diarrhoea (from cayman meat they had given him, as a delicacy) forced him to leave his hammock several times during the night. But when he returned he remained vigilant enough to hear the would-be killers approaching and whispering how they would do the deed. So Spruce got up again; but this time he went to the boat, took out his gun, and crouched behind a rampart of plant presses. He heard his men cursing him for not returning to the hammock, but when they saw him they knew the plot was up. Next day he dismissed the ringleader, and the others paddled him down the Negro as though nothing had happened.

Henry Bates's worst attack of malaria came at the end of 1858 when he was at São Paulo de Olivença on the Solimões. 'My ague seemed to be the culmination of a gradual deterioration of health, which had been going on for several years. I had exposed myself too much in the sun, working to the utmost of my strength six days a week, and had suffered much, besides, from bad and insufficient food.... I could not stir, and was delirious during the paroxysms of fever.' Bates took quinine. He was convinced that his liver and spleen would suffer permanent damage 'if the feeling of lassitude is too much indulged. So every morning I shouldered my gun or insect-net, and went my usual walk in the forest. The fit of shivering very often seized me before I got home, and I then used to stand still and brave it out.' Despite this characteristic but misguided fortitude, Bates then started to make his way homeward.

Bates had had many adventures, and he told them in one of the nineteenth century's most delightful travel books, *The Naturalist on the River Amazons*. When living at Ega, he often went with Pasé and Miranha Indians to net turtles – and 'I lived almost exclusively on them for several months afterwards. Roasted in the shell they form a most appetizing dish.' Once, when they hauled in their huge round net, there was a cayman among the turtles. 'No-one was afraid ... [and when] a lanky Miranha was thrown off his balance ... there was no end to the laughter and shouting.' A lad dragged the thrashing alligator ashore by the tail. Bates had armed himself with a strong pole and 'gave him a smart rap with it on the crown of his head, which killed him instantly. It was a good-sized individual: the jaws being considerably more than a foot long, and fully capable of snapping a man's leg in twain.' This was a Black Cayman, *Melanosuchus niger*. These can grow to be some of the world's largest crocodilians: eight metres (26 feet) in length and a metre wide. Normally docile, a mother Black Cayman becomes dangerous when protecting a nest of young: she will attack a passing canoe with the speed of a torpedo and her jaws can snap it in two. On another fishing trip, Bates amused himself by throwing scraps of meat to the caymans. 'They behaved pretty much as dogs do when fed; catching the bones I threw them in their huge jaws, and coming nearer and showing increased eagerness after every morsel.' He was then annoyed when 'every day these visitors became bolder; at length they reached a pitch of impudence that was quite intolerable'. One big cayman kept waddling into the hut at night, passing under the hammocks and trying to swallow a barking pet dog. So the men sallied forth in their canoes and spent a day killing saurians. (Black Caymans are now critically endangered. I saw some at the Mamirauá research station, not far from Bates's Ega. Although in the wild, these had learned to swim out when called and take bread thrown to them – just as Waterton's and Bates's had done.) Like Humboldt before him, Bates was also fascinated by the fish known as electric eels. He once got his friends to hold hands with him, then touched an electric eel with a knife, and caused much merriment as shocks passed along the line.

Bates loved birds. He deduced why toucans had evolved beaks as large as their bodies. This was to 'reach and devour immense quantities of fruit whilst remaining seated, and thus its heavy body and gluttonous appetite form no obstacles to the prosperity of the species'. We see from this passage that Bates had almost grasped the principle of evolution by natural selection that was to make his mentor Charles Darwin and friend Alfred Wallace so famous. For a time he kept a pet toucan, with 'a sly, magpie-like expression…. He ate of everything that we eat; beef, turtle, fish, farinha [manioc], fruit, and was a constant attendant at our table…. His appetite was most ravenous, and his powers of digestion quite wonderful.'

Bates once tried to collect a curl-crested toucan. 'I had shot one from a rather high tree in a dark glen in the forest, and … went into the thicket where the bird had fallen, to secure my booty. It was only wounded, and on my attempting to seize it, it set up a loud scream. In an instant, as if by magic, the shady nook seemed alive with these birds…. They descended towards me, hopping from bough to bough, some of them swinging on the loops and cables of woody lianas, and all croaking and fluttering their wings like so many furies.' The frontispiece to Bates's book shows him startled by the avenging toucans. He is wearing granny glasses, a moustache and curling sideburns, a broad-brimmed slouch hat, and checked shirt – a Woody Allen figure strayed into Alfred Hitchcock's 'The Birds'. Once he had killed the wounded toucan, its friends disappeared as suddenly as they had descended.

Spruce had some painful adventures. 'I have been stung by wasps I suppose hundreds of times – once very badly, having above twenty stings in my head and face alone. Yet I have always admired their beauty, ingenuity, and heroic ferocity.' These are the *acaba da noite* wasps that build tawny nests under low banana or other leaves. Trail-cutters give them a wide berth and fall silent as they tiptoe past – because if aroused scores of wasps will instantly attack an intruder. Spruce was also stung by terrible Amazonian hornets, *marimbondos*. Far worse was when he disturbed a colony of 'dreaded' *tocandira* ants (*Dinoponera grandis*). His feet were covered in stings from these 27-mm-long (over an inch) monsters. For hours 'my sufferings were indescribable – I can only liken the pain to that of a hundred thousand nettle-stings'. His feet and hands trembled as if from palsy, he was drenched in perspiration, and he wanted to vomit. Later, when on an Amazon headwater in the Andes, Spruce was stung on the wrist by a hairy caterpillar. To ease the pain, he foolishly applied a solution of ammonia to the wound. But after a cold rainy day collecting in the forest, his hand was swollen to double its normal size. 'That was the beginning of a time of the most intense suffering I ever endured. After three days of fever and sleepless nights, ulcers broke out all over the back of the hand and the wrist – they were thirty-five in all, and I shall carry the scars to my grave. For five weeks I was condemned to lie most of the time on a long settle, with my arm (in a sling) resting on the back.' At one time, Spruce feared that 'mortification seemed imminent' and considered showing his Indians 'how to cut off my hand, as the only means of saving my life'.

On another occasion, on the Trombetas river below Manaus, Spruce suffered three of the other hazards of life in the rain forest: dense undergrowth, getting caught by nightfall, and – most fearful of all – getting lost. He and his companions ran into 'flats of entangled bamboos and cutgrass, which were passable only on our hands and knees. The day was excessively sultry.... [Then came] torrents of rain and the incessant roll of thunder.' Then night fell, abruptly at six o'clock as it does every day on the Equator. Thoroughly drenched, 'we scrambled on – now plunging into prickly palms, then getting entangled in sipós [lianas], some of which were also prickly.... At one time we got on the track of large ants, which crowded up our legs and feet and stung us terribly.' They finally managed to regain their camp, but 'the effects of this disastrous journey hung on us for a full week. Besides the rheumatic pains and stiffness brought on by the wetting, our hands, feet, and legs were torn and thickly stuck with prickles, some of which produced ulcers.... Let the reader try to picture to himself [what it is to be lost or benighted in] the vast extent of the forest-clad Amazon valley; how few and far between are the habitations of man therein; and how the vegetation is so dense that ... it is rarely possible to see more than a few paces ahead.' He then told about people getting lost, even when not far from salvation. (Getting lost is one of the few fatal dangers in this environment. I have also experienced the panic of finding myself alone and disoriented in unexplored forests, far further from help than Spruce was at that time, knowing that if I continued in the wrong direction I would never survive.)

Movement in Amazonia depended entirely on indigenous paddlers. Boats had simple sails, but travellers still had to find native boatmen to propel them against currents and adverse winds or guide and haul them through rapids. All contemporary narratives are full of the tribulations of getting such helpers. Every one of the naturalists complained about the poor quality of his men, while simultaneously praising their stamina and skill. Spruce told how Brazilian traders got Indians blind drunk on cachaça rum and tossed them like logs into boats, where they awoke to labour as paddlers for months on end.

Bates learned a great deal about flora, fauna and ecology from local people, but he deplored their lack of intellectual curiosity and their rustic ways. He often described his helpers as lazy, useless or impudent. Wallace, as a utopian socialist, disapproved of slavery, but he observed that slaves on various plantations were well treated and seemed content. Spruce would hire only genuine 'bare-backed' Indians, since he was convinced that those who wore shirts had been corrupted by social aspirations: 'The least streak of white blood in an Indian's veins increases tenfold his insolence and insubordination.' (Yet pure Indians plotted to kill him on the upper Rio Negro.) Spruce admitted that with a few exceptions he disliked Brazilian caboclos, particularly 'free people of colour' – but not 'merry blacks'.

Spruce was normally an amiable man, quite ready to shed his English inhibitions when necessary. In June 1851 he was at Manaquiri on the Solimões not far from Manaus. The local people held a great celebration of the feast of St John. This was presided over by an elected 'Judge' and 'Lady-Judge (Juiza) chosen by the amount of her personal attractions'. After many preliminary revels, Spruce was invited to open the ball with the glamorous Juiza. He realized that 'I should be accounted very proud if I refused. I therefore led the lady out, first casting off my coat and shoes [to be like] the other performers. We got through the dance triumphantly, and at its close there was a general *viva* and clapping of hands for "the good white man who did not despise other people's customs!" Once "in for it" I danced all night.'

Bates often felt lonely without 'congenial company'. Soon after reaching Brazil he wrote to his agent: 'I should have liked a sympathizing companion better than being alone, but that in this barbarous country is not to be had. I have got a half-wild coloured youth, who is an expert entomologist.... If he does not give me the slip he will be a valuable help to me.' Bates was modest and uncomplaining. But years later, when in his sixties, he mesmerized a gathering of intellectuals in north London by reminiscing about the hardships of that decade on the Amazon. One of his audience described the scene: 'Bates told us with hushed breath how on that expedition he had at times almost starved to death; how he had worked with slaves like a slave for his daily rations of coarse food; how he had faced perils more appalling than death; and how he had risked and sometimes lost, everything he possessed on earth.' He spoke with 'child-like simplicity ... that brought tears to the eyes of grown men who heard him'.

One of Bates's claims to fame was 'Batesian mimicry'. He marvelled at camouflages that hide and protect so many rainforest insects. Some look uncannily like the bark or twigs of their favourite trees and 'many species of insects have a most deceptive resemblance to living or dead leaves; it is generally admitted, that this serves to protect them from the onslaughts of insect-feeding animals who would devour the insect, but refuse the leaf'. Other disguises have more sinister purposes, such as parasitic bees that imitate working bees among which they deposit their eggs, or jumping spiders that look just like flower buds as they wait for prey. What intrigued Bates was why different species of butterfly or gaudy caterpillar would resemble one another. He concluded that an insect flaunted bright colours because it was poisonous or unpalatable. 'So its imitator, not enjoying this advantage, would escape by being deceptively assimilated to it in external appearances.' For some tasty insects, the only survival strategy was to look like toxic ones. This was the observation named after him. 'Batesian mimicry' describes the situation in which a palatable mimic resembles an inedible one.

In the preface to his famous book Bates gave a breakdown of the 14,712 zoological *species* (not specimens, which would have been many times more) that he collected. The vast majority of these species – 14,000 – were insects, since these are super-abundant in tropical forests. He explained: 'The part of the Amazons region [near Ega] where I resided longest being unexplored country to the Naturalist, no less than 8000 of the species here enumerated were *new to science* [Bates's italics], and these are now occupying the busy pens of a number of learned men in different parts of Europe to describe them.'

Bates loved observing butterflies, moths and ants, but he is best known for his work on beetles. When he first visited Ega in 1851 he wrote to his agent Stevens that 'I worked very hard for Coleoptera.... Whenever I heard of beetles seen at a distance, I would get a boat and go many miles after them.' He employed a local man and his family to help him hunt. 'Every day he brought me from ten to twenty Coleoptera, and thus I got some of my best things.' Bates collected a staggering number of new species of beetle from this part of the Solimões. But he was keen to show that he was more than a mere collector – albeit one of the world's greatest – or a taxonomist concerned only with systematic classification of species. 'The discovery of new species forms but a small item in ... the study of the living creation. The structure, habits, instincts, and geographical distribution of some of the oldest-known forms supply inexhaustible materials for reflection.' Although the terms had not yet been coined, Bates saw himself as an animal-behaviourist and an ecologist.

Each of the three British naturalists in the Amazon in the middle nineteenth century went on to achieve fame, almost immortality. When Bates returned to England in 1860, both Joseph Hooker and Charles Darwin gave him fatherly advice on how to break into the elitist world of London's scientific establishment. In 1861 the Royal Geographical Society, which had been founded in 1830, decided that the time had come for it to be run by a full-time paid Assistant Secretary. Few applied for the post and, despite having no managerial experience but with Darwin as one of his supporters, Bates got it. Bates ran the Society for over thirty years until his death in 1892. In his quiet way he helped many travellers and explorers, through the Society's journals which he edited and the famous *Hints to Travellers*, and by personal encouragement. He was a modernizer who promoted the teaching of geography in British schools. Although he had left school at thirteen, Bates was elected a Fellow of science's most exclusive club, The Royal

Society. He was much loved, known as 'dear old Bates' or 'Bates of the Amazon', but some obituaries complained that administrative routine had stifled his creative research. (This author was the fifth paid head of the Royal Geographical Society. During the twenty-one years that I ran it, I had the inspiration of sitting beneath a portrait of my admirable predecessor, Henry Walter Bates. One of the Society's most coveted possessions is the tiny mauve pin-cushion that Bates fastened to his belt when he was chasing beetles and butterflies through the rain forest.)

Alfred Russel Wallace sailed for home in 1852 on the English brig *Helen*. He took a vast natural-history collection that represented virtually his entire wealth and capital. But three weeks into the voyage, when the ship was east of Bermuda, a fire broke out in the cargo of balsam and rubber. Wallace vividly described the efforts to douse the flames, the suffocating smoke, his own failure to rescue more than a couple of notebooks and a few of his many sketches, the chaos in launching leaky lifeboats, and the sight of the 'most magnificent conflagration' as the fire engulfed the sails and the combustible cargo. After ten days in the boats, when they were despairing of reaching Bermuda, the survivors were rescued by a passing ship. Back in England, Wallace wrote a moving letter to the President of the Royal Geographical Society, explaining the tragedy of his lost collection and asking for help to pursue his research in Southeast Asia. The RGS got him passage on a naval ship.

In the forests of the Malay archipelago, Wallace pondered the problems of evolution. In 1855 he published the idea that every species had come into exis-tence 'coincident both in time and space with a pre-existing closely-allied species'. Three years later, when recovering from malaria in the Moluccas, he had the inspi-ration that natural selection – survival of the fittest – was the method of this evolution. He rapidly wrote his idea in a paper that he sent for approval to Darwin, whom he knew to be working towards the same principle. Darwin was fourteen years older than the relatively unknown Wallace, but he had not yet published his own research. However, both men behaved with exemplary rectitude. Their work was presented jointly at a famous meeting of the Linnean Society in July 1858. Wallace never claimed primacy with the theory, and when Darwin published the *Origin of Species* Wallace read it six times, 'each time with increasing admiration'.

Wallace is also famous for observing the 'Wallace Line' – the total difference between fauna on either side of the Makassar Strait east of Borneo, a product of continental drift. He lived into his nineties and published extensively, ranging from excellent works on natural history, to unorthodox views on phrenology (the study of skull bumps), spiritualism, and against vaccination. He campaigned for the radical nationalization of land in Britain. Wallace, the humble surveyor from

Leicester, also became a Fellow of The Royal Society, which awarded him its first Darwin Medal, and in 1910 the King added him to the prestigious Order of Merit.

After Richard Spruce's three years' botanizing on tributaries of the upper Rio Negro and Orinoco, he rested and recovered in Manaus. In 1855 he took a steamer to Iquitos in Peru. The banks of the Amazon have changed little since then, and it is a pleasure to read the great botanist's joy at a view that the uninitiated might find monotonous. To his friend John Teasdale he wrote: 'I never tired of admiring the ever-varying forest panorama – the broad beaches densely clad with Arrow-reeds growing 20 or 30 feet high, behind which extended beds of slender and graceful willows (*Salix Humboldtiana*), their yellow-green foliage relieved by the occasional admixture of the broad white leaves of *Cecropia peltata* (a tree of the Mulberry tribe), while beyond rose abruptly the lofty virgin forest, composed of trees of the most different types growing side by side. Add to this the noble river, the innumerable islands (fixed and floating), the cranes and herons, the never-failing alligators, the fresh-water dolphins chasing one another and turning somersaults, besides numerous other sights and sounds....'

Spruce then continued by canoe up the Huallaga and was the first botanist to work extensively on the eastern slopes of the Andes. Because this region catches rain from clouds that sweep across the Amazon lowlands, and because it has the advantage of 'altitudinal zonation' – different ecosystems, as the land climbs from hylean rain forest into cloud and mist forests – it is one of the most species-rich places on earth. Spruce chose to settle on the Andean foothills above the rain forests. He spent almost two years at Tarapoto, an isolated village near the upper Huallaga (not far from where the ill-fated Ursúa and Aguirre had built their boats three centuries previously). He loved Tarapoto, where 'I am more agreeable [sic] placed than anywhere in my South American wanderings'. The townspeople, from the padre down, became his friends: they liked the tall and friendly man with a neat black beard who spoke good Spanish. The climate was lovely and the botanizing was spectacular. He found plants that reminded him of the Yorkshire dales – poppies, brambles, horsetails, and species of buttercups and hydrocotyle pond plants that looked familiar. Wallace later found that Spruce's notes recorded '1094 species of flowering plants and ferns, to which must be added several hundred species of mosses and Hepaticae [liverworts] – his favourite groups'. Spruce himself wrote that around Tarapoto he 'found 250 species of ferns and their allies, of which many were new, especially among tree-ferns'.

In 1857 Peru was disturbed by a revolution, and Spruce decided to leave Tarapoto and continue his collecting in Ecuador. He went with two local merchants in two open canoes paddled by fourteen Indians. The journey down the Huallaga, up a stretch of the main Amazon, and then up the empty, forested Pastaza and Bobonaza rivers proved to be a fifteen-week nightmare. He wrote to Bentham: 'Such a journey! I can hardly bear to think ... of what I saw and suffered.' One of the first perils was a fearful whirlpool, or *pongo*, on the Huallaga. Spruce had a beloved big dog, Sultan, that he had reared from a puppy. But, 'when my canoe was caught in the whirlpool, the horrid roar of the waters, which drowned our voices, and the waves, which splashed over us, so frightened the dog that he went mad!' Sultan refused to drink or eat, and went berserk whenever they landed, so Spruce had to shoot him. They were also plagued by mosquitoes. For fifteen days they saw no human being. They encountered villages completely deserted from fear of the warlike Huambiza – a subtribe of Jívaro (now called Shuar), whose speciality was to shrink enemies' heads. Then, the upper Pastaza was 'wearisome and monotonous, with almost continuous rains, rarely any dry land to sleep on, and not a single village or settlement of any kind.'

On the Bobonaza headwater the travellers survived one of the Amazon's great dangers: a flash flood. They were by now propelled by tribal Andoa Indians (Zaporoan-speaking, related to the Mainas), who saved their lives – just as their forebears had rescued Isabel Godin in the previous century. They had foolishly ignored distant thunder and settled for the night on a sandy beach. 'Then the storm burst over us, and the river almost simultaneously began to rise; speedily the beach was overflowed, the Indians leaped into the canoes; the waters continued to rise with great rapidity, coming in on us every few minutes in a roaring surge which broke under the canoes in whirlpools, and dashed them against each other.' The lianas holding the canoes finally broke. But the Indians clung onto branches through the stormy night, 'using all their efforts to prevent the canoes from being smashed by blows from each other or from the floating trees which now began to career past us like mad bulls. So dense was the gloom that we could see nothing, while we were deafened by the pelting rain, the roaring flood, and the crashing of the branches of the floating trees as they rolled over or dashed against each other; but each lightning-flash revealed to us all the horrors of our position. Assuredly I had slight hopes of living to see the day, and I shall for ever feel grateful to those Indians who ... stood through all the rain and storm of that fearful night, relaxing not a moment in their efforts to save our canoes.' The raging river did not start to subside until the middle of the following day. By then, 'we were wearied to death, and myself in a high fever.'

Once in Ecuador, Spruce survived many perils, not least clambering around slippery cliffs on bamboo bridges too fragile to take the weight of his collecting boxes. Once, to descend into the gorge of a rushing river, he had to climb 150 feet (46 metres) down notched poles hanging from a projecting rock. His reward was to be the first (and possibly the last) botanist in a very remote part of the Andean *montaña*, the mossiest place he had ever seen. His subsequent collections and discoveries were so rich that his friend Wallace, in his posthumous collation of Spruce's journals and letters, could not begin to quantify or describe them. Wallace simply listed *sixty* botanical *excursions* from the Ecuadorian towns Baños and Ambato in the two years 1857 to 1859.

At the end of 1859, Spruce was surprised to receive an official assignment. 'I was entrusted by Her Majesty's Secretary of State for India with a commission to procure seeds and plants of the Red Bark tree'. This was Cinchona, the famous 'fever bark' that contained the quinine palliative for malaria.

In 1852 a twenty-two-year-old former naval midshipman called Clements Markham had gone to see the Inca capital Cuzco and the headwaters of the Amazon in the Peruvian Andes. One of Markham's objectives in Peru was the Cinchona tree, *quina* to the Indians. As we have seen, indigenous people had long ago told Jesuits about the febrifugal properties of its bark (see p. 76). It was not until 1820 that French chemists extracted the alkaloid and called it quinine – this led to the first use of a pure chemical compound to treat a specific disease. Markham's quest was rewarded when he started the spectacular descent from the Andes towards the Amazon forests. 'Gradually the slopes covered with long grass were exchanged for a subtropical vegetation. There were many beautiful flowering plants. I here saw a cascarilla tree and afterwards another. The species was *Cinchona ovata*, not a valuable kind, but it made me acquainted with the genus.' Back in England, young Markham lobbied to get living Cinchona trees transplanted from South America to India, where malaria was becoming a scourge of the Indian army. He finally got official backing and organized three attempts to procure trees and seeds. Markham himself led the group that went to Peru. He descended as far as the lush forests of the Tambopata tributary of the Madre de Dios river east of Cuzco; but he was thwarted by Peruvians determined not to lose their valuable fever-bark trees and by perilous mishaps.

The only successful Cinchona-collecting venture proved to be by Richard Spruce – invited at the insistence of his admirer Sir William Hooker of Kew Gardens. Spruce was never robust, and by now he was exhausted and suffering from various severe ailments. Early in 1860 he had a physical breakdown, but he soldiered on despite 'unspeakable physical pain'. With characteristic thoroughness, Spruce charmed the authorities into allowing him to collect the valuable plants, learned all that the local bark collectors knew, and went on to discover more than anyone about the species, its habitat, and the right time to collect. He spent a year, alone, assembling some 2,500 Cinchona fruits with 100,000 seeds. He did this in Ecuador on the Pacific side of the Andes, built a special raft to get his material down a river, and shipped the precious cargo from the port of Guayaquil in October 1860. Then he returned to the sierra to gather 637 seedlings he had planted: he packed and shipped these a few months later. Spruce was shattered by losing all his modest savings, £700, in the failure of the Ecuadorian bank in which they were deposited, but he continued his bountiful botanical work in South America until 1864. The Cinchona seeds and trees he collected were successfully sent to India, where their quinine saved many lives. They also gave rise to 'gin and tonic'. Soldiers of the Indian army disliked the bitter quinine 'tonic' they were ordered to take, so their gin ration was added to make it more palatable – which it triumphantly did.

Spruce was intensely interested in hallucinogens, and described plants that the Indians used in their shamanistic rituals and to induce trances. He sampled ipadú coca (*Erythroxylon coca*) but found that it had little effect on him. 'Probably I took too small a dose.' The myrtle-like coca bush was sacred to the Incas and is beloved by Andean Indians to this day. They chew its leaves mixed with lime which, interacting with saliva, extracts some of the cocaine and frees the user from pangs of hunger. It also contains beneficial calories, vitamins, protein, calcium and iron. Lowland Indians never learned to mix their ipadú strain with lime, which is harder to find in the forest. The tragedy is that harmless coca contains the drug cocaine. This powerful alkaloid was isolated in 1860 and was soon in use as an excellent local anaesthetic, particularly by dentists. For a while coca was regarded as a wonder drug: it appeared in patent medicines and energizing drinks, of which the only survivor is Coca Cola (from which coca has long since been removed). Purifying the alkaloid to make cocaine is an elaborate process, now the province of organized criminals. This has given coca such a bad name.

Spruce noted 'an intoxicating drink known to all the natives of the Uaupés by the name of caapi'. He himself sampled caapi at an Indian feast, but the result was confused because his solicitous Tukano hosts also pressed on him, in quick succession, *caxiri* manioc beer, a huge cigar of forest leaves, and a cup of 'wine' from pupunha (peach palm) – all of which made him sick. However, he learned that caapi's source was a Banisteria (*Malpighiaceae*) twining liana with no botanical name, chemically analyzed its bark to prove the hallucinogenic property, and called it *Banisteriopsis caapi*. This was one of the first instances anywhere of a

The Spanish Jesuit mission of San Joaquín de Omaguas on the upper Amazon (Marañón) was the site of the rubber-boom city of Iquitos a century later. This watercolour is by Don Francisco Requena y Herrera, the chief Spanish Boundary Commissioner, sent to demarcate new frontiers between the Spanish and Portuguese empires after the treaties of Madrid (1750) and San Ildefonso (1777) gave Brazil roughly half the continent and the lion's share of the Amazon basin. Mainas Indians in canoes and frock-coated, tricorne-hatted boundary commissioners are shooting at turtles or a manatee in the river. The commissioners' sailing vessel is visible behind the sandbank.

Opposite above The Bavarians Johann Baptist von Spix and Carl Friedrich Philip von Martius were the first non-Portuguese scientists allowed to visit the Amazon, in 1819–20. Here Spix, together with a local priest in a broad hat, visits a village of Mundurukú, whose shamans wear tassels and bonnets of brilliantly coloured featherwork.

Opposite below Spix enters a hut of Mura, a people thought to be 'primitive' but brilliant boatmen and fighters who dominated the middle Amazon until they unexpectedly sought peace in 1785.

Right Alfred Russel Wallace, aged twenty-five in 1848, just before going with his friend Henry Walter Bates to collect natural history specimens in the Amazon. Wallace later worked in Southeast Asia, where he was a discoverer of the theory of evolution by natural selection.

Left The Yorkshire botanist Richard Spruce joined Wallace and Bates on the Amazon in 1849. During fifteen years in South America, Spruce became one of the greatest botanists of his century. This photograph shows him on his return.

Below Spruce's drawing of the village of Tarapoto near the Huallaga river in Peru, where in 1855–57 he had some of his happiest and most fruitful botanizing.

Above Although self-taught, Henry Walter Bates became one of the greatest naturalists of the Amazon, where in eleven years he collected thousands of species new to science. Here Bates is gathering a curl-crested toucan, but when the wounded bird shrieked, the naturalist was mobbed by a flock of its angry fellows.

Below At the end of the rainy season, in March and April, the Amazon river rises and inundates vast areas of its *várzea* floodplain. Boats can then glide amid the previously unattainable forest canopy.

Right The German anthropologist Karl von den Steinen in 1884 made first contact with the tribes of the upper Xingu river, and was then the first non-Indian to descend that great southern tributary. Here he is starting to descend the mighty cataract that had prevented access to the upper river (he named it after his compatriot Carl von Martius). Steinen's canoe capsized seconds after this scene, but the travellers survived the shipwreck and rescued their pet monkey and macaw.

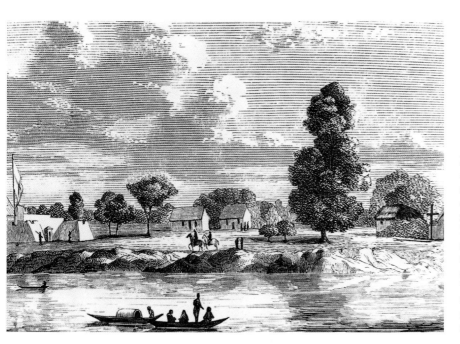

Left Fort São Joaquim (at the left), on the upper Rio Branco, defended the northernmost part of Portuguese Brazil against Indians and against its Spanish and Dutch neighbours. The British naturalist Charles Waterton recovered from malaria in this fort.

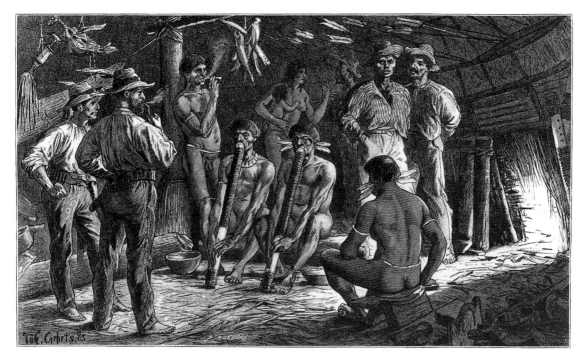

Above Karl von den Steinen was a perceptive and sympathetic anthropologist. Here he and his colleagues here watch upper-Xingu Bakairi Indians play sacred flutes inside a great *maloca* hut. The cluster of 'Xinguano' peoples survive into the twenty-first century with their cultures largely intact, thanks to the protective efforts of the Villas Boas brothers.

Right A Yanomami (on the right) recoils from hallucinogenic *epená* snuff blown up his nostrils by a shaman (on the left).

botanical explorer being a laboratory chemist. Spruce saw caapi again being inhaled and chewed by nomadic Guahibo at the Maipures rapids on the Orinoco. Five years later in the Ecuadorian *montaña*, he found Zaparo (Auca) Indians using the same hallucinogen, but they called it *ayahuasca* (meaning 'dead man's vine' in the Inca language Quechua). Further north in Colombia, Witoto and Bora of the Caquetá and Putumayo know it as *yagé*.

Spruce reported that 'all who have partaken of [caapi] feel first vertigo; then as if they rose up into the air and were floating about. The Indians say they see beautiful lakes, woods laden with fruit, birds of brilliant plumage, etc. Soon the scene changes; they see savage beasts preparing to seize them, they can no longer hold themselves up, but fall to the ground.' When an Indian awakes from this trance, he can violently attack the first person he sees; and he then collapses into a deep sleep. Amazingly, Indians have discovered two other plants – a madder and a liane similar to caapi – whose leaves contain a different hallucinogenic chemical, a tryptamine that powerfully enhances the effect of the drug. The user falls into a deep sleep and has dreams of extraordinary intensity: these not only seem precise, but they give an impression of clear understanding, and they are vividly recalled on waking. So shamans use caapi/ayahuasca/yagé for decisions about inter-tribal warfare, diplomacy, the authors of evil magic, cures for illness, or the love of their wives. Tukano Indians of Colombia have elaborate rituals surrounding the gathering, chewing and fermentation of caapi, its mixing in special sacred pots, and its drinking by a circle of men to the sound of rattles and pan-pipes in the red glow of pitch torches.

The Harvard Professor of Botany Richard Evans Schultes followed in Spruce's footsteps a century later and made further dramatic discoveries of these amazing hallucinogenic plants. When he sampled yagé mixed with another plant, 'the effect was electric; reds and golds dazzling in diamonds that turned like dancers on the tips of distant highways ... explosions of passion and dreams that collapsed one into another until finally, in the empty morning, only the birds remained, scarlet and crimson against the rising sun'. Although Professor Schultes was intensely conservative in manner, a journalist in *Life* magazine credited him with finding 'magic mushrooms' (peyote and others in Mexico) and thus inspiring the hippy drug movement of the 1960s. One of his students and lecturers at Harvard was Timothy Leary. Schultes was also the first serious academic to respect tribal shamans and learn much from them. So he is honoured as the founder of the discipline of ethnobotany – the study of indigenous people's uses of plants.

Spruce also studied the hallucinogenic snuff *yopo* or *niopo* inhaled by Indians on the upper Orinoco (as Humboldt had done in 1799). An aged Guahibo mixed his hallucinogens and said to Spruce in broken Spanish: 'With a chew of caapi and a pinch of niopo one feels so good! No hunger – no thirst – no tired!' The botanist found that yopo/niopo came from beans of the leguminous tree *Anadenanthera peregrina*, which is related to mimosas and acacias. Confusingly similar in name is *yoco*, a liana whose bark has a massive caffeine content. Tribes of western Amazonia eat no breakfast, but drink several gourds of yoco at dawn: this gives them tremendous stamina and no pangs of hunger until midday.

Another hallucinogenic snuff eluded Spruce because it is used by Yanomami peoples (of the Orinoco and northern Amazon), who were still uncontacted in his day. The Yanomami call this explosive snuff *paricá* and *epená* in their different dialects; further west in Colombia it is *yakee* to the Puinave and *viho* to the Tukano. It derives from reddish resin in the bark of *Virola theiodora* trees. Shamans blow it hard up celebrants' nostrils. (This author received blasts of it, in a Yanomami *yano* hut. Its effect was to convince me that I was thinking with great clarity and could solve any problem. It also affected my vision: people, and the poles supporting the mighty thatch, stood out from the gloomy background with startling sharpness.) The Yanomami use this snuff extensively in their rituals and divination. But – alone of Amazonian peoples – they also take it recreationally: gourds of the brown powder hang in huts and anyone who feels like a trip may inhale it. You see a solitary Indian dancing around, babbling or shouting, and then passing out from *epená*. The same resin from Virola bark is also used as poison on arrows and blow-gun darts – but as a curare it is taken straight from the trees, without the leaching (to remove poisons) and roasting for snuff.

Professor Schultes praised Richard Spruce again and again in his writings. He called him 'undoubtedly one of the greatest explorers of all times.... A man of extremely delicate health and plagued by chronic ills, he betook himself to one of the wildest and least known jungle areas of the world, to spend fourteen years of his life in hard physical work, constant exposure to the tropical elements and diseases, insufficient diet, and complete lack of even rudimentary comforts. A scholar with a thorough training and of outstanding cultural and scientific attainments, he divorced himself from all centres of culture and lived ... amongst Indians or unlettered half-breeds. A superb correspondent.... A botanist whose training and first love concerned mosses and hepatics – the most diminutive of land plants – he carried out painstaking research on ... gigantic tropical trees and lianas, even discovering hundreds ... hitherto unknown to science.... A mild-mannered and dignified person.... A student ... trained to handle masses of minute detail, he was able to cope with ... the organization and execution of cumbersome trips by canoe or on horseback of months' and even years' duration.'

Schultes also liked the way Spruce abhorred the notion that only things of immediate benefit to mankind were worthy of study. Spruce had said: 'I like to look upon plants as sentient beings, which live and enjoy their lives.... When they are beaten to pulp or powder in the apothecary's mortar, they lose most of their interest for me.' He admitted that his beloved liverworts yielded no food, hallucinogen, emetic or other medicine. 'But [even] if man cannot torture them to his uses or abuses, they are infinitely useful where God has placed them ... and beautiful in themselves – surely the primary motive for every individual existence?' Yet, despite this love of plants for their own sake, Spruce did in fact provide the first extensive descriptions of the rubber tree, massive information about quinine, and (in Schultes's words) 'studies on all manner of native economic plants, including gums and resins, fibres, foods, drugs, narcotics and stimulants, oils, dyes, and timbers'. Wade Davis, one of Schultes's most brilliant pupils, wrote that his mentor's 'love of Spruce, a raw atavistic association bordering at times on obsession, became his strength, allowing him to endure, encouraging him always to achieve more, and providing his closest experience of spiritual certainty. Asked in recent years whether it might be possible that he had, subconsciously or unconsciously, modeled his life and career on that of Spruce, Schultes replied, "Neither. It was conscious."'

After fourteen years in South America, Richard Spruce in 1864 returned to his native Yorkshire. He lived there for almost thirty years, very modestly in a cottage on the Castle Howard estate close to Gansthorpe parish where his father had taught and he had been born. Spruce published two monumental studies: 118 pages on palm trees, in the *Journal of the Linnean Society*, and a staggering 600-page book on 700 species in 43 genera of *Hepaticae* (liverworts) published in 1885 by the Botanical Society of Edinburgh; and he had many plants named after him. He died of influenza, aged seventy-six in 1893.

Spruce was highly respected, but he received no honours beyond a doctorate from Dresden and honorary fellowship of the Royal Geographical Society. In the last years of his life, his main income was a government pension of £50 a year that Markham obtained for him, and a later one of the same amount from India – a meagre reward for his services in bringing quinine to Asia. Fame came posthumously. In an obituary, his friend Wallace described him as 'tall and dark, with fine features of a somewhat southern type, courteous and dignified in manner, but with a fund of quiet humour which rendered him a most delightful companion'. He told plenty of jokes and anecdotes. Above all, Spruce was efficient, 'in the unvarying neatness of his dress, his beautifully regular handwriting, and the orderly arrangement of all his surroundings ... his writing-materials, his books, his microscope, his dried plants, his stores of food and clothing…. He was an enthusiastic lover of nature in all its varied manifestations, from the grandeur of the virgin forest or the glories of the sunset on the snowy peaks of the Andes, to the minutest details of the humblest moss or hepatic. In all his words and ways he was a true gentleman, and to possess his personal friendship was a privilege and pleasure.' Spruce was the quintessential 'botanist's botanist'.

In 1865, just after Spruce left South America, a grandiose scientific expedition reached the Brazilian Amazon. This was the Nathaniel Thayer Expedition, named after its rich American sponsor, but it was the indulgence of an ambitious society-scientist called Louis Agassiz. As a young man, the Swiss-born Agassiz had gone to Paris to help Carl von Martius classify Amazonian fishes collected by his colleague Johann Baptist von Spix (who had died in 1826). Agassiz taught as Professor of Natural History for thirteen years in Switzerland, and in 1846 when aged thirty-nine moved to Boston. The handsome Agassiz, who sported dark Byronic locks and spoke good English with a delightful French accent, made an immediate impact on Massachusetts society. He became Professor of Geology and Zoology at Harvard; founded a Museum of Comparative Zoology there; and his lectures on popular science were packed. He charmed the ladies of Boston and, when his spurned first wife conveniently died, married the heiress Elizabeth Cary from one of the top families. By the 1860s, the charismatic, energetic and supremely confi-dent Agassiz had made himself America's leading philosophical naturalist. So when his expedition sailed to the Amazon, backers were falling over themselves to finance him, provide free passage, and give letters of introduction to the Brazil-ian élite. The scientifically minded Emperor Dom Pedro II went onto his steamer to welcome Professor and Mrs Agassiz; and he enjoyed imperial support through-out his travels – in marked contrast to the solitary wanderings of the poor English collectors, who had struggled constantly to find boat crews and dispatch their specimens.

Agassiz collected quantities of Amazonian fishes. One of his team was William James (younger brother of the writer Henry James, and later a philoso-pher), who drew a humorous sketch of the Professor grinning over '4,000,000,000 species of new fish'. (Most of these trophies were discovered decades later in the Museum at Harvard, still in their original packing and pickling-alcohol.) The sar-donic young James noted that the Swiss professor's 'charlatanerie is almost as great as his solid worth'.

Apart from ichthyology, Agassiz's research was doomed by three glaring misconceptions. He went to the Amazon to try to refute Darwin, to establish that the Amazon valley was gouged by glaciation, and to prove racist views of the superiority of the white race. Louis Agassiz was a creationist who believed in 'God in Nature' and that each animal and plant species was fixed geographically. He hoped that his Amazon fishes and a collection of fossils would show that each species had been located by divine intervention in a separate stretch of river. He boldly proclaimed that biology was governed by topics, which could be classified. He then argued that the great Ice Age had been such a cataclysmic destroyer that it demolished Darwin's theory that evolution by natural selection occurred over many millennia. So he sought to find traces of glacial striation in the rocks of Amazonia – in vain since, although the ice ages affected the tropics, there were never lowland glaciers there. He also argued that the Biblical flood had covered this basin.

Professor Agassiz subscribed to theories of racial superiority that were all too common at that time. His expedition sailed in the final year of the Civil War and, although his team came from New England, Agassiz's attitudes seemed to be those of the Confederate states. He thought that human beings were divided into 'primordial' races, each created for a separate geographical location. Africans, of course, were intended to live in the tropics; Amazon Indians were autochthonous (originating there, and not migrating in from central Asia); and people of mixed race were degenerate. Louis and Elizabeth Agassiz jointly published a popular book about their journey. They wrote how shocked they were by the number of black and mulatto people in Rio de Janeiro. 'Let anyone who doubts the evil of this mixture of races … come to Brazil. He cannot deny the deterioration consequent upon an amalgamation of races … which is rapidly effacing the best qualities of the white man, the negro, and the Indian.' Once they had reached Manaus, Agassiz set up a backyard studio to photograph naked local people. The resulting pictures showed dignified people, mostly women, first in smart clothing and then naked, from the front, back and sides. All the models were black or mixed-race, none was white or a genuine forest Indian. Agassiz planned to include these pictures in albums of racial types that he was assembling at Harvard. To illustrate European perfection this collection included photographs of gleaming white marble busts of the Venus de Milo and the Apollo Belvedere. But the Manaus nudes were never published, perhaps because they failed to prove his theories of racial superiority or the virtue of eugenics.

Some of the best research to emerge from the often-ludicrous Agassiz expedition was by the Canadian geologist Charles Frederic Hartt. At first beguiled by his leader's glaciation theory, Hartt came to doubt it. He later returned to Brazil to make a geological study of its Atlantic seaboard; then in 1870 he organized the second American scientific expedition to that country. This was the Morgan Expedition, named in honour of its financier backer. It contained other fine geologists, including Orville Derby and Herbert Smith, and it worked throughout that decade. Some of its research was on fossils, but those collected in Amazonia proved to be *marine* and not the freshwater fossils that would have resulted from Noah's flood. Hartt and his colleagues published the first geological survey of the country, and the Emperor invited them to create and run an Imperial Geological Commission. They evolved the Hartt-Derby Theory, which has since been largely proven. They argued that in the earliest geological period, Archaean or pre-Cambrian, there had been two islands north and south of what is now the Amazon river. Over millions of years, these two plates closed and the channel between them became a river. Then plate tectonics (a concept unknown in Hartt's day) caused the Andes mountains to rise at the western edge of the continent. This may have reversed the flow of the Amazon river.

Charles Hartt's team were also pioneers in Amazonian archaeology, studying shell middens, ancient burials, and petroglyph carvings on river rapids throughout the region (see Chapter 9 for more details). These first forays into Amazonian archaeology were synthesized in a book by the Brazilian anthropologist Ladislau Netto, and in 1882 he organized an exhibition of newly excavated treasures. Ladislau was the first to link archaeological finds to contemporary Indians. Interest in indigenous peoples had been growing throughout the century, developing from travellers' or missionaries' descriptions into the new discipline of anthropology. The geologist Hartt also wrote a summary of the ethnography of the Amazon valley, and he was one of the first to appreciate the value of indigenous mythology. His Brazilian contemporary João Barbosa Rodrigues was a botanist specializing in palms and orchids, but he was also fascinated by Indians. He wrote monographs about the dances, folklore and artefacts of half a dozen tribes. He even made a peaceful (but short-lived) contact with the warlike Waimiri who live north of Manaus. This people and the related Atroari were suffering near-genocide from heavily armed expeditions, and they continued to resist gallantly for a further century.

As we have seen abundantly, by the 1880s the tribes of the Brazilian Amazon and its tributaries were shattered by 250 years of annihilation – by imported diseases, slavery, abduction to fill missionary villages, forced labour, the Cabanagem upheaval, and incursions to extract rubber and other resources. The banks of the main river and its great southern tributaries had been almost totally denuded of indigenous people. There was one remarkable exception to this depressing picture: the upper Xingu river. The lower half of the Xingu had been disturbed since the seventeenth century, but the upper river remained pristine, unpenetrated by whites. The main reason for this amazing isolation was a mighty set of rapids that prevented boats from moving upriver, and also the region's remoteness and lack of rubber, gold or other tempting resources.

Enter the twenty-nine-year-old German Karl von den Steinen. This young man had studied medicine in Berlin and the new discipline of psychiatry in Vienna. He sailed on a three-year circumnavigation of the world, during which he learned the rudiments of anthropology among South Pacific islanders. Then in 1884 Steinen took a steamer up the Paraguay river into Mato Grosso in central Brazil. In the former gold-mining town Cuiabá he heard about uncontacted tribes living in Amazon forests to the north. So he organized an expedition to have a look – with his brother Wilhelm, Paul Ehrenreich (destined to be another great anthropologist), a Frenchman, five Brazilian caboclos, and a military escort. A train of mules, oxen and dogs took the explorers across savannah to the accultur-ated Bakairi Indians, and these guided them to the uncontacted northern half of their tribe. A fortnight later they reached the headwaters of the Xingu, made eight bark canoes, and spent three weeks gliding down the idyllic, empty Batovi river. Steinen's expedition then saw its first sign of an Indian presence. They walked up a forest trail away from the river for almost an hour, in silence and increasingly apprehensive about what awaited them. The expedition suddenly entered a clear-ing with three enormous thatched huts. An Indian youth emerged and came towards them. One of Steinen's frightened Bakairi spoke in Carib and, to every-one's relief, was understood and answered. The two young men walked forward, leaning against one another and embracing, 'both talking at once, and both trem-bling all over their bodies from a mixture of fear and excitement. We were all overcome with a happy feeling of relief!' This was the first time an anthropologist was present at the thrilling moment of first contact with an isolated group.

Karl von den Steinen spent some days in this Bakairi village and then went on to contact seven other tribes, both then and on a second expedition three years later in 1887. We are fortunate that it was *he* who had the first glimpse of the para-dise of the upper Xingu, for Steinen was a fine anthropological observer, and he was also a wonderful writer and narrator. He gave good descriptions of Indian artefacts, set them in the context of tribal culture, and brought many back for museums in Berlin. He was interested in the origins of decorative motifs, the skill and artistry of manufacture, and the meanings of body paint. He told how the Waurá people had invented ceramics and twirling sticks for making fire. But he also delved into the abstractions of mythology and legend, which he told with sympathy and understanding. He described flute ceremonies and masked shamanic rituals. During his relatively short visits, Steinen penetrated indigenous imagination and beliefs more effectively than any previous commentator had done.

His classic books – *Durch Central Brasilien* about the first expedition, and *Unter den Naturvölkern Zentral-Brasiliens* (*Among the Native Peoples of Central Brazil*) about the second – had none of the pomposity that one might expect from a nineteenth-century German academic. He was young and inexperienced enough to write with naturalness. So he broke the mould of Brazilian anthropology. Up to then, the relatively small amount written about indigenous people was full of abstract theory and generalization. Steinen was the first to depict Indians as real people, individuals with distinct characters, even foibles. Although fully aware of the handsomeness of the Indians and the beauty of their world, he was no romantic beguiled by the myth of the noble savage. His Indians were intelligent and resourceful, some with a sense of humour but others bad-tempered, capable of being callous or quick-witted, spiritual or concerned only with the present.

In one passage Steinen described the rapture of an Indian with his first metal cutting blade, running through the forest slicing saplings with wild abandon. He also told how a Bakairi silently mimed the effort that went into felling a tree with a blunt stone axe, under an equatorial sun, chopping away, bent double, hungry and exhausted. The tree did not fall until the sun had almost set. The Indian actor then changed his manner to show the contrast with the white man's efficiency, and raised his imaginary metal axe with devastating strength and vigour. These two anecdotes show why metal blades have always been irresistible to forest peoples: to this day, they continue to be the main means of attracting isolated tribes.

Another Indian told Steinen about the topography that lay ahead. The river was drawn in the sand, and the rapids and tribes along it were marked with grains of corn. But Steinen's informant enacted the journey far more vividly than a Baedeker guidebook could have done. 'First you get into your canoe, *pepi*, and paddle, *pepi, pepi, pepi*. You paddle to the left and right, changing sides. You reach a rapids, *bububu*.... How high it falls: his hand goes down the steps with each *bu*.... There the *pepi* must plunge between rocks – a hard stamp on the ground with his foot. With what groans it is pushed through, and the baskets of baggage are wearily carried overland...' – and so on, throughout a wonderfully realistic day's journey.

In another passage, Steinen described his hard bargaining with a young couple of the Custenaú tribe, trying to acquire a hammock in exchange for some knives. 'The owner of the hammock was a young lad whose crafty and impudent expression reminded me of shoplifters in the Berlin police files. He was newly married. His wife was about twenty-five, with large shining eyes. Sitting there in her youthful happiness, she swung in her hammock and talked to me with animation.' Steinen was also struck by the beauty of another young mother, who had 'a finely cut European face with full lips, lightly reddened cheeks framed by thick waving hair, and the most beautiful eyes I had seen in all Brazil – which is saying a great deal.... With a body that had never been laced up or mishandled, she really looked like a young mother Eve. But, sadly, she scratched her head too often. This may sometimes have been done from embarrassment; but lice contributed to cause it.'

Steinen told his readers what it was like to be in a village full of naked people. 'After a quarter of an hour a visitor is no longer aware of this wicked nudity. But if you do deliberately remember it, and ask yourself whether these naked people – fathers, mothers and children who stand around or walk about so inno- cently – should be condemned or pitied for their nakedness, you must either laugh at your question as utterly absurd or protest against it as unworthy. From an aes- thetic point of view, lack of clothing like truth itself has its pros and cons. Young, healthy people may look enchanting in their unconstrained movements, but the old and sick are often dreadful in their decay.' Steinen also described the candour and total lack of prurience with which Indians referred to sexual activity. 'Our natives have no secret parts of their bodies. They joke about them in words and gestures with complete frankness that it would be idiotic to regard as indecent.'

Moving down the Xingu's headwaters, the expedition was camped on a sandbank when it was suddenly visited by a flotilla from the uncontacted and potentially hostile Trumai tribe. A long line of fourteen canoes glided silently into view. 'Two Indians stood motionless in each canoe with their bows ready, while a third sat in the middle and scarcely seemed to move his paddle. In perfect order, as if performing a carefully rehearsed theatrical production, the long narrow vessels glided noiselessly towards the forested far bank.' The Trumai warriors were painted for battle and wearing white feather headdresses. Then, equally suddenly, they started shouting fanatically, beating their chests and swaying their bodies and legs. Steinen commented that such movements while standing in a canoe would have pitched the Germans helplessly into the water. 'But we were on solid ground and the example was infectious. So we also howled and roared and beat our chests.' The tension was then broken by some nervous trading, with Steinen himself bravely wading into the river offering a piece of clothing.

The most exciting contact occurred further downriver, with the very belligerent Suyá people. 'Some forty men had assembled there, all naked, their bodies streaked unartistically with black and red dyes, some with white or orange feather headdresses, some with loose, tangled hair hanging down to their shoulders.' All were armed with bows and arrows and clubs, and they wore frightening lip-discs. 'None kept his mouth still for an instant, shouting "Suyá! Suyá! Tahahá Suyá!". The roaring of the frenzied pack always finished with these words repeated in every key. They brandished their weapons and leaped about with their eyes fixed on us.' Steinen again bravely went in the lead canoe. His dogs barked wildly – adding greatly to the danger, since these animals were unknown to the Suyá – so that for a time the Germans had to withdraw. After more adventures, they made contact and traded with the fearsome tribe.

On one occasion, Steinen introduced the Suyá to the concept of drawing on paper, and they portrayed the visiting expedition. They showed the five leaders with full bushy beards, but they chose to ignore their clothing altogether – the only other feature drawn on their matchstick bodies was their genitalia. At another time, three women and their men came to the expedition camp. 'The women came in the simplicity of paradise and no less innocence. They wanted to have intimate relations with us – something that did not conform to our rigorous discipline! Their male companions demonstrated this desire by sign language that could easily be understood by all peoples at all times.... The women then landed from the canoes and washed themselves in the most open manner, thus demonstrating a naïve innocence that prudish critics deny to the Medici Venus [by adding a fig leaf].'

Karl von den Steinen was an explorer as well as a groundbreaking anthropologist. His team were the first whites to descend the entire 1,500-kilometre (930-mile) length of the Xingu river. His canoe capsized and he was nearly drowned when they shot the great rapids that had previously protected the upper river. He named the waterfall after his compatriot Von Martius, who had been the first foreign scientist admitted to the Amazon almost seventy years previously.

During those decades, the Amazon and its forests and native peoples were seen in a new light. The region was recognized as the world's greatest tropical rain forest in the largest river basin. Although formidable, this was not just a fearsome wilderness: it contained untold scientific riches.

CHAPTER SIX

The Rubber Boom

When Richard Spruce returned to Manaus in 1853 after two years upriver, he found a social revolution in progress. 'All the way down the Rio Negro the smoke was seen ascending from recently opened seringales [rubber depots].... The extraordinary price reached by rubber in Pará at length woke up the people from their lethargy.... Throughout the Amazon ... the mass of the population put itself in motion to search out and fabricate rubber.... Mechanics threw aside their tools, sugar-makers deserted their mills, and Indians their roças [forest clearings], so that sugar, rum, and even farinha [manioc flour] were not produced in sufficient quantity.' Spruce reckoned that 25,000 men had already taken up rubber-gathering, mostly near Belém at that time. The Amazon forests were at last yielding a really profitable commodity.

Rubber had been known for a very long time. Christopher Columbus watched natives on Hispaniola (in modern Haiti) playing with bouncing balls – made from caucho, since the best rubber trees do not grow there. When the French scientist Charles-Marie de La Condamine descended the Amazon in 1743 he saw the Omagua using this elastic, waterproof and unbreakable material to make flasks and hollow balls. At their festivals, snuff was puffed from pear-shaped rubber syringes. Back in France, La Condamine delivered a paper about rubber to the Academy of Sciences. He noted that 'with a single incision [the tree] secretes a milky-white fluid that gradually hardens and darkens on contact with the air'. This milky fluid is *latex*, a hydrocarbon polymer found in the inner bark of many tropical tree species. It courses through tubes, apparently to protect the tree from insect predators, and it is elastic because its molecules are organized in long chains.

The Tupi-speaking Omagua called this wonderful fluid *hevé*, which led to the botanical name for the tall and graceful rubber tree being *Hevea brasiliensis*.

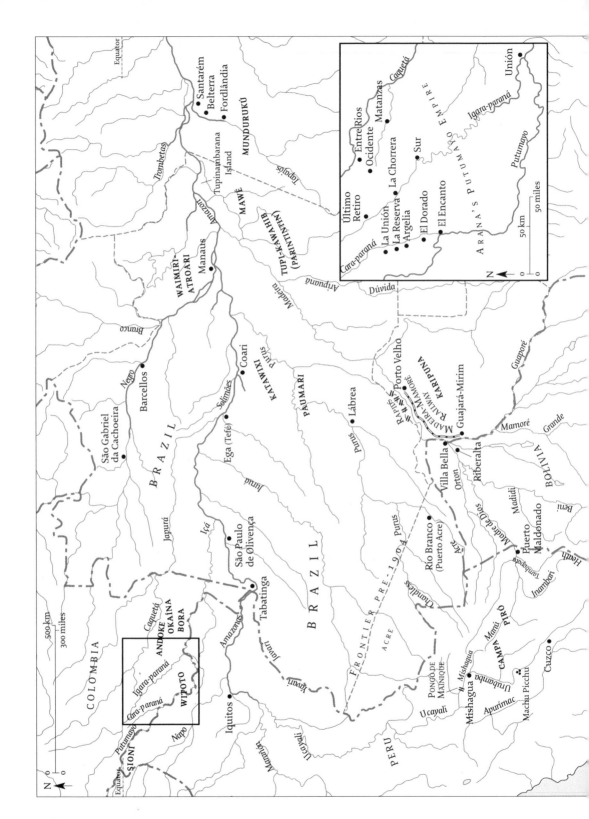

Upriver of them, La Condamine noted that Mainas people of the Pastaza river called their latex-bearer *cau-chu* meaning 'tree that weeps', which led to the French word for rubber *caoutchouc* and the Spanish *caucho* for the inferior Castilla latex found in western Amazonia. For Brazilians the tree is *seringa* because Indians used its milk for syringes to inhale hallucinogens; and from this came *seringal* (a stand or depot of wild rubber) and *seringueiro* (rubber collector). The English name was coined by Joseph Priestley, the discoverer of oxygen, who noted in 1770 that this gum was used to rub out pencil marks – hence 'rubber' or 'India rubber' because it came from Amazonian Indians.

Rubber was used on a small scale during the eighteenth century. La Condamine's friend François Fresnau, Sieur de La Gatandière, studied the plant for fourteen years while serving in French Guiana. In a memorandum in 1747 Fresnau brilliantly predicted rubber being used for waterproof cloth, fire-fighting pumps, awnings, diving suits, ammunition cases, boots and harnesses. His compatriot Fusée Aublet described the rubber tree botanically in 1755; but it was the German Karl Willdenow who first named *Hevea brasiliensis* in 1801. In the mid-eighteenth century the Portuguese sent army boots, rucksacks and other equipment to Pará to be waterproofed. The King dispatched a surgeon to the Amazon to investigate rubber's medicinal uses. On his return this doctor set up a small factory, and in 1800 he advertised in a Lisbon newspaper rubber probes, candles, and little bags to hold the urine of incontinent persons or 'even gonorrheal materials'. Three years later a Frenchman started a workshop making ladies' elastic garters. New Englanders were soon importing hundreds of pairs of rubber overshoes. Spix and Martius in 1819 noted that policemen in Belém wore rubber capes. They saw rubber poured into clay moulds to make souvenirs shaped like local fruits or 'animals (fish, jaguars, monkeys, manatees) and even figures of people or imaginary creatures, not always decent'. (Tourist shops in the Brazilian state of Acre still sell well-endowed bulls and sexy figurines made of solid rubber.) But rubber remained a curiosity. It suffered from two serious defects: it became sticky and smelly when hot, and rock-hard and brittle when frozen.

Rubber overcame these defects and became a phenomenal success thanks to a series of inventions. In the 1790s an Englishman patented a method of waterproofing materials with a mixture of rubber and turpentine. In 1820 Thomas Hancock, 'the father of the rubber industry', started large-scale production of rubber goods in England. Three years later Charles Macintosh found that if rubber was dissolved with low-boiling naphtha (waste from a gas works) it made a pliable

Opposite *Map showing rubber boom areas and (inset) the empire of Julio César Arana (see Chapter 7).*

coating for cloth. His factory in Glasgow produced the waterproof 'macs' that perpetuated his name. The big breakthrough came in the 1830s. A German and an American inventor both discovered that mixing sulphur into rubber gum eliminated its stickiness but retained its elasticity. In 1839 Charles Goodyear, a Connecticut hardware merchant, was experimenting with this mixture when he accidentally dropped some onto a hot stove. Suddenly, rubber turned into the stable, durable, waterproof, elastic and insulating material that we know. Goodyear called his discovery 'vulcanization' after the Roman god of fire. But Goodyear was a sickly young man and he failed to protect his invention: Hancock and Macintosh patented his idea in 1844 just before he could, so he died in poverty.

Rubber rapidly became an essential ingredient of the Industrial Revolution. It made the best gaskets for steam engines. It came to be used in pumps, machine belting, tubing, railway buffers, and later as coating for telegraph wires. Carriage wheels were rimmed with solid rubber, and in 1845 a pneumatic wheel was patented in England. The most spectacular modern use came in 1888 when John Dunlop, a veterinary surgeon in Belfast, created the first detachable pneumatic rubber tyre – to help his young son win a tricycle race. Dunlop patented 'a hollow tyre or tube made of India-rubber and cloth ... to contain air under pressure'. Bicycles became a craze that gave everyone freedom to travel. In France there were 250,000 bicycles by 1894, and five million by the start of the First World War. Then came automobiles. In 1888 André and Édouard Michelin founded a tyre company, and seven years later they used inflatable tyres to win a motorcar race between Paris and Bordeaux. World demand for rubber grew insatiably. And throughout the nineteenth century the Amazon had a monopoly of this wonderful commodity.

In Spruce's time rubber-gathering was still a cottage industry – his contemporaries Bates and Wallace scarcely mentioned it in their books. Some 1,500 tons a year were produced in Amazonia, and this was only a quarter of the region's meagre exports. The burst of activity that Spruce saw in the 1850s was just the start of the world's greatest boom based on a living plant product. During the next half-century rubber became 'white gold' (because its milk is white before smoking), succeeding and preceding the 'black gold' fossil-fuels coal and oil. Prices on world markets rose steadily, and so did the quantity collected. By the end of the century Brazil was exporting 21,500 tons of rubber worth £14 million, and a decade later the annual average had doubled to 42,000 tons worth £24.6 million. This was as much as Brazil's coffee exports: the two commodities accounted for 80 per cent of the nation's trade.

Hevea brasiliensis is a tree of the spurge family, with smooth grey bark and yellow-green flowers, which rises gracefully up to 40 metres (130 feet) into the forest canopy. It was gradually discovered that the trees grow best on *terra firme*, higher and better-drained ground away from rivers. They need constant heat, 1,800 mm (70 inches) of rainfall a year, and cannot grow at an altitude above 800 metres (2,600 feet). Most are found just south of the Equator on the Amazon's big southern tributaries, in a huge arc from the mouth of the river, to the Tapajós opposite Manaus, south into Bolivia, and westwards to the foothills of the Andes. Like many rainforest trees, *H. brasiliensis* scatters itself as protection against natural blights and predators, so there are only two or three tappable specimens per hectare. It has always been difficult to grow rubber trees in plantations in Amazonia because of insect predators and disease – particularly the fungal pathogen South American Leaf Blight (*Microcyclus ulei*). In fact, hardly anyone tried. Demand rose so fast that there was no time to wait a decade or two for planted trees to mature. The industry relied instead on wild-rubber tappers, called *seringueiros* in Brazil and *caucheros* in Spanish America.

Although Manaus is 1,500 kilometres (940 miles) from the Atlantic Ocean, it is a deep-water port throughout the year, and it is conveniently near the mouths of the great rubber rivers. In 1850 the town's name was changed from Barra to Manaus (in honour of Ajuricaba's vanished tribe), and it became the capital of the Province of Amazonas. Two years later a Company of Navigation and Commerce of Amazonas was created by Brazil's first major industrialist, Irineu de Souza, Baron of Mauá. He was a fervent anglophile who brought railways, factories and other wonders of the Industrial Revolution to his country. Mauá's shipping company started with three small steamers built in his own shipyard, and these plied the Amazon between Pará and Peru. Then in 1867 – under pressure from Britain and the United States – Brazil made the River Amazon an international waterway open to merchant shipping from every nation. Ocean-going vessels were soon cruising up the great river to Manaus. They also sailed far beyond to Iquitos, a city that the Peruvians created in 1863 (on the site of the former Mainas mission) by sending a steamer around Cape Horn and up the Amazon.

Manaus grew as fast as the rubber boom. In 1867 a German engineer described it as 'an insignificant little town of about three thousand inhabitants, with unpaved and badly levelled streets, and low houses and cottages of the most primitive construction without any attempt at architectural beauty.' But by 1890 it had ten thousand people, and a decade later it had become a city of fifty thousand. Life was very good at the top of the rubber boom's pyramid of exploitation. Manaus acquired all the municipal trappings. In 1893, soon after Brazil became a republic, a young colonel of engineers called Eduardo Gonçalves Ribeiro became governor of Amazonas. Diminutive, with receding hair and the obligatory handlebar moustache, Ribeiro was an energetic visionary who immediately started to transform Manaus. He laid out a grid of broad tree-lined avenues. Freighters that exported rubber returned with ballast of cobblestones for these streets and marble for the millionaires' palaces. Governor Ribeiro boasted: 'I found a village and turned it into a modern city.' The jungle city was hailed (with considerable artistic licence) as 'the Paris of the Tropics' and 'an amazing tribute to the energy of man'. To achieve this, Ribeiro had to protect Manaus's revenues from crooks and speculators. He was forced from office in 1900 to make way for a local politician more acceptable to the rubber barons. Ribeiro himself enjoyed all that his louche city offered: but he died in 1904, strangled during a sexual romp.

In 1897 Manaus got its famous opera house, the Teatro Amazonas. With its *art nouveau* cupola (coloured the blue, green and yellow of the Brazilian flag) shining in the tropical sun, its three-storey neo-classical portico surmounted by a curved pediment, colonnaded terrace, pavements with undulating mosaic patterns, and an extravagant bronze statue symbolizing Amazonia in its forecourt, the theatre is a fitting landmark for a boom-town in the midst of tropical forests. Ironwork came from Glasgow, tiles from Alsace, marble pillars from Carrara, mirrors from France, and chandeliers from Venice. The theatre boasted a ballroom decorated with Italian tapestries, and its 20-metre-high (65-foot) stage curtain glorified the Tupi water nymph Iara. The French geographer Auguste Plane marvelled at this 'majestic construction' with a foyer 'elegant and richly decorated, its ceiling an admirable masterpiece by the painter [Domenico] de Angelis. Well ventilated and well lit, it represents one of the sights of Manaus. The most refined civilisation has reached the Rio Negro!'

The Teatro Amazonas was inaugurated with Ponchielli's opera *La Gioconda* performed by an Italian company. But that was the only grand opera ever staged there. The theatre is too small: even if every one of its three tiers of boxes and every seat in the stalls were filled, it holds only 685 people. (Abandoned for decades, the theatre has recently been lovingly restored, even down to *belle époque* lettering and decorations. The author saw an operatic intermezzo by Telemann staged there, but this had a cast of only three singers and a dozen musicians.) The cost of bringing a full opera company and orchestra with all their paraphernalia up the river was also always prohibitive. So the greatest moments of the Teatro Amazonas were performances of plays and concerts – but none of these involved Enrico Caruso, Anna Pavlova or Sarah Bernhardt as legend has it.

In 1902 the covered Municipal Market was completed. Designed by the British architects Backus and Brisbane, its iron castings are marked by 'Francis Morton, Engineers, Liverpool'. Tons of river fish are still sold from its marble slabs.

That same year saw the opening of Manaus's famous *ponte flutuante*, designed and prefabricated on the Clyde by Scottish engineers. To cope with the Rio Negro's annual rise and fall of 14 metres (46 feet) this floating dock floats on great circular iron pontoons, and it is connected to the city by a 150-metre (490-foot) hinged ramp. A crane-and-cable system supported by 22-metre (72-foot) towers could swing 4-ton loads from ship to shore. The Booth Steamship Company, whose twenty ships sailed regularly between Manaus and Liverpool, paid for most of these harbour installations in return for management rights and docking fees. The dock leads to the Afândega or customs house, on the site of the old fort São José da Barra. Finished in 1908 by the English Manaus Harbour Ltd., this lovely building, with a facade of Lombard arches flanked by Corinthian pilasters, is an exact replica of one in Bombay (present-day Mumbai). Its reddish granite was also brought as ballast from England. The city's Palace of Justice was inspired by Versailles and cost £500,000. It and the nearby Palácio do Governo were built by Moers & Morton.

Manaus was one of the first cities in Brazil to have electric lighting, telephones (in 1897), and a university. In 1900 it got one of the world's finest tram systems: bottle-green American streetcars with 'Manaos Railway' in English on each car, eventually running on 25 kilometres (15 miles) of track that stretched out to rain forests surrounding the city. The trams were sponsored by the United States Rubber Company, which was buying a quarter of the city's exports. Manaus boasted three hospitals (one of them for the Portuguese, another for the insane), a public library, zoo, botanical garden, and ten private secondary schools. The Grand Hotel Internacional was 'the finest in Christendom', with electric lighting and electric-powered ventilators in the dining room. In its heyday 'Manaus also supported a racecourse, a bull-ring [the flamboyantly named Coliseu Tauromachico], thirty-six fashionable doctors, twenty-four bars, twenty-three high-class department stores, eleven fancy restaurants, nine modistes, nine gentlemen's outfitters, scores of barbers' shops, seven billiard saloons and seven bookshops.' There were cemeteries stuffed with ornate tombs to cater for an above-average death-rate from tropical diseases – and shootings. The region even inspired early Brazilian cinema, with *In the Steps of El Dorado* and other silent movies by Silvino Santos – whose beard and plus-four suit made him look like George Bernard Shaw.

Rubber tycoons enjoyed every possible luxury. Their palaces had chandeliered ballrooms, grand pianos or pianolas, and imported furniture, table settings and linen. Ships that exported rubber found that the best return cargo was delicacies for the newly rich. Robin Furneaux wrote that 'no extravagance, however absurd, deterred them. If one rubber baron bought a vast yacht, another would install a tame lion in his villa, and a third would water his horse on champagne.' This wine was the preferred drink at every party. Guests once knelt to lap champagne from the bathtub of the naked beauty Sarah Lubousk from Trieste. This bather in the bubbly was the mistress of Waldemar Ernst Scholtz, a clerk from Stuttgart with pince-nez spectacles and waxed moustache, who made a fortune as an importer and became Austria's honorary consul in Manaus. Scholtz belied his prim appearance by lavish spending on 'Babylonian' parties, on a lion, a motor yacht, sleek carriages and liveried footmen. His Palácio Scholtz, built by the French engineer Henri Moers, was one of the sights of Manaus with its three balustrades and deep verandas on Corinthian columns. (It now belongs to the State of Amazonas and is called the Palácio Rio Negro. I attended a banquet there that was a far cry from Scholtz's revels.) Another sought-after courtesan was the Polish Jewess Wanda. Adventuresses and society *grandes dames* flocked to this oasis of wealth. It was rumoured that the richest sent their dirty clothes to Europe to be laundered.

Most of Manaus's houses were said to have been brothels. One of the grandest was a floating palace that offered the most attractive girls. Its madam advertised: 'Frequent sailings to all parts of the river, with champagne on ice and a gramophone all included.' Less expensive was the Pensão das Mulatas ('Mulatto Girls' Pension'). These catered to every taste and pocket, from jaded millionaires to seringueiros escaping months without women on their lonely trails. The city throbbed with bars, cabarets and night-clubs – with enticing names like The Phoenix or High Life. The poet Anibal Amorim loved the cosmopolitan nightlife, with the Chalet Garden 'frequented by debauched men and women, where the hours passed amid beer and champagne' or the Café dos Terríveis (The Terrors), open all hours, with 'its tables at daybreak soaked in excessive spilled drinks'.

Meanwhile, the rubber boom also enriched Iquitos in Peru, which is 3,646 kilometres (some 2,265 miles) from the mouth of the Amazon, over twice as far as Manaus. Gustave Eiffel was said to have designed the frame and verandas of a two-storey 'Iron House' on the main square of Iquitos. It had formed part of the Paris Exhibition of 1889 and was shipped out in pieces by a rubber baron. The only problem now is uncertainty about its whereabouts: several buildings on the Plaza claim to be it.

Belém at the mouth of the Amazon also prospered from handling much of the commerce, banking and insurance of the boom. It gained many ornate buildings, including an improved Ver-o-Peso ('See the Weight') market whose wrought-iron is the work of 'MacFarlane, Glasgow'. This tree-lined eighteenth-century town, with Giuseppe Landi's baroque churches, grew gracefully into a modern commercial city.

The rubber trade in Manaus was run by a handful of merchant houses. There are photographs of their offices, panelled in local woods and with rows of clerks at mahogany desks using early typewriters. Every employee has oiled, centrally parted hair and a full black moustache (partly to show that he has no Indian blood). He wears a suit, white shirt and tie, but is allowed to remove his jacket in the equatorial heat. Overhead are big fans and electric lights in green shades, and there are venetian blinds on the windows.

Each trading house controlled a region of Amazon forests. The rich rubber rivers Purus and Juruá had a number of barons but also many independent wildcat rubber men. Manuel Vicente 'Carioca' was a burly seringueiro from Ceará, who somehow emerged from debt-bondage and came to control four hundred tappers on the Gregório headwater of the Juruá. The tall, blond Alfredo Arruda had 50 kilometres (30 miles) of forests on the Umari tributary of the Purus, and 'Colonel' Luis da Silva Gomes was extremely rich from his rubber on the Purus itself. Other colonels dominated less productive areas, on the Tapajós, the Xingu and the rivers flowing into the Solimões. Rubber on the upper Tapajós was run by one Paulo da Silva Leite. A French explorer wrote enviously that he 'disposes of an Indian tribe … as the boss and protector of the Apiaká'. Joaquim Gonçalves Araújo, always known as 'J. G.', became a major trader and shipper. He dominated the Negro and Branco basins, where there were few *Hevea* rubber trees but other rich pickings such as beef from savannahs of the upper Branco. The Içana source of the Negro was the territory of a tough Colombian called Don Germano Garrido y Otero. His press-gangs crossed into Brazil with impunity to terrorize its Arawak-speaking Baniwa, Hohodene and Warekena and the Tukano-speakers further south. Don Germano sired quantities of children, and he used his sons and god-children (in the manner of a Mafia godfather) to administer his empire.

The best rubber trees grew in Bolivia, on the headwaters of the Amazon's southwestern tributaries the Madeira, Juruá and Purus. Henry Pearson, editor of the American trade journal *The India Rubber World*, admired the self-made Bolivian rubber barons who dominated this trade. The richest, Nicolás Suárez, started bare-foot – and never really took to shoes. He contacted tribes of the Beni, Mamoré and Madre de Dios (all headwaters of the Madeira), 'savages whom no white man had ever dared to approach. Soon this man and his brothers obtained concessions which were little short of countries with sovereign rights. He ruled the wild Indians with a firm hand, exacting terrible reparations for the slightest insult or treachery.' By the end of the century, Nicolás Suárez had ten thousand employees on his payroll, dominated transport down the Madeira (with four hundred men hauling boats through its fearsome rapids), ran the towns of Riberalta and Villa Bella on the Beni, controlled eight million hectares of rubber forests, and eventually owned ranches with 250,000 head of cattle, a sugar mill, a power plant, an ice factory, and countless trading depots. The flamboyantly moustachioed Suárez was known as the Rockefeller of rubber. His brother Francisco went to England in 1871, established the family business Suárez Hermanos & Co. in the City of London, and became Bolivia's consul-general there. (This diplomat's son Pedro went to British boarding school, called himself Percy, and married Jessie, an aunt of the fashion photographer Cecil Beaton. Beaton wrote a delightful memoir, *My Bolivian Aunt*, about his exotic Aunt Jessie, her big house in Hampstead, and Uncle Percy's endless amorous tangles.)

Another big name in Bolivian rubber was Suárez's cousin Dr Antonio Vaca Diez, a thrusting young politician, scholar and medical doctor who came to control the Orton tributary of the Beni. Handsome until he became balding and portly, the young Vaca Diez sported the broad black moustache that was a trademark of rubber barons. (The Orton river was named after the American geologist and explorer James Orton by his friend the doctor-explorer Edwin Heath, who also worked for Vaca Diez. Heath also has a river named after him: a tributary of the Madre de Dios that now forms the boundary between Peru and Bolivia.) Vaca Diez owned almost 4,300 rubber trails (*estradas*), each with some 500 trees. In 1897 his company was floated in London with French capital. Between them, Suárez and Vaca Diez controlled an area of northern Bolivia half the size of France.

At the western fringe of the rubber forests was Carlos Fermín Fitzcarrald. The son of an American sailor who settled in highland Peru (and changed his name from the difficult Fitzgerald), young Fitzcarrald was educated in Lima, but he fled to the Peruvian Amazon because he was suspected of spying for Chile. He settled at an extremely remote place, Mishagua on the Urubamba (the river that flows past Machu Picchu), near the dreaded whirlpools of the Pongo de Mainique. During the 1880s Fitzcarrald became a caucho rubber boss, with the help of Arawak-speaking Piro and Campa peoples whom he won over with presents of knives and *aguardiente* brandy.

The Indians showed Fitzcarrald how the waters of the Mishagua river almost connect the Urubamba-Ucayali with the Manú-Madre de Dios-Beni-Madeira river system. This is still one of the least explored parts of the Amazon basin. In 1896 Fitzcarrald took a three-ton steam launch to this portage, had his Indians dismantle and carry it across, and sailed the reassembled little vessel triumphantly down to the Beni. This very circuitous route might have become a means of avoiding the terrible rapids on the lower Madeira. Dr Vaca Diez was impressed. In the following year the Bolivian rubber baron sailed up the Amazon to Iquitos, and Fitzcarrald took his launch *Adolfito* down to meet him. Then tragedy struck. In July 1897 Lizzie Hessel – a young Englishwoman whose husband was on his way to join Vaca Diez's rubber company – wrote that: 'Three days down [from] the Mishagua, the [drive-]chain of the *Adolfito* broke and the current took her and she went down, and the most dreadful thing of all, Vaca Diez was drowned together with [Fitzcarrald].... Poor Mrs Fitzcarrald has four children, she is, of course, dreadfully upset.' (Werner Herzog's film *Fitzcarraldo* portrayed him as an Irish eccentric madly making his Indians slice through a mountain to drag a large boat intact through the cutting, but in reality the link was a short portage on log rollers during the dry season and navigable on floodwaters during the wet; and the *Adolfito* was a modest craft. Herzog also fantasized that his hero adored Verdi operas and frequented the Manaus opera house, whereas this theatre was not yet opened and Fitzcarrald never went down the Amazon into Brazil.)

The Suárez brothers and other Bolivian rubber barons needed to get their white gold to the markets of Europe and North America, and the obvious route was down the Amazon rather than laboriously across the Andes. However, the Madeira river cascades off the Central Brazilian Shield in 30 kilometres (18 miles) of ferocious rapids upstream of Porto Velho. There are *cachoeiras* called Santo António, Teotônio with a 10-metre (35-foot) fall, and the raging Caldeirão do Inferno (Hell's Cauldron). Indians had to haul canoes up and down these falls. As the boom accelerated, the tonnage of rubber coming down and manufactured goods going up the Madeira multiplied. There was a series of portages around each rapid, with flotillas of boats to paddle on the stretches of river between them. But boats often capsized, with serious loss of profit and (less importantly to the bosses) manpower.

The Bolivians commissioned a German engineer, Franz Keller, to investigate ways of bypassing the rapids on the Madeira. He gave estimates for various solutions. Ramps for hauling boats would cost US$450,000; a paved road and a canal with locks, $10 million; and a railroad for $4,250,000. The latter seemed the best. So the Bolivians enlisted a dashing American engineer, Colonel George E.

Church, to build it. As a young man Church had designed the Hoosac tunnel in Massachusetts, had fought in the Civil War's Army of the Potomac, then worked for the Argentine government 'taming' indigenous peoples of Patagonia. In 1870 he registered the National Bolivian Navigation Company, raised the necessary finance, and engaged an English company to build the railway. Labourers were imported from Spain and northeast Brazil. But after a few months the English begged to be released from the contract: they wrote in 1873 that the country was a charnel house in which their men died like flies from malaria. The proposed railroad ran through a wilderness of swamp cut by porphyry ridges. 'With the command of all the capital in the world, and half its population, it would be impossible to build the road.' Colonel Church tried again in 1879, this time with the American company P. & T. Collins of Philadelphia. The Yankees started with great gusto. Over nine hundred Americans were sent out. Tragically, eighty of these drowned when their ship sank; and a further 141 American, 400 Brazilian, and 200 Bolivian engineers and labourers died during the eighteen-month contract – a few from accidents, one from an Indian arrow, but the vast majority from malaria. The Americans gave up the hopeless enterprise, P. & T. Collins went bankrupt, and in 1881 Colonel Church's concession was cancelled.

West of the Madeira, the Juruá and Purus rivers rise in the rubber-rich forests of Acre. The negotiators of the Treaties of Madrid (1750) and San Ildefonso (1777), who divided South America between the Portuguese and Spanish empires, had vaguely drawn the boundary from Porto Velho at the rapids of the Madeira westwards towards the unexplored source of the Javari. After independence, the Treaty of Ayacucho in 1867 redrew this boundary as a thousand-kilometre (620-mile) straight line, from the Madeira-Mamoré junction northwestwards to the upper Javari. This gave Brazil more of Acre's forests, but it definitely recognized that most of the rubber heartland lay south of this line in Bolivia. Many Brazilians were unhappy. They felt that their Foreign Ministry had made a serious mistake in yielding the headwaters of the Juruá and Purus rivers to Bolivia, which knew nothing about those forests.

The region was explored in the 1860s by the Brazilian mulatto Manuel Urbano da Encarnação and then by the English traveller William Chandless (who has a long headwater of the Purus named after him). During the following decade the Brazilian Colonel Antonio Labre started organizing the rubber trade in this richest of all areas. (Every boss in Amazonia was called 'Colonel', but Labre was one of the few who had actually served as an army officer, in the war against Paraguay.) He learned from Urbano da Encarnação how to enlist the help of local Indians, particularly Arawak-speaking Paumari and Katawixi. It was not long before thousands of Brazilian seringueiros poured up these meandering but rapid-free rivers. By 1890 there were an amazing 120,000 rubber men in the Purus valley – 22,000 of them in the town of Lábrea named after Colonel Labre.

By the end of the century, 60 per cent of all Amazonia's rubber came from Acre. The Bolivian authorities realized that tons of rubber were being removed from their side of the straight-line frontier. This was because Brazilians could easily sail up the Purus and Juruá, but it was very difficult for Bolivians to move overland to that remote forested part of their country. Despite this, the Bolivians rashly tried to impose an export duty of 30 per cent on every *bolacha* ball of rubber taken downriver to Brazil. The levy was to be collected by a customs post at a little place called Puerto Alfonso on the Acre river. A group of Bolivian businessmen and military officers went further. They drafted plans for a 'Bolivian Syndicate' that would tempt foreign powers, particularly the United States, to protect this remote territory. The Syndicate would buy Acre's forests for a few centavos an acre. Its investors would then enjoy tax-free trading for a few years, be allowed to enforce law and order, and be able to collect taxes with a percentage going to Bolivia. Some Americans were so taken by these ideas that they contemplated their government financing Bolivian military defence of Acre in return for half its rubber revenues and an American base there. An American naval captain who was taking this prospectus to Bolivia made the mistake of asking a young journalist in Belém to translate it. Instead, the journalist, Spanish-born Luis Gálvez Rodríguez de Aria, published the explosive plan in his newspaper the *Província do Pará*.

Brazilian seringueiros were already furious about the Bolivian attempt to tax them. News of the proposed Bolivian Syndicate roused them to action. On 3 May 1899 a Brazilian rubber boss called José Carvalho led a gang of his men in a pre-dawn attack on Puerto Alfonso: the Bolivian flag was torn down and its officials were hauled from their beds, packed into canoes, and ordered to paddle homewards upriver. Meanwhile the journalist Gálvez – a romantic idealist who knew all about the French Revolution but nothing about rubber or rain forests – was bringing 'an army of Bohemians and actors' up the Amazon and Purus in a comic-opera response. They arrived in late May. With the enthusiastic support of the seringueiros, Gálvez founded the Independent State of Acre to a cry of 'Acre for the Acreanos!' He made himself its president, wrote a constitution, and appointed a cabinet. He declared that it would be a democratic utopia created by 'an expedition of poets'. The muddy settlement was renamed Pôrto Acre and its potholed lanes were given Brazilian names. President Gálvez inaugurated his republic on Bastille Day, 14 July, from the verandah of the São Jerônimo rubber depot. There were banquets, for which the receipts have survived. The ruling junta consumed a case of American beer, a case of Veuve Cliquot champagne and 200 Donemann cigars, whereas 107 of their subjects on the riverbank ate their favourite foods – black beans, rice, jerked beef, bananas and guavas – washed down with Collares wine from Portugal, *cachaça* rum and Guinness beer, and smoked 500 Villar cigars.

Neither Bolivia nor Brazil welcomed this absurd rubber-rich state. The Bolivians managed to get a few soldiers through dense forests into Acre, and these defeated the separatists in a couple of skirmishes. A Brazilian naval flotilla meanwhile sailed up the Purus to extinguish the jungle republic.

Bolivia went ahead with the launch of its syndicate. The word 'rubber' was as magnetic as 'gold' or 'railways' in attracting speculators. So when the venture was floated in New York and London it was rapidly subscribed, with Vanderbilts, Morgans and Astors among its shareholders. Brazil, however, refused to recognize its neighbour's manoeuvres and closed the Amazon to traffic bound for Acre. In May 1899 the American warship *USS Wilmington* tried to slip upriver from Belém to reinforce the syndicate, but it was intercepted near Manaus and sent back to the United States with an angry diplomatic protest.

Brazilian rubber men were tough individualists who resented Bolivia's reoccupation of the Acre forests. In August 1902 a young South Brazilian called Plácido de Castro led a force of seringueiros to capture the rich region. Unlike Gálvez's 'poets', Castro and his men proved skilful guerrillas. For several months they outwitted an isolated contingent of the Bolivian army. In response, the Bolivian rubber baron Nicolás Suárez mobilized 250 of his men armed with Winchester rifles – but these were on the Beni, still separated from Acre by 250 kilometres (155 miles) of forested wilderness. In January 1903 Bolivia's president, General José Pando, himself led his army out of La Paz amid cheering patriotic crowds. But it took them three months of nightmarish travel just to reach Suárez on the Beni, and by that time it was all over in Acre.

Brazil again intervened to discipline its unruly nationals. It sent an infantry battalion under the ruthless General Olimpio da Silveira to disarm Castro, and he succeeded – even though beriberi and malaria killed two-thirds of his 417 men. However, this time the Brazilian military did not immediately withdraw. Their energetic Foreign Minister the Baron of Rio Branco had decided to annexe the lucrative region. Rapid negotiations resulted in the Treaty of Petrópolis of November 1903. By this, Brazil acquired the 191,000-square-kilometre (74,000 square miles) territory of Acre for £2 million and some 5,000 square kilometres (1,900 square miles) of land near the Madeira river. Much of the cash payment was to be used to complete the Madeira-Mamoré railway. It was a tremendous bargain for Brazil.

The aggrieved investors of the Bolivian Syndicate sued for damages, and eventually won £110,000.

Bolivia rewarded Nicolás Suárez for his patriotic gestures with an even larger concession on the Beni. But in 1904 his brother Gregorio was near the Madeira rapids meeting a group of normally docile Karipuna Indians whom he knew. There was a friendly shooting match, with seringueiro revolvers competing against native bows and arrows. But something went wrong: Gregorio Suárez was killed by an arrow through his heart and the Indians massacred almost all his companions. Two Bolivians escaped and told Nicolás Suárez. He was not a man to overlook his brother's death. His posse tracked the Karipuna into the forest and caught them allegedly ransacking captured cargo, drinking brandy, and with Gregorio's head on a pole. Their camp was surrounded, and every Indian was shot dead.

As promised in the Treaty of Petrópolis, Brazil made a fresh effort to build the infamous railway bypassing the rapids. This time the contract went to another American, Percival Farquar. He formed The Madeira-Mamoré Railway Company and engaged the civil engineers May, Jekyll and Randolph to build the line. This firm started landing men and materials in Brazil in 1907. It was an enormous enterprise: 22,000 men were employed during the five years of the construction, mostly from southern Europe, India and the West Indies, with three hundred Americans in charge. At any time there were four or five thousand men on the company's payroll in Porto Velho.

A great change had taken place during the twenty-eight years since Colonel Church's failure to build the line. There had been a series of breakthroughs in understanding malaria. As we have seen, the dreaded fevers appear to have reached Amazonia in the eighteenth century: Spix and Martius in 1820 said that 'malignant intermittent fevers' had arrived on the Solimões only 'very recently'. But the disease spread and it was soon the region's greatest killer. Every traveller and scientist caught malaria, as did countless seringueiros and indigenous peoples. In their annual reports, successive governors of Amazonas deplored the way riverbank settlements were being extinguished by this scourge. On average, two thousand people a year died of disease in the city of Manaus. An analysis during the five years to 1902 showed that 50 per cent of these deaths were from malaria (followed by intestinal complaints, 8.5 per cent; beriberi, 3.6 per cent; tuberculosis, 3.5 per cent; and dysentery and other ailments the remainder).

It is fascinating to see how intelligent observers sought to understand this disease. The name means 'bad air' and a common view was that it was caused by miasma rising from tropical forests and rotting vegetation. William Chandless and Richard Spruce both noted that malaria was worse at certain times of year, and they tried in vain to link it to the rise or fall of rivers. Others were convinced that it came from sweat-soaked clothing or sudden changes in temperature. The French geographer Elysée Reclus, the Brazilian poet-explorer Antonio Gonçalves Dias, and the English naturalist Henry Walter Bates all blamed bad hygiene. But Bates also advised people not to bathe when feverish or eat raw fruit. Food was often identified as malaria's cause – sugar cane, pineapple, too much brandy, or water-melons (there was a saying 'There's a shake in every melon'). Professor Louis Agassiz opined that people contracted malaria because of poor diet – too much salted fish and manioc and not enough milk. He seemed unaware that dairy cows could not find the pastures of his native Switzerland amid rain forests. But Agassiz was often wrong.

The understanding of malaria came from a succession of brilliant investiga-tions. People had often suspected that mosquitoes were involved, although it was hard to grasp that such tiny insects could transmit such a terrible disease. In 1880 a Dr Laveran with the French army in Algeria first saw under his microscope the living plasmodium parasite in blood from a malarial patient. Italian doctors pursued his research and identified different strains of malaria. In Amazonia the most common and benign is now called *Plasmodium vivax*. This is the one that can cause 'tertian' attacks every three days while the parasites spread from the liver into red blood corpuscles. (This author has twice had vivax malaria – and with fevers of 41°C (107°F) it seemed anything but 'benign'.) Far worse is *Plasmodium fal-ciparum*, which takes longer to manifest itself after infection (three to six weeks, as opposed to vivax's two weeks) but causes most deaths. Falciparum is cerebral malaria, which can induce a coma soon after it finally manifests itself: weak or infant victims never regain consciousness before they die. Dr Patrick Manson in England in 1894 and Major Ronald Ross in India in 1895 proved that mosquitoes transmit the disease. They showed how these blood-suckers pick up malaria from an infected victim, how the plasmodium multiplies in the insect, and how it is transmitted to other victims through the mosquito's salivary gland. In 1898 Italian researchers further identified the vector as the female Anopheles mosquito, particularly when she was reproducing and desperate for blood. Mos-quitoes have a flying range of only 2 kilometres (1.2 miles). So the spread of seringueiros throughout the Amazon basin brought the contagion to areas previ-ously uninfected.

Armed with this new knowledge, the Americans building the Madeira-Mamoré railway took appropriate measures. Workers were forced to sleep under mosquito nets; some pools in which mosquito larvae hatched were drained; and sanitation and hygiene were as good as possible, with drinking water drawn from wells rather than rivers. There was a hospital staffed by up to ten doctors and as many male nurses. Quinine was imported by the ton, and three laboratory workers were employed making it into pills. (Quinine does not prevent or cure malaria, but it suppresses the growth of protozoans in blood cells.) Despite all these precautions there was still much illness, with up to three hundred patients in the hospital at any time. In addition to malaria, they suffered from beriberi, black-water fever and dysentery.

These precautions succeeded, together with engineering skill and back-breaking labour. The first 92 kilometres (57 miles) from Porto Velho past the rapids were opened to traffic in 1910. A further 364 kilometres (225 miles) to Guajará-Mirim, a Brazilian-Bolivian border town far up the Mamoré, were finished by 1912. However, as we shall see, this coincided with the collapse of the Amazon rubber boom. So the extension of the line to Suárez's base Riberalta on the Beni was never built, even though this was stipulated in the Treaty of Petrópolis. In its heyday the railway was known as Mad Maria, and it was said – with some exaggeration – that a man died for every sleeper laid. (A train a week ran along it until 1971, spewing sparks from its burning logs, but most of the track was then converted into a road. In recent years, some rusting Philadelphia-built locomotives and station buildings have been restored as a museum in Pôrto Velho, and a short stretch of line now operates for tourists.)

By 1870 Britain was importing three thousand tons of rubber a year at a cost of £720,000. Sir Joseph Hooker, who had succeeded his father William as Director of the Royal Botanic Gardens at Kew, took note of the amazing rubber tree. So did his friend Clements Markham of the India Office – the traveller in Peru, who in 1860 had got Richard Spruce to bring Chinchona trees from Ecuador. The two decided to repeat this transplanting with rubber. In 1871 a young Englishman called Henry Wickham published a travel book, *Rough Notes of a Journey through the Wilderness*, about a journey up the Orinoco and down the Negro. It was an unremarkable book. But it described a few weeks he spent as a caucho-tapper on the Orinoco, and it had drawings of the *Hevea brasiliensis* tree (even though this does not grow on the Orinoco) with the suggestion that it might be planted elsewhere. By 1873 Wickham was trying to develop a tobacco and sugar plantation near Santarém, and he had brought his bride Violet (daughter of his book's publisher) and his widowed mother to live with him. Wickham's farm was failing, so the young man was delighted when he received a letter from Sir Joseph Hooker commissioning him to send *Hevea* seeds. He asked how much he would be paid. Markham had persuaded his masters at the India Office about the importance of rubber, and in July 1874 he told Hooker that 'they have agreed to pay Mr Wickham £10 for every 1,000 seeds'. There was further correspondence about the difficulty of this enterprise, and in April 1875 Hooker wrote to ask Wickham to collect ten thousand seeds – but only of 'the tree which produced the true Pará rubber of commerce…. Spare no expense to get me living seeds.'

Over thirty years later, Henry Wickham published a lively account of how he fulfilled this daunting commission. He was pleased that it was 'a straight offer to do it; pay to follow result'; but 'question came home to me, how on earth to bring it off'. As he pondered what to do, Wickham and others 'were surprised and startled by news of the arrival on the great river of a fully-equipped ocean liner', the S. S. *Amazonas* of the new 'Inman Line steamships – Liverpool to the Alto-Amazon district'. The liner's Captain Murray invited Wickham and others to a splendid dinner on board. 'We were entertained by two gentlemen, as in charge of "inauguration of the new line".' A few weeks later, 'the startling news came down the river, that our fine ship, the "Amazonas", had been abandoned, and left on the captain's hands, after having been stripped by the two gentlemen supercargoes (our late hospitable entertainers!), and that without so much as a stick of cargo for return voyage to Liverpool. I determined to plunge for it.' Wickham had no money, but the seeds were rapidly ripening on the rubber trees. 'I knew that Captain Murray must be in a fix, so I wrote to him, boldly chartering the ship on behalf of the Government of India; and I appointed to meet him at the junction of the Tapajos and Amazon rivers by a certain date.'

Since, as Wickham told it, 'there was no time to lose', he took an Indian canoe up the Tapajós and plunged into the *terra firme* forest where the *Hevea* trees grew best. 'Working with as many Tapuyo [detribalised] Indians as I could get together at short notice, I daily ranged the forest, and packed on our backs in Indian pannier baskets as heavy loads of seed as we could march down under…. I got the Tapuyo village maids to make up open-work baskets or crates of split *Calamus* canes for receiving the seed, first, however, being careful to have them slowly but well dried on mats in the shade, before they were put away with layers of dried wild banana leaf betwixt each layer of seed…. Also I had the crates slung up to the beams of the Indian lodges to insure ventilation…. I had got to look upon the heavy oily seeds in their dappled skins as become very precious, after having backed them down so many long days tramping across the forest plateaux, and so lost no time in getting them carefully stowed under the *tolda* [awning] of the canoe, and starting away down stream, duly meeting the steamer, as appointed, at the mouth of the Tapajos.' He found Captain Murray 'crabbed and sore' about the way he had been cheated by 'his two rascally supercargoes': they had sold all his trade goods, but vanished before bringing the return cargo of rubber.

'The fine ship sped' down the lower Amazon, with Wickham satisfied that his seeds were well housed in a roomy forehold. 'We were bound to call in at the city of Pará [Belém], as the port of entry, in order to obtain clearance for the ship before we could go to sea. It was perfectly certain in my mind that if the authorities guessed the purpose of what I had on board we should be detained under plea for instructions from the Central Government at Rio, if not interdicted altogether.... Any such delay would have rendered my precious freight quite valueless and useless.' But Wickham's friend the British Consul Thomas Green 'quite entering into the spirit of the thing, went himself with me on a special call on the Barão do S____, chief of the "Alfandiga" [customs] and backed me up' because the young man explained to the diplomat that he had on the ship 'exceedingly delicate botanical specimens specially designated for delivery to Her Britannic Majesty's own Royal Gardens at Kew'. The Baron appreciated the urgency. 'An interview most polite, full of mutual compliment in best Portuguese manner, enabled us to get under way as soon as Murray had got the dingey [*sic*] hauled aboard.'

This entertaining story was often repeated. Unfortunately for a good yarn, Professor Warren Dean of New York University has blown holes in Wickham's version. He wrote in 1987 that Wickham 'refined his tale for twenty years.... The garrulous old man with the handsome sunburned leonine head and drooping mustachio was the very image of a planter-hero.' But Wickham's memory (or imagination) was flawed. Although there was an *S. S. Amazonas*, operated by the Royal Mail Steam Ship Company in which the E. S. Inman Line had an interest, her maiden voyage to Brazil was two years before Wickham's adventure. Her captain was J. L. Beesley, not Murray. He would not have owned his ship's cargo, and the merchant houses on the Amazon were too efficient and powerful to let 'two rascally supercargoes' get away with stealing an entire shipload. Even had they done so, a return cargo of rubber would certainly have been secured. The ship's manifest in 1876 included 141 cases of rubber shipped at Manaus, but no mention of any seeds. In any event, the captain of such a ship would never have accepted a charter from the penniless young Wickham; and there were plenty of other vessels stopping at Santarém that could have taken his cases of seeds. There was no 'Barão S____' in charge of the customs at Belém. The only baron living in Pará whose title started with S was an aged gentleman called Santarém (whom Wickham may have known); but he had nothing to do with the customs service, which was run by a man called Ulrich.

Brazilians have always been incensed by what they regard as one of the greatest thefts in history. However, Professor Dean showed that the idea of propagating rubber trees outside the Amazon was not new. In the early 1860s the Brazilian João Martins da Silva Coutinho had grown *Hevea* trees in Rio de Janeiro and predicted that tapping wild rubber would be insufficient to meet demand. In 1867 he was sent by his government to the Exposition Universelle in Paris to demonstrate that Brazilian rubber was the finest in the world and should respond to growth in plantations elsewhere. In England, Hooker and Markham first heard the suggestion to transplant rubber from James Collins, curator of the Pharmaceutical Society's museum, who published papers about it during the 1860s. Markham later wrote: 'In 1870 I came to the conclusion that it was necessary to do for the caoutchouc-producing tree what had already been done with such happy results for the cinchona [quinine] trees.' In 1872 the India Office asked Collins to investigate. His *Report on the Caoutchouc of Commerce* described the various types of rubber and latex tree, and he favoured *Hevea brasiliensis*. Then in 1873 Collins's friend Charles Farris, who lived at Cametá on the Tocantins, brought two thousand rubber seeds to London. Markham heard that the French and Americans were bidding for these and got the India Office to buy them, but they were in poor condition so that only six seedlings were eventually shipped for planting in Calcutta. In May 1875 another collector, Ricardo Chavez, sent the India Office 485 pounds (220 kg) of rubber seeds, which he had collected with indigenous helpers. Incompetence in the India Office led to these seeds languishing for ten days because no-one knew what to do with them. They were then bundled off to India and all died.

Warren Dean further argued that the authorities in Santarém would have known about Wickham's collecting activities. So would the owners of the rubber seringals, whom he probably paid and who may even have helped him. In 1913 the Brazilian Ministry of Agriculture published a report on *Rubber in Brazil*. This credited Wickham with the 'honour' of having exported to Kew 'the first fresh seeds of *Hevea brasiliensis*, thanks to the benevolence of the Government of Brazil which had these seeds collected by Indians in rubber groves on dry land situated in the Lower Tapajós valley. This historic consignment amounted to 70,000 seeds.' This may have been a face-saving gloss, but it was hardly in the language of a wronged nation.

It was also possible that the shipment of the seeds was legal. There was no law prohibiting the export of rubber. The relevant customs regulation allowed foreigners to remove boxes of plants for botanical gardens without having these opened, provided that they made a declaration verified by a diplomatic official.

Wickham's export went initially to the Royal Botanic Gardens at Kew, but it was *only* of rubber seeds and was for commercial rather than scientific purposes. So he complied with the letter but not the spirit of the law.

Dean commented that there is a whiff of hypocrisy in Brazilian fury at the 'theft' by Wickham, whom they vilify as 'the Prince of Smugglers' and, in modern jargon, 'the greatest eco-pirate'. They themselves are proud of Major Francisco de Melo Palheta, a handsome envoy to the French colony Cayenne in 1727. The French had recently acquired seeds of *Coffea arabica* from the Dutch (who had got them from Arabs of Mocca in Yemen) and were jealously guarding this rare plant. Palheta was negotiating a border dispute, but his instructions told him to try to secrete some coffee beans about his person. Dressed in the latest fashion, he charmed the wife of Governor Claude d'Orvilliers. She served him a cup of coffee, which he had never drunk but praised profusely, so she generously plucked a handful of berries from a tree and told him to enjoy a cup of coffee when he was back in Belém. Instead, he planted them and other beans he had managed to obtain. Palheta soon had a thousand coffee trees on his property near the town. His seeds formed the origin of Brazil's gigantic coffee industry – which became its most lucrative export, greater and more enduring than rubber. Modern supermarkets commemorate the diplomat's theft by selling brands of coffee called Palheta and d'Orvilliers, although few shoppers know their derivations.

Whatever the truth about his story, Wickham's rubber seeds crossed the Atlantic successfully. The *Amazonas* stopped at Le Havre (another sign that she was not specially chartered) and Wickham landed there in order to hurry to London. Hooker acted decisively. He emptied Kew's orchid and propagating houses (to the dismay of flower lovers and curators) and chartered a special train to bring the rubber seedlings from Liverpool to London. Wickham boasted that 'A fortnight afterwards the glass-houses at Kew afforded (to me) a pretty sight – tier upon tier – rows of young *Hevea* plants – 7,000 and odd of them.' Actually, 2,800 of the seeds germinated, but this was a very high ratio, given the delicate nature of rubber seeds which have a high sugar content and can easily ferment, and the fact that they had come from only 26 trees and endured a rigorous voyage. These survivors were shipped out to British India in 'wardian cases' (sealed glass boxes invented by one Nathaniel Ward, in which seedlings could grow from their own condensed moisture). Wickham was paid just £1,505.4s.2d. for his feat. But he later received thousands of pounds from various grateful rubber interests, an annuity of £400, and in 1920 a knighthood. Sir Henry Wickham died in 1928 aged eighty-two, but his wife had left him thirty years earlier – possibly bored at hearing his rubber story too often.

If any one man was responsible for the collapse of the Amazon rubber boom, it was not Henry Wickham but Henry Ridley. When Wickham's seeds were shipped to Ceylon in 1874 most died, because they were planted in wet ground from a mistaken belief that the Amazon was all humid. Trained at Kew, Henry Ridley was in charge of the botanical gardens in Singapore. He experimented boldly, to refute three beliefs of Amazonian seringueiros: that rubber trees could be tapped only infrequently; that only mature trees yielded good rubber; and that they could not grow in plantations. By the simple expedient of a herringbone pattern of cuts (rather than parallel sloping incisions) Ridley showed that trees could be milked of their latex *every day*. He then proved that trees as young as four years could be tapped constantly. He also showed how to grow rubber trees in neat rows provided that they were not too close to one another.

It was not until 1888 that a plantation experiment was attempted in Ceylon – and that was too near a swampy river. In 1895 Ridley finally persuaded some Malayan tea-planters to devote a few acres of drier ground to rubber trees. The first four tons of Malayan rubber reached London in 1900, by which time planters were rushing to convert to rubber. They imported thousands of Chinese workers to milk the trees, and their plantations were close to deep-water seaports. By 1908, Malaya had ten million trees covering 1,300 square kilometres (500 square miles). Not only was Malayan rubber becoming abundant, it was also very cheap – a *fifth* the price of the Amazonian product. Plantations in Southeast Asia were well managed. Improvements in plant selection, breeding, cloning and husbandry of the trees, as well as in every stage of the extraction process, meant that their yield increased ninefold – from some 400 kilograms of rubber per hectare per year to 3,500 kilos within a few decades. Thus the world's burgeoning rubber industry had a dependable supply of high-quality produce at low price – none of which could have come from the exhausted seringals of Amazonia. 'Rubber' Ridley, as he became known, continued to improve every aspect of rubber growth and extraction throughout his long life. He witnessed a jump in demand during the First World War, and the Japanese invasion of the plantations in the Second. In a history of Kew Gardens, Wilfred Blunt wrote with delightful understatement: 'Ridley, whose active life was cut short in 1956 at the age of 101, played an important part in the establishment of rubber in Malaysia.'

Amazon rubber output continued to grow until 1912, but static prices and rising costs meant that the rubber barons suffered a net loss of £9 million in that year. Malaya and Sumatra were then producing 8,500 tons compared to the Amazon's 38,000 tons. But only two years later in 1914 the Asian output had multiplied eightfold to 71,400 tons which easily surpassed the wild rubber of the seringals. During the five years 1910–15 exports from Brazilian Amazonia collapsed in value by 80 per cent. In 1919 Amazonia's 34,000 tons of rubber represented only 8 per cent of the world total. By 1923 oriental plantation rubber totalled 370,000 tons, whereas that from the Amazon was down to a mere 18,000 tons. The Amazon rubber boom had burst.

The effect on the glamorous riverbank cities was devastating. In 1912 there were £4 million worth of bankruptcies in Pará alone. Upriver in Manaus, trading houses folded and fortune-seekers and courtesans deserted the sinking ship. Many left so fast that they said their farewells through newspaper advertisements. Alfredo Arruda's marble-faced house and warehouse full of rubber were confiscated by the Bank of Amazonas; and Carlos Montenegro's luxury yacht was taken by the Bank of Brazil. The orgy-giver Waldemar Scholtz lost his mortgaged palace, fled to the Putumayo, and committed suicide. The riverboat operator João Antunes was bankrupted, but he stayed on in the streets of Manaus as a lottery-ticket hawker. Shops, bars and brothels went out of business. In that black year 1912 the auctioneer Agente Leon held 140 sales. From his research in Manaus, Richard Collier wrote that everything went under the hammer: 'the stock of the "Casa 22" department store and the gentlemen's outfitters "Havana House" ... the "Golden Globe" jewellers ... house after fancy house on Joaquim Sarmento Street ... luxury carriages ... sparkling crystal ... Steinway grands, chinoiserie tables, panther-skin rugs.... The "Paris in America" fashion store slashing £20,000 worth of perfumes to half price.' Up the Amazon in Peru, Iquitos's Malecón promenade gradually crumbled into the river.

CHAPTER SEVEN
The Black Side of Rubber

The rubber bonanza exacted a heavy price – but the victims were human, not environmental. Fortunately, tapping does not destroy rubber trees. Seringueiros' clearings and trails were mere scratches on the immensity of the Amazon forests and, since movement was all by river, there were no roads apart from the Madeira-Mamoré railway. So there was little deforestation. Fish, game and particularly turtle resources were depleted to feed and light the lamps of the rubber men and their masters in the cities. But the greatest cost of 'white gold' was in the misery of those who extracted it.

In the early decades of the boom, from the 1850s to 1880s, rubber-tapping was a form of liberation for the Amazonian working class. Because there was an acute labour shortage, caboclos could demand good treatment if they were to continue to work in plantations, public works or as boatmen. Hundreds chose to migrate up the tributaries in search of rubber. The British consul in Pará described this exodus, in 1870. 'A family gang or a single man erect a temporary hut in the forest and, living frugally on the fruit and game which abound and their provision of dried fish and [manioc] farinha, realize in a few weeks such sums of money, in an ever-ready market, with which they are able to relapse into the much-coveted idleness and enjoy their easy gains until the dry season for tapping the rubber-trees ... returns.' At first the provincial authorities resented this drain on their labour supply. One president of Pará lamented that the white-gold-rush 'is leading into misery the great mass of those who abandon their homes, small businesses and even their families to follow it. They surrender themselves to lives of uncertainty and hardship, in which the profits on one evening evaporate the following day.' Such condemnation, however, changed when presidents started to appreciate the value of rubber exports. All that money easily wiped out any scruples about how it was acquired.

The system was lubricated by itinerant traders known as *regatão* ('hawker' or 'haggler'). A regatão took his boat far up forested rivers and sold essential goods to seringueiros in return for their rubber crop. He of course made the maximum profit, selling shoddy goods at grotesquely inflated prices and buying cheaply. There was much official fury against the regatão, sometimes tinged with xenophobia because many were Levantine or Jewish. But these traders supplied seringueiros with the few goods they needed as well as some companionship, and they provided an outlet for the rubber. As the boom progressed, individual hawkers gave way to better-organized *aviadores* ('suppliers'), often equipped by and working for the big rubber companies in Manaus or Belém. Aviadores were just as shameless as regatão traders in exploiting tappers, but some were also liked because they brought supplies and friendship to isolated workers.

Some indigenous tribes entered the rubber system voluntarily, others were forced into it, yet others fled from the madness deeper into their forests. The Mundurukú was a large and formerly warlike tribe on the upper Tapajós river that took to tapping rubber – and they still do to this day. Working hard, the Mundurukú gathered large quantities of rubber. But they were woefully uncommercial, easily duped because they did not understand arithmetic. Regatão traders sold them goods at a fourfold mark-up, including quantities of cachaça rum and useless patent medicines. They were of course paid poorly for their rubber. But the tribe was at least its own master.

Far to the west, some indigenous peoples of what are now the Brazilian states of Amazonas and Acre were forced to gather rubber and kept in a state of perpetual indebtedness. Others had to work at gunpoint, with their families kept as hostages for the men's hard labour. But forest Indians were generally shunned as rubber-tappers, because most could not be persuaded to work voluntarily for the derisory goods on offer, and because as superb woodsmen they could easily escape. Some fought back, ambushing seringueiros who had wronged them – but then often suffering murderous reprisal attacks on their villages. In the lawless world of Brazil's western forests, one seringueiro told a missionary who reprimanded him for violating Indians' rights: 'We do not respect the Constitution here. We have our own constitution with one article in it – Article 44 of the Winchester constitution!' (The lethal Winchester .44 carbine was their favourite weapon.) Cândido Rondon, an army officer who became the great champion of indigenous peoples, lamented: 'What innumerable atrocities! Raids were the rule, bringing death to all the *malocas* [tribal huts or villages].... When the onslaught had passed, women knew nothing of the whereabouts of their children. Wandering, helpless tribes could scarcely recognize the sites of their former dwellings, such was the devastation!'

In the early years, the brunt of rubber labour fell to detribalized Indians, descendants of the mission and Directorate villages. Wicked rubber bosses seduced such people with 'presents' of food, cachaça rum, guns and clothing on credit, so that they ran up huge debts to be repaid in rubber. This they were of course unable to do. 'These Indians were soon victims of slavery and dishonour, and were lucky if their troubles ended quickly in death. In this way ... families and whole villages were completely extinguished.' A president of Pará wrung his hands about the exploitation of these people. From all their toil 'they achieve, instead of the dreamed-for wealth ... ruin and death. A society such as ours, of Christian morality, should not remain indifferent to the ruin, destruction and death of their inexperienced and blind class.'

Acculturated Chiriguano and Chiquito – descendants of Jesuit missions on the Mojos llanos – were brought downriver as virtual slave labourers. They worked hard to collect rubber but were paid only about 3 per cent of its value, whereas they were charged ludicrous prices for even candles and matches. A Brazilian officer was appalled by the exploitation of these native Bolivians, but when he told their masters that it was illegal to enslave Indians in Brazil, they were amazed. On the upper Madeira docile Panoan-speaking Pakawara and Karipuna were also put to work on the rubber trails. An American visitor saw a seringal manager give alcohol to these bedraggled, deculturated and impoverished people. They grimaced when they swallowed. The drink turned out to be kerosene or paraffin, but the manager 'assured us that kerosene would not hurt Indians'.

The commodity that isolated, lonely seringueiros wanted most from indigenous peoples was their women. Some indigenous partners were willing enough, but others were seized in raids, raped, or acquired by barter. Rubber bosses flaunted their power with harems of native women. A Karipuna woman who tried to escape this sexual bondage was going to be executed by being fired from a cannon, but a Brazilian officer prevented this. A Mawé girl called Francisca rebelled against the demands of a seringueiro on the lower Tapajós, and eventually shot her tormentor. At her trial in Santarém in 1871 she raised her skirt to show scars from leg-shackles. 'Before a numerous and horror-stricken audience, the Indian girl reported scenes of barbarity and disgusting licentiousness that had taken place in the depot of that ferocious man.' The jury absolved her, but it sent her accomplice, an Apiaká boy 'of sweet and attractive appearance', to life imprisonment. In a dispute between an Italian missionary and other seringueiros, the missionary complained to the President of Pará that rubber men invaded his village of Mundurukú, got Indians drunk, and stole all their possessions and food. 'They practised public prostitution by day and night in the doors of houses.... There wasn't a family of the poor Indians whose honour and dearest decorum was not abused in a horrible manner.... The mission became a veritable den of vice.' A friend of the Bolivian Suárez rounded up six hundred Indian girls on the Madre de Dios river and invited his friends to impregnate them, so that their children would grow to be slave labourers. These cases achieved public attention. Countless other sexual abuses doubtless went unnoticed in the depths of Amazonia.

One tribe at least waged successful war against rubber men. The Kawahib (known for years as Parintintin, the Mundurukú word for 'enemies') terrified anyone venturing into their forests on eastern tributaries of the middle Madeira river. An anthropologist said that the Kawahib were at war with all strangers, whites and Indians alike. 'They have not the slightest respect for the lives or property of others. For the Parintintin, war is not a tough and deplorable necessity: it is the preferred sport of boys from the age of twelve onwards.' They could attack at any hour of day or night, preferably in the dry season along a network of trails, but also during the rains using canoes that they had hidden all over their territory. They were fearless and ruthless; they killed hundreds of people; and they kept their area free of rubber seekers. But the warlike Kawahib were the exception. Most indigenous peoples were no match for the guns of the invaders: their only defence was flight.

As the world's appetite for rubber grew exponentially, demand for labour far outgrew the native population of Amazonia. The northeastern 'bulge' of Brazil met the shortage. This was a tough, dry region, where sugar grew in profusion near the Atlantic coast and the interior was cattle country, with scrawny animals driven between water-holes on the parched plains. In 1877 there was a terrible drought in the province of Ceará. During the following five years 60,000 northeasterners decided to try their luck in the Amazon. There was plenty of transport, and the government even helped some migrants with small subsidies. But the illiterate workers were easily duped. 'The seringueiro begins to owe, from the very day he leaves Ceará. He owes his steerage passage to Pará and the money he receives to equip himself. Then comes the cost of transport to the distant *barracão* [rubber depot] to which he is destined, in a *gaiola* [two-decker] launch.' He was supplied with basic possessions: 'a two-handled cooking pot, a pan, an iron hatchet, an axe, a machete, a Winchester carbine with two hundred bullets, a coffee pot, two reels of fishing line and a case of needles. Nothing more.' This kit, and some food, were supplied on credit. His boss ensured that he never emerged from that debt for the rest of his life.

Seringueiros led wretched lives. Once again, extraction of the Amazon's resources depended on exploitation of people at the base of the economic pyramid. A seringueiro typically rose long before dawn, clambering into the pitch-dark forest with a hurricane lantern. He twice plied a wearisome 8- to 10-kilometre (5–6 mile) trail to draw latex from between 70 and 150 trees. On his first round he renewed diagonal incisions in the barks and fixed up to ten gourds or metal cups per tree. He then returned to collect the latex that had oozed into the cups – before the midday heat caused it to coagulate, hence the early start. He carried the heavy harvest of nine litres of latex back to his hut in metal buckets.

Then the nastiest work started. The seringueiro had to harden the latex milk in layers around a paddle on a pole. The densest smoke for this curing came from dampened palm nuts (which also had to be gathered) burning in a beehive-shaped earthenware oven. This was a dangerous operation: an inexperienced operator could be asphyxiated by the creosote fumes billowing up from the oven. Joseph Woodroffe, an expert on the rubber industry, felt that its conditions were tougher than in the worst of Britain's satanic mills. 'At the end of the [eleven-hour] day it is not difficult to realize the state of the *seringueiro*, for he will be found after he has finished smoking his day's collection of latex with tired, sore eyes, sunken and smarting from the effects of the smoke; his body racked with spasmodic coughing and covered with smoke, dirt and soot.' The layers of rubber around the paddle formed *bolas*, great balls weighing 30 to 40 kilos (66 to 88 pounds). The creamy-white latex turned a beautiful yellow-brown from curing, and then the familiar black of commercial rubber when left in the sun.

Rubber latex did not flow well from November to January when the trees were flowering and their fruit growing. This was the height of the rainy season south of the Equator, so collecting ceased. 'During such times the weeks are grey and sad, and the seringueiro passes day after day in his hammock without any profitable occupation.' He watched the river waters rise around his hut, which was of course raised on poles. He and his family 'pass several months of the year perched in such a poor habitation, sharing it with his dogs, fowls, and a host of insects, all unable to move far owing to the water that surrounds them.' Of necessity, these immigrants learned how to hunt and fish in the rain forests.

Malaria was rampant throughout the region. But there were other diseases such as beriberi, a debilitating and often fatal condition that attacked non-Indians living in rain forests. (Beriberi is now known to be caused by deficiency of vitamin B-1, coupled with low intake of calories but excessive carbohydrates. As late as the 1930s, a lengthy expedition to survey Brazil's northern frontiers lost many men from beriberi: its leader was convinced that this was caused by masturbation, which he punished mercilessly.) There were endemic scourges like Chagas disease (transmitted by *barbeiro* bugs, still incurable, and fatal when it attacks the muscles of the heart), intestinal parasites, botflies and other bugs that lay eggs in human skin, and snake bites. The British missionary Kenneth Grubb wrote that 'the life of the seringueiro is the most miserable that could be imagined…. He has no knowledge of sanitary precautions, is barely acquainted with the use of quinine, and the effect of the constant attacks of the intolerable *pium* [biting black-fly] … is seen in a body covered with ulcers…. Under-nourishment is always present, the peril of loss and starvation in the forest constantly threatening, and the rifle the only known remedy for abuses and wrongs.' Oswaldo Gonçalves Cruz was a Brazilian doctor who gallantly tried to combat disease during the rubber boom. He lamented that 'addicted to alcohol, which they abuse to an incredible extent, the seringueiros have no proper food – and yet they pay fabulous prices for what they get. Their basic foods are dried meat and *farinha d'agua* [flour from fermented manioc]. The former almost always arrives rotting, which happens easily because of the appalling conservation and the humidity in the region.' By the late nineteenth century, some food was tinned. But vacuum-packing was unknown, so that the food inside these cans could be poisonous. Unscrupulous importers employed people called 'tin-solderers' whose job was to pierce tins swollen by bacteria or putrefaction, release the gases, and then resolder the container. 'Seringueiros in remote regions … have to eat these rotten substances or die of hunger.'

Kenneth Grubb felt that the gloom of the forests 'brings out the worst instincts of man, brutalizes the affections, hardens the emotions, and draws out with malign and terrible intention every evil and sordid lust'. Two British engineers met seringueiros who were idling away the rainy months in a riverbank town, but found them boring men who thought about nothing but rubber and money. The great Brazilian novelists José Verissimo and Euclides da Cunha chronicled the rubber trade as vividly as Victor Hugo or Charles Dickens were dramatizing the grim factories in Europe. An author who thrilled his readers with the horrors of this 'green hell' was the Colombian José Eustacio Rivera in *La Vorágine* ('The Vortex'). He wrote that 'labourers in rubber know full well that the vegetable gold enriches no one. The potentates of the forest have no credit beyond that on their books – against peons who never pay (unless with their lives), against Indians who waste away, against boatmen who rob what they transport. Slavery in these regions becomes life-long for both slave and owner.... The forest annihilates them, the forest entraps them, the forest beckons in order to swallow them up. Those who escape ... carry the curse in body and soul. Worn out, grown old and deceived, they have only one desire: to return, to return to the forest – well aware that if they return they will perish.' Euclides da Cunha wrote that when immigrant labourers entered the 'exuberant surroundings of the Hevea and Castilla trees, awaiting them was the most criminal employment organization ever spawned by unbridled selfishness'. Cunha called for a law to protect these victims; but the rubber barons ridiculed him as ignorant and demented – and for using convoluted prose.

As the demand for pure rubber exceeded supply, there was an upsurge in collecting inferior caucho latex from Castilloa trees of western Amazonia. Since those forests near the Andes had hitherto produced no commercially attractive product, they had been largely ignored by the Spanish-speaking republics that owned them. The frontier between Peru and Colombia was not even clearly defined – apart from a desire by those two larger nations to stop little Ecuador from expanding southeastwards towards the main Amazon. There was thus a political vacuum in that scarcely explored region. It provided a breeding-ground for the most evil of all the rubber barons.

Julio César Arana was born in 1864 in Rioja, a small town of the Peruvian *selva*. The son of a hat-maker, his first job was selling straw hats in the sleepy villages of the eastern Andes. At twenty-four Arana opened a trading post to supply the needs of rubber-collectors, at Tarapoto on the Huallaga river. Because he sold on credit based on rubber and the price of rubber was spiralling, he was soon making a fourfold profit. In 1890 he bought a latex-rubber circuit and spent six years in Manaus learning the rubber business. Some of his wealth came from trading rubber on the Javari/Yavari river that is the boundary between Brazil and Peru, but Arana almost died of beriberi there. In 1896 he first made his way up the Putumayo, a big northwestern headwater that joins the Amazon inside Brazil (where its name changes to Içá).

Because Peru and Colombia could not agree whether that river was the boundary between them, they submitted the matter for arbitration by Pope Pius X. In July 1906 he ruled that, pending a final agreement, all armed forces must be removed from the disputed region. The result was a political no-man's-land that Arana could exploit. A score of Colombian *caucheros* were gathering caucho latex in the middle-Putumayo region. Arana organized a flotilla of launches to take their produce down to Manaus – the only outlet they could reach by river. He thus controlled the Colombians' trade, and he got them into his debt. In his own words: 'I entered into business relations with the [Colombian] colonies [rubber depots], exchanging merchandise for rubber, buying produce and making advances.' In 1901 he went into partnership with Benjamín and Rafael Larrañaga at La Chorrera ('Rapids'), and in 1904 he bought them out for £25,000. Other Colombians followed: the Calderón brothers at El Encanto ('Enchantment'); Hipólito Pérez at Argelia; José Cabrera at Nueva Granada; and others from depots with names like Abisinia and Último Retiro ('Last Retreat'). This was done at knock-down prices, through debt-enforcement and coercion.

Arana resented the difficulty and cost of luring workers up from Brazil, particularly since his caucho latex was worth less than pure rubber from *Hevea brasiliensis*. So he turned to indigenous people for his collectors. The forests of the middle Putumayo were home to Witoto and related Bora, Andoke and Ocaína. These were populous and unwarlike peoples. They had suffered little contact – a few visits by missionaries in the seventeenth and eighteenth centuries, some trading of their sarsaparilla and cacao for tools, beads and trinkets, and glimpses of travellers who sailed up their river. So the Witoto and Bora quietly hunted and farmed forest clearings. Observers guessed that there may have been thirty thousand of them before the arrival of white settlers.

In the early days of the rubber boom, Witoto and Bora gathered caucho and exchanged it with the Colombians for the usual trade-goods. Arana changed this into a system of slave labour enforced by institutionalized violence. He divided his empire into districts, each controlled by a white 'chief' who took a commission on his area's rubber. Such a trading station or 'section' was protected by fifteen to twenty heavily armed guards. Some of these henchmen were young natives known as *muchachos* or *cholitos* (little Indians), boy-soldiers given rifles and trained in marksmanship and brutality, but who also had inherited skills in tracking down fugitives. In 1904 Arana sent his brother-in-law Abel Alarco to the British colony Barbados to recruit black overseers. Alarco signed up 196 tough West Indians on two-year contracts. About half of these reached the Putumayo, where they were soon embroiled in the brutal system. They were loathed by the Indians – both for their cruelty and because indigenous and African races generally despised one another – so they had to be loyal to their Peruvian masters.

The Putumayo's *Castilloa* trees could not be tapped but had to be felled for their caucho. At first there were plenty of Castilloa trees, each of which when destroyed yielded up to 45 kilos (100 pounds) of latex. Coagulated by smoking with soap and potassium, this was made into long rolls for Indians to carry. The resulting 'Peruvian slab' was *jebe débil* (weak rubber), used for household articles such as bath-mats or garden hoses. In 1903 the region produced some 230,000 kilos (500,000 pounds) of rubber, but by 1905 this had doubled – even though the trees were getting harder to find.

As Arana's business grew, he took his dissolute brother and more efficient brothers-in-law Abel Alarco and Pablo Zumaeta into partnership. He called his growing company J. C. Arana y Hermanos, and in 1904 opened a branch in Manaus. Julio César himself took over, worked an 18-hour day, and built it up to be the sixth-largest trading house in the city. Arana was rather different to other flamboyant rubber barons. He fancied himself as an intellectual, a sober family man and pillar of the establishment. He married a respectable wife, Eleonora, ensured that his daughters were well educated, took pride in the best library on the upper Amazon, dressed in suits and starched collars, and eventually sported a trim spade beard instead of a wild moustache. He moved his family to a fine house in Iquitos, with the motto 'Activity, Constancy, Work' over the lintel, and his sobriety and industry caused a journalist to dub him the Abel of the Amazon. In 1904 he sent his wife and daughters to Europe, to live in luxury in Biarritz.

In 1907 Arana spread a rumour that Colombia was violating the Papal arbitration by sending armed forces to the Putumayo. So he persuaded his Peruvian government to investigate in force. Forty soldiers were sent upriver, in one of Arana's boats of course. The arrival of Peruvian troops added muscle to Arana's intimidation of the few Colombian rubber-traders still active in the region. One, José Cabrera at Nueva Granada depot was forced to sell, when he himself was shot at and his men removed; the black Ildefonso González at El Dorado was equally coerced; and the magistrate Gabriel Martínez was kidnapped at gunpoint from Remolino ('Whirlpool'). David Serrano refused to sell his post La Reserva. So in December 1907 Miguel Loayza, Arana's brutal young overseer at El Encanto, sent a contingent to collect a small debt from Serrano. These enforcers tied Serrano to a tree and 'forcibly entering his [Indian] wife's room, dragged the unhappy woman out on the porch, and there, before the tortured eyes of the helpless Serrano, the chief of the [gang] outraged his unhappy victim. Not satisfied with this, they took [Serrano's] entire stock of merchandise … together with his little son and the unfortunate woman who had just been so vilely outraged.' Serrano 'heard that [down at El Encanto] his wife was being used as a concubine by the criminal Loayza, while his tender son acted as servant to the same repugnant monster.' Everything seemed set for Julio César Arana to become sole master of this very remote and lawless corner of the Amazon basin.

Arana became more ambitious. In October 1907 he incorporated his company in London and changed its name to Peruvian Amazon Rubber Company Ltd. It was controlled by Arana and Alarco, but four British and one French director lent respectability – these included the banker Henry Read and establishment figure Sir John Lister Kaye, Baronet. In December 1908 the Peruvian Amazon Company (having dropped the word 'Rubber') tried to raise capital on the London stock exchange. It offered a million £1 preference and ordinary shares. The prospectus was full of lies – that the company had legal title to its territories; that its depots were surrounded by cultivated lands; that it had the finest rubber trees as well as minerals; and that its '40,000 Indians' were being educated and civilized. Despite this hyperbole, the issue flopped.

At this critical moment a curious craft appeared on the Putumayo. It was a dugout canoe, stuffed with belongings, and paddled by two very young, dishevelled and poor Americans. The leader of the intruders was Walter Hardenburg, aged twenty-one, and his friend was William Perkins, two years older. But this Hardenburg was to become the nemesis of the mighty Arana.

Walter Hardenburg was the son of a farmer in Youngsville, New York. Soon after graduating from high school, Walter left home, did some teaching, moved to an aunt in New York, briefly enlisted in the Navy, worked for a while in the Panama Canal Zone, then helped build a railway inland from the Colombian Pacific port Buenaventura. Ambitious and motivated, Hardenburg taught himself Spanish and some engineering, and was soon earning good money managing a survey crew. He had always dreamed of seeing the Amazon, so he persuaded Perkins to join him in seeking work with the American engineers building the Madeira-Mamoré railway.

The two young adventurers decided to reach the Amazon by the Putumayo, since that river flowed in the right direction. They travelled with horses and porters through the Andes of southern Colombia and bought a big canoe on the upper river. They hired two Sioní paddlers, who skilfully steered the canoe through turbulent rapids, but after a few days these declared that they were beyond their territory, and quit. Hardenburg and Perkins paddled on. They had fun on the empty river, shooting at every sort of game – monkeys, birds, tapirs, caymans, even a big anaconda – and soon had their craft stuffed with trophies and souvenirs on top of their baggage and surveying instruments. They once ran aground and were marooned on a sandbank for six days; and Perkins had a bad attack of malaria.

Just before Christmas 1907 Hardenburg and Perkins reached their first big caucho depot, Yaracaya. Its owner Jesús López told them about the threat from

Arana's men and the Peruvian troops further down-river. After a few more days of paddling, drenched with rain and plagued by blackflies, they reached Remolino – leaderless after the kidnapping of its owner Martínez. Hardenburg decided that they must leave the Putumayo, to avoid Arana's empire by portaging south to the Napo river. So, in order to find porters, an Indian guided him for two days' walk to La Reserva, where the wretched David Serrano had just been so cruelly abused. (La Reserva was on the Cara-paraná which, with the Igara-paraná, was a northern tributary of the Putumayo. These rivers' forests contained most Castilloa latex trees and many rubber 'stations' were along their banks. *Paraná* means 'large river' in Tupi; *cara* means 'canoe' since that river was navigable; whereas *igara* means 'rough water' because of its rapids.)

Hardenburg then accompanied the outraged Serrano, two government emissaries and others down the river to confront Arana's man Loayza in a parlay at El Dorado. Loayza never came. So the group started to paddle back up the Cara-paraná. When they tried to pass Arana's Argelia post, the government official Jesús Orjuela was seized at gunpoint. Hardenburg and one other man were allowed to continue upriver. On the night of 12 January 1908 Arana's 148-ton double-decker boat *Liberal* and the smaller gunboat *Iquitos* suddenly swept down on them. Their Witoto paddlers scrambled off into the forest. Searchlights picked out their canoe, and there was a barrage of gunfire with orders to sink the small craft. Hardenburg and his companion were as overwhelmed as Humphrey Bogart and Katharine Hepburn by a similar riverboat in the film *The African Queen*. Summoned to approach the *Iquitos*, Hardenburg later recalled that 'we were jerked on board, kicked, beaten, insulted, and abused in a most cowardly manner by Captain Arce Benavides of the Peruvian army ... and a gang of coffee-coloured soldiers, sailors, and employees of the "civilising company", without being given a chance to speak a word'. They watched in horror as 'a Captain' raped Pilar Gutiérrez, the Indian wife of Rafael Cano of La Unión. She was 'in an advanced state of pregnancy.... This human monster, intent only on slaking his animal thirst of lasciviousness ... and, in spite of the cries of agony of the unfortunate creature, violated her without compunction.' The ship took them back down to Arana's western base El Encanto, where the Cara-paraná river joins the Putumayo. Perkins was already a captive on the *Liberal*, and the two Americans were 'expecting to be shot or stabbed at any moment, for our captors were drunk and in a most bloodthirsty mood'. At El Encanto they and several Colombians were thrown into a bare prison cell.

Their Peruvian captors had been reinforced with more soldiers and returned from two bloody 'victories' over heavily outnumbered Colombians. At La Reserva they killed two men and David Serrano escaped into the forest mortally wounded. At nearby La Unión, the Colombian Colonel Gustavo Prieto defiantly ordered the invaders to depart, but in the ensuing shootout between 140 men from the boats and 20 settlers, five Colombians were killed and the rest fled. Both depots were plundered of quantities of rubber and other belongings, and then burned. Arana's company was triumphant. He now controlled over 30,000 square kilometres (12,000 square miles) of rubber forests in that remote region, to which access was only by his fleet of 23 trading launches.

At El Encanto, Hardenburg obtained the Americans' release by brandishing a letter they had from a US congressman and by pretending that he and Perkins were important executives of Farquar's railway company. Miguel Loayza could not read English, so he was impressed and promised them passage to Iquitos on the *Liberal* in a few days' time. It was during those days at El Encanto that the young Americans glimpsed some of the horrors of the evil empire. They were already appalled by the attacks on Colombian rubber men – flagrant violations of the arbitrated truce – and by their own mistreatment.

All this started to change Walter Hardenburg. Despite his youth and insignificance, he decided that he must do something. In *The Putumayo, The Devil's Paradise*, a book he wrote three years later, his attitude to indigenous people changed dramatically. At first he mocked Indians as ugly little people who drank too much and were lazy and improvident. But after his walks and river journeys with the Witoto, he described them as 'a well-formed race' whose men wore bark-cloth breech-clouts but both sexes were otherwise naked. The women stooped from carrying heavy loads and 'when they walk their thighs strike against each other as though they were afraid. Notwithstanding these defects … many of these women are really beautiful, so magnificent are their figures and so free and graceful their movements…. Their breasts are periform and always prominent, even among the old, in which case they diminish in volume but never hang down.' Hardenburg marvelled at the Indians' skill in making lethally accurate blow-guns for hunting. He admired their elaborate system of *manguare* bush-telegraph. A pair of large hollowed tree-trunks was suspended from the roof of a hut, each giving a different note when pounded. 'A code is arranged, based upon the difference of tones and the length and number of the blows struck, so that all kinds of messages can be exchanged.' Hardenburg himself heard such exchanges carried over 10 kilometres (6 miles). By hitting these logs with a rubber-tipped drumstick, in different rhythms, the 'telegrapher' could announce festivals, summon council meetings, or send other information. Another traveller was equally enchanted by these indigenous peoples. The young British cavalry officer Captain Thomas Whiffen was on the Putumayo just after the two Americans. Although untrained as an anthropologist, Whiffen amassed a wealth of valuable information about the Bora, Witoto and related peoples. Most aspects of their life impressed him – from magnificent huts and elaborate dances to hunting skills, the powers of shamans and spiritual beliefs. He even explained and excused their occasional ritual-eating of executed captives. He loved the Indians' appearance, with the men slim but strong, and the women with 'a beautiful figure, well proportioned and supple, with high, straight shoulders'.

At El Encanto Hardenburg watched emaciated and malaria-stricken men and women unload the boats. They were given only a handful of manioc flour and occasionally a quarter share of a tin of sardines. 'And this was to sustain them for twenty-four hours, sixteen of which were spent at the hardest kind of labour!' It was 'pitiful to see the sick and dying lie about the house and out in the adjacent woods, unable to move and without anyone to aid them in their agony. These poor wretches, without remedies, without food, were exposed to [the elements] until death released them from their sufferings. Then their companions carried their cold corpses ... to the river, and the yellow, turbid waters of the Caraparaná closed silently over them.' Hardenburg was outraged by this 'perpetual and devilish carnival of crime'.

The two Americans decided that Hardenburg should sail to Iquitos, to see whether he could do anything about these horrors. Perkins would remain at El Encanto in the hope of recovering their stolen possessions. During his journey Hardenburg visited Arana's other main base, La Chorrera on the Igara-paraná river. It was run by Victor Macedo, as brutal a psychopath as Loayza at El Encanto. This was the home of Bora Indians who were also slaves of the company. The launch Liberal sailed down into Brazil and back up the main Amazon to Iquitos. The American was in his hammock on deck, but nine Colombians (including the government official Orjuela and the magistrate Martínez) were in the hold, crammed into a tiny cage in which they could scarcely move.

Hardenburg reached Peru's rubber city in February 1908. Iquitos was still quite small, with only 12,000 inhabitants. Buildings around the central square were faced in bright tiles, but other houses were of split-bamboo and thatch. Many people lived – as they still do – over Amazon waters in the picturesque but primitive district of Belén, where huts are on stilts or floating on rafts linked by rickety gangplanks. Hardenburg had no money, but he was soon earning £10 a month by teaching English at a school and £30 a month for helping to design a hospital. He also wired home to ask his mother for $300 she was keeping for him. He looked up the American Consul, a dentist called Dr Guy King. To the disgust of the young idealist, Dr King 'contented himself with congratulating me upon my narrow escape from death at the hands of the assassins of Arana and informing me that, owing to various circumstances, he could do absolutely nothing for us!' The Consul said that his predecessor had in 1907 told the US Secretary of State that investors should avoid the Putumayo because of Arana's gun-law abuse of Colombians. The widower Dr King did, however, provide lodgings for Hardenburg during what proved to be a seventeen-month stay in Iquitos.

The city was dominated by Arana – his brother-in-law had been its mayor, and he himself was president of the chamber of commerce and controlled many activities through his family, employees and agents. Soon after Hardenburg's arrival he heard that Arana was in town and bravely went to call on him. He hoped that the tycoon might be unaware of the horrors in his rubber domain. Julio César Arana was dignified and aloof, but the American realized that he was not only aware of what was happening but had organized it. So when Arana asked Hardenburg what he had seen on the Putumayo, the young man was noncommittal and spoke only about his stolen belongings.

Hardenburg watched the demolition of the printing business of one Benjamín Saldaña Rocca who had dared to publish a newsletter attacking Arana. This periodical, called *La Sanción* and then *La Felpa* ('The Thrashing'), had given eyewitness accounts of the Putumayo atrocities by men who had worked there. Not surprisingly, it lasted for only a few months in 1907–1908 and most copies of it were destroyed. But before being expelled from Iquitos, Saldaña and his son gave Hardenburg their notarized depositions and helped him track down others to tell their dreadful revelations. In April William Perkins arrived from the Putumayo, weak and ill, without any of their stolen baggage, and with more atrocities to add to his friend's dossier – including the murders of every Colombian who had been captured with them. Perkins was desperate to leave the Amazon, so Hardenburg bought his passage home from the $300 sent by his mother.

The eyewitness accounts published in Saldaña's newsletter or obtained by Hardenburg were gruesome. But they were crucially important in the saga of the Putumayo. They were given by ordinary employees, who wanted to do something to end the reign of terror they had witnessed. These men did so under oath before a notary public, Federico Pizarro, and said that it was to help the Indians, for justice, or for the good name of their nation. Their accounts were full of circumstantial details and were entirely convincing. It was these testimonies that changed young Walter Hardenburg from an appalled and angry traveller into a passionate crusader against evil.

La Felpa told how Arana's section chiefs – the 'famous bandits' Armando Normand, Abelardo Agüero, Miguel Loayza, the brothers Aurélio and Arístedes

Rodríguez, and others – imposed on every Indian a quota of 5 *arrobas* (75 kilos; 165 pounds) of rubber every quarter. When they and their wives and children staggered into the depot with this impossibly heavy load, it was weighed. If the needle reached the required amount, they laughed with delight; but if not, they prostrated themselves to await punishment. 'They are generally given fifty lashes with scourges until the flesh drops from their bodies in strips, or else are cut to pieces with machetes. This barbarous spectacle takes place before all the rest, among whom are their women and children.' A witness called Julio Muriedas testified that at Normand's depot La Chorrera if an Indian fled, 'they take his tender children, suspend them by their hands and feet, and in this position apply fire so that under this torture they will tell where their father is hidden'. Muriedas had seen Indians with insufficient rubber 'shot, or their arms and legs are cut off with machetes and the body is thrown around the house'. He also reported the thrashing of four tribal chiefs. Chief Cuyo 'was flogged to death and the others, after the flagellation, were kept chained up for several months, all for the "crime" of their people in not delivering the number of kilos of rubber fixed by the company'.

The witness Anacleto Portocarrera swore that when he was at Último Retiro in 1906 its boss José Inocente Fonseca committed countless crimes. On one occasion, Fonseca saw several Indians going to fetch water. He took a revolver and carbine and, saying to his white companions '"Look, this is how we celebrate the *sábado de gloria* [the day before Easter] here", wantonly let fly at the Indians, killing one man and hitting a girl of fifteen' who was then dispatched with a rifle bullet. One of Fonseca's nine concubines was accused of 'infidelity' during his absence. 'Enraged, he tied her up to a tree by her open arms and, raising her skirt to her neck, flogged her with an enormous lash, continuing until he was tired out. He then put her in a hammock inside a warehouse, and as the scars received no treatment in a few days maggots bred in them; then by his orders the Indian girl was dragged out and killed.'

Carlos Soplín told Saldaña that during ten weeks at Monte Rico, 'I have seen more than three hundred Indians flogged' with between 20 and 200 lashes, 'this latter number being given when they wish to kill him on the spot by flogging.' Then, during four months at Esmeraldas station, Soplín watched over 400 people flogged, of all ages and both sexes. The 'Inspector of Sections', Bartolomé Guevara, killed two chiefs there. 'This is the individual who introduced the method of having men tied to four stakes and flogging them.... He says that Indians must either work or die, for he does not wish to return to his country poor. This terrible man must have flogged over five thousand Indians during the six years he has resided in this region.' He was also said to have shot many white Colombians.

Another witness said that he had seen nine of Arana's bosses – all of whom he named – personally murder Indians with their own hands, and another, Andrés O'Donnell, order over five hundred to be killed. In just over a year at Matanzas, under the orders of Normand, 'I saw ten Indians killed and burnt, and three hundred were flogged who died slowly, for their wounds are not treated, and ... they kill them with bullets and machetes and afterwards burn some of them. Others are thrown aside and, as they rot, emit an insupportable stench. This section stinks so that at times it is impossible to remain there on account of the rotting flesh of the dead and dying Indians.'

A Brazilian, João Batista Braga, had been a fireman on one of Arana's launches on the Putumayo and then in 1904 rejoined the company as boss of 65 Peruvians. His section head, Abelardo Agüero, showed him how he treated prisoners. 'Taking eight Indians out of the *cepo* [tree-trunk stocks] where they had been barbarously martyrised, he had them tied to eight posts in the patio and, after drinking a bottle of cognac with his partner [Augusto] Jiménez, they began to murder these unfortunates, who perished, giving vent to horrible shrieks.' Their crime was attempted escape. Three months later, Braga was ordered to shoot 35 chained men, for the same offence. He refused, on the grounds that he was a Brazilian who could not do this. So Jiménez was told 'to murder those thirty-five unfortunates, still in chains, in cold blood'; but Braga was then victimized by starvation (forced to survive on forest plants, which he listed) and prevented from leaving. 'During these three years and eight months of prison I had the opportunity of seeing an infinity of atrocities.' A chief called Iubitide was tied up and shot because he refused to surrender his wife to Jiménez. Another chief, Tiracahuaca, and his wife were held in chains for a month so that their people would come to work for the depot. When 'the tribe did not come, [Jiménez] ordered a can of kerosene to be poured over them, and then, striking a match, he set fire to these unfortunates, who fled to the forest uttering the most desperate cries.' Braga finally escaped by night in an Indian canoe with two other white victims, while Arana's men were drunk after an orgy on Peru's National Day, 28 July 1908.

Hardenburg contacted other potential informants during his months in Iquitos. Juan Rosas testified that at Abisinia in August 1903 he observed Agüero behead a man, cut off women's limbs, burn dead bodies, and put some fifty Indians in the stocks. 'As he gave them neither water nor food, the poor Indians began to dry up like pieces of wood, until they reached such an extreme as to be quite useless and dying. Then he tied them up to a post and exterminated them by using them as targets for his Mauser revolver.' Rosas was moved to Morelia. He saw its boss, the psychopath Jiménez, put fifteen Indian prisoners in the stocks.

As one, dying of hunger, begged to be killed outright, Jiménez released him by cutting his leg off with his machete and ordered him to be dragged off, killed and burned. In 1904 Rosas was under Aurelio Rodríguez at Santa Catalina and watched one raiding party bring back forty indigenous prisoners. These were put into the stocks, but they were already stricken with smallpox. 'Although they were in a most pitiable condition, Rodríguez took them out, one by one, and used them as targets to practise shooting at.... The vicinity of the house where this man lives is sown with skeletons.' O'Donnell, chief of Entre Ríos, was equally cruel to any Indians who failed to bring in enough rubber, punishing, mutilating and murdering them. Rosas repeatedly emphasized that 'I can vouch for these crimes as I saw them with my own eyes'.

One Celestino López told Hardenburg that at Abisinia Abelardo Agüero kept a harem of eight 'girls from nine to sixteen years'. One of these was seen talking to a Peruvian. 'They suspended the poor woman from a rafter ... and lashed her for two hours without compunction, and then, regardless of her sex, they removed her garment and exhibited her naked body, bruised and cut to pieces by the lash.' López witnessed Indians being punished for bringing too little rubber. 'They were scourged with such fury that their backs and hips were completely cut to pieces, the blood rushing from their wounds.... I withdrew, for I could not endure it nor the diabolical jokes and laughter of those fiends upon seeing the desperate agony of their victims.' At Santa Julia he 'saw three Indian women flogged most barbarously, without the slightest reason, by order of the notorious Manuel Aponte.... This flogging, like all the rest I have seen in this awful region, was excessively inhuman; but, not content with this, these fiends, after flogging the poor women, put salt and vinegar into their wounds so as to increase the pain.'

Another witness was at Armando Normand's section Matanzas. In June 1907 he saw a gang return from a raid, bringing thirty Indians in chains. Normand went up to three elderly women and their two daughters and asked them where the rest of their tribe was. They said that they did not know – its people had dispersed into the forest to escape his raiders. 'Normand then grasped his machete and murdered these five unfortunate victims in cold blood.' Their bodies were left near the house, and Normand's dogs soon dismembered them: 'The morning is rare that they do not appear with an arm or a leg of a victim at the bedside of this monster.' The rest of the captives were locked in tree-trunk stocks, and Normand ordered that they get no food. Before long, 'they began to fall ill and utter cries of pain and desperation; whenever this occurred, Normand grasped his machete and cut them to pieces.' Three weeks later, another gang led in a chief with his family. He was asked why his people had failed to deliver enough rubber, and said that the

with some of his men. While prisoners were being taken back, five were beheaded with machetes – including Katenere's six-year-old daughter – and the raid's leader boasted that he had left the trail looking 'pretty': strewn with headless corpses. Katenere later died a hero's death while leading an attack on Abisinia station.

Walter Hardenburg became increasingly aware that he could achieve nothing in Arana's base, Iquitos. The rubber baron's spies were everywhere. When the American tried to get some of his depositions copied, the photographer refused and reported him to Arana's agents. Hardenburg sailed down to Manaus, partly to get another confession, and also to see whether he could stir up opinion in the Brazilian rubber metropolis. In June 1908 the Colombian government had persuaded the Manaus newspaper *O Jornal do Commercio* to publish accusations against the Peruvian aggressors. But Arana's company was an important trader in Manaus and in that boom-town money spoke louder than wronged Colombians or terrorized indigenous people, so the exposés ceased.

Back in Iquitos, young Hardenburg made an extraordinary decision. He guessed that the only place where he might obtain justice was in faraway London, the financial capital to which Arana had moved his nefarious company. So in June 1909 he bought a passage on a Booth Line steamer. Even though he travelled steerage this cost him £40 (then almost $100) – a large part of his meagre wealth. When he reached London, Hardenburg took lodgings opposite St Pancras station and went the rounds of the national newspapers. Not surprisingly, no editor would touch the twenty-two-year-old American farm-boy's wild accusations. He alleged horrors in the most distant corner of the Amazon jungles, and defamed a company whose directors included pillars of the British establishment.

Hardenburg's breakthrough came when he met the Reverend John Harris of the Anti-Slavery Society, which was then merging with the Aborigines' Protection Society. Founded in 1839 and 1837 respectively, these were the world's oldest human rights organizations. Harris's Society had just waged a successful campaign to expose rubber-trade horrors perpetrated by the Belgian King Leopold in the Congo 'Free State'. King Leopold posed as the enlightened bringer of Christianity to darkest Africa, when he was in fact turning the Congo into his personal commercial fiefdom. The Belgians had imported Amazonian rubber seeds to Africa, just as the British, Dutch and French had done to Southeast Asia. To get this latex, the King's agents terrorized Africans as ruthlessly as Arana did Amazonians. The Belgian King's pious hypocrisy was exposed by two men – a shipping clerk called Edmund Morel and a British consul Roger Casement. Morel noticed that Elder Dempster ships brought lucrative cargo from the Congo, but went out carrying little more than guns, ammunition and shackles. Morel resigned from the shipping company, wrote a powerful diatribe, *The Congo Scandal*, and became a passionate campaigner. Casement, a Protestant from Northern Ireland, joined the consular service in 1892, and after postings in southern Africa was sent in 1903 to establish a consulate in the Congo port of Boma. Casement went inland to investigate the rubber traffic and was appalled by its brutality. His angry despatches were published as a government White Paper, and the allegations were confirmed by an official Belgian report in 1905. The Rev. John Harris was a missionary in the Congo when Casement was there and had also seen the rubber atrocities. So the Anti-Slavery Society, which Harris was now running, vigorously pursued the campaign.

Harris was the first to believe Hardenburg's terrible revelations about the Putumayo. He introduced him to Sydney Paternoster, assistant editor of a weekly called *Truth* – a curious mixture of doggerel verse, gossip and often-outrageous political crusading. The editors of this magazine obtained corroboration from Colombian diplomats and, more guardedly, from David Cazes, the British honorary consul in Iquitos who happened to be home on leave. They were impressed that the Peruvian government offered to compensate Hardenburg and Perkins with £500 for their sufferings – almost an admission of guilt.

Truth started to publish Hardenburg's revelations on 22 September 1909, under the headline: 'The Devil's Paradise. A British-Owned Congo'. The magazine opened with an electrifying article from *La Sanción*. This told how Arana's agents forced the Putumayo Indians to work on rubber extraction day and night without pay or food. 'They rob them of their own crops, their women and their children, to satisfy the voracity, lasciviousness and avarice of themselves and their employees, for they live on the Indians' food, keep harems of concubines, buy and sell these people wholesale and retail in Iquitos; they flog them inhumanely until their bones are laid bare...; they mutilate them, cut off their ears, fingers, arms and legs; they torture them by means of fire and water, and by tying them up, crucified head down; they cut them to pieces with machetes;' – and so on, in horrific detail. The story ran for six weeks, giving most of Hardenburg's and Saldaña's notarized eyewitness accounts.

A Member of Parliament tabled a question asking whether the Foreign Secretary knew about the activities of the Peruvian Amazon Company and its British subjects from Barbados. The Foreign Office was taken by surprise: papers later made public showed that the diplomats knew absolutely nothing about the Company or the region. They put these terrible accusations to Arana, who sent a typically suave reply. He dismissed everything as the ravings of aggrieved employees – all of whom had been dismissed and some of whom were serving prison sentences (he named their jails). His company attempted to blacken Hardenburg's character, claiming that in Iquitos he had forged a letter of credit and had demanded £7,000 as hush-money for not revealing his evidence. The amateur anthropologist Captain Whiffen was also accused of attempted blackmail. The *Morning Leader*, a rival of *Truth*, gleefully published these stories. But Arana's staff then made a mistake. They pressed an envelope of money on a journalist from the *Morning Leader*, in gratitude but unaware that the British press did not welcome bribes. So this newspaper changed its stance, with a damning article: 'Our Congo; Strange Story of a Banknote; Peruvian Amazon Company and the *Morning Leader*'.

Walter Hardenburg, who alone had told the world about the Putumayo, was poorer than ever. *Truth* did not pay for campaigning articles, and he could not get a job in London. Early in 1910 he married a young friend of his landlady, and when the first compensation money arrived from Peru the couple emigrated to Canada. Julio César Arana moved his family from France to a large house north of Hyde Park. His daughters were enrolled in a Catholic school; and his household staff of fourteen included two governesses and, ironically, a Witoto boy whom Arana placed in a school in Kent in the hope that he would eventually become a doctor. But Arana was not able to enjoy a life of respectable affluence. The Foreign Office continued its correspondence against him; there were more questions in Parliament; and the Dean of Hereford denounced the Company's abuse of Indians.

In June 1910 the Peruvian Amazon Company suddenly announced that it was sending a commission of enquiry to the Putumayo – at the request of Mr Arana and his aggrieved Peruvian employees. The commission consisted of the tropical agronomist Louis Barnes, a rubber expert, a trader, and the Company Secretary Henry Gielgud, all of whom were likely to give a whitewash. So John Harris of the Anti-Slavery Society wrote to Roger Casement telling him about the Putumayo and asking him to join the team. Casement was the ideal man for this. After helping to expose the Congo rubber atrocities, he had spent two years of sick leave in Ireland (during which he started to become passionate about Irish nationalism). Casement was then sent to Brazil, briefly as Consul in Belém do Pará and in 1908 as Consul-General in the capital Rio de Janeiro. In 1910 Casement was again on leave in Ireland, so he hurried to London. Harris and some concerned MPs persuaded the Foreign Secretary Sir Edward Grey to send Casement to join the Company's commission, in order to investigate British interests and the British subjects from Barbados.

Casement and the commission reached Iquitos at the beginning of September 1910. After two weeks interviewing Barbadians and others in the town, the group sailed to the Putumayo. They reached the depot La Chorrera on the 22nd; moved up the Igara-paraná to Occidente where they stayed for a week; then more sailing and a few days at the notorious Último Retiro station. Returning down-stream, they made a tough 20-kilometre (12-mile) walk to Entre Ríos (between the Putumayo and Caquetá rivers) where they were based for a fortnight apart from two rugged excursions – four days to Matanzas (in Andoke territory near the Caquetá) and a day southwards to Atenas. They then walked and sailed back to La Chorrera, where they stayed during the first half of November. The other commissioners moved on, for a further two months at the western base El Encanto, but Casement left after almost eight weeks in Arana's Putumayo empire.

As a British diplomat, Roger Casement held his main purpose to be the welfare of the men from Barbados. By 1910 most of these had left Peru – many to seek work building the Madeira-Mamoré railway – so there were only a few in Iquitos and a score in the various stations on the Putumayo. Casement handled these men brilliantly. Many had been forced to commit atrocious crimes, and they were understandably frightened and suspicious of the tall white diplomat. Casement treated them with respect and patience, and thus coaxed their horrible stories from them. Some lied or said that they had seen nothing. But the majority confirmed the atrocities in Hardenburg's testimonies, often adding circumstantial evidence, confessing their own roles, or giving details of other crimes. By the end, some who had lied returned to Casement to apologize and give their true accounts. Casement reported to the Foreign Secretary that 'the Barbados men were not savages. With few exceptions they could read and write, some of them well. They were much more civilised than the great majority of those placed over them – they were certainly far more humane.' Their statements left no doubt in Casement's mind, 'nor in the minds of the commission sent out by the Peruvian Amazon Company, that the method of exacting rubber from the Indians was arbitrary, illegal, and in many cases cruel in the extreme, and the direct cause of very much depopulation'.

Casement often recorded his reactions to these Barbadians in his journal. A typical entry was about James Chase who 'asserted in the most painfully timid manner, that was all the more convincing, that he had seen Indians shot and flogged to death'. On that same afternoon at La Chorrera, Stanley Sealy 'spoke like a man throughout and my heart warmed to the ugly black face, shifting from side to side, his fingers clasping and unclasping, but the grim truth coming out of his lips. Yes, he had flogged Indians himself – many times – very many times – at Abisinia.... The [station's] Chief decided which Indian was to be flogged. It was always for not bringing in rubber – some getting 25 lashes, some 12, some 6; and some only 2 – according as the rubber was "short".' Augustus Walcott told Casement how he saw an Indian burned on the orders of Aurelio Rodríguez. '"He had not work *caucho*. He ran away and he kill a *muchacho* a boy, and they cut off his two arms and legs by the knee and they burn his body." Question: "And he still living?" Answer: "Yes, he still living." ... Question: "Are you sure he was still alive ... when they threw him on the fire?" Answer: "Yes, he did alive, I'm sure of it. I see him move – open his eyes, he screamed out."'

If the Barbadians ever refused to inflict tortures or commit murders, or if they had any argument with their white bosses, they themselves were savagely punished. Walcott had been hung up with his arms behind his back and beaten, so that he had to be carried in a hammock and could not use his arms for two months. Another, Joshua Dyall, was put in stocks with holes far too small for his ankles and with his legs extended four holes apart, so that he suffered acute pain. He could not walk when released, and bore scars for life from his ordeal.

The two months in Arana's rubber forests were a terrible ordeal for Casement. He worked very hard, extracting dozens of confessions, discussing the situation with his colleagues and Arana's employees, writing his journal late into the night, and sending letters and reports. He travelled extensively, in the enervating humidity. He personally measured the tree-trunk stocks, weighed loads of rubber, photographed all possible evidence, and inspected the Company's account books to show how outrageously it cheated its own workers. He wrote to a Foreign Office friend: 'Since coming to Iquitos I have been ill and my eyes are very weak. The heat has been stifling up here, and mosquitoes day and night....' The mental strain of hearing and seeing so many horrors must also have been intense for such a sensitive man. He confided to his journal: 'One is surrounded by criminals on all sides. The host at the head of the table [Macedo] a cowardly murderer, the boys who wait on you, and the whole bag of tricks.' He hated having to live alongside 'the snake-like Velarde and the burn-em-alive Jiménez' or Abelardo Agüero, a 'rapacious-faced individual – bold and hawk-like'. Even worse was the 'stout, rather gentlemanly-looking' José Inocente Fonseca. Casement wrote: 'I shuddered, positively, when I had to shake hands with this monster', because he had just heard the Barbadian Stanley Lewis tell how Fonseca shot girls at Último Retiro, and James Chase declare that 'this awful wretch killed a man in the *cepo* [stocks] by smashing his testicles and private parts with a thick stick – a poor young Indian who had simply run away from working rubber'.

Worst of all was Armando Normand, who had been running Matanzas station near the Caquetá since 1904. Casement reported to Sir Edward Grey that Normand was a Bolivian of foreign parentage, largely educated in England. The crimes alleged against him 'seem wellnigh incredible. They included innumerable murders and tortures of defenceless Indians – pouring kerosene oil on men and women and then setting fire to them, burning men at the stake, dashing the brains out of children, and again and again cutting off the arms and legs of Indians and leaving them to speedy death in this agony.... Westerman Leavine, whom Normand sought to bribe to withhold testimony from me, finally declared that he had again and again been an eyewitness of these deeds.... Normand ... had directly killed "many hundreds" of [Andoke] Indians – men, women, and children. The indirect deaths due to starvation, floggings, exposure, and hardship of various kinds in collecting rubber or transferring it ... must have accounted for a still larger number.' In addition to the testimonies of the Barbadians, the visitors saw enough to persuade them that they were, in the words of Casement's journal, in 'a pirate camp ... a vile squalid place'.

The Witoto and Bora delighted in traditional dance festivals. Whiffen devoted two chapters of his book to dance, because 'it gives opportunity for the aesthetic, artistic, dramatic, musical, and spectacular aspirations of the Indian's nature. It is his one social entertainment, and he invites to it every one living in amity with him.' The preparations were extremely elaborate, in food and drink, body paint and decoration, and in hundreds of people walking in from a wide catchment. Everything was governed by ritual, in the music and dances, in the chiefs' songs, and the movements of the men and women for hours on end. The visiting commission was twice 'entertained' by such dances, performed by Indians who had delivered their rubber to stations. But the effect was not as intended by the Peruvian masters. These dances, by emaciated and exhausted people far from their villages, were listless affairs. Most dancers bore 'Arana's mark' – scars from flogging. The commissioners learned that the number of dances permitted to the Indians was rationed to four a year – in order not to inter-fere with their rubber-gathering.

In his diary Casement exploded with rage. 'Poor Indians! Everything they like, everything that to them means life, and such joy as this dim forest at the end of the world can furnish to a lost people, is not theirs, but belongs to this gang of cut-throat half castes. Their wives, their children are the sport and playthings of these ruffians. They, fathers of families, are marched in, guarded by armed ruffi-ans, to be flogged on their naked bodies, before the terrified eyes of their wives and children. Here we see all before us, men and husbands and fathers, bearing the indelible marks of the lash over their buttocks and thighs, and administered for what and by whom? For not bringing in a wholly lawless and infamous toll of rubber, imposed on them ... by an association of vagabonds, the scum of Peru and Colombia, who have been assembled here by Arana Bros. and then formed into an English Company with a body of stultified English gentlemen – or fools – or worse – at their head.'

Casement was delighted by the beauty of the indigenous people. He described Bora men as 'not tall or big really, yet wonderfully graceful and clean limbed. They walked as steadily as machines.... Many of them had fine limbs, strong arms and beautiful thighs and legs, although nowhere any remarkable development of muscle. It was simply that they were all over well and perfectly made children of the forest, inheriting ages of its wild free life.' Casement deplored how an Indian was robbed of everything but 'his fine healthy body capable of supporting terrible fatigue, his shapely limbs and fair, clean skin – marred by the lash and scarred by execrable blows. His manhood has been lashed and branded out of him.... One looks then at the oppressors – vile, cut-throat faces: grim, cruel lips and sensual mouths, bulging eyes and lustful – men incapable of good.' The Company's agents did absolutely no physical work. 'It is this handful of murderers who, in the name of civilisation and of a great association of English gentlemen, are the possessors of so much gentler and better flesh and blood.'

In addition to hearing the appalling depositions, Casement and his colleagues themselves saw abundant evidence of cruelty and slavery. They inspected stocks at each station (some of them crudely hidden under palm fronds), saw harems of delicate girls everywhere, and frequently examined, photographed or tried to heal scarred and gashed Indians. Casement told his Foreign Secretary that 'the implement used for flogging was invariably a twisted strip, or several strips plaited together, of dried tapir-hide ... sufficiently stout to cut a human body to pieces.' When the observers were walking back from Matanzas they were alongside a column of two hundred Andoke and Bora carrying loads of rubber. They thus saw the difficulty of the trail, the great distance walked (up to 100 kilometres, or 60 miles), the huge weight of loads (some they weighed were over 45 kilos, or 100 pounds), the emaciated state of some of the men, women and children porters, the armed *muchachos* guarding the column, Peruvians forcing the Indians to walk for twelve hours on end, and Normand with an armed gang at the rear to catch fugitives or stragglers. They were appalled to see that these porters received no food whatever and were reduced to grabbing forest seeds as they walked; and when they reached their destination they were forced to sleep in the forest, unfed. Casement occasionally succoured exhausted, sick or dying individuals.

Casement was dismayed by the commission's inefficiency. It had little discipline, and an inadequate recording system. But, one by one, the inspectors came to acknowledge the horrors. Even the Company Secretary Gielgud changed from 'seeing no evil' to vowing that things must change. But by the end of the investigation, Casement and the commission member Barnes felt that it was all so rotten that no remedy was possible. The Peruvian Amazon Company must be liquidated and disappear. However, the Indians still seemed doomed. Casement wondered whether an international outcry could compel these countries to protect their indigenous peoples.

Casement's 135-page Report to the Foreign Secretary of 17 March 1911 included all the unspeakable crimes told by the Barbadians. Sir Edward Grey said that 'of all the things I have ever read that have occurred in modern times ... the accounts of the brutalities in Putumayo are the most horrible'. The Foreign Office sent Casement's report to its diplomats in Peru. President Augusto Leguia of Peru said that he was horrified and would act. Finally, in July 1911 a Putumayo Commission was sent under Dr Rómulo Paredes, owner of the Iquitos newspaper *Oriente* and related to Arana's manager. Perhaps surprisingly, this Peruvian commission fully confirmed the crimes and issued an amazing 215 arrest warrants. Dr Paredes's newspaper praised Casement. But nothing else happened. There was a xenophobic reaction in the Lima press, declaring that Arana was innocent and the hypocritical British should mind their own business.

Perhaps more worryingly, evidence emerged early in 1911 of abuse of Indians by British rubber companies in other parts of Peru. These companies were active on the Inambari and Tambopata headwaters of the Madre de Dios in southwestern Peru. The Lima newspaper *La Prensa* drew attention to the practices of the Inambari Pará Rubber Company (related to Harrison and Crossfield Ltd.) and the Anti-Slavery Society tried to take up this cause. Then missionaries accused the nearby Tambopata Rubber Syndicate (a subsidiary of the guano fertilizer producers Anthony Gibbs and Sons) of disgraceful oppression of indigenous peoples. American companies were also named. But these areas had no Walter Hardenburg to arouse public opinion. So they – and others throughout the rubber forests of Peru, Brazil and Bolivia – were never investigated, and no guilty parties were punished.

Meanwhile, in London, Casement's report was sent to the Peruvian Amazon Company, whose British directors were at a loss what to do. They tried in vain to dismiss guilty employees; they were flabbergasted to learn that Arana's brother-in-law Pablo Zumaeta had mortgaged all the Company's rubber interests to Arana's wife for a mere £65,000, to settle a debt it was alleged to owe the Aranas; they wanted to send an Englishman to run the Putumayo estates but found that the Company was too poor to afford this. The board finally decided to wind up the rotten Company. But the liquidator appointed to do this was none other than Julio César Arana!

Roger Casement's excellent investigation was recognized by a knighthood, conferred by King George V in July 1911. (The King, Casement and Arana all sported identical dark and neatly trimmed spade beards.) In the following month, the

Foreign Office sent Casement back to the Peruvian Amazon to see whether the Peruvian authorities had done anything. He was furious to learn that two of the worst torturers, José Inocente Fonseca and Alfredo Montt, had escaped with ten kidnapped Bora slaves – with the connivance of the Peruvian police sent to arrest them – and were tapping rubber on the Javari river. When Casement reached Iquitos in October, his worst fears were confirmed. The Peruvians' commission had visited all twenty-six stations in the Putumayo, but it returned with only one minor official in custody. 'All the rest of the accused were stated to have "escaped", in some cases ... taking with them ... captive Indians, either for sale or for continued forced labour in other regions of the rubber-bearing forests.' The Commissioner, Dr Paredes, showed Casement his powerful 1,300-page report, which described the Company's agents as 'all drunkards, chewers of coca, idlers corrupted to the lowest possible degree.... Diseased in their minds ... they slaughtered and slaughtered without pity entire Indian tribes.' But of the 215 men named in warrants, only nine had been arrested. The only important criminal in jail was Aurelio Rodríguez – and he was released soon after. The chief of police admitted to Casement that everyone knew that Pablo Zumaeta was living comfortably in Iquitos; Elias Martinengui had been seen in Lima; and Victor Macedo was openly in the capital city. A disillusioned Casement wrote: 'We may expect the ... trial [of the criminals] to begin long after we are dead and the last Putumayo Indian has been gathered, in fragments, to his fathers.'

The British tried to involve the United States, and in October 1911 it promised that its Minister in Lima would support the campaign. The new American and British consuls in Iquitos went to inspect the Putumayo. But they had to travel in one of Arana's vessels, and they were accompanied by a Peruvian diplomat Carlos Rey de Castro (who had been given a large loan by Arana's company) and by Julio César Arana himself. The British consul, George Michell, was impressed by his hosts' determination to watch the foreigners' every move. 'Though totally unfitted physically for severe exercise, [the Peruvian diplomat] followed us over fatiguing roads, through heat and storms wherever we went, while Señor Arana, a heavy man, no longer young, and suffering acutely from sciatica, also accompanied us, uncomplaining but indefatigable.' Predictably, they saw nothing other than dances by apparently contented Indians who had been coached to call their boss 'Papa Arana'. Sir Roger Casement was ordered to return to England via the United States in order to rouse it to action. In January 1912 the British Ambassador in Washington arranged for Casement to meet President William Howard Taft. They discussed the Monroe Doctrine and what the United States could do about the rubber-trade atrocities.

The Foreign Secretary Grey noted that a greater tonnage of rubber was shipped from the Putumayo in the first quarter of 1912 than throughout the previous year. 'These figures can only have been rendered possible by a continuance of the old system of forced labour.' In July the exasperated British government took the unusual decision to publish Casement's full report of the previous year as an official *Putumayo Blue Book*. It was written in his passionate style rather than the usual dry Foreign Office prose – full of emotional words such as 'unspeakable', 'atrocious' and 'revolting', Arana's agents were 'villains', and indigenous people 'souls'. There was public outrage. Members of Parliament tabled repeated questions. Newspapers were full of indignant editorials – *The Spectator*, unaware of the Andes mountains, thundered that the Pacific coast of Peru should be blockaded to prevent the export of rubber. Canon Herbert Henson of Westminster Abbey denounced each director of the Company by name from the pulpit.

H. H. Asquith's Liberal government had to respond to the public outcry. Three weeks after the publication of the *Putumayo Blue Book*, it announced a Select Committee of the House of Commons to investigate the Peruvian Amazon Company's conduct and decide what should be done to avoid similar disgrace in future. The twelve-man Select Committee included such luminaries as William Joynson-Hicks (a future Home Secretary) and the famous MP and KC Swift Mac-Neill. The Company was allowed to be defended, and its legal team included the Prime Minister's son Raymond Asquith and Douglas Hogg (the future Lord Chancellor Lord Hailsham). Work began in November 1912, with witness after witness confirming events that had taken place in London, Barbados and Peru. Casement appeared before the Committee twice to reiterate the evidence in his report, illustrated by horrible photographs of scarred Indians and the instruments of torture. Under savage cross-questioning, the Company's directors admitted that they had investigated none of the criminal charges, never visited the Putumayo, did not resign, and had left everything to Arana who owned most of the Company.

Arana had been in Manaus but decided that he must return to England to clear his name. At first he made an excellent impression on the Select Committee, answering questions about his employees' flogging and hunting down Indians 'calmly and confidently' and radiating 'an impression of energy and determination'. But the parliamentarians wore down Arana's protestations that he knew nothing about atrocities or rifles used against indigenous people. He repeated the allegation that Hardenburg had tried to pass a forged letter of credit and to blackmail his company. While he continued to defame the young American, Swift MacNeill was able to launch a master-stroke. He suddenly said to Arana:

'Turn around. Turn around and see Hardenburg before you.' The man who had first exposed the Putumayo scandal four years previously was sitting in the House of Commons committee chamber.

After Walter Hardenburg and his new wife Mary had emigrated to Canada, they went to try their luck in the prairie town Red Deer, Alberta. Hardenburg built them a log cabin and they had two sons. He had almost forgotten the Putumayo. But the Rev. John Harris decided that they must get him back to London. The Anti-Slavery Society paid for the young man's passage, by train across Canada and the cheapest Atlantic crossing, just in time to reach Parliament for the hearing on 10 April 1913. Now it was the American farm-boy's turn to impress the Committee. His calm, brief and factual replies demolished Arana's trumped-up accusations of wrongdoing. He was asked, 'Was it common knowledge in Manaus and Iquitos that Indians were being done to death by torture and starvation in thousands?' 'Yes.' ... 'Did you see the healed scars on the backs of the Indians, the *marca de Arana*?' 'Yes: Arana's trade-mark.' By contrast, Arana's imperturbability started to crumble when his interrogation resumed. Swift MacNeill asked the Peruvian what he meant by claiming that his company made Indians more civilized. 'Didn't you mean ... that they were becoming more amenable to floggings and outrages and murders – more broken-spirited?' In a company prospectus Arana had written that there was 'an abundance of labour, the Indians being naturally submissive, and eight or ten civilised men can control 300 or 400 of them'. The Member of Parliament asked whether this 'control' was enforced by Winchester rifles? Arana admitted that 'in order to make themselves respected it was necessary that each employee should carry a Winchester'. The rubber-baron became increasingly flustered by hours of such questioning. He eventually abandoned the hearings altogether.

The Select Committee finally found that, although the Company's British directors had not directly oppressed Indians, they 'cannot escape their share of collective moral responsibility [for] gross abuses'. They deserved severe censure, and had 'exposed to risk the good name of England'. As for Arana, he knew about and 'was responsible for the atrocities perpetrated by his agents and employees in the Putumayo'. Unfortunately the impact of these stinging rebukes was lessened because they were issued on 4 June 1913, the day that the suffragette Emily Davidson threw herself in front of the King's horse in the Derby.

Roger Casement, William Cadbury and his rich friends subscribed £15,000 to a Putumayo Mission Fund, which eventually sent a group of British Catholic Franciscans. They reached the Putumayo in early 1913, but initially reported favourably of well-fed Indians who greatly appreciated English steel machetes.

The Peruvian media continued to react with patriotic xenophobia, dismissing the revelations as 'a large and disgusting amount of sensational rot', while a German magazine accused the British and Americans of double standards because of atrocities that they had committed in their colonies and in the Far West.

What became of the principals in this extraordinary saga? Walter Hardenburg said goodbye to his friends in London and returned to his family in Canada. He lived there happily and obscurely, dying in 1942 aged fifty-six. Sir Roger Casement was rightly praised as a great humanitarian. In August 1913 he resigned after almost twenty years in the Foreign Service. He had become increasingly anti-colonialist and passionate about Irish independence, and started campaigning for the militant wing of the Irish cause. When Britain went to war with Germany in August 1914, he was addressing rallies of Irish supporters in the United States. So in October Irish Americans sent Casement to Germany in a neutral Norwegian ship. The Germans were unsure what to do with this tall, knighted, former British diplomat. He remained in Germany for eighteen months, trying to recruit prisoners-of-war to his cause and to persuade the Kaiser's government to send a force to help liberate Ireland. The Germans agreed to do this, but only if their fleet gained control of the seas.

In April 1916 a German ship was sent to smuggle arms to what proved to be the Irish Easter Rising. Meanwhile a U-boat took Casement and a colleague and landed them at Banna Strand in the southwest corner of Ireland. However, British intelligence had cracked German codes and knew all about these moves. The gun-running ship was blown up off Cork. And as Casement was rowed ashore on Good Friday, a policeman arrested him and asked 'Sir Roger' whether there was anything he wanted – to which he wryly replied that he thought he was going to need a shroud. The Irish Republic was proclaimed; the Easter Rising was crushed after five days and its leaders executed; and Casement's trial took place in London from 26 to 29 June. The trial was the most publicized legal event of the war, with F. E. Smith (later Earl of Birkenhead) leading the prosecution, Casement defended by three American barristers, and Rufus Isaacs (later Marquis of Reading) as judge. Casement was found guilty of high treason for his activities in Germany at the height of the war, and was sentenced to death.

Although the Battle of the Somme was raging, there was a stream of petitions for clemency because of Casement's great humanitarian record. His supporters included George Bernard Shaw, Sir Arthur Conan Doyle, W. B. Yeats, the Webbs, Jerome K. Jerome, G. K. Chesterton, Dora Carrington and Lytton Strachey. But the movement to save Casement from execution collapsed when rumours circulated that he had been a very active homosexual. When the police searched his belongings, they discovered four small notebooks that have become known as the 'Black Diaries'. Casement was a prolific diarist, often writing over a thousand words a day even when he was in the heat and humidity of the Amazon. He also liked names, facts and figures, which he jotted down in parallel notebooks. As he was going up the Amazon in 1910 and again in late 1911, he recorded the ship's run, how deep the river was, butterflies, vegetation, people met, games of bridge, and any other interesting data. But among these thousands of entries were details of his male conquests in riverside towns. Some were men or boys he had known when he was Consul in Pará in 1908. Typical of these many encounters were: in Belém on 8 August 1910, after dinner 'Senate Square & caboclo (boy 16–17). Seized hard. Young stiff, thin.'; or three days later, again after dinner with English friends, 'at 12.30 Darkie policeman 'en paisana' [in plain clothes] – enormous = 5$'; or in Manaus on 16 August, 'One lovely schoolboy. Back & forward several times & at 8.15 to Chambers [Hotel] & stayed all night there in good bed & room.' The 'black diary' during Casement's return journey in 1911 contained more erotic fantasies; but it, too, was clearly written by him. The only remarkable thing about the diplomat's frequent liaisons with consenting partners was that he was never molested, caught, betrayed or blackmailed – apart from an attempt by his Norwegian valet/lover Adler Christensen en route to Germany in 1914.

The British Home Office kept these so-called black diaries locked away until recently. This secrecy fuelled a conspiracy theory that they were forgeries, commissioned by the British secret service to blacken Casement's reputation during the few weeks between his trial, unsuccessful appeal, and execution on 3 August 1916. Leading forensic handwriting experts now agree that the writing in the 'black' and 'white' diaries is by the same hand; and the strange gay jottings could never have been invented by a forger. The pity is that they, and the furious debate about their authenticity, have distracted attention from the achievements of an extraordinary man.

When Casement was in the Tower of London awaiting trial, he received a telegram from Arana that gloated with *Schadenfreude*. The Peruvian asked the prisoner to admit that he had fabricated his Amazonian evidence, 'inventing deeds and influencing Barbadians to confirm unconsciously facts never happened, invented by Saldaña, thief Hardenburg, etc., etc.... You tried by all means to appear humaniser in order to obtain titles fortune, not caring for the consequences of your calumnies and defamation against Peru and myself doing me enormous damage. I pardon you, but it is necessary that you should be just and declare now fully and truely all the true facts that nobody knows better then yourself.' Arana's empire was collapsing: the British Company had been liquidated, and in 1914 he closed his office in Manaus. He brought his family back to Peru. But he had siphoned off enough from his nefarious activities to live comfortably for thirty-six years after Casement's execution. He died in Lima in 1952, aged eighty-eight.

Arana's brutal henchmen had mixed fortunes. Warrants were issued for the arrest of Arana and his brother-in-law Pablo Zumaeta, but these were annulled on appeal, and Zumaeta went on to be briefly elected Mayor of Iquitos. An attempt to get Andrés O'Donnell extradited from Barbados failed on a technicality, but he was later caught in Venezuela and tried in Lima. The evil Armando Normand was extradited from Bolivia to Peru. There were eulogies of him in the chauvinistic Lima press under headlines such as: 'The European and Anglo-American wolves and the ewes of Spanish origin'. Appeals and counter-appeals delayed proceedings until May 1915 when, just before a verdict against them, Normand, Aurelio Rodríguez and another were allowed to escape from jail. Abelardo Agüero and Augusto Jiménez went to tap rubber in the Bolivian Beni; they were arrested by the authorities there and returned to Peru, but they also escaped long imprisonment.

Some Witoto, Bora, Andoke and other indigenous groups survived the oppression of the rubber years, but with their numbers badly diminished. The British Franciscan missionaries, who had been welcomed by the Indians in 1913, reported three years later that: 'Though the wholesale crimes of former times have disappeared ... still the Indian has constantly been punished with whips, logs, chains, kicks and stocks for shortage of rubber.' Some Indians attempted armed resistance, but this was crushed and its leaders punished – far more quickly and violently than any retribution against their former torturers. The Franciscans were hated by the Peruvians, and finally abandoned their mission in 1918.

What saved the Indians was the collapse of the Amazon rubber boom. Surprisingly, exports of low-grade Peruvian caucho continued unabated throughout the war years, but the price did not rise and demand for such rubber then disappeared altogether. Largely because of this, the Peruvian government in 1922 ceded to Colombia the entire region north of the Putumayo – which included all Arana's stations along the Igara-paraná and Cara-paraná tributaries. As a postscript, President Barco of Colombia in 1988 chose the once-infamous La Chorrera to declare a gigantic 60,000-square-kilometre (23,000-square-mile) Predio Putumayo indigenous reserve. This embraces far more than the former caucho forests. There are now several thousand Witoto and Bora. A group of each lives in adjacent villages down on the main Amazon near Leticia, where they welcome passing cruise ships. For several decades these peoples were little molested. Their main problems now come from FARC revolutionaries, from traffickers wanting to grow coca to be processed into cocaine, and from sometimes overzealous missionaries.

The ending of the rubber boom did have two welcome outcomes. The cruelties of the rubber-tapping industry ceased and seringueiros drifted away from their debt-bondage. Indigenous peoples who survived or had escaped into the forests enjoyed a half-century respite. Looking back, Colonel George Church (the American engineer who tried to build the Madeira-Mamoré railway in the 1870s) asked the glaring question: 'What has civilized man been able to accomplish during the four centuries he has occupied the [Amazon] valley? ... In reality, with all his advantages, he is worse fed there than were his aboriginal predecessors, since there are probably not twenty square miles of the Amazon basin under cultivation.' Colonists and immigrants – Church's 'civilized man' – had decimated indigenous peoples with their diseases, guns and oppression, but had proved hopelessly unable to 'combat the forces of nature' and live sustainably in those teeming forests and rivers. So the natural world continued its exuberant and turbulent existence, unmolested by man for a few more decades.

CHAPTER EIGHT

Explorers and Indians

With the collapse of the rubber boom, Amazonia returned to a half-century of environmental tranquillity. It now held few attractions for outsiders. Slavery was firmly outlawed, and in any case there were hardly any indigenous peoples left on the accessible rivers. Medicine had moved on from the *drogas do sertão* – sarsaparilla, ipecac, false cloves and some herbal remedies – that had driven eighteenth-century expeditions into the forests. Now that ships were built of metal there was little demand for timber for masts or lianas for cordage. Other natural products grew better elsewhere. Coffee flourished on the more temperate plateau of São Paulo; rice, cotton and sugar were farmed in northeastern Brazil and even better in the southern United States and Caribbean; cacao plantations in West Africa exceeded those in Amazonia.

After the departure of most rubber-tappers and their flamboyant bosses, those who remained were small-scale fishermen, slash-and-burn farmers and forest collectors. Usually of mixed blood, these hardy people were the first outsiders to adapt to the problems and potential of Amazonia. They were the river-bankers – *ribereños* in Spanish, *ribeirinhos* in Portuguese – and they knew the tricks of survival, particularly on the rich *várzea* floodplain. They learned about plants, hunting and fishing from the Indians, whom they replaced on the banks of the main rivers. Their fishing, logging and rubber-tapping was on too small a scale to damage the pristine rain forests and rivers. Cattle was raised where there was natural savannah, particularly on the island of Marajó in the river's mouth, on the upper Rio Branco (now Roraima) at the north of the basin, and in the Bolivian llanos to the south. But this ranching was nothing like the burgeoning meat industries of Argentina, Uruguay and southern Brazil. In the flooded parts of Amazonia, river-bankers still raise water buffalo who happily wallow in water during the day and are herded into corrals raised on platforms at night. Fishermen have houses high on stilts or floating, with rafts alongside for little gardens and pens for domestic animals. No-one bothered to fell forests to clear land for ranching or farming.

The Amazon's 'decline' confounded the visions of economic Darwinians who believed in never-ending human progress. With the crash of the rubber boom, writers echoed Colonel Church in wondering what had gone wrong. The American geographer Roy Nash in the 1920s noted how badly Amazonian cabocolos were fed and housed. There was virtually no agriculture or roads. Nash's inelegant analogy was: 'The first four hundred years of Portuguese-Brazilian nibbling has not even made a hole in the rind of this mammoth green cheese.' Those centuries of 'paddling up and down the river' had yielded only 'the destruction of most of the aboriginal population and the mutilation of a few rubber trees'. Nash blamed rain. To him, Amazonia was 'damp, steaming, muggy in the "dry" season. During the "rainy" season, slippery, soft mud; roaring, flooded streams; soaked, drowned, disheartened inhabitants.' Nash was right, but for different reasons. The high rainfall and tropical climate meant that vegetation grew constantly. It greedily absorbed virtually all nutrients that reached the ground, so that the soil was impoverished. When cleared, topsoils exposed to heavy rainfall instantly eroded, and were then baked into pink clay by the intense sun.

In July 1911, when Arana's evil empire on the Putumayo was starting to collapse, there was a thrilling discovery in Peruvian Amazonia 1,600 kilometres (1,000 miles) to the south. The American adventurer Hiram Bingham stumbled across the Inca ruins of Machu Picchu. The discovery was the embodiment of everyone's secret dreams, the inspiration for countless adventure yarns.

The young Bingham was trekking out of Cuzco with a group of Yale college friends on a bid to 'find Inca ruins'. On only their third night out, they were camped beside the turbulent Urubamba headwater of the Amazon when a local farmer, Melchor Arteaga, said that there were ancient buildings on the forested hillside opposite his hut. Bingham alone decided to investigate. He and his Peruvian guides crawled across the raging river on rocks and logs, then spent a hot morning clambering up the mountainside. They paused for a lunch of cold sweet-potatoes. Then, rounding a promontory, 'we were confronted with an unexpected sight, a great flight of beautifully constructed stone-faced terraces, perhaps a hundred of them, each hundreds of feet long and ten feet high'. They struggled upwards through thick cloud forest. Then came the amazing reward. 'Suddenly

I found myself confronted with the walls of ruined houses built of the finest quality of Inca stone work. It was hard to see them for they were partly covered with trees and moss, the growth of centuries, but in the dense shadow, hiding in bamboo thickets and tangled vines, appeared here and there walls of white granite ashlars carefully cut and exquisitely fitted together.' They scrambled over slippery stones and pushed through the choking vegetation. 'Without any warning' Bingham came upon a rock crevice carved into a three-dimensional sculpture of stark beauty. Above was a jewel-like temple whose 'flowing lines ... symmetrical arrangement of ashlars, and gradual gradation of the courses, combined to produce a wonderful effect.... It seemed like an unbelievable dream. Dimly, I began to realize that this wall and its adjoining Semicircular Temple over the cave were as fine as the finest stone work in the world. It fairly took my breath away.... Surprise followed surprise in bewildering succession ... and held me spellbound.'

This was one of the most thrilling moments in the history of archaeological exploration. Other archaeologists have found older or artistically more important ruins – Agamemnon's or Tutankhamun's tombs, Petra, Angkor Wat, Lascaux, or Sian's terracotta army – but Bingham was the one who pushed tropical creepers aside to reveal superb stones. Machu Picchu was the archetype of lost cities – an intact Inca site of several hundred structures of incomparable stonework, unknown to the outside world, and perched amid breathtaking granite pinnacles. None of the world's other great ruins can compare with Machu Picchu's location. It is on a knife-edge ridge, amid tropical rain forests often cloaked in Wagnerian clouds, with the Urubamba roaring through a hairpin-bend canyon far below, the sugar-loaf of Huayna Picchu like a rhinoceros horn at the end of the spur, and snow-capped mountains shining in the distance.

Not content with this amazing discovery, Bingham's 1911 expedition pressed on down the Urubamba and up its Vilcabamba tributary. They penetrated the wild Vilcabamba region, where Manco Inca and his sons had ruled a neo-Inca enclave between 1537 and 1572. In quick succession, Bingham discovered and identified its two most important archaeological sites: Vitcos, where Manco was almost caught by conquistadors in 1537 and where he was murdered by his Spanish guests in 1545, and then in dense forest three days' walk to the northwest, the ruins of Manco's exiled capital, Vilcabamba city. In the second half of the twentieth century, American, Peruvian and British explorers, archaeologists and adventurers have ransacked the daunting forested hills of Vilcabamba. But none has discovered ruins to compare with those found by Bingham during that glorious month in 1911.

There have been attempts to belittle Bingham's achievement. Others claimed to have been to Machu Picchu before him. It was said that he had been told where to look by the scholar Carlos Romero in Lima – which Bingham freely acknowledged. He was lucky to be the first to use a mule trail recently blasted along the Urubamba canyon to extract caucho rubber, and he was amazingly fortunate to stumble across the three exciting ruins. Another allegation is that Bingham failed to appreciate the significance of Machu Picchu. It is true that he spent only a few hours at the ruins on 24 July 1911 and did not bother to revisit the lost city on his return a few weeks later. It was the *National Geographic* magazine that trumpeted the importance and glamour of the find. But these criticisms of Hiram Bingham were trivial. One definition of an explorer is that he has to discover something unknown to his society and then return and give a full report about it. By these criteria, Bingham *was* the discoverer of Machu Picchu, because he was the first to tell the world about the stupendous find. The Peruvian authorities graciously acknowledge this, with a plaque at the site and by naming the zigzag road that takes tourist buses up to the ruins the 'Carretera Hiram Bingham'.

At the time of the discovery Bingham was 35, very tall, ruggedly handsome, fit, adventurous and an able leader. He dressed in a safari shirt and jodhpurs, puttees, jaunty kerchief, and a slouch hat. Harrison Ford, the actor of the Indiana Jones movies, was given a similar early-explorer outfit. Bingham's career was colourful. Born in 1875 to strict Protestant missionaries in Hawaii, he grew up amid cliffs festooned with orchids, bromeliads and tropical vegetation that he later compared to the approaches to Machu Picchu. He went to the smart boarding school Andover and then to Yale, where his charm and looks propelled him into the fast set. He married a Tiffany heiress and promptly moved into a thirty-room mansion. After Yale, Bingham got a doctorate from Harvard (in history and political science), followed by minor teaching and administrative posts in those two Ivy League universities. But he was an adventurer at heart, and his wife's money enabled him to pursue a series of expeditions.

In Peru in 1909 Bingham had his first taste of the Incas when a sub-prefect invited him to join a treasure-hunting foray to the remote ruins of Choquequirau (southwest of Machu Picchu, and recently cleared and restored as a major tourist destination). Back in the United States, he tried to get his Yale classmates to back his next venture. He suggested climbing a mountain, descending an Amazon river, studying the Maya, or looking for Inca ruins. Luckily, it was the last that appealed to his rich friends. The result was the wonderfully successful Yale Peruvian Expedition of 1911. Bingham then persuaded the National Geographic Society and others to fund massive expeditions to investigate, excavate, photograph, map, and start to clear and restore Machu Picchu. He himself led these fine projects, in 1912–13 and 1914–15. 'We made a determined effort to uncover everything that had been hidden by nature in the course of the centuries and ... to restore the beauties of the Inca's favourite residence.' He gave names and guessed at functions of the various temples and buildings, and many of his attributions have endured.

After the series of Machu Picchu expeditions, Bingham took up flying. He was with General Pershing fighting Pancho Villa in Mexico and then the Germans in France. As a colonel in the Army Air Corps and a famous explorer, Bingham got elected first as Governor and then Senator for Connecticut. A Republican, he lost his Senate seat in the Roosevelt landslide of 1932. So he turned to business, making money in a savings-and-loan bank and the petroleum company Colmena Oil. In 1937 he divorced his patient wife Alfreda, after she had borne him seven sons and he had spent her money; aged sixty-two Bingham married a younger second wife. His final job was chairman of the Loyalty Review Board of the Civil Service Commission during the McCarthy witch-hunts. This lively career was fitting for a restless adventurer. But the world owes Hiram Bingham a debt for discovering Machu Picchu and initiating the rescue of the most beautiful ruin in the Americas.

At the beginning of 1914 another remarkable American appeared in the Amazon basin. Theodore Roosevelt had been the hugely popular twenty-sixth President of the United States of America, from 1901 to 1908. Now aged fifty-five, Roosevelt was overweight, but a vigorous outdoors man who loved nature: he initiated the world's first national parks during his presidency. He was also an avid African big-game hunter, but a friend persuaded him to try his next adventure in South America. When he approached the Brazilians they warmly welcomed his visit. However, they said that he might collect Amazonian fauna for American museums but not indulge in shooting for sport: in any case, the Amazon had no big trophy animals apart from jaguars. Roosevelt lectured in São Paulo and Buenos Aires and then took a steamer up the Paraguay river to Mato Grosso. He was greeted by Brazil's finest explorer, Colonel Cândido Rondon.

Rondon was Brazil's answer to Dr David Livingstone – an intrepid explorer and great humanitarian. Livingstone used his fame as an explorer to crusade against African slavery. Rondon was a brilliant Army engineer and a devout follower of the Positivist creed, who turned *his* reputation to the cause of indigenous peoples.

Born in 1865 in a humble house in Mato Grosso, Cândido Rondon was orphaned when both his parents died of smallpox when fleeing from invasion by Paraguay. Brought up by his grandparents, one of whom was part Bororo Indian, Rondon learned the lore of the Brazilian backwoods. He was educated locally and won a place at the prestigious military academy in Rio de Janeiro. Hard work and brilliance earned Rondon top marks of his class of cadets, so he became an officer of the elite engineers. His inspiring tutor at the Academy was Benjamin Constant, tutor to the children of Emperor Dom Pedro II but also a republican and a passionate Positivist. Followers of this cult were morally upright and preached human progress towards social perfection. When Brazil stumbled bloodlessly and almost inadvertently into becoming a Republic, in 1889, the Positivists sought to implant their noble values in the constitution of the new secular state. The Positivist motto 'Order and Progress' is still emblazoned on the Brazilian flag.

During the war with Paraguay, the Brazilian government had been alarmed by the precariousness of its communications with the interior. It took months to get messages from the capital on the Atlantic coast to the Amazonian heartland. This problem was exacerbated when the rubber boom made Porto Velho on the Madeira strategically important and when in 1903 Brazil gained rubber-rich Acre. In those days before the invention of wireless telegraphy, the solution seemed to be to drive a telegraph line for thousands of kilometres across the unexplored forests and savannahs of the *sertão*.

Rondon spent the 1890s erecting the telegraph between the old gold-mining town of Cuiabá and the headwaters of the Araguaia-Tocantins. This was through the territory of the Bororo, and part of this nation was still uncontacted and defending its forests against invasion. Rondon's commanding officer, Major Gomes Carneiro, taught his young protégé a wealth of forest-survival lore. He also instilled respect and love of Indians. Carneiro ordered his men to defend and protect indigenous people, and to avoid fighting the people whose territory they had entered. One night Carneiro woke Lieutenant Rondon and whispered to him: "'Cândido, are you listening?" The forest was becoming animated. At some distance around our campsite, apes yelled and howler-monkeys roared, *prego* macaques were whistling, *jaós* and partridges were chirping…. It was as if all the wildlife around us was conversing. "I can hear the chirps of partridges. But they do not chirp at night like jaós. Apart from that, it is unnatural for all this animal life to decide to converse at this hour of the night." "What do you think, then?" "That these are Indians communicating with one another at a distance."' The Major was sure that the Bororo were planning an attack. So, rather than have a conflict, the engineer-explorers struck camp and disappeared into the darkness. Their telegraph line skirted the southern headwaters of the Xingu, where Karl von den Steinen had recently contacted ten tribes. Rondon then spent four years in command of a contingent driving another telegraph line southwards around the huge Pantanal swamplands of the Paraguay.

Back in Rio de Janeiro in early 1907, Rondon was asked by the President of Brazil to undertake a stupendous challenge: to build a telegraph from Cuiabá northwestwards for 1,100 kilometres (almost 700 miles) to Porto Velho. Most of this was unexplored, a vast tract of forests, savannahs and occasional hills and scarps. It was the watershed between the upper Guaporé-Madeira and the sources of the Tapajós. For four years, Rondon drove his men into this wilderness in one of the twentieth century's great feats of exploration. Not only did the army engineers discover, survey and map hundreds of kilometres of tough territory and countless rapid-strewn rivers, they and their scientists also undertook much research and published a huge corpus of books and reports. Rondon became a heroic explorer, ramrod-stiff, rising long before dawn, eating and sleeping very little, and yet neatly uniformed in even the harshest terrain. He was a stern disciplinarian – he had to be, for his men were often mutinous after months of labour, undernourishment and hardship in the gloom and heat of the Amazon forests; but he was invariably a just and caring officer. Legends grew about his stamina. Rondon worked himself mercilessly, even when in raging malarial fever. He could sleep while riding; he once spent a day swimming back and forth across a river to ferry supplies; and there was nothing that he did not know about rainforest survival and natural history. He formed a cadre of brilliant young officers, who of course worshipped their morally upright commander. Several of them died during those arduous years of discovery.

In the first phase of these explorations, Rondon mapped the Sepotuba and Juruena headwaters of the Paraguay and Tapajós rivers. Further west, he found that the Ji-paraná (Machado) tributary of the Madeira was a full 2 degrees (almost 200 kilometres; 120 miles) out of place on existing maps. So Rondon's next expedition, starting in May 1909, was to descend and map this unexplored river. Despite all his team's experience and planning, the task proved appallingly difficult. By August, food supplies were exhausted and the men survived for three months on the sparse game, wild honey and berries that they could hunt or gather. Many were so weak that they could scarcely crawl, far less paddle or heave canoes through rapids. But they did reach the Madeira by Christmas, utterly exhausted, starving, and wracked with diseases.

Rondon was a fine orator, in the flowery, patriotic style of that era, and he had amazing adventures to recount. He achieved pop-idol status. Whenever he returned to the capital city, he was greeted with garlands of flowers, and his lectures in the largest theatres were packed by everyone from the President down. Rondon used his fame to further the Indian cause. In one speech he described an atrocity in which rubber-men mercilessly gunned down and burned a village of innocent Paresi. The explorer told his distinguished audience to 'tremble with indignation and shame' at this genocidal slaughter. As his teams had advanced westwards, they entered the territory of the semi-nomadic Nambiquara. Rondon riveted another audience by describing how, riding across a campo savannah, he suddenly 'felt a puff of wind on my face and glimpsed something like a small bird crossing my path, at eye level and very close. I turned to look to my right, and then understood: the shaft of an arrow was vibrating with its point buried in the sandy soil. A second deadly messenger passed close to the nape of my neck, grazing my sun helmet. In front of me, some twelve paces away, two Nambiquara warriors were drawing their bowstrings.' They were tall, naked, powerful men, and they stared at Rondon with 'a hard, penetrating [gaze] as implacable as the points of their silent arrows'. Rondon grabbed his gun and fired twice into the sky. A third arrow broke when it struck the butt of his rifle. (This author saw another group of Nambiquara, from the Galera river, at the time of their first contact sixty-five years after Rondon's close shave. These looked exactly as he had described their relatives.) The famous explorer stressed to his listeners that he later learned that these Nambiquara had also been victims of a seringueiro attack, and he told how he made a large detour around their land to avoid a confrontation. He ordered his men on no account to retaliate. After several brushes with Indians during these years, Rondon evolved a famous creed for men confronting hostile tribes: 'Die if you must, but never kill!' The humanitarian told how he won the friendship of each tribe, how they gave invaluable help to his explorations, and how they were fine, industrious people and brilliant hunters and woodsmen. These were revelations to people who had heard only derogatory accounts of Indians, from missionaries who patronized them, or from settlers who exploited, despised and feared them.

A pro-Indian movement grew among some Brazilian intellectuals during these years. It was a mixture of romantic nationalism and guilt at past injustices. Indigenous people were seen as the original Brazilians, at a time when the nation was seeking a non-European identity. Novels and epic poems had Indian heroes in the Hiawatha mould. Now that tribal peoples were a shattered minority who presented no threat to the expanding nation, it was easy to pity and wish to help them.

The Positivists particularly wanted special protection for Indians in the new Republic's constitution, and they were determined that treatment of indigenous peoples should be taken away from missionaries. Since the expulsion of the

Jesuits in 1760 'catechism' of Indians was largely left to Catholic missionaries from European countries. There were not many of these, and they had little experience of the Brazilian backlands. They tended to be proselytizers bent on changing native culture, and thus achieved few genuine conversions. Italian Salesians were active among the Bororo in Mato Grosso and peoples of the upper Rio Negro, and they imposed a rigid theocracy in areas they controlled. French Dominicans fared better with some Kayapó on the Araguaia; German Franciscans arrived among the Munduruku of the Tapajós; and Belgian Benedictines on the Rio Branco (Roraima) in the extreme north of Brazil clashed violently with local cattle-ranchers and freemasons.

The non-missionary Indian sympathizers were few in numbers, but they cleverly manipulated nationalist sentiment in parts of the press and influential learned societies. They argued that Indians were authentic Brazilians who needed to be defended against foreigners. In 1910 they persuaded a new Minister of Agriculture, Rodolfo Rocha Miranda, of the need for a new Indian Service staffed by disinterested soldiers and civil servants rather than missionaries. In February of that year, Rondon returned on one of his rare visits to Rio de Janeiro and was duly lionized. Minister Rocha Miranda invited Colonel Rondon to lead this new service. The explorer accepted, but with conditions. These included: that there should be no attempt at religious or other conversion; that protection of Indian lands (and restitution of stolen territories) was the Service's main purpose; and that tribal societies and traditions must be respected – even though Indians would be encouraged to change gradually to become settled agricultural workers.

The Indianists moved very fast. The Minister got the consent of all state governors, largely by claiming that the new Service would pacify hostile tribes and convert them into docile labourers. Rondon agreed to lead the Indian Protection Service in March 1910; regulations for the organization were drawn up in May; and it gained presidential approval and became law in June. The Service was known by its Brazilian initials SPI, and its motto was Rondon's dictum: 'Die if you must, but never kill.' The Catholic Church and its missionaries awoke to the loss of their monopoly of Indian affairs (and the government subsidy that went with this) and mounted a determined rearguard action, but it was too late. The religious lobby did, however, persuade the army in 1912 to transfer Rondon and many of his ablest officers to other duties. This damaged but did not stifle the fledgling Service. After a glorious start, the SPI had a chequered fifty-seven-year history of successes and failures. But in its patchy way, it and its successor Funai (the National Indian Foundation) were to have a profound effect on the indigenous peoples of Brazil and, by example, of other Amazonian nations.

⊙

In 1914, Rondon was the obvious person to guide Brazil's distinguished visitor ex-President Theodore Roosevelt. The two got on famously. Roosevelt wrote that 'Colonel Rondon immediately showed that he was all, and more than all, that could be desired. It was evident that he knew his business thoroughly, and it was equally evident that he would be a pleasant companion.' He was 'neat, trim, alert and soldierly'. The President was impressed that his guide had spent the past 24 years exploring his country's western highlands. 'During that time he has travelled some fourteen thousand miles [22,500 kilometres], on territory most of which had not previously been traversed by civilized man, and has built three thousand miles [almost five thousand kilometres] of telegraph. He has an exceptional knowledge of the Indian tribes, and has always zealously endeavoured to serve them and indeed the cause of humanity....' After dinner, host and guest would sit 'under the trees in the hot darkness and talk of many things.... Colonel Rondon is not simply "an officer and a gentleman" ... he is also a peculiarly hardy and competent explorer, a good field naturalist and scientific man, a student and a philosopher. With him the conversation ranged from jaguar-hunting and the perils of exploration in the Mato Grosso, the great wilderness, to Indian anthropology, to the dangers of a purely materialistic industrial civilization, and to Positivist morality.' Rondon told how piranha had bitten him and killed one of his officers. The two outdoorsmen agreed (correctly) that the greatest dangers were from insects and the diseases they transmitted, from dysentery and starvation, and from accidents in rapids rather than from snakes, jaguars, caymans or bloodthirsty fish.

As the expedition moved northwestwards along the line of the new telegraph, they met indigenous peoples. Rondon was delighted that the amiable Paresi 'received me as a friend and a beloved and respected chief.... I had been introducing the benefits of civilization among them gradually.' At that time, and as a Positivist, both he and his North American guest were convinced that progress meant that Indians should acquire the 'benefits' of European society. (Later in his long life, Rondon came to doubt the wisdom of trying to 'acculturate' tribal people.) Roosevelt admired the 'good humour, consideration, and fundamentally good manners' of the Paresi, and how gentle they were to their children – 'friendly little souls, accustomed to good treatment'. He was also impressed by the tribe's wild sport of headball. Handsome warriors butted a rubber ball with the tops of their heads, leaping and diving with reckless bravado. They 'throw themselves headlong on the ground to return the ball.... Why they do not grind off their noses I cannot imagine.'

Further west, they entered the territory of the now-peaceful Nambiquara. Roosevelt marvelled at their arrival at his camp in 'an interminable file, completely naked, with the women carrying the small infants and all the baggage, while the men carry only their bows and arrows.... They were a laughing, easy-tempered crew, and the women were as well-fed as the men, and were obviously well-treated, from the savage standpoint; there was no male brutality.' When the Nambiquara crowded into his hut, the ex-President reacted to their nakedness in the same way that Steinen had done. The men wore penis-strings and pierced their nose septums to take ornamental feathers, but 'the women did not wear a stitch of any kind anywhere on their bodies. They did not have on so much as a string, or a bead, or even an ornament in their hair. They were all ... as entirely at ease and unconscious as so many friendly animals.... The behaviour of these completely naked women and men was entirely modest. There was never an indecent look or a consciously indecent gesture.'

A series of great rivers flows northwards towards the Amazon from this plateau – a region that is now the State of Rondônia, named in honour of the explorer. Like a bizarre travel agent, Rondon offered Roosevelt a choice of four rivers for them to descend. The gung-ho traveller chose the toughest, a river that one of Rondon's officers had named Rio da Dúvida, the 'River of Doubt' because no-one knew where it emerged. The 22 men embarked in seven dugout canoes at the end of February 1914. This was almost the end of the wet season, a good time for shooting rapids or sailing over fallen logs, but the swollen river's current was ferocious and there was often rain. There were three Americans (Roosevelt, his son Kermit and the experienced naturalist-ornithologist George Cherrie), three Brazilian officers (Rondon, Lieutenant João Lyra and a doctor), and 16 woodsmen. Roosevelt was delighted by these *camaradas*. 'The paddlers were a strapping set. They were expert river-men and men of the forest, skilled veterans in wilderness work. They were lithe as panthers and brawny as bears. They swam like water-dogs. They were equally at home with pole and paddle, with axe and machete; and one was a good cook and others were good men around camp. They looked like pirates....' Whenever the going got tough, he praised these men's 'good will, endurance and bull-like strength ... and the intelligence and unwearied efforts of their commanders'. He was scornful of armchair 'impostors and romancers' who belittled the qualities of 'men of the tropics' and the fatigue, hardship and danger of genuine exploration.

After a few days' paddling, the unexplored river started to cascade off the Parecis plateau. Roosevelt later wrote to the Brazilian Foreign Minister that, beyond the raging Navaité falls, rapids were 'continuous and very difficult and dangerous'. Many were so bad that the expedition had to cut portages through the vegetation to drag canoes and carry stores and equipment around them. This was (and still is) backbreaking and time-consuming work. Canoes split and five of the original boats had to be abandoned or replaced. A big dugout that took the men several days to build was lost when it was being lowered, unmanned, over a fierce rapids. Tragically, a small canoe commanded by Kermit Roosevelt was caught in an eddy, swept over a fall, and capsized when caught by another whirlpool. The paddler Simplicio drowned and his body was never recovered. Kermit was plunged into the river and 'the water beat his [pith] helmet down over his head and face, and drove him beneath the surface; and when he rose at last he was almost drowned, his breath and strength almost spent'. He was saved by another Brazilian *camarada*. The Brazilians blamed Kermit's rashness for this accident: they said that he had insisted on inspecting the rapid too closely.

The expedition saw many signs of Indians. Once, Rondon's beloved dog Lobo (Wolf) howled with pain and was found killed by two arrows. His death may have saved his master. The warriors responsible were probably from a Mondé/Tupi-speaking people now called Cinta-larga ('Broad-belt', from a girdle of black nuts) who live in that remote region. Later, one woodsman-soldier went berserk, killed his sergeant and ran off into the forest. He was sighted briefly, gesticulating from a bank. Roosevelt wanted to abandon the killer, but the morally correct Rondon insisted on mounting a (fruitless) search to bring the criminal to justice. Rondon also demanded a full traverse to survey the unknown river, even though the ex-President urged them to press ahead as fast as possible.

After three weeks of arduous travel it was clear that the Dúvida was an important river. Rondon named one tributary the Kermit. Next day he had the men erect a large post and drew them up in parade order. He then read out a government proclamation formally christening the river 'Rio Roosevelt'. The ex-President was taken by surprise. 'We felt that the "River of Doubt" was an unusually good name; and it is always well to keep a name of this character. But my kind friends insisted otherwise, and it would have been churlish of me to object longer. I was much touched by their action, and by the ceremony itself.'

Roosevelt often admired the river's beauty. One camp had 'a beach of white sand, where we bathed and washed our clothes. All around us, and ... on both sides of the long water-street made by the river, rose the splendid forest. There were flocks of parakeets, coloured green, blue, and red. Big toucans called overhead, lustrous green-black in colour, with ... huge black-and-yellow bills.' However, like so many of his contemporaries, Roosevelt wrongly equated tropical luxuriance with the rich soils of his temperate land. He imagined this place becoming a coffee plantation. 'Surely such a rich and fertile land cannot be permitted to remain idle, to lie as a tenantless wilderness, while there are such teeming swarms of human beings in the overcrowded, overpeopled countries of the Old World.' He thought that the rapids could generate hydroelectric power. This would 'drive electric trolleys up and down its whole length … and run mills and factories, and lighten the labour on farms.'

The rapids, races, whirlpools and waterfalls got worse as they descended the newly named Roosevelt. Weeks were spent overcoming them. On a typical day, 'Lyra, Kermit and their four associates spent from sunrise to sunset in severe, and at moments dangerous, toil among the rocks and in the swift water.' With so many canoes lost, supplies were running low and food was rationed. Most men suffered from malaria, dysentery, sores, or limbs swollen from insect bites. Roosevelt gamely tried to help with the work. But he hated the many insects, particularly the mosquitoes, sweat-bees, and *borrachudo* black-flies that left an itchy red bite. He modestly admitted that he was a blundering novice in this strange environment. 'Now, while bursting through a tangle, I disturbed a nest of wasps, whose resentment was very active; now I heedlessly stepped among the outliers of a small party of the carnivorous foraging [*Eciton*, army] ants; now, grasping a branch as I stumbled, I shook down a shower of fire-ants [*tocandeira*, *Dinoponera*], which stung like a hornet, so that I felt it for three hours…. We were bitten all over our bodies, chiefly by ants and the small forest ticks. Because of the rain and the heat our clothes were usually wet when we took them off at night, and just as wet when we put them on again in the morning.' Roosevelt hurt his leg badly while pushing a canoe and it became abscessed: 'I could hardly hobble, and was pretty well laid up.' Rondon recalled that: 'This was not all. He was overcome by a tremendous attack of fever and it was necessary to interrupt the journey. Roosevelt was delirious. He called me and said: "The expedition cannot stop. On the other hand, I cannot continue. Leave without me!"' Rondon could hardly arrive at the foot of the river having abandoned the former President! So they pressed on, with the sick man being nursed in a covered canoe. His malaria 'gave rise to such extreme bodily weakness that his back became covered with boils and he was forced to lie face downwards in the canoe to avoid excruciating agony.'

The ordeals – and the exhilaration of exploring virgin territory – ended when the expedition encountered the first rubber-tappers' huts. After a few more days on the by now placid Roosevelt river they joined the equally large Aripuanã, descended it to the Madeira, and then to the main Amazon near Manaus. An American there found Roosevelt 'wasted to a mere shadow of his former self; but his unbounded enthusiasm remained undiminished'. The Roosevelt-Rondon

Right Prosperous Manaus during the rubber boom was one of the first cities in South America to have electric trams – green streetcars sponsored by the United States Rubber Company and marked 'Manaos Railway' (in English).

Below The boom-town Manaus boasted hundreds of bars and brothels. The noticeboard in this all-night 'High Life Bar' advertises all the Amazonian favourites, from manioc tapioca and *farinha d'agua* to German lager beer (Schopp), *cachaça* rum, cheroots and cigars, and coffee, chocolate and 'iced or hot milk'.

Above Belém do Pará, at the mouth of the Amazon, flourished as a financial centre and trading port during the rubber boom. Its bustling waterfront was lined by warehouses, some designed by the Italian architect Giuseppe Landi in the mid-eighteenth century.

Left The Madeira-Mamoré railway was built to transport Bolivian rubber past thirty ferocious rapids on the Madeira river. Its construction through forest and swamps cost thousands of lives, mostly lost to malaria. The ill-fated railway was largely finished only in 1912, when the rubber boom was crashing.

Right The flamboyantly moustachioed Bolivian Nicolás Suárez was the greatest of all the rubber barons. Despite his vast wealth, however, he preferred to go barefoot as in his humble boyhood.

Below Walter Hardenburg, the young son of an American farmer, single-handedly exposed the atrocities of the Putumayo rubber empire to world attention.

Below left and right Two adversaries in the Putumayo rubber scandal both wore trim spade beards. The Peruvian Julio César Arana (below) rose by ruthless ambition to be the most powerful baron of *caucho* rubber of the upper Amazon, but he instituted a regime of utmost cruelty to force Indians to labour in his 'evil empire'. Sir Roger Casement (below right) was the British consul in Brazil, sent in 1910 and 1912 to investigate the Putumayo atrocities, about which he wrote a devastating report.

Above Indians resting from backbreaking work in gathering rubber. Their chief wears a Brazilian army uniform, given as a badge of honour.
Below Walter Hardenburg's heartbreaking photograph (from a water-damaged negative) of chained Witoto. Indians were flogged, often to death, for failing to bring enough rubber or for trying to escape their bondage.

Right Manioc is the 'wonder food' plant of Amazonia – easy to grow and harvest, and rich in carbohydrates and calories. Here a Yanomami woman roasts manioc flour into *beijú* pancakes.

Below Each Indian's rubber was weighed and, if it was below his quota, he was savagely beaten or starved in the stocks. 'Peruvian slab' *caucho* came in long rolls.

Below right A *seringueiro* rubber-tapper had to smoke each day's haul of latex to harden the rubber into large balls. This was done over a brazier of poisonous creosote.

Right There was friendship and mutual respect between ex-President Theodore 'Teddy' Roosevelt and Colonel (later Marshal) Cândido Rondon, Brazil's greatest explorer and the humanitarian founder of its Indian Protection Service. Roosevelt was allowed to shoot animals 'for the pot' but not as big-game trophies. The two explorers pose here with a brocket deer, during their tough first descent of a river later named Roosevelt, in 1914.

Below Hiram Bingham in 1911 discovered Machu Picchu, the most spectacular ruin in the Americas. Tall and handsome, Bingham was the epitome of an explorer and adventurer.

Below right Richard Evans Schultes was an outstanding botanist and explorer. He created the discipline of ethnobotany and was fascinated by hallucinogenic plants. Here he inhales snuff from a Yukuna near the Caquetá river in Colombia.

Left Rock art is an enduring legacy of early man in Amazonia – most of whose artistic creations were perishable. There are thousands of petroglyphs throughout Amazonia. Here a Barasana boy of the upper Caquetá in Colombia stands beside an engraving on 'the Rock of Nyi', which was recently defaced by a missionary zealot who condemned it as devil worship.

Above Betty Meggers and her husband Clifford Evans of the Smithsonian Institution were pioneers of Amazonian archaeology and environmental history. Here she is, in 1949, excavating a magnificent pot on Marajó Island.

Left Professor Anna Roosevelt at work in Pedra Pintada ('Painted Rock') cavern, north of the lower Amazon. Her excavations revealed very early dates for the arrival of human beings. She also argued that pre-conquest chiefdoms on the main rivers were larger than had previously been thought.

Left Orlando Villas Boas with apprehensive Ikpeng (Txikão) women at the moment of first contact in 1964. Orlando and his brother Cláudio were outstanding champions of indigenous people in the second half of the twentieth century. They were also great explorers and creators on the first huge indigenous and environmental reserve, on the upper Xingu.

Below The charismatic Chico Mendes led Acre's rubber-tappers against landowners who wanted to destroy their forests for cattle ranching. In 1988 he was murdered for this. Here Chico is standing on the newly built BR-364 highway, which brought thousands of settlers into Rondônia and Acre, and led to massive deforestation and environmental destruction.

Scientific Expedition lasted for five months, and its descent of over a thousand rugged kilometres (620 miles) of river took eight weeks. Roosevelt said goodbye to Rondon at the mouth of the Amazon. He praised the Brazilians as 'a fine set, brave, patient, obedient and enduring.... Together with my admiration for their hardihood, courage, and resolution, I had grown to feel a strong and affectionate friendship for them.... I was glad ... that I had been their companion in the performance of a feat which possessed a certain lasting importance.'

Since Amazonia offered so few commercial prospects, its main attractions in the first half of the twentieth century were exploration, anthropology and natural sciences. A series of German anthropologists followed Karl von den Steinen into the idyllic upper Xingu: Paul Ehrenreich, Hermann Meyer, Theodor Koch-Grünberg and Max Schmidt. They were generally welcomed by the Xingu tribes. Meyer ran out of food, but was saved by indigenous hospitality and spent delightful evenings splashing in the river with the Kamayurá and then Trumai boys and girls. Schmidt went to the area alone in 1901, guided by acculturated southern Bakairi – just as Steinen had been. He approached a village playing a popular tune on his violin and was well received because of (or despite) this. But things went wrong with the nearby Nahukwá. Schmidt tried to barter his trade goods for artefacts, but the Indians misunderstood this ungenerous behaviour, stole his goods and even reclaimed some of their own objects in order to trade them again. When he went on to the Aweti, the porters carrying his remaining possessions simply went off with them. Schmidt fled, but he was surprised when the Aweti later caught up with him and returned most of his goods. He was by now hungry and feverish, but he was nursed by the Indians and woken from a delirium by 'the beautiful Tuirki, a slender young girl with a figure still in its first bloom, who was well aware of her charms'. Other visitors were less fortunate. In 1898 five Americans visited the warlike Suyá. This fierce group appeared to welcome the strangers but, when these were seated in a hut, each was clubbed to death from behind. In the following year a Brazilian colonel Paula Castro led a large treasure-hunting expedition in search of supposed gold mines called Os Martirios (The Martyrs), but most of his men perished from starvation and disease and Paula Castro went mad.

Theodor Koch-Grünberg was with Meyer on the Xingu, and went on to become one of the finest anthropologists in the north of the Amazon basin. In 1903 he went to study the peoples of the upper Rio Negro, paddling deep into

Colombia to live with them. Koch-Grünberg then spent the years 1911 to 1913 crossing from the savannahs near Mount Roraima westwards up the Uraricoera headwater of the Rio Branco to the upper Orinoco in Venezuela. It was an amazing journey, previously done by only one European – the German-British explorer Robert Schomburgk, in 1838–39. Both travellers were of course guided and paddled by Indians, Yekuana (also called Maquiritare and Maiongong) who know every rock, rapids and bend of this labyrinth of forested rivers. This brought Koch-Grünberg into fleeting contact with two villages of Yanomami, the largest surviving nation of undisturbed indigenous people.

American explorers also penetrated these northern regions. In 1914–15 William Curtis Farabee led a remarkable expedition into Brazilian Guiana. Striking eastwards from Boa Vista in Roraima (then called Rio Branco), Farabee moved overland between the headwaters of the Amazon's northern tributaries. It was a very tough journey, into what is to this day one of the least-known Amazonian rain forests. Farabee's team from the University of Pennsylvania Museum was rewarded by contacts with a series of virtually isolated Carib-speaking tribes. First came the Wai Wai, the tall and handsome warriors whose piled-up hair may have inspired the Amazon legend (see p. 33). Their most prized possessions – and sought-after trade goods – were trained hunting dogs. These animals were pampered more than the pets of any other tribe, well fed and groomed and sleeping on special platforms. Beyond the Wai Wai came the related Parikotó, and east of them the Tiriyó. Most of these peoples welcomed the American expedition with speeches, hand-shaking with every member of the tribe (down to tiny feather-ornamented children), and hours of dancing or ritual club-battles or wrestling, all washed down with mildly intoxicating manioc cauim. But some villages were hostile. In one, the Americans had to advance, slowly and bravely, into a semicircle of warriors with taut bows pointed straight at them. The arrows were finally lowered when it became clear that the strangers came in peace and bearing gifts.

Among the Tiriyó, Farabee observed the horrific initiation ordeal of boys at puberty. After dancing all night in beautiful feather costumes, each initiate was strapped into a hammock in a specially built hut. A basketwork frame containing up to a hundred huge fire-ants, each held by the centre of its abdomen, was then applied to the wretched boy, while stinging wasps were similarly placed on his forehead. Anyone bitten by a single *tocandira* fire-ant never forgets the excruciating pain. So when boys were repeatedly bitten by scores of these monsters, the agony made them writhe uncontrollably – their shelters shook so much that they seemed about to collapse – until they fell into a coma and were carried away like little corpses. Those who survived such agony had earned the status of manhood.

Dr Alexander Hamilton Rice was a Harvard-trained eye surgeon who became an explorer. After learning surveying from the Royal Geographical Society in London, Hamilton Rice in 1907 descended the Vaupés/Uaupés from Colombia to its junction with the Negro in Brazil, medically studying indigenous peoples along the river. He was back in 1912, 1917 and 1919, exploring the rivers of the upper Rio Negro and mapping the Casiquiare Canal between it and the Orinoco. He gathered information about Indians' health and their knowledge of medicinal plants. On the upper Orinoco his men were attacked by Yanomami but escaped after firing into the air. In 1924–25 Hamilton Rice approached Yanomami territory from the northeast. He led a well-financed expedition that used the latest radio equipment and the first float-plane ever seen in this region. The team went from the Rio Branco up its Uraricoera headwater, but its boats were too cumbersome to surmount the endless rapids on the watershed crossing to the Orinoco, as done previously in Indian canoes by Schomburgk and then Koch-Grünberg. (At the very remote Purumame waterfall, there is a rock on which Schomburgk, Hamilton Rice and Rondon – who got there in 1927 – all carved their names. I was photographed on it, but did not add my grafitto.) Hamilton Rice's Yekuana (Maiongong) guides took him up a side stream to visit a group of Yanomami. He was impressed by the Indians' huge conical *yano* hut, but not by their 'squalor' and diet of little more than bananas. This was a mistaken impression: other observers love the attractive looks and body paint of the Yanomami. These consummate hunters in fact have a rich diet of game, plantation crops and protein-rich termites, but their favourite food is now bananas (not originally native to Amazonia), which they cultivate extensively.

Rondon's new Indian Protection Service had to prove itself by contacting hostile tribes. This was known as 'pacifying' at that time, and the hope was that indigenous people would then undergo 'acculturation' with a view to eventual 'assimilation' into Brazilian society. The SPI's early contacts were all in southern Brazil, outside the Amazon basin. There was, however, one warlike group that gallantly defied and terrified rubber-tappers near the Madeira river. These were the Tupi-Kawahib, then called Parintintin, who lived in forests west of the lower Roosevelt and Aripuanã rivers. Rondon ordered various officers of the SPI to try to pacify the ferocious Parintintin. Each failed, because he used the wrong techniques (such as aggressively invading Parintintin territory, or having their Indian enemies on his contact team) and because the tribe was implacably hostile and justifiably suspicious of all whites.

In 1922 Rondon sent a remarkable 39-year-old German to make another attempt. Born Curt Unkel to a humble family in Jena, this man had no university education and he travelled to Brazil in 1903 as a penniless immigrant. He soon chose to live among the dirt-poor Ñandeva Guarani of the interior of São Paulo state. Slight and slim, reserved and precise, with a neat moustache that he trimmed every day, Curt Unkel looked like a stern bank manager. But he became an outstanding self-taught anthropologist and champion of indigenous rights. He developed an empathy for Indians' thinking and society by spending so much time among them. He explained that he did this because 'it is necessary to feel in your own flesh the problems of the group as if they were your own – to fear the same threats, raise the same hopes, grow angry at the same injustices and oppressions'. The Guarani loved the quiet German and decided to adopt him into their tribe. They gave him the title Nimuendajú ('He who resides among us') in an elaborate night-long ceremony and 'when the sun rose behind the forest, its rays illuminated a new companion of the Guarani tribe who, despite his pale skin, faithfully shared with them for two years the misery of a moribund people'. When Unkel later became a Brazilian citizen, he took the name Curt Nimuendajú.

After a decade living with and studying tribes of southern Brazil, Nimuendajú in 1915 started working with Amazonian peoples. In 1921 he was among the demoralized tribes of northern Amapá, near the border with French Guyane. Then he lived with Mura and Tora of the lower Madeira, survivors of colonial wars, slavery and missionary efforts. He was thus on the spot when Rondon asked him to try to make peace with the feared Parintintin.

Nimuendajú's technique was to build an outpost in the midst of these warriors' territory, and settle down to await their reaction. His men built a hut, defended only by corrugated-iron walls and surrounded by a small clearing and wire fence. Presents were left in shelters in the nearby woods. There were minor skirmishes during several months, and his men became fearful and rebellious. The decisive encounter happened one morning. In Nimuendajú's words: 'The Parintintin ran in through the gate to attack me, amid their war cries and a hail of arrows.... At the instant I shielded my body behind a corner of the house, arrows struck beside me. The veranda was immediately riddled with them and the yard was strewn with others that fragmented when they hit the walls.... I could see a group of attackers advancing against the house, continually shouting and shooting.... I called to them, but they shouted so frenetically that I could hardly hear my own voice.' Nimuendajú was about to order his men to fire into the air to scare off the Parintintin, but the Indians suddenly decided to withdraw. 'I immediately exchanged my gun for an axe and a machete, which I showed and offered to them.... Then I quickly jumped down into the yard and, showing them some strands of beads, approached them. They were very excited and suspicious, and recoiled before me. So I had to follow them outside the perimeter where, at their request, I laid the beads on the ground and then withdrew a little so that they could come to pick them up.' There were further arrow shots and war cries during that day and the next. But Nimuendajú's bravery, tact and knowledge of the Parintintin's Tupi-Guarani language (learned from the people who gave him his name) finally achieved a dialogue and the all-important first physical contact. Some Indians visited the house and were fed. He commented on his success: 'The "indomitable wild beasts, the man-eaters with whom one could talk only through the barrel of a rifle" had conversed peacefully with me and exchanged presents during almost three hours!'

The 'pacification' of the Parintintin went horribly wrong. This gallant tribe was decimated by alien diseases, and as soon as they laid down their weapons their lands were invaded. A friend of Nimuendajú's later wrote that he deplored his heroic action. 'He realized that the happiest Indians are those who keep themselves independent by their fighting valour and by intransigent hostility to any usurper of their lands.' Tragically, contacts with isolated tribes throughout most of the twentieth century had a similar outcome. The first encounter was often done by skilled and well-intentioned officers of the Indian Protection Service or its successor Funai. But, almost inevitably, there was soon a terrible epidemic – measles, influenza or tuberculosis – for which there was no remedy or for which inadequate medical provision had been made. Also, all too often, when a feared tribe ceased to fight its forests and rivers were invaded.

Curt Nimuendajú was on an expedition to a tribe or on an archaeological excavation every single year from 1910 until his death in 1945, when he was sixty-two and living among the Ticuna of the Amazon-Solimões. This was a prodigious achievement, in the days before roads or planes when travel was only by river or on foot or horse. Nimuendajú of course suffered frequent attacks of malaria and periods of malnutrition. In a moment of depression he wrote that the life of forest Indians was incredibly miserable, full of penury and privations, persecutions and danger. With one tribe, he became desperately ill from dysentery and fever and was convinced that he was cured by the rituals of a shaman – and he wrote as much in a learned German journal of anthropology. Nimuendajú generally loved the tranquil life in most indigenous villages. He entertained his hosts with stories about other Indians, and they warmed to him. Women of the Canela (Ramko-kamekra) of Maranhão spent hours painting him from head to foot and decorating him with bird down gummed to his skin. The related Apinayé of the Tocantins-Araguaia also gave him an honorific name and formally married him to a young girl.

A meticulous observer and scholar of the history of Indians, Curt Nimuendajú produced anthropological studies of no fewer than *forty-five* tribes. Perhaps because he was self-taught, he wrote in jargon-free prose. He told stories about every aspect of village life, down to children's games or adolescent girls' attitudes to sex. He was fascinated by mythology, which forms such an important element in each people's cultural and spiritual heritage. So he was an instinctive anthropologist, accurately recording every aspect of indigenous society. Nimuendajú was just as interested in tribes battered by the advancing colonial frontier as by glamorous uncontacted peoples. He was the first anthropologist to study the pathetic remnants of tribes along the Atlantic seaboard, who had borne the brunt of European invasion since the sixteenth century. He tracked down the last survivors of three tribes in other parts of Brazil and wrote heartrending accounts of the extinction of these once-proud peoples.

In 1927 Nimuendajú visited Indians far up the Rio Negro and its Uaupés and Içana headwaters. These peoples were forced to labour for rapacious *cauchero* bosses, whose gangs prostituted their women and stole their few possessions. Nimuendajú even wished that these docile Indians would take up arms and use their blow-guns and poisoned darts to kill their evil masters. Some respite came from Italian Salesian missionaries, who established a virtual theocracy in that part of Brazil and neighbouring Colombia. These protectors were, however, intent on the conversion and regimentation of the tribes in their care. Nimuendajú watched in horror as Salesian fathers ordered the demolition of the magnificent great huts, *malocas*, of the Tucano and Desana. These houses were architectural masterpieces, dry and cool in all weathers, spotlessly clean, and with their facades decorated in handsome geometric patterns. Each family had its hammocks and hearth in part of the hut, and there was an area for collective meetings and ceremonials. They were preferable in every respect to the hot little boxes with which the missionaries replaced them. The anthropologist knew that 'the principal reason for the missionaries' aversion to communal habitations is ... that they see in them ... the symbol, the veritable bulwark of the former ... social order that is so contrary to their plans for conversion, for spiritual and social domination. The Indians' own culture is condensed in the *malocas*: everything in them breathes tradition and independence. This is why they have to fall!' Nimuendajú deplored every abuse of indigenous peoples. He was the first anthropologist to campaign for their rights and act in their defence.

Curt Nimuendajú was deservedly honoured during his lifetime, with his work published in books and journals by academic institutions in Brazil, Germany, France and the United States. He left a posthumous *Ethno-Historical Map* that showed the locations and movements of every indigenous people in Brazil since 1500. This map and the massive accompanying notes were monuments of scholarship. When he died, one of Brazil's most distinguished anthropologists wrote that this uneducated immigrant from Germany was 'without any doubt the principal figure of Brazilian ethnology' during the first half of the twentieth century.

A very different type of stranger appeared in Amazonia at this time. Colonel Percy Harrison Fawcett had become an officer in the Royal Artillery in 1886, later took a course in boundary surveying from the Royal Geographical Society, and in 1906 was seconded by the British Army to help Bolivia survey its northern frontier. He spent a year sailing along the main rubber-boom rivers and visiting the Suárez brothers' bases on the Beni and Orton. He mapped the Abunã and upper Acre rivers, which formed the new frontier between Bolivia and the territory of Acre that Brazil had recently purchased.

In 1910 and again in 1911, Fawcett did an impressive survey of the Heath River, a tributary of the Madre de Dios headwater of the Madeira. The Heath is the boundary between Bolivia and Peru, in the forests east of Cuzco. Rubber-men at the river's mouth were terrified of its Warayo Indians, a Tupi-speaking people who defended themselves against would-be slavers with arrows and some captured firearms. Fawcett's canoes were greeted with a hail of arrows, but he bravely stood up and called to them. Although he later learned that he was shouting the wrong things in the wrong language, no arrow or shot hit him, and he established friendly relations with this people – partly by his men sitting on a sandbank, playing an accordion and belting out popular songs at the tops of their voices. Once the Warayo were convinced of the explorers' good intentions, they gave them plenty of fish. Further up the Heath lived an even more amiable people, the Echoca. Fawcett loved the Echoca for their kindness, generosity, cleanliness and modesty. To him, their 'inherent nobility was far greater than that of many "civilized" people's.'

Fawcett's attitudes to Indians were curiously mixed. He admired the honesty, intelligence and sobriety of some tribes and was appalled by the rubber men's cruelty to them. The rubber firms 'kept forces of armed toughs for hunting Indians, and wholesale butchery went on'. Captive Indians were given a shirt, tools and some rice, and forced to work incessantly to collect excessive quotas of rubber. Fawcett was disgusted by rubber men who boasted of murderous raids on indigenous villages, of beating Indians to death or drowning them, or who 'never tired of telling me that the half-caste and Indian understood only the whip'. The atrocities were almost as bad as Arana's on the Putumayo. In contrast to this liberal outrage, the British officer developed ugly racist notions. He wrote that 'There are three kinds of Indians. The first are docile and miserable people, easily tamed; the second, dangerous, repulsive cannibals very rarely seen; the third, a robust and fair people, who must have a civilized origin.' He became convinced that parts of South America were once inhabited by a 'superior' race, who of course had fairer skins and hair and bluish eyes. Alongside such eugenic gibberish, Fawcett was fascinated by the paranormal. He came to believe that the Amazon forests contained ruins of lost civilizations that were perpetually lit by enigmatic forces.

President Ismael Montes of Bolivia was delighted by the British major's maps. He therefore sent him to survey the Verde River, a headwater of the Guaporé that forms the boundary with Brazil in the extreme northeast of Bolivia. In late 1908 Fawcett took a steamer up the Paraguay river and then had a very tough expedition up the little-known Verde. The explorers almost starved to death in this area of swamps, rapids and moss-draped vegetation, on a bed of rugged pre-Cambrian rock. In the distance were the table mountains of the Ricardo Franco Hills (named after the eighteenth-century Brazilian officer Ricardo Franco de Almeida Serra, who first mapped them). Fawcett wondered whether there might be primeval animals isolated above those cliffs. Back in England, he told his thoughts to his friend Arthur Conan Doyle, who shared Fawcett's interest in the occult. The outcome was *Lost World*, serialized in the *Strand* magazine and then published as a classic book. Fawcett returned to the Verde in 1909, with a Bolivian-Brazilian boundary commission that cut a mule trail to plant markers on that remote frontier.

Fawcett was back in the region in 1914, having resigned from the Army and spent some months travelling for pleasure in Peru and Bolivia. From Mato Grosso City, a near-derelict ruin of a former gold-mining town, he paddled down the Guaporé river for eleven days to its Mequens tributary on the Brazilian side. The English traveller was impressed by a large tribe, some days' walk inland. He called this people Maxubi, but they were probably those now known as Arikapú. He admired their great conical hut, their cleanliness, good looks, plantations (particularly of tobacco and peanuts), music, astronomical knowledge, and orderly society. But he spoiled this favourable picture by writing: 'I believe that these people ... are the descendants of a higher civilization ... rather than [being] a people evolving from savagery.'

After five days' walk through virgin forest to the northeast, Fawcett's team came across men of a tribe he called Maricoxi. (From the location, these were probably Tuparí or Tupi-speaking Aruá, both as handsome as any other Indians.) Fawcett's description of these 'savages' was prejudiced by contemporary interest in the 'missing link' or the Piltdown Man fraud. To him, they seemed 'large hairy men, with exceptionally long arms, and with foreheads sloping back from pronounced eye ridges – men of a very primitive kind, in fact, and stark naked'. One of these 'hideous ape-men' had 'pig-like eyes half hidden under overhanging brows'. They hopped from leg to leg and jabbered in 'a barbarous, merciless din'. Their huts were primitive shelters, and they were 'some of the most villainous savages I have ever seen ... great ape-like brutes who looked as if they had scarcely evolved beyond the level of beasts'. All this was, of course, ludicrous racism: no Indians have body hair, Neanderthal brows or ape-like arms, and they move with graceful agility not hopping on bowed legs.

Percy Fawcett returned to England in 1915, to rejoin the Royal Artillery and fight in France. He ended the War as a colonel with a DSO. The Royal Geographical Society had awarded him a gold medal for his boundary-survey expeditions. In a lecture to the Society in 1910 he said that he had heard 'rumours of old ruins ... hidden in the forests of the Amazon basin'. He was told about a document of 1743 in which a band of adventurers tried to find a gold mine seen by a *bandeirante* slaver-explorer over a century earlier. By the 1740s Brazil's gold mines in Minas Gerais (General Mines) were in full production, but the explorers apparently struck far north of them, and found and entered a ruined ancient city. He marked its 'possible site' on his map, south of the bend of the São Francisco river in the state of Bahia – an area well known and settled by cattle ranchers by the twentieth century.

Disillusioned by post-war Britain, Fawcett left his wife and family to return to Brazil to pursue his chimera. For some reason, he sought the mysterious city in Mato Grosso – 1,200 kilometres (745 miles) southwest of where the explorers imagined that they had sighted it. He took a steamer up the Paraguay river to Cuiabá and in early 1921 rode out of that old mining city towards the Xingu. Fawcett's two non-Brazilian companions proved hopelessly incompetent, and the expedition was abandoned ignominiously beyond a cattle ranch on the trail to the source of the river. Later that year he moved his quest to the Atlantic coast south of Bahia. He was still with a useless lad called Felipe from Mato Grosso, and their venture was a fiasco reminiscent of Don Quixote's. The picaresque colonel then spent three months alone, 'researching' for ancient ruins among diamond prospectors at the railhead west of Bahia. None of these failures dimmed his conviction that Amazonian tribes had 'once been dominated by a "White Race" expert in the arts of civilization' who had left fabulous ruins. Back in England with his family, Fawcett admitted that 'the failures, the disappointments, have been bitter' and 'the last few years have been the most wretched and disillusioning in my life'. But he was obsessively determined to 'give the world the most stupendous discovery of modern times'.

In 1925 Colonel Fawcett, now aged fifty-seven, returned to Cuiabá. This time he took his eldest son Jack, aged twenty-one and 'big, very powerful physically, and absolutely virgin in mind and body. He neither smokes nor drinks.' The third member of the tiny expedition was Jack's friend Raleigh Rimell, a jolly public-school boy who was 'keen as mustard' but knew nothing of Brazil, foreign languages or forest survival. The trio took twelve pack animals and muleteers to the ranch Fawcett had reached four years previously. They moved on to the SPI's post for the southern Bakairí. During the forty years since Karl von den Steinen's expedition this was always the entry point to the Xingu, because the less-contacted northern Bakairí still lived on its Batoví source and there was an easy trail between the two halves of the tribe. While the Englishmen were at the post, it was visited by some Mehinaku from the Xingu. Fawcett wrote home that these Xinguanos were 'of the brown or Polynesian type, and it is the fair or red type I associate with [lost] cities'. He told his young companions that they should soon see 'a long rectangular rock pierced with three holes ... and behind it an inscription of fourteen strange characters', or 'a great stone carved in the shape of a mushroom – a mysterious and inexplicable monument', or 'a sort of fat tower of stone. [The Indians] are thoroughly scared of it because they say at night a light shines from door and windows!' He never explained where he had heard about these oddities.

The trio sent their local men and some animals back, and pressed on across the savannah with eight mules. In his last letter home, dated 29 May 1925, Fawcett wrote: 'I expect to be in touch with the old civilisation within a month, and to be at the main objective in August.' He had previously explained his modus operandi. This 'will be no pampered exploration party, with an army of bearers, guides and cargo animals.... Where the real wilds start ... it is a matter of cutting equipment to the absolute minimum, carrying it all oneself, and trusting that one will be able to exist by making friends with the various tribes one meets.' This was a dangerous philosophy. Although the tribes of the upper Xingu had generally welcomed the score of expeditions who visited them since Steinen, they had come to expect plenty of presents, particularly axes, knives and beads. They would take a dim view of Fawcett's 'making friends' by enjoying their hospitality but keeping unopened the bag of presents intended for the inhabitants of the lost city. And Fawcett should have known, from near-death on his survey of the Verde river, that three men cannot cut a trail through Amazon forest while carrying all their supplies, particularly if one is elderly and feeling his age and the other two are novices. It was criminally irresponsible to sacrifice the two young men to his quixotic obsession and incompetent methods.

Nothing more was heard from the three explorers. The disappearance of a British colonel on a quest for lost cities in the jungle was a journalistic dream. It became a top international story. To this day, it continues to intrigue many with an interest in the exotic, and conspiracy theorists still speculate about the fate of the Fawcett expedition. During the next decade there were rumours of Fawcett living as the grey-bearded patriarch of some tribe, and sightings of a crazed Englishman in different parts of central Brazil. Many people visited the Xingu during the 1930s – Indian Service staff, missionaries, anthropologists, film-makers, surveyors – and all advanced theories about what happened to Colonel Fawcett. Expeditions were organized to search for him. The most successful of these was in 1928, led by Commander George Dyott, RN. It learned much from the upper-Xingu Indians and collected objects left by the English trio, but it had to flee down the river when its stock of presents was exhausted and the Indians became increasingly importunate. In 1932 another Fawcett-search expedition led by a bombast called Colonel Churchward got no further than the Araguaia – the tributary of the Amazon east of the Xingu. But Peter Fleming, an irreverent young member of this team, wrote a brilliant book about it. His best-selling *Brazilian Adventure* wittily debunked the imagined horrors of the Amazonian 'green hell', the exaggerations of the exploration game, and the boasts of his expedition's ludicrous leader.

It seems likely that Fawcett's group were killed by indigenous people soon after their arrival on the upper Xingu. They were said to have done various things that were unacceptable to these Indians. When they reached the first headwater they saw two canoes tethered on the bank and purloined these, even though their owners were obviously hunting nearby. Walking with guides between the Nahukwá and Kalapalo villages, Fawcett shot a duck, snatched it from an Indian who ran to pick it up, and tried to have only the Englishmen eat it. He did not know that in the Xingu hunters invariably share their catch with everyone and are the last to consume it. Fawcett later hit a boy who was examining his knife. Xinguanos are protective parents who never reprimand their young and would be infuriated by a stranger striking a child. These seem trivial offences but, coupled with Fawcett's lack of generosity with his bag of presents, they would have marked his group as undesirable intruders. The head of the Indian Protection Service lamented that 'Colonel Fawcett ... was deaf to all advice. He went ahead ... without reaching an understanding with the SPI, which could fully have guaranteed [their safety] with all the tribes of the sources of the Xingu.' An outstanding Indian expert later commented that 'Fawcett was the victim, as anyone else would have been, of the harshness and lack of tact that all recognized in him'.

Assuming the group were murdered, the question remains: which tribe did it? Chief Aloique of the Nahukwá used dramatic sign language to tell Commander Dyott that the fierce Suyá further down the Xingu had appeared to welcome the Englishmen but then murdered them with club blows from behind. (The upper-Xingu tribes feared and hated the Je-speaking Suyá; and such clubbing was how the Suyá were said to have despatched the five Americans in 1899.) The Kalapalo gave a similar version of the crime, but they said that it was the Nahukwá who did it – and Dyott tended to agree with this. The most convincing account came in 1946, when three brothers called Villas Boas reached the Xingu on a government-sponsored project, loved the idyllic place, and spent the rest of their lives championing its peoples. Soon after their arrival, Chiefs Izarari and Komatsi of the Kalapalo assembled their villagers and told them and the Villas Boas exactly what had happened to Fawcett's party twenty-one years previously. They said that three Kalapalo guides (Cavuquiri, Araco and Culili) decided to kill the English-men – without the approval of their then-chief Caiabi. They hid on the far side of a small lake, later called Verde. A Kalapalo boy ferried the explorers across this water and as they clambered up the bank each in turn was hit on the head with a club. Fawcett died from two blows; the young men tumbled into the lake and were drowned. Chief Caiabi was angry when he heard what had been done. He feared retribution and ordered his men to bury the bodies or secure them on the lakebed.

The Villas Boas brothers got Indians to dive and scour Lake Verde, but they could find only one skeleton buried in its far bank. These bones were sent to London in the diplomatic bag. The Brazilian ambassador, a flamboyant publisher called Assis de Chateaubriand, recognized a good story and organized a lavish reception at Claridge's Hotel to show the relics to the world. But palaeontologists and Fawcett's surviving son Brian felt that these were not the right bones – the teeth in the skull seemed wrong and a shin bone was too short. The bones were returned to São Paulo. Brian Fawcett died, and his surviving sister refused to give a DNA sample that might have resolved this mystery. In the 1960s the American anthropologist Ellen Basso worked among the Kalapalo. To her, they emphatically denied that their people had murdered Fawcett. They said that the Villas Boas asked them to find bones of a tall man, so they exhumed those of a tall chief called Mugika – although it would be unusual for Xingu Indians to treat their grand-father's bones so casually. The Kalapalo now suggest that the Englishmen journeyed onwards and were either killed by a different tribe or perished of starvation, lost in the forest. The latter was the verdict of the German anthropologist Max Schmidt, who was in the Xingu two years after the tragedy.

In 1922 British and Dutch rubber planters in Malaya and Sumatra formed a cartel known as the Stevenson Plan, to limit production and force up prices. They did this because their huge acreage of tappable rubber trees had matured sufficiently to be milked, so the owners feared a world glut. The British-Dutch cartel angered Henry Ford – who was manufacturing half the world's motor cars. Some Americans were also growing rubber outside the Amazon. Harvey Firestone had a plantation in Liberia; Paul Litchfield of Goodyear in Panama and Costa Rica; others in Haiti, the Philippines and Mexico; and the great inventor Thomas Edison's last experiment was to try to produce latex from North American plants that he grew in vast quantities. The big companies United States Rubber and Goodyear also owned plantations in the British and Dutch colonies in Southeast Asia.

In 1923 and the following year, the US Departments of Agriculture and of Commerce sent teams to Brazil, to report on potential sites for rubber production in the Amazon. The Brazilians co-operated fully with this research, since they wanted to retaliate against the Asian plantations and they hoped for lavish American investment. The main reason for the failure to grow plantation rubber in the Amazon was the parasite *Dothidella ulei*, known as South American Leaf Blight or SALB. This microcyclus attacked the leaves and then the fruit and peticles of *Hevea* rubber trees. It was virulent, jumping from one tree canopy to the next, and it was devastating. So the American teams reported extensively on SALB, hoping that it might be controlled or that rubber trees might survive if planted outside its normal geographical range.

Henry Ford was planning his own tyre company and was eager to grow his own rubber. A Brazilian consular official told him about tax concessions that his government offered to anyone establishing plantation-rubber there, and Ford determined to go ahead. As the historian of rubber Warren Dean commented: 'The occasion was ripe for a swindle.' Jorge Dumont Villares, scion of a São Paulo coffee family, obtained options on some 2.4 million hectares (9,270 square miles) from the State of Pará. This land was on the Tapajós river, close to where Henry Wickham had collected his seeds half a century earlier, but it was half a continent away from Acre and the Beni where *Hevea brasiliensis* trees flourished best. Villares went to the United States and offered his land for 50 cents an acre first to Firestone and then to Ford. The giant motor company sent an employee to Brazil to 'find a good area somewhere' and his team contained Carl LaRue, a leader of the US government's earlier investigation. LaRue had changed his opinion and now favoured the lower Amazon rather than Acre. Dean suspected a conspiracy: 'Curiously, the ... entourage made a beeline for one of the Villares concessions, an 80 kilometer [50-mile] stretch of the east bank of the lower Tapajós River, spent one month traversing it, and returned to Dearborn having visited no other site.' LaRue's brief report to Ford ruled out all locations other than Villares's concession. He neglected to say that, apart from being so far from the heartland of *Hevea* growth, its climate was too dry, its soils too sandy, the river too shallow for large ships during part of the year, and the site too hilly for easy management. In June 1927 Henry Ford paid the Brazilian agent $125,000 for land that the State of Pará might well have granted for nothing.

The Ford Motor Company plunged into its Brazilian adventure with characteristic gusto. It rapidly built a city known to Brazilians as Fordlândia, which became the fourth-largest on the Amazon, after only Belém, Manaus and Iquitos. This had two hundred houses, dormitories for a thousand single men, a large hospital, cinema, churches and schools. These were on avenues lined with mangos, palms and eucalyptus, all lit by electric street lamps. There were two social clubs for the managers, one for Americans and one for Brazilians, complete with tennis courts, swimming pools, plazas for square-dancing, and an eighteen-hole golf course. Fordlândia was serviced by water and sewerage pipes, 50 kilometres (30 miles) of roads and railways, warehouses, machine-shops, and a port. Much of this infrastructure and machinery arrived on the Tapajós at the end of 1928 in a company-owned freighter.

Within Brazil there was some opposition to such a vast area being granted with generous tax breaks to foreigners. A partner of Villares, disgruntled at getting too small a share of the payout, revealed to the press how the state governor had been bribed. But in October 1930 a 'Liberal Revolution' elected Getúlio Vargas as President of Brazil. He was determined to reduce the power of the old élites in the states, and his fifteen-year control of Brazil developed into the fascist-leaning Estado Novo (New State). President Vargas visited Fordlândia and was impressed. So his regime strongly supported Ford's initiative.

In contrast to the building of Fordlândia town, the rubber plantation developed very slowly. In the early years it was delayed by a decision to extract any good timber for logging rather than burn it. Thus, by 1931 a mere 1,300 hectares had been cleared for planting – a tiny proportion of the vast concession. This was done by hand with axes. It was calculated that at this rate it would take a thousand years to convert the entire area. The Ford management sensibly sought seeds from the rubber areas of the upper Madeira, but 600,000 of these were planted for propagation on an island in the main Amazon that was just inside the State of Amazonas. Inter-state jealousy caused the seeds to be impounded, and a legal battle ensued to get them into Pará. Local seeds were hastily used, but these proved inadequate and were ploughed-in. There were other blunders. Time was wasted on an attempt to find oil in the concession. Amazingly, during the first five years there was no-one at Fordlândia with scientific training in either tropical agriculture or rubber planting.

Finally, in 1932 there was an attempt to learn about a bud-grafting technique that was proving successful in Asian and African plantations. In 1934 a new manager, James Weir, brought seeds from trees in Goodyear's plantations in Sumatra. These were descended and cloned from Wickham's original seedlings, which had been gathered from a perilously small gene pool of only 28 trees. They had been bred to be highly productive, but they were known to be vulnerable to South American Leaf Blight. At first things went well, and by the end of that year 3,400 hectares (8,400 acres) had been planted with almost 1.5 million rubber trees. Then, in 1935, disaster struck. The rubber trees had grown to a size where their canopies touched one another. The dreaded leaf-blight innoculum spread virulently. Weir wrote that 'Practically all the branches of the trees throughout the estate, but especially on the poorer sites, terminate in naked stems. Each successive elongation of the shoot becomes smaller and smaller … with the result that … the growth impetus ceases altogether.' Trees grown from Asian seeds – those from Wickham's original Tapajós stock – were the most sensitive and died quickest.

Weir recommended that new trees be planted on a plateau called Belterra, near the mouth of the Tapajós 50 kilometres (30 miles) south of Santarém. He hoped that this drier and windier site would be less vulnerable to SALB. Henry Ford was fed up that, after an investment of almost seven million dollars, his Amazonian plantations had yielded no rubber and little was in prospect. But he authorized Weir's move to Belterra, where in 1934 an even larger version of Fordlândia was constructed on a 281,000-hectare concession. This time there were eight hundred houses, several movie theatres, three recreation halls and five football fields. Five million seeds were planted at Belterra. (Tourists now visit the remains of the American town, with its grid of streets, suburban houses surrounded by verandahs and gardens, typical iron fire-hydrants, and a splendid water tank.)

By 1941 the Belterra plantation seemed to be thriving and it looked as though it could finally rival those in Malaya. It had seven thousand people and 3.6 million trees. But the young trees were developing canopies large enough for

SALB to spread. There was another devastating epidemic. The only glimmer of hope was that other types of *Hevea* seemed to be more resistant than *H. Brasiliensis*. So the managers at Belterra embarked on the vast task of top-budding all their trees. This meant lopping each tree at two metres (some seven feet) and then carefully grafting on branches from resistant species. The result was SALB-resistant foliage on trunks that yielded plenty of rubber latex. Two million trees were grafted in this way – a gargantuan task that took six hundred labourers four years to complete. It was in vain. The company had sunk almost ten million dollars into its plantations on the Tapajós, but in 1945 Henry Ford II finally abandoned the enterprise without having tapped any rubber. He sold Fordlândia and Belterra to the Brazilian government for half a million dollars.

In the Second World War the Japanese captured all the Asian plantations. Rubber was essential to the war effort, and there was no time to wait for Ford's trees to mature to tappable age. The American government therefore sent the Harvard botanist Richard Evans Schultes to scour Amazonia for blight-resistant trees. Schultes made heroic journeys, particularly in the western Amazon in Peru and Colombia. Covering thousands of kilometres of largely unexplored forests and rivers, he suffered many of the region's diseases and near-starvation, and survived accidents in waterfalls and getting lost in forests. He was starting to identify suitably hardy trees that yielded various types of rubber, but the war effort could not wait. The Americans abruptly switched to synthetic rubber and, with their habitual amazing energy, rapidly produced enough of it to help win the war.

CHAPTER NINE

Archaeologists Find Early Man

⊙⊙

During the past century and a half, archaeologists have struggled to discover more about the people who occupied Amazonia before the devastating arrival of Europeans. It is hardly surprising that archaeologists came late to this obscure field of study. Compared to excavations in the open deserts of Egypt, Mesopotamia or Peru, the Amazon gave archaeologists a seemingly impossible challenge. This difficult region offered few prizes of museum-quality artefacts. Early people in the Amazon naturally used its wealth of plant and animal products for daily needs. Almost all their creativity was thus ephemeral. It went into lovely architecture of wood and thatch, fantastic feather ornaments, body paint, and elegant artefacts of wood, bone, shell and basketry. Outcrops of stone are rare in a rain forest, and with such profusion of organic building materials there was no need to work stone into building blocks. Household containers could be made from gourds and basketry, so many tribes flourished without ceramics. Thus, almost all creations of early man have perished – rapidly consumed by termites, bacteria, fungi and the decay of the humid tropics.

Against these obstacles, Amazonian investigators have a few advantages. There is still some 'living archaeology' – indigenous peoples who exist now as they have done for millennia. European explorers also left some valuable chronicles of the peoples they encountered. Friar Gaspar de Carvajal's account of Orellana's first descent in 1542 was the most important of these. And there *are* some surviving artefacts of ceramic and stone as well as remains of massive agricultural works. Caves provide shelter from destructive forces of nature, and a few

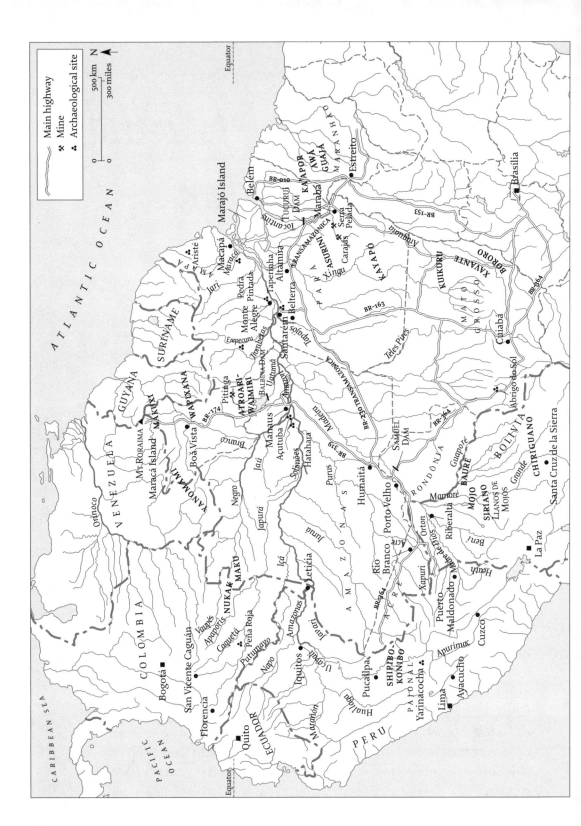

of these have man-made detritus, paintings or burials. Early people along Brazil's Atlantic seaboard and the mouth of the Amazon left *sambaquis*, huge middens of the shells of molluscs and seafood that they consumed. Sambaquis sometimes contain burials and datable material.

The great German naturalist and polymath Baron Alexander von Humboldt lamented the lack of a spectacular archaeological legacy. When he reached the northern edge of the Amazon basin in 1800, he deplored the fact that 'no oasis recalls the memory of previous inhabitants; no carvings, no ruins, no fruit trees once cultivated but now wild, speak of the work of former generations'. But as Humboldt travelled through Spanish South America, he grasped that its indigenous inhabitants originated in Asia and formed 'one unique race ... one single organic type modified by circumstances which will for ever remain unknown'.

The first investigations of the prehistory of Amazonia were by Brazilian naturalists – Alexandre Rodrigues Ferreira in the 1780s, then Domingos Ferreira Penna, Ladislau Netto, João Barbosa Rodrigues and others a century later. These reported on tribal cultures and their pottery and petroglyphs. Other pioneers of Amazonian archaeology came from further north. The Canadian geologist Charles Hartt in the 1870s published the first major studies of carvings on river rocks and the excavation of a sambaqui on the lower Amazon. In the early twentieth century, the work was carried forward by the Swedish anthropologist Erland Nordenskiöld and his American pupil Helen Palmatary. Nordenskiöld led a series of excavations, and he also employed the remarkable self-taught German-Brazilian anthropologist Curt Nimuendajú to dig among the ceramic-producing cultures of the Amazon. These archaeologists struggled with the paucity of evidence, at a time when their discipline relied on stratigraphy for dating and when the world was dazzled by glamorous discoveries in Egypt, the Fertile Crescent and among the Incas and Maya.

Understandably, archaeologists started by studying ceramics. Orellana's Spaniards had been impressed by the pottery they found among some riverbank tribes. They saw huge jars capable of holding 450 litres (100 gallons), plates, bowls, and vessels they called 'candelabra'. These glazed polychrome pieces seemed to them equal to the finest porcelain. One chronicler said that it was better than Spanish Málaga-ware. It was 'thin and smooth, glazed and with colours shading off into one another in the manner of that made in China'. This style is now known as Santarém, from the town on the south bank of the lower Amazon.

Opposite *Map showing twentieth-century activities and main archaeological sites.*

The most famous ceramic style is Marajoara, named after the flat island Marajó that sits like a cork in the mouth of the Amazon. The size of Switzerland, much of Marajó is flooded during the rainy months and its forests and mangroves are a labyrinth of channels as the waters recede. It benefits from being at the meeting of river and ocean waters since this dissolves sediments and yields abundant fishing. Jesuits and other Europeans also found that its expanses of savannah made good cattle and water-buffalo country.

Marajó's pottery was first excavated in the 1870s by Ferreira Penna and Hartt. Its masterpieces grace the Goeldi Museum in nearby Belém, the National Museum in Rio de Janeiro, and others as far afield as Geneva, Barcelona and Sweden. Marajoara funerary urns are a metre (over 3 ft) high and easily able to hold a dismembered corpse. They are covered with elaborate incised and painted geometrical tracery. Everything is stylized, self-assured, intricate and beautiful. Human faces are reduced to components, as in a Picasso portrait, and there are snakes, lizards, caymans, tortoises and birds. Important animals are often sculpted in high relief. Many pots depict females, with every feature (eyebrows, nose, bean-shaped eyes and mouth, nipples, navel, pubic triangle, vagina, feet) reduced to geometric simplicity with the elegance of Cycladean art from the eastern Mediterranean. Between these creatures in relief, the entire urn is covered in a graceful, swirling arabesque of symmetrical patterns, in red, white or brown paint generally outlined by incisions. The clay used in Marajoara pottery starts light-grey but turns orange-red on firing.

There are also ornamental ceramic *tangas*, curved triangles that covered women's genitals, possibly during rite-of-passage ceremonies. Tangas are always of the finest clay, thin and smooth, and they have holes at the corners for cords to hold them in place. (These distinctive triangles gave their name to tiny modern bikini bottoms worn on Brazilian beaches.) Marajoara pottery also comes in utilitarian shapes – bowls, dishes or manioc pans. It is associated with large settlements in the heart of Marajó Island, some of which had fields for farming and mounds for religious purposes. People were still making pottery there when the Europeans arrived, but it was of a simpler style known as Aruã. The great Marajó chiefdom had ended two centuries earlier, but the Arawak-speaking Aruã were probably descendants of the great pottery-makers. Marajoaran culture may have been shattered by a 'mega-Niño' (ferocious drought or storms caused by an El Niño change in Pacific Ocean currents) and then overrun by its equivalent of barbarians invading the Roman Empire.

Northwest of Marajó Island, a small river called Maracá flows into the north bank of the mouth of the Amazon. Here, pioneers of Amazonian archaeology became aware of an excitingly different style of ceramics. But it was not until recent decades that the Brazilians Mário Simões and then Vera Guapindaia really tackled sites filled with this beautiful Maracá pottery. These explorers hacked through dense vegetation to find several undisturbed cave burials. They had the thrilling sight of a mass of pottery figures seated on or protruding from the earth floor. They got there before the grave robbers. This was the Amazonian equivalent of Howard Carter breaking into Tutankhamun's tomb.

The most distinctive Maracá ware is funerary urns shaped either as humans seated on stools or as four-legged animals. A typical urn is only 66 centimetres (26 inches) high, so bodies must have been dismembered and the bones ground or burned before burial – as is still done by various tribes. The lid is the head, with the facial features modelled with an elegant simplicity that would have inspired sculptors from Matisse to Brancusi. Stylized body parts clearly show the sex of the dead person, many of whom were women. There are traces of geometric painting all over the urns. Seated figures have long arms with their hands on their knees, but curiously their elbows bend upwards instead of down towards their waists. There are holes in these inverted elbows, possibly to pour ash into the arms during funerary rites. The figures all sit on sculpted stools, which are still a symbol of rank in some indigenous societies.

Intriguingly, very different funerary urns have been discovered in other parts of Amapá, the Brazilian state north of the Amazon's mouth. Some are from Aristé, far north near the frontier with French Guyane. Others are from sites still to be fully excavated. And we have to keep reminding ourselves that this magnificent pottery is but one survival of chiefdoms that must have been quite large and creative. These undoubtedly produced a wealth of other artefacts and ornaments that perished centuries ago. In 2006 archaeologists found a 'Stonehenge' circle of 127 carved stone blocks on top of a hill in this part of Amapá. It was apparently an astronomical observatory to plan agricultural seasons. Associated pottery indicated that the stones were erected at about the time of Christ.

Further up the Amazon is the Santarém pottery that so impressed Orellana's men. It is also of a simplicity that appeals to modern taste. Many pots are in human shape, mostly of women and delightfully naturalistic – one is of a seated girl with her arms holding a leg so that she can suck her toes. Such pieces have traces of paint showing that bodies were covered in geometric painting, with complicated hairdos, coronets containing *muiraquita* amulets in greenish stone, and pierced earlobes. Once again, of course, we see only the few durable objects – pots and muiraquitas – that survive from a culture full of artistic expression. Other Santarém ceramics are extremely complicated, of baroque extravagance, covered in stylized animal shapes and fantastic volutes. Some vessels are known as 'caryatid' because they have three crouching human figures supporting ornate dishes, like the tiers of a wedding cake. The symbolized decorations are often cayman snouts, beaks of king vultures, or frogs.

In the early twentieth century Erland Nordenskiöld worked among the Shipibo-Konibo, a people of the Ucayali in Peru who still make pottery decorated with lovely geometric designs. He was so impressed by the sophistication and antiquity of this pottery that he postulated that his Shipibo had taught other Peruvians their art. A later student of the Shipibo was the American Donald Lathrap who in 1970 published a radical theory – that the lower Amazon from Manaus to the Atlantic Ocean, far from being an imitator of the advanced civilizations of Peru, was their cradle, a hub from which ceramic techniques spread *up* a web of rivers. Interestingly, the Asurini people near the lower Xingu – whom I saw at their first contact in 1972 – made glazed pottery with geometric designs similar to those on Shipibo ware.

Hundreds of rock outcrops, rapids and caves throughout the Amazon's tributaries carry engraved designs. These petroglyphs are impossible to date, difficult to interpret, and often eroded by water cascading over them.

Jesuits and other early travellers remarked on the profusion of rock carvings. Humboldt, Spix and Martius, Wallace, Ferreira Penna and others tried to interpret the meaning of these enigmatic, usually geometric designs. Spruce asked Baré Indians to tell him what they thought was represented – they guessed everything from a circular manioc oven, to river dolphins, and maps that identified rapids and villages by the animal symbol of each chief or tribe. Charles Hartt made the first serious study of these petroglyphs, in a paper in 1871 called 'Brazilian rock inscriptions'. In 1907 the German anthropologist Theodor Koch-Grünberg admitted that they 'have called forth among scholars so many varied and contradictory explanations' – from animalistic creator-deities to fertility symbols (phalluses and vaginas), geometric patterns that may have been tribal or geographic symbols, hunting prey, household objects, some form of writing, or primitive cartography depicting a river's rapids. The great Colombian anthropologist Gerardo Reichel-Dolmatoff was sure that some of these abstracts 'are almost wholly derived from drug-induced inner-light experiences' since they are so similar to drawings made by shamans during hallucinogenic trances.

A major study of rock art carried out by Edithe Pereira of the Goeldi Museum in Belém focused on many sites on the Erepecuru tributary of the

Trombetas (which flows from the north into the lower Amazon). She found engravings clustered at three types of location: near black-earth archaeological sites, alongside powerful waterfalls, and at places where fishing is best. Almost half the designs are geometric, particularly spirals, circles and rectangles. There are also representations of human figures, faces or body parts, as well as zoomorphic glyphs of birds, monkeys, fish and snakes. Whatever their meaning, the petroglyphs are evidence of human creativity and spiritual symbolism. A number of caves and rock shelters contain engravings and paintings. There are also a few stone artefacts, some of them carved with skill and simple beauty.

In 1971 the American archaeologist Betty Meggers published a seminal book, *Amazonia: Man and Culture in a Counterfeit Paradise*. She and her husband Clifford Evans had worked in the region for twenty years, and had in 1954 written an equally challenging paper on how a harsh environment inhibits cultural development. Meggers argued that agriculture depends on extracting nutrients from soils into edible crops, so that societies in Amazonia could never grow large because the underlying soils were too impoverished. The exuberant and evergreen vegetation recaptures every scrap of nutrient, leaving the soil as acidic sand. Thus, *terra-firme* forests away from riverbanks are a 'counterfeit paradise' that look luxuriant but are difficult to exploit. This, coupled with a lack of domestic animals, meant that Amazonians could never produce advanced civilizations, since 'the level to which a culture can develop is dependent upon the agricultural potentiality of the environment it occupies'.

Meggers accepted that fish and turtle resources of the main rivers enabled Indians to build the long villages that Orellana's men saw as they descended the Amazon in 1542. But she dismissed as exaggerated Carvajal's guesses of tens of thousands of people in those settlements, and she was sure that they did not extend far inland. In support of this theory, the Omagua, one of the greatest chiefdoms observed by Carvajal, were riverbank people who regarded the hinterland forests as a barbaric wilderness. Meggers also noted the great stretches of uninhabited river banks between the chiefdoms.

Modern forest tribes keep their villages below a thousand inhabitants so that they do not outgrow surrounding game and vegetable resources. (They do this by birth-control customs, infanticide if a baby has any defect, or fragmentation and migration if a community's population becomes too large.) Meggers was convinced that it had always been thus. There was no forgotten secret that once enabled men to create great civilizations in this inhospitable environment. She always stressed the contrast between evergreen tropical rain forests and temperate forests: 'namely, most of the nutrients and all the calcium are stored in the *biomass* of the former and in the *soil* of the latter'. She and other experts are convinced that, although humans can manipulate the growing vegetation, they cannot markedly alter soil properties.

Central to Meggers's theory is a conviction that food can be grown in tropical forests only in small slash-and-burn clearings. Such 'forest gardens' are called *roça* in Brazil, *roza* in Spanish-speaking countries, and to some anthropologists the technique is swidden farming. Some trees are felled at the start of the dry season and burned a few months later. The resulting clearing is farmed for several years and then gradually abandoned when its feeble soils are exhausted.

Scientific advances came to the aid of the deprived Amazonian archaeologists. First, radiocarbon dating of the time of death of any organic material (vegetable or animal) had been discovered in 1947; then in the 1970s thermo-luminescence told when ceramics were fired; recently improved techniques can date when stone was chipped; and there were advances in pedology (soil studies) and palynology (analysis of pollen and seeds preserved in lake or river beds).

New techniques, coupled with fine research in widely separated parts of Amazonia, led to challenges to accepted theories. In the final years of the twentieth century fierce debate erupted about four issues: the date when humans first arrived on these forested rivers; how soon they developed agriculture and ceramics; whether they farmed in forest clearings or manipulated the forest itself; and the scale and sophistication of pre-conquest societies.

The antiquity of swidden farming was challenged in the 1980s. The anthropologist Robert Carneiro and the geographer William Denevan argued that it would have been too laborious for indigenous peoples to clear forest for agriculture using stone axes (Carneiro himself tried to clear a *roça* using such tools, and found that it took over 150 days of hard labour – this notwithstanding the plethora of other tasks the Indians would have had to perform). But Carneiro and Denevan had underestimated the Indians' skills. By exploiting natural tree falls or patches of *cerrado*, by judicious use of fire, communal effort and patient labour with reasonably sharp stone implements, indigenous peoples did often manage to open *roças* large enough to feed their villages. This has been shown repeatedly when first contacts have been made with tribes.

Also in the 1980s, anthropologists and botanists learned far more about indigenous peoples' knowledge of plants and their *manipulation* of forests. Darrell Posey went on hunting expeditions with Kayapó (on the plateau between the Tocantins and Xingu rivers) and found that, at their infrequent rests, they always seemed to have the produce they wanted. He realized that they were planting desirable trees when they defecated at these places. Posey later collaborated with William Balée of Tulane University to study the hundreds of species of plants used by the Ka'apor people (in the area between Pará and Maranhão). They found that this ingenious tribe surrounded its villages with patches of forest rich in plants that delivered everything it needed or that attracted game or even edible grubs. The Ka'apor were using half the species in their managed forest, whereas they would have used only a fifth of species in pristine forest. Similar studies of plant-use by peoples like the Atroari-Waimiri (north of Manaus) and Yanomami (between Brazil and Venezuela), by Ghillean Prance and William Milliken of Kew Gardens and others, reached the same conclusions. All these ethnobotanists were amazed by the quantity of plants known to and used by the tribes they studied. Balée suggested that over 12 per cent of Amazon forests has been changed by human beings. That is a vast area. But it would still leave 87 per cent pristine.

A leading revisionist in these debates is Anna Roosevelt of the University of Illinois, who told me that she is the great-granddaughter of President Theodore 'Teddy' Roosevelt. She revisited a huge cavern called Pedra Pintada (Painted Rock) in a spur of sandstone that runs south from the geologically ancient Guiana Shield. Pedra Pintada is 10 kilometres (6 miles) north of Monte Alegre, a town on the Amazon roughly 300 kilometres (185 miles) from its mouth. As well as rock paintings, this cave contained a nondescript mound that proved to be a midden full of exciting refuse. There were 24 worked stone tools and thousands of flakes, burnt wood from hearths, many seeds, bones of animals and fish, and tortoise shells. Roosevelt's team obtained 56 radiocarbon dates that ranged from 9,200 to 8,000 BC. She concluded that this very ancient culture 'with its ... economy [based on] tropical-forest and river foraging, shows that the earliest foragers were neither primitive in culture nor unable to adapt to the humid tropical environment'. Pedra Pintada also had sherds that were said to be the oldest pottery in the Americas, but these have not been fully described, and in a few illustrations they look more recent. The 'Amazonian palaeo-Indians' who made it are known as Paituna, after a nearby modern village. Datable material of similar antiquity was found in a rock shelter called Abrigo do Sol ('Shelter from the Sun') far away to the south, near a source of the Tapajós river. Digging below what she thought was the lowest stratum of habitation, Roosevelt found evidence of a culture as much as 13,000 years old. The discovery of such ancient human presence was a bombshell in the recondite world of Amazonian archaeology.

The accepted wisdom had been that human beings moved from Central Asia into the Americas. They made the crossing in successive waves after 22,000 years BC, during the ice ages when the shallow Bering Strait would have been exposed as a windswept land-bridge between Siberia and Alaska. They may have sailed round the coast – which was then 200 feet (60 metres) lower than now – in pursuit of fish or other marine game. Skirting the vast glacial sheet that covered most of Canada, humans migrated south into the great plains of North America. A site near the town of Clovis (in dry badlands of northeastern New Mexico) in the 1930s yielded a mass of animal bones and artefacts of their human hunters. Organic material at Clovis was dated to 11,500 BC, while artefacts at other sites, such as Cactus Hill in Virginia, might be from 16,000 BC. DNA research by molecular geneticists confirmed that there were probably two paths of migration from 'Beringia', in 13,000 and 15,000 BC. Descendants of the 'Clovis people' moved southwards, into Mexico and Central America and on to the coastal plain of Peru and the forests of the Amazon. The more ancient dates of Roosevelt and others were presented in 1999 at a conference in Santa Fe, New Mexico (not far from the Clovis excavations). They provoked a row between the 'Clovis mafia' (who questioned the scientific techniques used on the earliest samples and clung to their later dates) and the new guard (with growing evidence of earlier human arrival).

Apart from the discrepancy in dates, there is much to support the conventional model. Native Americans of both continents resemble Central Asians – in skin colour, straight black hair, eyelids, noses, even blood groups and DNA. People who adapted to life in the high Andes (through enlarged spleens and lungs and a higher ratio of red to white blood corpuscles) look just like those of Mongolia or Tibet, even down to the rosy cheeks of their children. And infants of some American indigenous tribes are born with the 'Mongol spot', a bluish birthmark at the base of the spine that soon disappears. This is true of the Yanomami, the largest native nation of Amazonia to survive with its culture relatively intact.

Recent discoveries challenge the dating and routes of internal migrations, but not the main theory. They show that man arrived in the Americas far earlier than was previously thought, perhaps as much as 30,000 years ago, but the pattern of occupation is still thought to be from north to south. It might seem surprising that human beings spread over such an immense area, or that they migrated for such long distances and past barriers of mountains, deserts, or the rain-drenched Darien Gap between Central and South America. But they *did* fragment in this way. Hunter-gatherers and subsistence farmers are self-sufficient, so that when they move with their families and few possessions they can travel very far in a few decades. (For example, in the late sixteenth century eighty-four villages of Tupinamba migrated away from Portuguese oppressors on the Atlantic seaboard, moved right across the continent to the foothills of the Andes in Bolivia – where Spaniards recorded their arrival – and then descended the Madeira river system to settle on Tupinambarana Island downstream of Manaus. When the Portuguese saw them there in 1639 old men recalled their homeland in Pernambuco. This migration of some 5,600 kilometres – 3,500 miles – was done in only two generations.) Indigenous peoples of the Americas developed a bewildering variety of languages and each tribe had peculiarities of ornament, customs, beliefs, dwellings and artefacts. But the broad similarities between them far outweighed the differences.

So human beings apparently found agreeable homes in the Amazon in the late Pleistocene age, over 11,000 years ago. It was the time of the last Ice Age, when Amazonia was cooler and drier than now. Dating of cores from lake and river beds (and of the pollen these contain) indicates that there was then as much tree-cover in the region as at present. But it was differently distributed, with more forests on the slopes of the Andes and more grasslands further east. Those early settlers then grew in numbers and they lived and hunted in bands, as most other primates do.

There was a very long hiatus in the human remains excavated from Pedra Pintada cavern. Pottery appeared there again, datable from about 2,000 BC. Anna Roosevelt found that by then 'the Indians of the lower Amazon were growing crops – at least 138 of them according to a recent tally'. So early humans in Amazonia evidently foraged, fished and hunted, used crude pottery, and congregated into larger groups and tribes, centuries before they started farming. The staple crop became manioc (discussed above: see pp. 25–27). At first this was sweet manioc, grown in more open savannah or campo; then humans learned how to leach poison from more nutritious bitter manioc. This wonder-plant may first have been domesticated in about 7,000 BC in what is now Brazilian Rondônia and western Mato Grosso. It grew best in more rainforest-clad areas, so the spread of its farming led to anthropogenic or man-manipulated soils under many Amazon forests.

We are fortunate to have living examples of foragers in the twenty-first century. At least two tribes of nomadic hunter-gatherers are still active: Maku, Nukak and Hupdu bands between Brazil and Colombia, and the Awá-Guajá in ancient forests in Maranhão (the Brazilian state southeast of the mouth of the Amazon). Both these groups of peoples prefer to be nomadic, stopping only briefly in temporary shelters beneath the forest canopy. They lead remarkably good lives. Their knowledge of forest resources is astounding and they are skilled hunters. The British anthropologist Peter Silverwood-Cope learned about the Maku's deep understanding of their environment and their rich mythology and culture. 'They live in small family groups, prefer the deep forest to the rivers, and are constantly on the move. In fact, they never stay in one place for more than a few days. As they are so mobile it means that they can have few possessions, and what they have must be easily portable. At a minute's notice, therefore, they can wrap up their fibre-string hammocks (which are their only real furniture), put their pots and few remaining items in home-made rucksacks, and move on.... The Maku eat fish, game, turtles, fruit, vegetables, nuts, insects and honey. Indeed, it is hard to think of a healthier or more balanced diet.' When the Maku abandon a campsite, they know that their detritus will sprout into their favourite trees and plants. So when they return, months later, they camp alongside but not on top of the forest they have manipulated.

An archaeological site that yielded evidence of very early foragers from over 7,000 BC is Peña Roja ('Red Outcrop') – and this is near the forests of present-day Maku, on the Caquetá affluent of the Amazon in Colombia. Forests there are lower, drier and less luxuriant than in western or central Amazonia. Flying over these apparently pristine forests, one is struck by huge patches of palm trees. They were probably altered by millennia of human interference, for excavations at Peña Roja showed quantities of seeds of popular palms like buriti (*moriche* in Spanish, *miriti* in English, *Mauritia flexuosa* botanically), bacaba (*Oenocarpus*) and najá (*Maximiliana martiana*) alongside flaked stone implements.

Palms are wonderfully useful to foragers. They are easy to fell. The tall and stately buriti/moriche 'supplies building materials for houses, carbohydrate food, cork for bottles, fibre for weaving, a fermented beverage, [logs for rafts], and diverse other products important in tribal economies'. The tucumã/cumare (*Astrocaryum*) has hideous porcupine-like spines up its entire trunk to repel climbers, but it is the Indians' great friend. Its leaflets yield a tough fibre that makes the best hammocks and cords, the spines have myriad uses, the orange fruit is fish bait, and the wood is good for boats and houses. Down on Marajó Island the best-loved palm is açaí (*Euterpe oleracea*), which yields clusters of purple fruit the size of large blueberries. Amazonians have always been voracious drinkers of açaí juice:

second only to manioc and fish, this is a staff of life in the region. Local people are right: modern nutritionists see açaí as 'the world's most complete natural food' – full of thirty times as many antioxidants as red wine and all the vitamins of olive oil. And there is the all-purpose peach palm (*Bactris gasipaes*), so useful that it has a host of names including pupunha, chontaduro and tembé. Tall and straight, with many stalks, its wood is ideal for hut beams, and strong enough for bows, clubs or even saws. Its clusters of orange-red fruits are also a major source of calories, oil, vitamin C and protein. Dried fruit can make flour for unleavened bread; cooked and fermented it yields beer. Protective rings of spines around the trunk deter climbing foragers, but these spines have plenty of uses – including the 'feline whiskers' that adorn Yanomami women's cheeks.

Carvajal in 1542 and other later explorers saw extensive villages along the banks of the main Amazon and its large tributaries. Much of this is *várzea*, the region of massive annual flooding from the river's rise between January and May. The main food of *várzea*-dwellers was of course the profusion of fish and turtles in their sediment-rich white-water rivers. None of their fishing apparatus survives, but we observe modern tribes using most techniques, including trellis traps across rivers, basketry nets, shooting fish and turtles with bows-and-arrows or harpooning larger fish, and damming streams to stun fish with poison from *timbó* lianas. Vegetables were farmed and animals hunted in riverside forests, and people learned which foods could be stored under the floods and recovered when the waters receded. So the wonderfully rich *várzea* is thought to have supported a population seventy times that of normal *terra-firme* forest – 14.6 persons per square kilometre compared to 0.2. This density is after allowing for the long stretches of empty riverbanks observed by Orellana's expedition.

These riverbank communities produced the 'chiefdoms' of Anna Roosevelt and other modern revisionists. These argue that there was nothing counterfeit about the riverside part of the Amazonian paradise. They say that great chiefdoms evolved during the two millennia before the arrival of Europeans. Because of the problems of Amazonian archaeology described above, exponents of the chiefdom theory have to rely on four sources: raised terraces that required large labour forces; elaborate ceramics that showed hierarchical societies; observations by the first Spanish explorers; and black-earth sites.

Roosevelt revisited Marajó Island and felt that its chiefdom had been greater than Meggers and Evans concluded when they worked there in the 1950s to 1960s.

She was able to use modern remote-sensing techniques – topographic mapping from satellites, side-looking aerial radar that can penetrate surface soil, and scanners that detect variations in magnetic or electrical fields. This, coupled with Marajoara pottery and discoveries of more agricultural platforms, led Roosevelt to conclude in 1991 that 'Marajó was one of the outstanding indigenous cultural achievements of the New World', with over a hundred thousand inhabitants, Such chiefdoms had 'territories tens of thousands of square kilometres in size' and societies stratified from deified chiefs down to vassals and captive slaves. This seems exaggerated. Marajó was abundantly rich in fish resources, but its soil has always been weak. Even though the Marajoarans enhanced their flat island with raised platforms and irrigation, their staple crops were probably from palm trees. I find it impossible to imagine this Amazonian culture rivalling the civilizations of Peru and Mexico – as some chiefdom proponents have suggested. In lowland Amazonia there were no domesticable animals (such as the llamas and guinea pigs of the Andes), no easy crops other than manioc (no potatoes, quinoa, maize), little open terrain, few stone quarries and no metals; in addition, no South Americans had writing as we understand it, or wheels, or beasts of burden.

Betty Meggers fought back. She was still director of the Smithsonian Institution's Latin American Archaeology Program in the twenty-first century, when in her eighties. In 2001 she even accused the revisionists of endangering all Amazon rain forests by suggesting that these could be felled to create large-scale farming. 'Adherence to "the lingering myth of Amazon empires" not only prevents archaeologists from reconstructing the prehistory of Amazonia, but makes us accomplices in the accelerating pace of environmental degradation.' She scoffed at Roosevelt as a beginner who confused sporadic occupation of a site with remains of a single great society. Charles Mann summed up the feud between the two formidable archaeologists: 'Over time, the Meggers-Roosevelt dispute grew bitter and personal; inevitable in a contemporary academic context, it featured charges of colonialism, elitism, and membership of the CIA.'

Meggers's arguments were reinforced by palaeo-ecologists led by Mark Bush (a Britisher at the Florida Institute of Technology). This team in 2007 published findings from lake-bed analysis of pollen and charcoal at sites in Peru, Ecuador and Brazil. In each location, people always lived in one lakeside village but didn't stray far from home. In each of the study areas, 'there is evidence of long, continuous occupation of more than five thousand years that did not spread to the adjacent, 8- to 10-kilometres-distant lakes'. Thus, in terra-firme forest away from the main rivers, villages were small and widely dispersed. Dr Bush's research also challenged the notion that much Amazonian forest is a 'built landscape' manipulated by generations of human beings. His team agreed with William Denevan who in 1996 suggested that 'occupation was centred on sandy bluffs overlooking navigable channels and floodplains. This ... suggests local alteration of landscapes extending five to ten kilometres around settlements, but with vast interfluvial areas where humans had little impact on the biota.' The research also coincided with Nigel Smith's contention in 1980 that *terra-preta* deposits averaged over 21 hectares on riverside sites, but only 1.4 hectares under *terra-firme* forest. Thus, 'we see long histories of disturbance at ... a central location, with relatively small impacts on nearby systems and no apparent impacts ... 50 kilometres away'.

Early archaeologists were intrigued by *terra-preta* (black-earth) sites, which occur near rivers all over Amazonia. This wonderful black soil contrasts strikingly with the miserable yellow or pink earth under most rain forests. *Terra-preta* soil can be 50 cm (20 inches) deep, and it contains plenty of carbon, nitrogen, calcium and phosphorus. These sites were clearly occupied for centuries by early man: they are usually littered with masses of potsherds. In the 1870s the American geologist Herbert Smith (a pupil of Charles Hartt) wrote how excited he was by 'rich *terra preta*, "black land", the best on the Amazons'.

Experts still differ about the origin of black earth. A few think that these sites are natural occurrences (perhaps caused by volcanic intrusion or lake sediment), merely discovered by man. Some wonder whether ancient man created *terra preta* by some now-forgotten process. But the majority relate it to sustained human habitation. Nutrient-rich black earth, often full of artefacts, is where houses and refuse middens decomposed; nearby paler *terra mulata* is where agriculture took place and there was more burning of vegetation and removal of crop plants. One theory is that human beings mixed charcoal into the soil – and far richer maize was the result. Michael Heckenberger of the University of Florida and Susannah Hecht of Los Angeles watched Kuikuro Indians of the upper Xingu burn vegetable waste with a gentle, constant smouldering, then mix the resulting charcoal into the soil to create a form of *terra preta*. Wood charcoal helps to retain carbon in the soil, but itself contains few nutrients: these must have come from waste matter.

Some gardeners believe that black-earth soil is 'alive' and can regenerate itself. Modern settlers seek such locations because they know that they will yield good harvests, and urban horticulturalists pay high prices for this miraculous product. The geographer William Woods tried moving a large patch from near Santarém to a new site where, to his surprise, it 'grew back' in three years. He suggested that it 'should be treated as a living organism and that [soil] micro-organisms are the secret'. Here again, Betty Meggers is sceptical: 'The idea that the indigenous population has secrets that we don't know about is not supported by anything except wishful thinking.... The myth just keeps going on and on. It's amazing.'

Whatever its nature and origin, there is no debate about *terra-preta*'s fertility. It is less acidic and contains a humus with more nitrogen and phosphorus than soils nearby. These sites have been occupied for many centuries and are often densely littered with sherds of ancient pottery. Surviving *terra preta* tends to be found on bluffs or levées some distance from riverbanks – where it could not be washed away by river currents. There is also a dark brown soil known as *terra mulata* that contains no potsherds and is probably the remains of a farmed garden.

The earliest black-earth sites are dated from a few centuries BC, coinciding with the first intensive agriculture and settlement. One of the oldest such sites is near Yarinacocha on the lower Ucayali in Peru, dated 200 BC. A huge complex is Açutuba, a forested farm above the Rio Negro opposite Manaus, and Hatahara a few kilometres away but overlooking the Solimões *várzea*. James Petersen of the University of Vermont and Eduardo Neves of São Paulo started a project here in 1994. Açutuba's *terra preta* can be carbon-dated from about 360 BC to AD 1450, just before the arrival of Europeans; but there is 'tentative evidence of an earlier occupation at 4900 BC'. These vast sites cover many square kilometres, and they are littered with millions of potsherds. Neves reckoned that a single mound contained forty million sherds, deliberately broken, possibly to aerate or drain the soil. This pottery ranges from fine ceramics ornately painted in black and white, to coarse ware – clear evidence of a class structure. Orellana's first Spaniards called a settlement near here 'Pottery Village' because of the abundance of what archaeologists now refer to as Guarita ware. Açutuba and neighbouring sites could easily have supported a population of ten thousand people.

Another *terra-preta* deposit is Taperinha on the lower Amazon, near modern Santarém and the mouth of the Tapajós river. Taperinha's black earth stretches for 5 kilometres (3 miles) along the riverbank and is over a kilometre (half a mile) wide. This was clearly the homeland of the people who made 'Santarém' ceramics. And we have seen how the Tapajó remained a powerful tribe with an elaborate religion, witnessed by Orellana's men in 1542 and finally enslaved by the Portuguese in 1640. William Woods argued that if the Tapajó chiefdom farmed this patch of *terra preta* intensively it could have supported tens of thousands of people – which would have made it one of the most densely populated places on earth at that time.

Ancient mounds and terraced fields are dispersed through Amazonia, from Marajó in the river's mouth, to upland plains of modern Bolivia thousands of kilometres to the southwest, and to Colombia far to the northwest. These extraordinary raised fields were clearly the work of large and well-organized communities. All were in more open terrain outside high *terra-firme* forests.

At the southern extremity of the Amazon basin, anthropologists and archaeologists have long been fascinated by hillocks rising above featureless flatness. These are in Bolivia's Beni province, on the Llanos de Mojos where the long Rio Grande (or Guapay) flows northwards to become the Mamoré and then the Madeira. In 1620 Antonio Vázquez de Espinosa described this land as 'vast plains which they call pampas, which pass out of sight into the far distance with horizons like those at sea. They call the mounds in them "islands" and use them as guideposts, so as not to get lost in such extensive plains.... This country has wonderful land and skies, with a good climate and pleasant breezes: it is so fertile and prolific that it seems almost like Paradise.' This chronicler wrote that these savannahs were covered with countless Indian tribes, including the Chimané, Mojo, Sirionó, Bauré and others, with the populous Chiriguano peoples to the southeast (near the now-booming city of Santa Cruz). The plains were flooded for almost half each year, until the shallow waters drained off towards the Amazon; during the dry season indigenous people burned the grasses to enhance growth. In the 1680s Jesuit missionaries introduced cattle, horses and other European livestock to these Indians, who took to ranching. The herds multiplied, and there were eventually fifteen thriving mission 'reductions' among the Mojo. After the Jesuits' expulsion in 1767 animals and missions were destroyed by marauders, and the Indians were almost extinguished by diseases, neglect and removal for forced labour on estancias and during the rubber boom.

Erland Nordenskiöld excavated some mounds in the early twentieth century, but he and the French ethnographer Alfred Métraux concluded that they were natural outcrops because they contained no burials or other deposits. In the 1960s the young American geographer William Denevan flew low over the Beni and was amazed to see that much of it was an op-art canvas of zebra-striped ridges and rectangular copses linked by straight lines of vegetation. Modern investigators have returned to these rectangular mounds and are now sure that they were man-made, in order to raise trees and crops above the flooding. Straight causeways joined the mounds and alongside them were canals from which their earth had been taken. Indians could move either along the raised roads or in their canoes on the canals. Agriculture on raised fields could have supported tens of thousands of people, on what are now weak and thinly populated grasslands. Such earthworks were clearly the work of populous and well organized societies.

The mounds are now called *camellones*, or camel humps. There are thousands of them in the Beni, with the highest rising to 18 metres (60 feet). Alf Hornborg of the University of Lund in Sweden argues that raised fields were the invention of Arawak-speakers, since they occur on plains occupied by those mobile and industrious peoples, from Caribbean islands, to northern Colombia and Venezuela, Marajó Island, the Pajonal in eastern Peru, and Bolivia. Mounds in all these places can be full of broken pottery – like black-earth sites on the lower Rio Negro. In addition to providing refuges from seasonal floods, raised fields were useful for drainage and 'soil aeration, reduction of root rot, increased nitrification, pest reduction, less acidity, moisture retention (in the ditches), enhancement of fertility [with] muck from the ditches' and easier weeding and harvesting.

North of the Llano de Mojos, at Baures on a southern tributary of the Guaporé, archaeologists were excited by low earthworks zigzagging across 500 square kilometres of savannah. It was Clark Erickson of the University of Pennsylvania who realized that this had once been a gigantic fish farm. The earthworks change direction every 10 to 30 metres (30–100 feet), so they were *weirs*. During the annual flooding, fish at each kink were funnelled into 2-metre-deep (6.5 feet) ponds. They could be kept there as the waters receded during the dry season. Erickson reckoned that a hectare of pond would have yielded a metric tonne of fish a year. There were also edible *Pomacea* snails, quantities of whose shells are piled round the abandoned ponds.

Michael Heckenberger and James Petersen recently found traces of large, sophisticated settlements near the village of the Carib-speaking Kuikuro of the upper Xingu. In a decade of work amid the roots and leaf litter of scrubby forests, they discovered three concentric circular moats, the largest about 1.6 kilometres (a mile) in diameter, some 4 metres (12–15 feet) deep and 15 metres (50 feet) wide. This moat's mound has regular holes, apparently for upright posts of a defensive palisade. There is also evidence of broad roads linking this site to others in the region, and within the circular defences there may have been broad plazas and regular town planning – although the buildings were of course made of perishable timber and thatch. Heckenberger found traces of 'bridges, artificial river obstructions and ponds, raised causeways, canals and other structures ... a highly elaborate built environment'. Potsherds, black-earth and other finds date these settlements to just before European arrival elsewhere: AD 1250–1400. This chiefdom may have had a population of many thousands. But it is worth noting that the upper Xingu is in fairly open country at the southeastern edge of the mass of Hylean rain forests, where the trees are lower and less dense and the rivers teem with fish. Also, when the dozen tribes of the upper Xingu were first contacted by Karl von den Steinen in 1885 – apparently before they had suffered depopulation from alien diseases – they all (including the Kuikuro) numbered only about three thousand.

So, who is right in the 'Meggers-Roosevelt' debate? I agree with both camps to some extent. Roosevelt's very early dates of human arrival in the Amazon, and the development of tribal societies and pottery before agriculture, are now accepted. But I do not accept Lathrap's theory that the lower Amazon was a hub from which culture radiated to influence Peru's early civilizations – since antecedents of the latter are thousands of years earlier than chiefdoms such as Marajó and Santarém, and the environments are totally different. However, Arawak-speaking peoples do seem to have taken their mount-building knowledge in their migrations through the Amazon basin.

Modern swidden clearings undoubtedly depend on metal axes and saws. However, pre-conquest man could to some extent have relied on such agriculture: some forest peoples did open large *roças* before they acquired metal blades. For instance the Panará of central Brazil, who were contacted in 1973, had several hectares of farms in the forest near their villages. These were planted with peanuts and other crops arranged geometrically in curious circular patterns, which baffled Brazilians flying over before contact was made on the ground. Many other groups had vegetable gardens before they acquired metal blades. I saw sizeable farms alongside villages of the Asurini and the Parakanã (both in Pará, between the Xingu and Tocantins) at the time of their first contacts. So it is clear that some pre-contact tribes exploited natural tree-falls as well as bare patches of *cerrado* and savannah or did manage to fell trees with stone axes, hardwood saws and burning. Some plains Indians also used fire to surround game during their hunts. The practice of annual burnings was adopted by European settlers, who call it *coivara*. Such fires sometimes rage into adjacent forest when it is at its driest, and lightning storms can also spark conflagrations. Whatever the cause, there is evidence of burning under many forests. The ecologist Chris Uhl commented that 'in much of Amazonia it is difficult to find soils that are not studded with charcoal'.

There is no question that large and well organized chiefdoms flourished along some of the main rivers. Archaeological evidence (from pottery, black earth and rock engravings) confirms the reports of large populations by the first European explorers – not just by Carvajal in 1542 but also by others like Raposo Tavares who descended the Madeira in 1650. Meggers conceded that such chiefdoms existed, but she also noted that the first reports spoke of long expanses of uninhabited banks, particularly on upper rivers and between warring chiefdoms.

Having myself studied accounts of exploration and first contacts throughout Brazilian history, I agree with Meggers's contention that dense settlements did not extend deep into *terra-firme* forest. Humans in such forests kept their villages small in order not to exhaust the surrounding plant and animal resources. Tribes at first contact had far larger populations and more villages than after they were decimated by alien diseases. But during the past century the ratio of destruction after contact was ten to one at its very worst – usually far less. At their nadir in the mid-twentieth century, forest peoples throughout the Amazon basin numbered about 200,000, so by this maximum extrapolation they might once have been two million. The chiefdoms on the great rivers and surrounding savannahs bore the brunt of enslavement, depopulation and extinction. In their heyday they could have added a larger population than the forested areas. This would have given the entire Amazon basin a pre-conquest total of four to five million.

CHAPTER TEN

Planes, Chainsaws and Bulldozers

By the mid-twentieth century the Amazon's forests had defeated the mighty Ford Motor Company and frustrated the American war effort, just as they had baffled conquistadors, colonists and rubber barons. Its rivers reverted to sleepy backwaters peopled by a few resilient caboclos; its towns and cities were in decline. The world's richest ecosystem might have continued as a pristine paradise. That tranquillity was destroyed by three inventions: the plane, the chainsaw and the bulldozer.

Civil aviation gave the Andean countries access to their cities on the Amazon. Planes could service places previously reachable only by backbreaking mule rides through the mountains and river journeys past rapids and whirlpools. Peru now had regular flights to Iquitos on the Amazon, Pucallpa on the Ucayali and Puerto Maldonado on the Madre de Dios. Bolivia was better linked to former rubber depots like Riberalta on the Beni and what became its second city Santa Cruz de la Sierra on the llanos; and Colombia could reach Leticia, its distant toehold on the Amazon. Brazil, with the lion's share of the Amazon basin, made the most of planes. Capitals of states or territories – Belém in Pará, Cuiabá in Mato Grosso, Manaus in Amazonas, Rio Branco in Acre, Porto Velho in Rondônia, Boa Vista in Roraima, Macapá in Amapá – all had new leases of life from aviation. Towns, villages, missions and Indian posts on the vast network of rivers acquired airstrips.

The Brazilian Air Force FAB operated regular flights to remote airstrips in an admirable service called CAN (national aerial postal service). Its daring pilots flew the wartime workhorse Dakotas and their C47 successors, as well as elegant

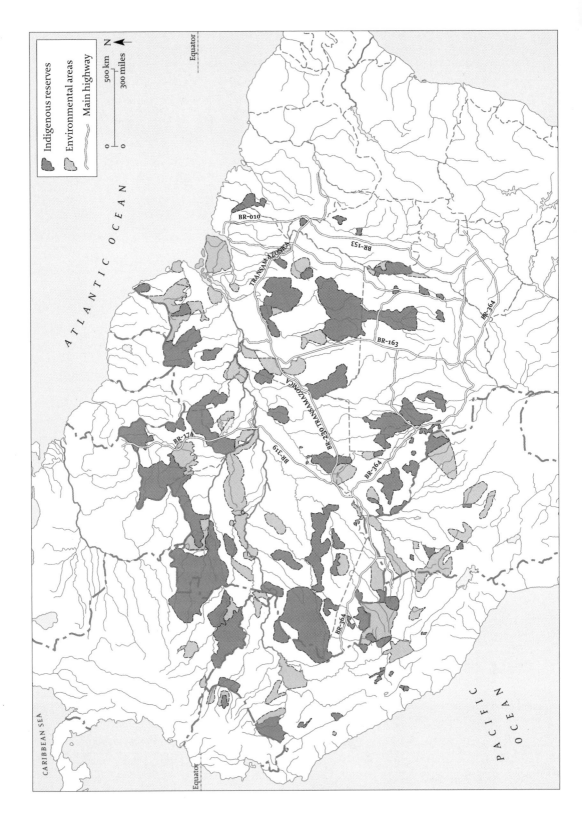

Catalina flying boats, but they could land on unlit jungle clearings or rivers only during daylight hours. This author had scores of flights with the CAN. Its planes carried a mix of service personnel, missionaries, forest woodsmen and civil servants, seated around a cargo of food (including bloody meat carcasses), petroleum, beer, tools and other paraphernalia of frontier life, and the occasional corpse or injured victim of a barroom shooting. One Air Force brigadier kept the men in his isolated outposts happy by sending a couple of prostitutes on their monthly supply flights.

In the 1940s, the Vargas government created the Central Brazil Foundation with a mission to open the heart of the country. It launched an expedition to cut a trail from the upper Araguaia northwestwards across unexplored country to the Xingu and then on towards the Tapajós. The objective was to clear airstrips that could be used for emergency landings by planes flying to North America and as weather stations. Three young brothers from São Paulo left routine city jobs to join this exciting venture. With their education, these Villas Boas brothers soon took charge of the three-year expedition. After months of arduous cutting across the plains and hills of the warlike Xavante (pronounced Shav-ante), the explorers in 1944 reached the Xingu's headwaters. They were enchanted by the tribes that had welcomed Von den Steinen sixty years previously (and had probably killed Colonel Fawcett twenty years before). So they never left this tropical Eden. Orlando and Cláudio Villas Boas lived there for the next thirty years, and they succeeded Rondon as the champions of indigenous peoples. (The third brother Leonardo died in 1961 during a heart operation.)

Planes and their airstrips revolutionized movement in the Amazon basin, but they did not destroy much forest. Chainsaws were another matter. Metal blades (machetes, axes, hand-saws) had made it possible for men to fell trees in a few hours of physical effort. They proved irresistible to Indians, and have always been the lure in contacting isolated tribes. Chainsaws, with their portable motors, represented a huge advance for the loggers. Gigantic trees could be felled in minutes with little exertion. This destruction was coupled with burning of cleared vegetation or nearby *campo* grasslands – a practice inherited from some plains Indians who burned savannah each year to help them hunt its game. Suddenly, the great rain forests were prostrate at the feet of man.

The rain forest's third nemesis was earthmoving machines and the roads they could build. To the south, the Bolivians had roads from La Paz north to the

Opposite *Map showing major protected areas and highways in the Amazon Basin.*

Beni and northeast to the Mojos plains. In the west, the Peruvians built a highway through the Andes to Pucallpa on the navigable Ucayali. They later cut rougher and more tortuous roads through the mountains, in the south from Cuzco to the Madre de Dios headwater of the Madeira, and in the north to Chachapoyas and Richard Spruce's botanizing base Tarapoto on the Huallaga. Ecuador had always had a trail from Quito down to its Oriente province on the upper Napo, and this was widened for motor vehicles. That country's economy was transformed when, in 1964, Texaco struck oil in those forests. This was the largest petroleum find in the Amazon basin: it has always provided over half Ecuador's gross national product. Colombia eventually cut a road south from Bogotá across the mountains to Florencia at the source of the Caquetá.

As with aviation, it was Brazilians who launched an onslaught into the Amazon by road-building. This was, of course, far easier for them because they did not have to surmount the barrier of the Andes. In 1953 the government created a 'Superintendency' to develop the stagnant Amazon region. This was known as SPVEA and, when it collapsed from inefficiency and corruption, its successor's acronym was SUDAM. The first two new roads skirted the great mass of tropical rain forests. In 1958–60 the 'Road of the Jaguar' (BR-010 and BR-153) was built for 1,900 kilometres (1,180 miles) from the new capital Brasília north to Belém at the mouth of the Amazon. This highway often ran through natural savannah, in the mesopotamia between the Tocantins and Araguaia rivers, so it opened a region of good farming and ranching country. In its first decade, this Belém-Brasília road helped that region's population increase twenty-fold to two million, living in 120 towns where there had been ten, and with a cattle herd grown from almost none to five million head. The road made it cheap for migrants to settle, easy for them to travel to the rest of Brazil, and above all economic to move their farm produce and animals to market.

The Amazon Superintendency's other planning success was to declare the city of Manaus a duty-free zone. This surprising move – to make a moribund boom-town far up the Amazon into a free port – succeeded because Brazil had artificially high tariffs and taxes. Rich Brazilians flew to Manaus to buy duty-free goods, and manufacturers located there to enjoy generous tax breaks. In time, Manaus became Brazil's centre for producing domestic appliances, white-goods and scooters. By the end of the century, Manaus had mushroomed into a sprawling, chaotic metropolis of two million people. It has always contained roughly half the inhabitants of the huge, forested State of Amazonas. But its heart was still the grid of avenues laid out at the height of the rubber boom, looking up from the floating port to the Teatro Amazonas opera house.

The next new highway skirted the southeastern edge of the rain forests. It ran northwestwards from Cuiabá in Mato Grosso to Porto Velho on the Madeira. This BR-364, built a decade after the Road of the Jaguar, followed the route of Rondon's strategic telegraph line across what was named after him as the Territory (later State) of Rondônia. The BR-364 was also on the geologically ancient Central Brazilian Shield, partly on the watershed between two Amazon tributaries. Some of it ran across open campo, entering Hyleian forest only when it approached the Madeira or crossed other rivers. There was a rumour that it occasionally struck patches of purple soil, highly fertile *terra roxa*. After a slow start, the BR-364 became the artery for the greatest migration into virgin territory in South American history. These two roads, built in the 1960s on more open land that frames the mass of Amazon forests, created a tremendous 'arc of deforestation'.

By 1980 half a million settlers had moved along the BR-364, and transmigration accelerated during the next decade. Many colonists were industrious farmers from southern Brazil, displaced by mechanized agribusiness. (In the 1970s I watched truck after truck trundling along the dusty or muddy highway, each with a family living in the back amid its furniture and possessions.) As with any rush, there were violent clashes. Land wars broke out between colonists and Indians, peasants and *latifundários* (owners of vast tracts of land), the government's land agency Incra and property speculators, squatters and legal owners. Loggers, wildcat miners, ranchers, and truckers all tried to make a killing in this frenzy. Among the genuine settlers, there were hired-gun *pistoleiros*, conmen peddling bogus title deeds, and prostitutes operating from shacks with names like 'Paradise' or 'A Thousand and One Nights'. As the migration continued, and after the BR-364 was paved (in 1985, helped by a controversial World Bank loan), a grid of roads sliced into forests on either side of the highway. There was massive deforestation along each of these side roads. The BR-364 became notorious as the greatest destroyer of rain forests.

A military president of Brazil was moved by the suffering caused by severe drought in the arid northeast of his country. Emílio Médici in 1971 vowed to open the Amazon forests to these poor people, to provide 'a land without people for a people without land'. With no research or planning, he launched the Transamazonica Highway. This was a 'penetration road' – in other words a road going nowhere, just piercing the forest. The Transamazonica (or BR-230) ran a few hundred kilometres south of the lower Amazon and its Madeira tributary. It started at Estreito and Marabá on the Tocantins and thence westwards to the rapids where each southern tributary plunges off the Central Brazilian Shield. There was always a town at these locations, since this was as far as river boats could sail upstream – Altamira on the Xingu, Itaituba on the Tapajós, Humaitá on the Madeira, then on to Porto Velho (already reached by the BR-364) and west across Acre, to peter out towards the Peruvian frontier. The construction of this pioneering road was an amazing feat. I saw teams of tough woodsmen hack trails for hundreds of kilometres between the rivers. They lived rough and were guided and supplied by planes which threw food down onto their camps. Other labourers widened their trail with chainsaws, creating a 70-metre-wide (230-feet) swathe of cleared forest. Behind them, big yellow earthmovers sliced, graded and surfaced a straight dirt road, which crossed streams on wooden bridges and big rivers on pontoon rafts. The 2,232-kilometre (1,386-mile) stretch from the Tocantins to the Madeira was completed by 1974; the full Transamazonica, if placed on a map of Europe, would stretch from Lisbon to Moscow. To complement this east-west highway, other roads were pushed into the Amazon forests roughly from south to north: from Cuiabá in Mato Grosso towards Santarém on the Amazon; from Porto Velho to the Amazon river opposite Manaus; and from Manaus to Roraima, and thence eventually to Venezuela and Guyana.

These penetration roads violated the pristine forests of Amazonia, but planners justified them with talk of *faixas* ('swathes of social occupation') that connected 'dynamic growth poles'. Expert *sertanistas* of the Indian service Funai were ordered to contact and 'pacify' isolated indigenous peoples before they were hit by the road-workers and their bulldozers. It was hoped that a million colonists would have settled along the Transamazonica by 1980, half of them on government-cleared 100-hectare plots and the rest as spontaneous migrants. In the event only two thousand families were settled by that date, and those I visited were dismayed by the hardships – poor soil, myriad insects, choking weeds, no market for their meagre produce, extremely expensive basic necessities, and a highway that was an impassable muddy quagmire in the rainy season and a potholed dust track in the dry. It was a far cry from the slightly higher and far more fertile land along Rondônia's BR-364. Other highway schemes were even greater failures. A plan to build a Northern Perimeter highway east-west to the north of the Amazon was abandoned after the construction of only some stretches – but not before it brought disease, disruption and invasion to indigenous peoples along its route. Far to the west, President Fernando Belaúnde of Peru in 1980 had a vision of a Marginal Highway along the eastern slopes of the Andes, to attract settlers to Peruvian Amazonia. It, too, was rapidly abandoned.

In the four decades between 1960 and 2000, however, the population of Brazilian Amazonia increased tenfold, from two to twenty million. This demographic explosion was caused by internal migration, but a high birthrate among

the frontier settlers also helped. Almost all the migrants lived in the 'arc of deforestation' (near the BR-010/153 and BR-364 highways flanking the main mass of rain
forests) and around the city of Manaus. It was not until the new millennium that
many settlers pushed along penetration highways into hitherto inaccessible
forests.

During these decades, Amazonia was the scene of several major projects. In 1965
the American shipping tycoon Daniel K. Ludwig got a concession to buy, for a
dollar an acre, between 3.5 and 4 million acres (over 1.5 million hectares) of forest
on the lower Jari river, which enters the Amazon from the north not far from its
mouth. Ludwig's plan was to create a gigantic plantation of softwood trees for
timber and pulp. To overcome the blights that had defeated Henry Ford, Ludwig
imported seventeen million fast-growing *Gmelina arborea* and other species from
Southeast Asia. He hoped to reverse what Henry Wickham had done in the 1870s
by taking rubber trees from across the world to tropical forests free of their parasites. He also planned the world's largest rice plantation and big cattle ranches.

Things went wrong from the outset. Ludwig brought a huge floating pulp
mill and wood-fired generator across the world from Japan, at a cost of $250
million. He hired highly qualified foresters, but they were Americans unfamiliar
with tropical forests. Trees were felled and the timber sold, carefully leaving
branches in situ for nutrient. Millions of softwood seedlings were planted to
replace them. However, bulldozers were used to clear the forest, and these scraped
off any fragile soil. Many seedlings therefore failed, and others did not grow as
well or as fast as had been hoped. The experts' projections were never remotely
attained. The Jari Project eventually employed thirty thousand Brazilians in a
paternalistic and morally correct enterprise. (Their bars and brothels were on the
far bank of the Jari.) The Project had a stroke of luck when it stumbled across one
of the world's largest deposits of kaolin or china clay, but this was not enough to
save it. Xenophobic Brazilian media started to complain about this imperial-sized
concession to a foreigner; some of the original tax concessions were withdrawn;
and in 1981 the reclusive billionaire angrily abandoned his costly folly. Lovers of
rain forests were encouraged by his high-profile failure.

During the late 1960s the Brazilian government paid for a survey of the
region by aircraft equipped with SLAR (side-looking aerial radar). This
Radambrasil Project could locate mineral deposits beneath the forest cover, in the
years before remote-sensing from satellites. Its planes, and geologists on foot,

located the world's largest iron-ore deposit in the Carajás hills between the lower Araguaia and Xingu rivers. The Vale do Rio Doce company (CVRD) that operated this huge mine sought to minimize its environmental damage, but a railway built to take its ore to the Atlantic coast caused great destruction, from a 'development corridor' along its track and timber-fuelled pig-iron smelters. A bauxite deposit discovered on the Trombetas (a northern tributary of the lower Amazon) was also mined environmentally, by Alcan, in such a way that it discharged almost no effluent into the rivers.

One of the world's largest hydroelectric dams was built on the lower Tocantins, largely to generate electricity to convert the Trombetas bauxite into aluminium. This Tucuruí dam, described by its critics as a 'pharaonic enterprise', caused massive flooding from its 200-kilometre-long (125-mile) reservoir. Another hydroelectric dam, Balbina on the Uatumã river north of Manaus, was a disaster. Opened in 1987 amid a barrage of criticism, it flooded an unacceptable 400,000 hectares (1,500 square miles) of virgin forest – much of it indigenous land – and because of seepage and silting its output was a paltry 250 megawatts. North of the Balbina reservoir, the world's largest open-cast cassiterite (tin) mine Pitinga reached full capacity by 1985, but it invaded the lands of Waimiri and Atroari Indians. There were other cassiterite mines in Rondônia, a region that had Amazonia's third largest hydroelectric dam, Samuel, just east of Porto Velho on the Madeira.

Land in lowland Amazonia is less than 90 metres (under 300 feet) above sea level, and it is too flat to generate power without flooding appalling areas of forest. In the late 1980s there was a plan to build a series of hydroelectric dams on the lower Xingu near the Transamazonica town of Altamira. These dams' reservoirs would have drowned territories of Kayapó indigenous peoples. However, the Kayapó are a bellicose and politically astute nation, and they had a charismatic leader Paulinho Paiakan. Encouraged by Brazilian and foreign NGOs and media, the Kayapó in 1988 organized a huge rally in Altamira. A Kayapó woman shouted at a power-company executive: 'We don't need electricity. Electricity won't give us food. We need the rivers to flow freely – our future depends on them. We need our forests to hunt and gather in. We do not want your dam.' When the engineer spoke about progress to relieve poverty, the Kayapó answered with devastating logic: 'Don't talk to us about relieving our "poverty". We are not poor: we are the richest people in Brazil. We are not wretched: we are Indians.' The rally appeared on the world's television screens, and international banks refused funding. So the Xingu dams were shelved – for the present. They have reappeared on planners' agendas in the twenty-first century.

Kayapó self-assurance came partly from mining revenue. In 1979 a farmer stumbled across a nugget of gold in the mud of Serra Pelada ('Bald Hill'), roughly between the Carajás iron-ore mine and the start of the Transamazonica at the scruffy frontier town of Marabá. Tens of thousands of wildcat prospectors, *garimpeiros*, poured in to the resulting gold rush. Their feverish prospecting gouged a vast crater, and the world's press showed heartbreaking photographs of columns of near-naked men scrabbling in the mud in antlike frenzy. Gold fever spread southwards when the precious metal was found in streams within Kayapó indigenous reserves. The garimpeiros were self-regulated by their own cooperatives, and they were forbidden firearms. The warlike Kayapó were thus able to intimidate far greater numbers of invaders with well-publicized shows of force. As a result, the Indian service Funai helped Chief Paiakan and others negotiate a levy on extracted gold. Indian warriors strip-searched departing miners and took the agreed royalty of gold dust. The Kayapó used their wealth quite judiciously, in policing their immense tribal frontiers, buying supplies collectively in the nearest town, filming tribal ceremonies for the education of their young, and financing public relations and political lobbying. The price they paid was to see some of their lands churned into eroded lunar landscapes and their rivers polluted with mining effluent.

The second half of the twentieth century was a turbulent time for Amazonia's surviving indigenous peoples. Tribe after tribe was contacted by government Indianists or occasionally by missionaries. Most had decided that they wanted accommodation with the strange white intruders, because they had learned of the power of their metal blades and their weapons. The Brazilian, Peruvian and Colombian Indian services launched arduous and often dangerous contact expeditions deep into the forests, most of which finally achieved a face-to-face encounter without loss of life. But, tragically, almost every tribe that emerged from isolation was struck, first by the trauma of cultural shock, then by epidemics of alien diseases, then by despair caused by devastating depopulation. These indigenous peoples were just as vulnerable to measles, influenza or malaria as their predecessors had been ever since the arrival of Europeans and their African slaves. There were disorganized attempts to inoculate or treat newly contacted peoples, but this was difficult in their remote malocas, and a satisfactory measles vaccine was not available until the 1960s. So thousands perished. Small tribes lost up to two-thirds of their number, and their grief and social disruption were overwhelming. The total population of tribal Indians in Brazilian Amazonia fell to almost 100,000. Anthropologists predicted that by the end of the millennium they would be extinct.

Then, in the final decades of the century, the situation of the indigenous peoples of Amazonia started to improve. This recovery was helped by the remarkable Villas Boas brothers, the young men from São Paulo who reached the upper Xingu in 1945 and stayed with its Indians. Orlando and Cláudio Villas Boas spent a lifetime among the handsome and amiable tribes. They were pioneers in many ways. The first non-missionaries to live for many years among the same Indians, they developed an extraordinary empathy with them, treating them as equals and understanding the politics of each group. They themselves were very different personalities. Orlando was portly and extrovert, with tousled hair and an 'imperial' moustache and beard: one friend likened him to a Turkish-bath attendant. Cláudio was quieter and more introverted, a shambling figure with granny glasses and baggy shorts. He was a voracious reader of philosophical works, full of semi-marxist theories that he expounded at length. He loved to lie in his hammock conversing for hours with the Indians, all of whom he knew personally. Both men were superb woodsmen: tough, resilient and experienced.

The Villas Boas brothers gradually contacted the remaining isolated or hostile tribes of the Xingu. Then, miraculously, they persuaded them to stop fighting one another, to bury ancient feuds, reconstitute tribes that had fragmented, and regain lost pride. The Villas Boas were the first to give the indigenous peoples real control of their lives, within the Brazilian system. (Other Indian-service posts were run by government officials, most of whom were dedicated and well-intentioned, but some were inept, dishonest, lazy or cruel.) Soon after their arrival in the Xingu, its indigenous groups were struck by alien diseases, particularly the dreaded measles and influenza. The upper-Xingu tribes fell to fewer than 1,200 people in total. The brothers were in despair, but they managed to get medical supplies and doctors to administer vaccinations. The São Paulo medical school, under Orlando's great friend Dr Roberto Baruzzi, brought teams of volunteer doctors every year from the mid-1960s onwards, so that by the end of the century every Xingu Indian had a full medical record and health care as good as anyone in South America.

The Villas Boas were the first to appreciate the importance of public relations and national politics. They courted politicians of every persuasion, giving them – and their wives – a glimpse of the idyllic world in which they were operating. They relied on regular supply by Air Force planes, so were equally hospitable to military personnel, who tended to be pro-Indian. And they appreciated the publicity value of beautiful, largely naked indigenous people in the heart of a bustling, modern nation. They welcomed journalists and camera crews. The resulting media coverage meant that Indians came to be highly regarded by educated Brazilians, most of whom never saw an Indian but felt guilty about the centuries of oppression of them by their forebears. However, indigenous peoples were often feared or envied by frontier society. The Villas Boas evolved a policy of 'change, but only at the speed the Indians want'. So they admitted manufactured goods, clothes, tools and motors, but not items that competed with native arte- facts on which some groups depended for inter-tribal trading. They did not allow missionaries into the Xingu. As a result, frustrated proselytizers spread false rumours that the brothers were operating a 'human zoo' for the delectation of politicians and the media, or that they were enriching themselves or interested only in self-glorification. Anyone who experienced the spartan life in the Xingu knew how wrong this was and that, although the brothers did become famous, everything they did was for the benefit of their indigenous friends.

The greatest achievement of the Villas Boas and some anthropologists was the designation of the upper Xingu as a gigantic reserve to protect its tribal peoples and their natural environment. This audacious idea became law in 1961 after eight years of political struggle. The 'Xingu Indigenous Park' covered 22,000 square kilo- metres (8,500 square miles) of pristine forests and rivers. (After various vicissitudes, its area is now 26,500 square kilometres, or 10,200 square miles.) This was the proto- type. In the following decades, a score of other huge indigenous reserves were decreed in Brazil, Colombia, Peru, Venezuela and all the Amazonian nations.

Most of these protected areas were achieved only after long struggles. Ama- zonia's Indians gradually learned about politics and the strange concepts of law and ownership. They had to appreciate that their forests, which to them were as free as air or water, could be acquired by an alien. They were coached by a growing regiment of supporters – anthropologists, Indianists, missionaries (particularly the more enlightened Catholics who espoused liberation theology), lawyers, jour- nalists and many other activists. These formed non-government organizations in South America and in every industrialized nation. (In 1969 I was a founding trustee of one of the most dynamic of these NGOs: Survival International in London.) However, the Indians gradually learned how to fight their own political battles. Ironically, in Brazil it was buses, pounding along the penetration roads which had caused them so much damage, that enabled tribal leaders to travel to meetings with other indigenous peoples. Most tribes are tiny democracies, with village affairs discussed on a daily basis. This gave the tribal leaders experience as orators, sometimes rambling but forceful and passionate. The first indigenous assemblies were organized by Catholic missionaries in the mid-1970s. These gath- erings showed Indians from all over the country that they had common cause against similar threats. At an assembly in his village, Meruri in Mato Grosso, the

Bororo chief Txibae lamented that 'White men, those who call themselves civilized, have crushed not only the earth but also the soul of my people. The rivers rose and the sea became more saline because our tears were so plentiful.' But he declared defiantly: 'All I know is that we are inspired by great hope and are determined to change the path of our history.' So tribes gradually created their own community-based organizations (CBOs), representing a particular ethnic grouping or a river valley or forest region, with umbrella non-government organizations (NGOs) alongside these. By the end of the century there were an extraordinary 130 such indigenous pressure groups in Brazil, helped and encouraged by some thirty NGOs of sympathizers.

Indigenous spokesmen emerged from these assemblies. The first was Mário Juruna, a Xavante chief born before his people were 'pacified', who in 1982 became the first (and so far, only) Indian to be elected as a Brazilian national congressman. Portly and forceful, Juruna's trademark was a tape-recorder with which he noted the lies that white men told Indians. The Kayapó were particularly aggressive in political lobbying, and rich from gold and timber royalties. They produced some charismatic spokesmen, including Paulinho Paiakan and Raoni (chief of a group of Mentuktire contacted by the Villas Boas), both of whom toured the world and dealt calmly with encounters with presidents, kings, religious leaders, celebrities and the international media. Paiakan organized the great gathering in Altamira in 1988 to protest against proposed Xingu dams, but he was brought down four years later by a dubious rape allegation. The Kayapó instinctively understood public relations, grabbing television coverage by stunts in which they always wore body paint, feather headdresses and wooden lip discs. They and non-Indian sympathizers lobbied hard and successfully for indigenous rights in a new Brazilian Constitution in 1988, after the nation had emerged from 21 years of military government. From southern Brazil came Marcos Terena, a leader of the Union of Indigenous Nations, and the fine orator Marçal Tupã-I, a Kaiowá Guarani who was chosen to speak on behalf of all Indians to Pope John Paul II when he visited Brazil in 1980; but Tupã-I was murdered, either by a rival within his tribe or by a rancher who coveted its land. The Yanomami, the large indigenous people whose forested hills straddle the Brazilian-Venezuelan border, produced the articulate shaman Davi Kopenawa who continues to tell the world about the Indian cause and philosophy.

All this political activity resulted in the legal protection of large tracts of Amazonian forests for their indigenous inhabitants. In Brazil a huge reserve was finally decreed in 2005 for the Makuxi and Wapixana in Roraima. Other large reserves will follow, so that Indian areas will cover 12 per cent of that large country

– an area as great as the original European Community. Colombia has decreed vast indigenous reserves in its southern provinces Amazonas and Vaupés, including the Predio Putumayo reserve for survivors of the tribes victimized by Julio César Arana during the rubber boom. Venezuela has national parks for its Yanomami that are almost as large as the Yanomami Indigenous Park in Brazil – which was decreed in 1992 after twenty years of tenacious campaigning. Peru, Bolivia and Ecuador also have protected areas of forest that contain indigenous peoples.

There are three main benefits from these reserves. One is their effect on tribal morale. Land means everything to Indians. It supplies their hunting, fishing and material needs; it is the cement of their beliefs, heritage and tribal identity; they know and love the trees, rivers and sacred places of their environment; and it is a buffer against aggressive outsiders. Almost every Amazonian tribe recovered from the post-contact onslaught of diseases and disruption. Far from becoming extinct, indigenous populations have quadrupled since 1960. This is thanks to the security afforded by land protection, and better health care including preventive medicine and natal care.

Another great benefit of reserves is that indigenous people tend to be good custodians of their rainforest environment. A few tribes are suborned by loggers, prospectors or wildlife hunters, but most value their habitats too highly to permit destructive invasion. With rampant and accelerating deforestation, indigenous territories are increasingly vital as refuges within precious forests. The urban electorates in Amazonian countries approve of Indians having large forest reserves, precisely because they are perceived to be excellent custodians of the environment. (Attitudes are less favourable among the landless poor of the colonization frontiers, but even they admit that indigenous people are the only ones who can survive sustainably in rain forests.)

The third benefit of reserve areas is that they contain most of the forty or fifty isolated and uncontacted groups that are thought to exist in Amazonia – and probably nowhere else on earth. The man in charge of isolated peoples in Brazil was Sydney Possuelo, a sertanista who inherited the mantle of Cândido Rondon and the Villas Boas brothers as the region's greatest explorer and protector of Indians. Bearded and balding, Possuelo was lean and fit from almost forty years of expeditions, which included making first contacts with seven indigenous groups. He ran the Indian service Funai for two years in the early 1990s, and during his tenure the area of legalized reserves in Brazil doubled. Possuelo then escaped from the political jungle of Brasília to the real jungles in which he was expert: he resumed the job he had created as head of Funai's department of isolated peoples.

Amazonia's luxuriant forests have provided cover for revolutionaries and religious sects, terrorists and narcotics traffickers. Fidel Castro's charismatic lieutenant Ernesto 'Che' Guevara decided in 1965 to try to export Cuban communism. After an unsuccessful foray into the Congo, Che hoped to rouse Bolivia's Indians from their political apathy. Unable to operate in the open altiplano, he tried to win over Bolivia's forest peoples. He had learned some Quechua of the highlands, but this was no use with the Tupi-Guarani speakers of the eastern lowlands. Guevara had assumed that the Bolivian army was incompetent, but was unaware that American military instructors had trained an elite contingent of Rangers. These troops knew more about rainforest survival than his small band did. In October 1967 they hunted Che Guevara down and killed him, at a place called La Higuera, southwest of Santa Cruz de la Sierra, at the source of the Grande headwater of the Mamoré-Madeira in the southernmost extremity of the Amazon basin.

The previous year 1966 saw the formation of FARC, the Revolutionary Armed Forces of Colombia. Far more serious than Che Guevara's blunders in Bolivia, the FARC was to become Latin America's most formidable, most enduring, and richest left-wing insurgency. It was a reaction to rightist excesses during the 'Violencia' of the 1950s. Although formed as the armed wing of the Colombian Communist Party, the FARC was nationalistic and anti-capitalist, rather than Cuban-Soviet communist (as was its counterpart the ELN, National Liberation Army). By the 1990s, after the death of its founder Jacobo Arenas, its new leader Manuel Marulanda described it as a Marxist-Leninist organization inspired by Simón Bolívar. In its early decades, the FARC's strength was among the rural poor and urban shanty-dwellers of northern Colombia. It came to control the wild hills around the country's two intramontane rivers, the Cauca and Magdalena. But to escape campaigns by Colombia's armed forces, the FARC also moved southwards and east to the slopes where the Andes plunge into Amazon forests.

It was drug money that made this revolutionary force so successful. It operated in forests that yield the hallucinogenic plants that had so fascinated botanists from Richard Spruce to Richard Evans Schultes. The FARC organized plantations of coca, marijuana and even Asian poppies (for opium), and it protected factories where Colombia's notorious drug barons converted innocent coca into addictive cocaine. Estimates of the FARC's annual income range from 300 million to a billion dollars, and no-one doubts that two-thirds of this comes from its 'coca taxes' on narcotics passing through its regions. This wealth supports armed forces reckoned to be between six and sixteen thousand troops. In 1998, in one of the periodic attempts to bring the FARC into mainstream politics, it was granted a 110,000 square kilometre (42,000 square mile) safe haven known as the Despeje (clearing). This was near San Vicente del Caguán, three hundred kilometres (185 miles) south of Bogotá on a source of the Amazon's Caquetá-Japurá tributary. When that ceasefire failed, the Colombian army in 2002 invaded the Despeje. The revolutionary army then changed tactics and parts of it moved deeper into Amazonia. It was active to the east in forests near the headwaters of the Rio Negro, and in 2005 it paralyzed the southern province of Putumayo by cutting off electricity and blockading roads. Truck drivers were too terrified to move, and bewildered indigenous peoples had to accommodate the ruthless new administrators.

Colombian *narcotraficantes* also sought coca from Peru, where the leaf had been a staple of Andean society since the Incas and the civilizations that preceded them. In 1980 Peru got its own brand of murderous revolutionaries, when armed militants tried to disrupt the presidential election in a Central Andean village. The movement was led by Abimael Guzmán, a sociology professor at the University of Guamanga in the poor colonial city of Ayacucho, on the road between Lima and Cuzco. (Ayacucho is technically in the Amazon basin, since its river flows into the Apurímac which becomes the Ucayali.) Guzmán had been in Mao's China, and he wanted his new movement to be the 'Fourth Sword of Marxism' (after Marx, Lenin and Mao) but with overtones of Inca messianism and Andean Indian spirituality. He called it *Sendero Luminoso*, a Shining Path that followed the 'luminous' teaching of José Carlos Mariátegui, Peru's 1920s home-grown Marxist and Inca revisionist. Although its origins were idealistic, the Shining Path degenerated into bloody anarchy. Like other revolutions, it sought to destroy the social order and create its egalitarian, Indian utopia on the ruins. So it terrorized peasants and murdered prominent Peruvians, from village mayors, priests or teachers to philanthropists, doctors and aid workers. Like Colombia's FARC, the Shining Path appealed to the urban poor and idealists among the underpaid middle class.

Peru's armed forces were ruthless in trying to eradicate this scourge. Innocent Andean Indians were caught in the crossfire and brutalized by both sides. With the election in 1990 of Alberto Fujimori, the military offensive against the Shining Path was intensified. The murderous movement was losing its appeal, and it was almost obliterated when in 1992 Abimael Guzmán was captured (hiding above a ballet school in a middle-class district of Lima). The Peruvian government did not make a martyr of Guzmán by executing him – even though his movement had caused sixty thousand deaths. Instead they made a fool of the insignificant, portly, ranting sociologist, and sentenced him to life imprisonment.

When under pressure the Shining Path, like Colombia's FARC, retreated to sanctuaries in the Amazon forests, and it was financed and armed by an unholy alliance with drug syndicates. One stronghold was (and still is) the Huallaga valley in northern Peru – the river on which Ursúa and Aguirre built their boats in 1560 and Spruce had his happiest botanizing three centuries later. Peru had attempted to attract colonists to its eastern forests. Most of these settlers were failing, for the same reasons that their counterparts in Brazil made no headway with plots along the Transamazonica highway. So when a Senderista or a Colombian trafficker offered cash for coca, it was manna from heaven for these desperate smallholders. Coca grows like a weed in Peruvian Amazonia. As we have seen, chewing coca has always been a staple of life in the Andes. In its chewed form, it has no adverse effects and in fact contains beneficial vitamins. The tragedy is that this shrub can be converted into cocaine. It is as though the plant that produces an innocent drink like tea, coffee or beer was found to be the source of a powerful narcotic. Attempts to eradicate coca are as fruitless as would be the elimination of one of these popular Western beverages.

In the 1980s there was a struggle that epitomized the 'good' of poor workers who wanted to save rain forests versus the 'evil' of richer landowners bent on deforestation to create cattle pasture. In Acre (the state that Brazil acquired from Bolivia during the rubber boom) some seringueiros were still tapping *Hevea brasiliensis* rubber trees. This was a modest operation, since most of the world's rubber now came from Asian plantations. A newspaper described Acre as 'a state in agony' because huge tracts of forest were being sold to property developers and would-be cattle ranchers. In 1984 the BR-364 highway was paved as far as Porto Velho, thus hugely accelerating inward migration to Rondônia; and two years later paving started on its extension westwards to Rio Branco, capital of Acre. That town mushroomed to 250,000 people, some of whom tried to create cattle ranches while others were engaged in the other reason for felling forests – logging. Within two years of the paving of the highway, Rio Branco had forty sawmills working incessantly to process logs from convoys of timber trucks. Some of the best rubber trees grew in the valley of the Xapuri, a headwater of the Acre river south of Rio Branco. Rubber-tappers of the Xapuri were appalled that their forests were disappearing at the rate of 10,000 hectares (25,000 acres) a year – and with them the *Hevea* trees that provided their sustainable livelihood. These seringueiros created a trade union to defend their rights. They devised a tactic called *empate* (stalemate), whereby labourers and their families formed human walls to stop earth-movers or chainsaw gangs. This was dangerous in the lawless wilds of Acre. Some empates succeeded, but others ended in bloodshed and failure.

The first leader of Acre's Union of Rural Workers was assassinated. His successor was Chico Mendes, a chubby man with tousled hair and a black moustache, eloquent, quietly determined, energetic and charming. An NGO headed by the Brazilian Mary Allegretti and American Stephan Schwartzman took up the rubber-tappers' cause, and they projected Chico Mendes onto a world stage. He was so impressive and his struggle so patently worthy that he was lionized and honoured wherever he went. But, back home, he got death threats and inefficient police protection. One night in December 1988 Chico Mendes stepped out of his kitchen to take a shower in his garden bathhouse, and was shot dead. There was outcry at the murder of this champion of the poor and their rain forests. Everyone suspected a small-time rancher, land speculator and logger called Darli Alves, but it took several years of tortuous legal proceedings – and the removal of the trial from Acre – to gain a conviction of Alves's sons. There were many books and television programmes about this tragedy, and Robert Redford and other movie moguls vied for the film rights from Chico's widow. The best outcome of his martyrdom was that the Xapuri became Brazil's and the world's first 'extractive reserve' – a protected area in which environmentally friendly rubber tapping was permitted. It was named in Chico Mendes's honour. But deforestation of Acre along the Transamazon highway continued apace.

The British film-maker Adrian Cowell made a powerful television series called *The Decade of Destruction* about the appalling deforestation, lawlessness and environmental mayhem of the 1980s. Scientific reports and books alerted the world to the scale of the threat to the world's greatest expanse of tropical rain forests. This had a profound effect, which culminated in the 'Earth Summit' UNCED (United Nations Conference on Environment and Development) held in Rio de Janeiro in 1992. More heads of government attended this gathering than any previous event: it took place in the country that held most tropical forests and rivers, and ironically it was in the 500th anniversary of Columbus's discovery of the Americas. I was at this huge, vibrant conference and experienced the resulting feeling of optimism. We hoped that something might be done to check deforestation and other environmental follies before it was too late. Sadly, those aspirations were misplaced.

There are only two reasons to fell tropical forests – either to get at the soil beneath them, or to take their timber. During the decades after the advent of chainsaws and road-building machinery, most deforestation was to clear land for other uses. It was hoped that cattle ranches could replace forests, and that settlers could feed their families from small farms. In the early days, all the Amazonian nations gave subsidies for 'improving' land by clearing it of forest cover. As we have seen abundantly, these plans were flawed. They were based on the old misconception that luxuriant forest could be converted into fertile farming. Politicians said (and some still say) that northern countries have created success-ful farms by clearing their forests, so they have no right to dissuade tropical nations from doing the same. They equated tropical and temperate forests, unaware that these ecosystems are radically different. The fallacy in this thinking was demonstrated repeatedly by scientists, and it was opposed by environmental-ists. More persuasive were the failures of farmers and ranchers. Many settlers lured into the Amazonian 'land without people' were defeated by its impover-ished soils, difficult climate, and hostile insects and parasites. Cattlemen tried to use tough grasses like *colonião* and humped zebu cattle that could withstand heat and ticks better than European stock. Even such bovines were an alien species. They could not grow fat without lush pasture, and they were reared hundreds of kilometres from slaughterhouses and markets.

Destruction of forests was so obvious that the authorities started trying to quantify the loss. This was no easy matter in a region as vast and remote as Ama-zonia. Earth-observation satellites helped. Brazil had a new Space Research Institute (INPE) which could see the largest areas of deforestation on Landsat imagery. The grid of destruction on feeder roads along the BR-364 in Rondônia was particularly glaring. It looked like a fish skeleton, with the highway as the backbone and ribs of treeless strips jutting out from it. Brazilian scientists and the Food and Agricul-ture Organization of the United Nations calculated that in that frontier state 51,000 square kilometres (almost 20,000 square miles) of forests had been destroyed by 1987 – 22 per cent of Rondônia's total. Some of this had been converted into cattle pasture and a small amount planted for agriculture, but the majority (32,000 square kilometres; 12,500 square miles) degenerated into useless *capoeira* brushwood.

Dennis Mahar, in a report to the World Bank in 1988, calculated that an appalling 600,000 square kilometres (230,000 square miles) of tropical forests in Brazilian Amazonia had already been cleared. Eighty per cent of this destruction had occurred in the previous decade. That represented 12 per cent of Brazil's forest cover, and there was further deforestation at a lesser pace in the surrounding Spanish-speaking countries. A weather satellite from the American NOAA atmospheric agency could record heat and light from burning, so there was an attempt to calculate forest loss from the number of fires this detected. In 1987 it indicated a staggering area burned in Brazil, but that might have been a peak since less than half that amount appeared in the following year. All these figures were disputed. Fires picked up by the satellite clearly included some annual clearance of savannah grasslands. It may have recorded the same fires more than once: one politician sneered that it was monitoring backyard barbecues. In 1989 President José Sarney announced a plan called 'Our Nature' to try to curb rainforest destruction. He strongly disputed the World Bank's estimate of 12 per cent destruction, arguing that it was nearer 5.1 per cent; his authorities later revised this to 7 per cent. Whatever the correct figure, the world was becoming alarmed.

President Fernando Collor, who hosted the 1992 Earth Summit, was more of an environmentalist than his predecessors. His radical environment minister, José Lutzenberger, was appalled to find that tax breaks encouraging forest clearance were still in place. At a time of rampant inflation, companies and rich individuals found that land was a safe hedge. Cheap forested land was particularly attractive, with minimal tax on agricultural profits, depreciation of animals and other fixed investments allowable several times over, and in some states subsidies for 'improvement' by deforestation. Many of these incentives were abolished, but the land agency Incra continued to promote migration into Amazonia by small farmers.

For a time it seemed, to optimists like me, that rainforest destruction would steadily abate and even cease. We felt that everyone, from politicians to migrant settlers, had realized that soils beneath cleared forest were unsuitable for conventional agriculture and cattle-ranching. The influential – and often anti-environmental – newsmagazine *Veja* lamented in 1989 that: 'Intensive occupation promoted by the government in Brazilian Amazonia has been a disaster. It devastated an area greater than Japan to yield less than the national product of [Brazil's poverty-stricken neighbour] Suriname. Over 30 million hectares of trees were uprooted to give way to a hundred ruinous cattle projects.' Surely rainforest clearance would end because it was a waste of time and money.

Any hopes of abatement in the rate of deforestation were dashed by a surge in logging. The tropical forests of Southeast Asia were being stripped of their accessible trees, but the demand for hardwoods was unabated – particularly in Japan, which accounted for over half the world's international timber trade, then by voracious China. So loggers turned to the Amazon, the greatest repository of such forests. It was difficult to monitor destruction from logging, since its clearings rarely showed on satellite imagery and they generated few fires. But the explosion in logging in the 1990s was evident to everyone. Sawmills sprang up every few kilometres along the forest highways, and towns like Paragominas (south of Belém in Pará) became one of the world's logging capitals. The roads were full of trucks piled high with the trunks of mighty trees that had once towered over the forest canopy and been home to thousands of creatures. Every Amazonian river seemed clogged with endless rafts of logs.

Mahogany (*Swietenia*) is the most sought-after tree. These lovely hardwoods were hunted down everywhere, even deep inside nominally protected environmental or indigenous reserves. It is reckoned that every mahogany tree that is felled causes the destruction of 27 other trees. This is because a tree crashing in the forest brings down neighbours linked to it by creepers, and there is collateral tree mortality. Loggers cause a chain of destruction: first the tree-falls, then 'skid trails' where trunks are hauled out by tractors or skidders, then dock clearings where logs are loaded onto trucks, and a labyrinth of roads to reach highways. All these trails open areas of forest to migrant settlers, expose soils to erosion, and leave stumps to rot and release carbon into the atmosphere. Hungry loggers and colonists slaughter forest fauna with their hunting.

The environmental situation worsened in the new millennium. Logging continued unabated, despite efforts to regulate and control it. Multinational timber companies moved into the Amazon, particularly from Asian countries after they had exhausted the rain forests of Southeast Asia. I have seen Japanese tugs towing seemingly endless rafts of logs down rivers that had been devoid of traffic. Domestic companies in every Amazon nation are equally predatory. These are supposed to log 'sustainably', but a government inspection of thirty-four operations around Paragominas found that not one was mitigating forest damage in the approved manner. In 1997 the Brazilian government controversially opened thirty-nine of its National Forests (*Florestas nacionais*, known as 'Flonas') to 'selective' logging, with the dubious safeguard that companies who behaved irresponsibly would not have their licences renewed. In that same year, an official study feared that 80 per cent of logging in Amazonia was illegal. Occasional raids impounded quantities of stolen timber, but the forests are too remote, the controls too porous and the enforcement officers too few to stop this massive traffic. In 2005 a team led by Gregory Asner of Stanford used an extremely accurate system of remote-sensing analysis to reveal terrible damage done by 'selective logging' – extraction of valuable trees. This estimated that 10–15,000 square kilometres (4–6,000 square miles) of forest are logged each year in Brazil alone – which is as much as is deforested for agriculture. It concluded that 'selective logging causes widespread collateral damage to remaining trees, subcanopy vegetation, and soils; with impacts on hydrological proceses, erosion, fire, carbon storage, and plant and animal species'.

1997 was a year of devastating fires, all of them man-made. Satellites picked up 45,000 conflagrations in Brazil and neighbouring countries. Then came an El Niño phenomenon (when change in currents across the Pacific Ocean causes freak warming along the coasts of the Americas) and the resulting drought meant that the annual burning of savannah in Brazil's northernmost state Roraima raged into the forests. Three or four million hectares of trees went up in flames: fire-fighters were powerless to control the disaster, and it was ended only by miraculous and unexpected rains in early 1998.

To the dismay of environmentalists, cattle-ranching made a comeback. By the end of the century, large and medium-sized ranches were reckoned to cause three-quarters of all deforestation in Amazonia. This was caused by a variety of factors. There were incentives for converting forest to grazing during the two decades of military government in Brazil. At a time of high inflation, deforestation was important in securing a landowner's title and 'improving' his holding for profitable resale. Cattle were a cheap way of maintaining cleared land, and the animals were an excellent liquid investment. Soaring world demand turned Brazil, which used to supply only its domestic market, into the world's leading beef exporter with the largest herd. Meat exports increased fivefold between 1997 and 2003 – and 80 per cent of this growth was supplied from Amazonian ranches. The herd in the Brazilian Amazon doubled in the final decade of the twentieth century, to 57 million. It occupied 340,000 square kilometres (130,000 square miles) of pasture, which was six times the area devoted to crops. Paving of forest high-ways made it easier to move animals and carcases. There were almost as many slaughterhouses and meat-packing plants along the roads as sawmills. The resurgence was also due to new techniques of planting grasses on forest soils and of cattle husbandry in the tropics. Exports boomed because successive states were declared free of foot-and-mouth disease, thanks to vaccination campaigns; and Amazonia was spared BSE 'mad-cow' disease (although this – or possibly rabies spread by vampire bats – had destroyed half the cattle in Roraima in the 1930s).

Second to the large ranchers, small farmers account for a significant quantity of forest destruction. A migrant family establishes a claim by slash-and-burn clearing. This supports a crop for two or three years, after which the colonist moves on to open another *roça*. The average small farmer in Amazonia clears a hectare of forest each year, and the cumulative deforestation by this practice is massive.

All this clearance – for ranching, small farming, and timber extraction – produces widespread forest fragmentation. Closed-canopy forest that is suddenly exposed to open fields or roads suffers in many ways. Ecological processes such as pollination, seed dispersal, nutrient cycling and carbon storage are severely damaged; food chains are shattered as animal species shun the open spaces; disruptive winds enter the closed forest; and there can be less rainfall. Logged or fragmented forest is more likely to catch fire. Trees and brushwood at its edges become desiccated, so the annual burnings of nearby settlers can rage deep into the forest fragment. Scientists estimate that the area of forest that is fragmented is half as much again as that actually deforested.

Alongside the resurgence in ranching and logging came another massive threat to the forests – from soya-bean plantations. The bean is cheap, and rich in proteins. It is added to many human foods, but its main use is as animal feed for poultry and livestock. Most soya exports initially went to Europe, where demand for it was vast and spiralling. This surging demand is driven by two factors: people everywhere want a higher standard of living, which means better food; and the world's population is growing at a terrifying pace – from 1.5 billion in 1900 to 6.5 billion a mere century later, and set to reach 9 billion by 2050. China and India between them contain over a third of the human race, their economies are booming, and they want Amazonia's three products – soya, timber and (for China) beef. The numbers of chickens and cattle in the world are at an all-time high and increasing constantly. So people need ever more soya to feed these animals – and the money available to buy it is prodigious.

Soya (or soybean) was introduced to Brazil a century ago by Japanese colonists, and Brazil is now second only to the United States as its largest exporter. Soya is grown largely in the more temperate southern part of the country and in northern Argentina. This plant is remarkable for its nitrogen-fixing properties. It was found that it is one of the few crops that can grow on poor soil beneath rain forests. So a vast and expanding area of Mato Grosso, Rondônia and Pará is being stripped of its forests to make way for fields of soya that stretch to the horizon. Some of these are farmed on an industrial scale by lines of tractors and harvesters. Soya is an insignificant-looking shrub that grows to the height of a man's thigh, and each of its many pods contains four or five beans. To be farmed most profitably, soya should be planted on flat land – which rules out parts of Amazonia.

The Governor of Mato Grosso state, Blairo Maggi, became the world's wealthiest soya producer. Mato Grosso means 'Dense Forest', and the large state contained great expanses of it. During the year 2004, when Maggi took office, the rate of deforestation in Mato Grosso *doubled*. Governor Maggi declared: 'I don't feel the slightest guilt over what we are doing.... It's no secret that I want to build roads and expand agricultural production.' One of Maggi's properties is the 82,000-

hectare (202,000-acre) Tanguro *fazenda* south of the Xingu Indigenous Park (to the distress of the Xingu Indians whose rivers it and others pollute). The Governor insists that his operations are all legal and environmentally correct, with danger-ous chemicals kept away from rivers and some reforestation. To facilitate soya exports, he urged the rapid paving of the BR-163 road from his state capital Cuiabá north to Santarém on the Amazon. This highway looks set to be a more violent destroyer than the BR-364 across Rondônia, because it slices through rather than skirts the main mass of forest. 1,800 kilometres (1,100 miles) long, it soon had a string of booming frontier towns, and its network of side roads and loggers' trails are thought to amount to a staggering 170,000 kilometres (105,000 miles).

Trees are felled, and then burned at the end of each dry season. Observers were appalled as 'a smoke haze blurs the frontier between the world's mightiest forest and its biggest threat: the humble soya bean. The four-month burning season is when the giant trees, felled to make space for crops, are reduced to ashes. Even after being slashed and burned, the trunks of the *tauari* and *maçaranduba* are so huge that their embers glow for more than two years.... Brazil's boom crop [soya] and [the world's] growing appetite [for it] are clearing more forest than logging, cattle farming and mining.' The American soybean expert Kory Melby saw plantations of it stretching to the horizon for hour after hour as he drove along a paved stretch of the BR-163 in 2001. 'We were all in shock.... When I saw with my own eyes how *two* D7 Caterpillars could flatten 80 acres of trees per day, I was completely amazed. I learned that hundreds of Caterpillars were working in the forest at any given moment.' One activist who tried to stop farmers felling trees was Father Edilberto Sena. He lamented that 'they see soya as a commodity, but we see it as the death of the forest'.

I have walked in vast fields of soya on what had a few months earlier been magnificent forest, home to millions of species of animals and plants. Local farmers told me that soya in fact grew successfully for only the first two or three years. After that it had to be drenched in fertilizers, so lasting profits were made by chemicals salesmen rather than growers. Scott Wallace commented in the *National Geographic* that 'a casual observer might marvel at the bright green luster of the plants, unaware of the toxic mix required to achieve that sheen. Soybeans need large amounts of acid-neutralizing lime, as well as fertilizers, pesticides, and her-bicides. From scientists to native villagers, nearly everyone but [Governor] Maggi spoke to me with alarm about toxins seeping into the watershed' where they poison water and fish. With so many expensive chemicals needed to keep soya growing on weak acidic soils, small growers may be ruined in a 'two-headed catas-trophe: environmental and economic'.

As with rubber a century earlier, it is exporters of soya who make fat profits. Three of the largest traders of American grain moved into the soybean market, led by Cargill (possibly the world's largest family-owned business, with revenues of $63 billion in 2003). Cargill, Maggi and others transported soya down the BR-364 from Rondônia and Mato Grosso to Porto Velho on the Madeira, and thence by barge to ships on the main Amazon. Cargill soon had thirteen soya-storage silos in Amazonia. Anticipating the paving of the BR-163 'soy highway', it built a soya washing-and-drying plant (essential before the beans can be shipped without rotting) at the road's northern terminus, Santarém. In 1999 Cargill made its own deep-water port there, with facilities that could handle over 60,000 tonnes a day. This harbour was initially condemned because it was built without the necessary environmental-impact assessment. After it became operational, however, its conveyor was used to take the beans up to three drop-pipes which rapidly fill an ocean-going container ship moored in the Amazon. Cargill reckons that, when the BR-163 is all asphalted and its port legally opened, it could move two to three million tonnes of soya a year through Santarém. Belterra, just south of the city, has become a centre of soya growing. Thus, American interests revived the town created by Henry Ford's rubber-growers seventy years earlier, and some of its soil is *terra preta* from the pre-conquest Tapajós chiefdom.

In 2003 a record 25,000 square kilometres (9,600 square miles) of forests were destroyed – which was 55 per cent more than the average for the previous five years. The pace of deforestation continued to grow in successive years. In 2005 Brazil's economy shrank, but Mato Grosso's domestic product grew by 8 per cent, thanks largely to soya and beef, and this helped Brazil achieve a trade surplus. The combination of logging, cattle-ranching and soybean farming accelerated the rate of rainforest destruction. Throughout Amazonia, 640,000 square kilometres (almost 250,000 square miles) of rain forests – 13 per cent of the total – vanished in the four decades since chainsaws and bulldozers started to make devastation so easy. That was an area the size of Texas and larger than France, gone forever. Other estimates reckon deforestation by 2005 at as much as 16 per cent of the total.

Although the rainforest destruction was appalling, soya grown on soils under felled trees represented only five per cent of Brazil's total. The great majority was grown on open land in the more temperate south of the country, where it causes less environmental damage. Campaigners from Greenpeace traced soya grown on illegally cleared Amazon forest as it moved to Europe and entered famous supermarkets and fast-food chains. So, by threatening a consumer boycott, Greenpeace got these giant outlets to put pressure on the big exporters – Grupo Maggi, the Americans Cargill, ADM and Bunge, and French-owned Dreyfus.

In 2006 these companies pledged not to buy soya from illegally cleared rain forest in the future. They would also try to make farmers on land already illegally deforested obey Brazilian law, which says that no more than 20 per cent of a closed-canopy holding (or 50 per cent of a 'transitional' low forest) may be stripped of trees. But such pledges and laws are circumscribed in scope, widely flouted and difficult to monitor and police.

Since the 1970s, local and foreign scientists have been doing tremendous research throughout Amazonia. They have been learning about the complexities of rainforest dynamics and discovering thousands of new species of plants and animals in the world's richest ecosystem. In Brazil the government's scientific effort was based in INPA (National Amazon Research Institute) in Manaus and the Emilio Goeldi Museum of Pará in Belém. Each of the other Amazonian nations had institutes researching the secrets of this extraordinary region.

Individuals and teams from the United States and other countries contributed in every branch of science. There were some major research programmes – such as Projeto Flora Amazônica (led by Ghillean Prance of the New York Botanical Garden, which sent teams of botanists to different forests every year to inventory the wealth of flora); a Forest Fragments project north of Manaus to ascertain the minimum critical size of forest needed to sustain biodiversity (led by Tom Lovejoy of the Smithsonian Institution); the Maracá Rainforest Project in northern Roraima, in which some 200 scientists and technicians sought to learn more about forest dynamics and natural regeneration (led by me, for the Royal Geographical Society, the Amazon research institute INPA, and the Brazilian environment secretariat); and many others. This great corpus of research demonstrated the bewildering intricacy of tropical rain forests. Each of their millions of species occupies a distinct niche in its own food chain or habitat and interacts with others in innumerable systems of immense complexity. It was shown that if rain forests were cleared over an area of more than a few hectares they would probably never recover.

In 2002 Brazil published a five-year development plan called *Avança Brasil* ('Forward, Brazil'). This anticipated spending $40 billion, with half going to infrastructure in Amazonia. New roads were to be cut into the forests, and 7,500 kilometres (over 4,500 miles) of highways paved so that they could be used in all seasons. As we have seen, the most damaging of these was the north-south BR-163 Cuiabá-Santarém highway. The BR-174 from Manaus north to Boa Vista was also paved, to increase access to the ranchlands and mineral resources of Roraima and then on towards the Caribbean in both Venezuela and Guyana. This BR-174 was originally announced in the 1970s as a 'surgical cut' that would not harm pristine forests or the territory of the Atroari-Waimiri tribes that it traversed. But in 1997 six million hectares of land along it was opened to settlement. The next road to be paved would be the BR-319, which runs through fine forests from Porto Velho to the Amazon opposite Manaus. Philip Fearnside, the most experienced monitor of rainforest destruction, fears that paving this road will be particularly pernicious in opening large, previously inaccessible areas to migration.

The 'Interoceánica' is a highway from Rio Branco in Acre heading south-westwards to Puerto Maldonado in Peru, thence through the selva and up tortuous, landslide-prone roads over the Andes. These reach the Pacific coast either via Cuzco and Ayacucho, or southwards past Lake Titicaca and Arequipa. From Rio Branco to the Peruvian port of Matarani is 2,600 kilometres (1,600 miles), and the cost of improving this highway with much paving and bridge-building – including a long bridge across the Madre de Dios river – has come to over $1.3 billion. The highway traverses punishing terrain, and the civil-engineering project has been described as the biggest in Peruvian history. This is the first major initiative of a Brazilian-inspired plan to integrate infrastructures of South American nations, and most of its funding has come from Brazilian development banks because of the perceived boost to Brazilian exports. With the completion of the project, the journey-time for trucks is halved to some three days, and eager Asian markets can get Amazonian timber, beef and soya far quicker across the Pacific than via the Amazon and Cape Horn.

Environmentalists are worried about the deforestation that will result from opening this remote region in the heart of the continent. Being in well-watered western Amazonia and on the foothills of the Andes, its forests have some of the highest biodiversity on earth. An 'Amazon Basin Conservation Initiative' seeks to control environmental damage near this new road and the watersheds it crosses, but illegal logging, unofficial roads and spontaneous settlement are widespread. Land speculators, drug traffickers and prostitutes pile in, as they did to Rondônia when its BR-364 highway was paved. In 2005 there was serious drought in this region, with fires spreading into primary forest, followed by devastating flooding. There is a gold rush at Huaypetue near the Andean part of the road, with the resulting influx of prospectors and rivers polluted by mercury (used to separate gold). Many welcome the boost to the economy of Madre de Dios Department, not least from a new hydroelectric generator in the mountains, and more tourists coming to the beautiful Tambopata and Manú national parks. Other Peruvians fear that efficient Brazilian producers will undercut their western neighbours.

There is another threat – to extend the Transamazonica from its western extremity in Acre to Pucallpa on the Ucayali in Peru. The distance of this link is only 250 kilometres (155 miles), and it then takes trucks little more than a day to drive from Pucallpa to Lima. Such a road would be disastrous. It would traverse pristine forests that are home to a score of isolated indigenous peoples. One of these uncontacted groups was photographed in 2008 shooting arrows at a low-flying plane – an act of defiance that caught the world's imagination.

Research has shown repeatedly that roads are the greatest cause of deforestation. One study found that 'two-thirds of all forest clearing in Amazonia is within 50 km of a major road'. The damage is exacerbated when a road is paved, so that people and produce can move in and out throughout the year. 'Paved roads have had much farther-reaching effects on the landscapes they traverse than have unpaved roads….'

Not surprisingly, a proposal to build or pave a road sends land values soaring. Property speculators play a nefarious role in Amazonian development and deforestation. They are known in Brazil as *grileiros*, from *grilo* meaning cricket, grasshopper or locust. When Brazil's agrarian-reform agency Ibama examined some title deeds in Amazonia, it cancelled over sixty thousand of them because they were probably fraudulent. In 2005 gunmen hired by a *grileiro* shot dead Dorothy Stang, an elderly missionary and activist who was trying to help poor land-squatters. Because Sister Dorothy was American her murder provoked a police reaction, but other killings in the 'wild west' of Amazonia are commonplace and unnoticed.

Brazil's development plan also anticipates building eighty hydroelectric dams, even though the flatness of Amazonia means that their reservoirs would flood 12 million hectares (half the area of the United Kingdom) and cause appalling release of carbon from the drowned trees. The new dams include those on the lower Xingu that were halted by the Kayapó protest in 1988. The proposal for a huge Belo Monte dam at Altamira resurfaced two decades later, but another protest meeting had little impact in trying to stop it.

The authorities have tried to control the situation with a series of plans: the G7 industrialized nations put aid money behind a Pilot Program to Preserve Brazilian Rain Forests (PP G7); then came the Sustainable Amazon Plan (PAS); and the System for Protection of the Amazon (SIPAM). These all helped to mitigate the effects of deforestation, but none of them was strong enough to stop the forces of destruction. In 2006 Brazil opened a huge area of forest to 'sustainable' logging. This involved 40-year contracts to the highest bidder, in 130,000 square kilometres (over 50,000 square miles) – which is an alarming three per cent of the region's forests.

Recipients of these licences were supposed to comply with tough regulations and a management plan to replant trees, none of which is easy in a complex rain forest.

The situation is not hopeless – yet. There are many large protected areas. In Brazil, indigenous reserves cover 12 per cent of that huge country (or 23 per cent of Brazilian Amazonia), an area equivalent to France, Germany and Italy combined. Most tribes are fine custodians of their beloved forests and rivers (although a few are suborned by loggers or mineral prospectors). Indians are admired as environmental protectors by Brazilian public opinion. Stephan Schwartzman (champion of Chico Mendes, expert on the Panará people, and now an activist with the Environmental Defense Fund) summed up their crucial role: 'Where Indian land begins is where deforestation ends.' In addition there are some huge environmental reserves, notably the national parks of Jaú (off the lower Rio Negro) and Tumucumaque (on the border with French Guyane, alongside large indigenous reserves), and many national forests ('flonas') – although their protective legislation is weak and policing often non-existent. By 2006, these environmental areas covered some 11 per cent of Brazilian Amazonia – roughly half as much as the indigenous reserves. Half these environmental areas (195,000 square kilometres; over 75,000 square miles) were fully protected, and the same area was in 78 units of 'sustainable use'. Further areas were added during the first decade of the twenty-first century, including indigenous reserves (such as Raposa/Serra do Sol near Mount Roraima and Trombetas/Mapuera straddling the states of Amazonas, Pará and Roraima) and a vast corridor of environmental protected areas stretching westwards from Jaú for 650 kilometres (400 miles) to the north of the Solimões river.

Colombia has most of its lowland forests protected, as either indigenous reserves (Predio Putumayo, Vaupés and others) or national parks such as Chiribiquete on the upper Apaporis, La Paya on the Putumayo headwaters, or Puinawai on the sources of the Guainía and Cuiari. Peru was a pioneer with its Manú and Tambopata-Candamo national parks off the Madre de Dios source of the Madeira, followed by the huge Pacaya-Samiriya reserve between the Huallaga, Ucayali and Marañón rivers. These all protect the magnificent biodiversity of westernmost Amazonia. But it was not until the early twenty-first century that Peru added a series of indigenous and environmental areas in its eastern forests bordering Brazil and Colombia. Venezuela long ago protected its Yanomami and neighbouring peoples with the Neblina and Parima-Tapirapecó national parks (which are as large as the Yanomami park in Brazil) and has added other environmental reserves in its Amazonas province. Bolivia has 'flora and fauna sanctuaries' on the old rubber rivers Heath and Orton, on the ancient forests and savannahs south of the upper Guaporé, and elsewhere in its slice of the Amazon basin. Ecuador protects

Above The Brazilian archaeologists Mário Simões and Vera Guapindaia made a thrilling discovery of undisturbed burial urns in Caretas Cave near the small Maracá river north of the mouth of the Amazon. The 'Maracá' culture flourished at the start of the second millennium AD.

Right No-one knows how early man in Amazonia created highly fertile *terra preta* (black earth) soil. The black earth at Hatahara archaeological site, which overlooks the Solimões river, is littered with millions of sherds of pottery that had apparently been deliberately broken.

Left Burning rain forests releases thousands of tonnes of carbon into the atmosphere, as well as destroying countless plants and animals. Some fires are deliberate – to clear forest for ranching or soya; other conflagrations result from the annual burning of grasslands that rages into surrounding forest. Very few fires are caused by lightning.

Below Cattle enter a burned forest. Humped zebu and guzerat cattle from South Asia are better able to stand the heat and ticks of Amazonia. In the past ranches on cleared forest often failed because soils were too weak, but this has been counteracted recently with tougher tropical grasses, better husbandry and slaughterhouses along the new roads. Brazil now exports more beef than any other country, much of it from Amazonia.

Above In 1979 gold was discovered in the mud of Serra Pelada ('Bald Hill') near Marabá at the eastern end of the Transamazon highway. Thousands of wildcat prospectors gouged a crater in their antlike frenzy to find gold.

Right Soya is one of the few crops that can be grown on the weak soil under cleared rain forest. There is soaring demand for the protein-rich soybean, as cattle and poultry feed, and as a food additive. This field near Santarém has just been planted after destroying forest that appears behind it. It may soon require heavy spraying with fertilizers and pesticides.

Above The Transamazon highway in the 1970s was an extraordinary engineering feat, cut into thousands of kilometres of virgin forest. Such 'penetration' roads are the main cause of deforestation, particularly when they are later paved to allow movement at all seasons.

Right Chainsaws make it all too easy to fell mighty rainforest trees. This kapok stands on huge buttress roots, like the fins of a space rocket on its launch pad. It is reckoned that every large tree cut down by loggers destroys some 25 other trees by the time it has been toppled and dragged to a road.

parts of its Oriente forests. In the first decade of the new millennium, every one of these nations still had isolated or uncontacted tribes. There were known to be some fifty such groups, mostly in Brazil and Peru where many fortunately live in forests that enjoy protected status.

All the Amazonian countries have environmental legislation in place and claim to favour protection of natural resources. Public opinion and the media are generally pro-environmental – at least in the cities far from the ecological frontier. But the forces of destruction are powerful and driven by huge financial and social imperatives. Local politicians often thwart good intentions of distant national governments, as do poor and landless pioneers, and a host of business interests. Brazil in particular is a 'federative' republic where states have considerable autonomy. Its largest state, Amazonas, changed from the 'anti-environmental' governor Gilberto Mestrinho to the conservationist Eduardo Braga, whereas Mato Grosso's voters did the opposite when they chose Governor Maggi.

Amazonas State still has 98 per cent of its forests intact. Its Secretary of Environment Virgilio Viana (who was a forest ecologist on the Maracá Rainforest Project that I led) says that it is possible to regenerate some felled forest. He is also encouraging sustainable use of forest produce, as is done in Acre's rubber-tapping forest named after Chico Mendes. Nigel Smith (an Englishman at the University of Florida) has shown the luxuriant range of local plants and fish used by river-side settlers. The challenge is to get these exotic foods and fibres appreciated elsewhere so that they can be marketed.

Although the reserves are admirably large, two-thirds of Amazonia does not enjoy protected status. Also, it is almost impossible to police reserves whose boundaries run for thousands of kilometres of tough terrain. It is therefore imperative that those who preserve tropical rain forests get income from so doing. The economic value of the Amazon's carbon stocks and biodiversity is vast, so compensation for their protection should be made through the region's governments. They must be rewarded by the rest of the world, via carbon credits or some other mechanism. It is equally important that payments reach the custodians who actually save the forests – which includes indigenous peoples who are desperately short of cash. The need for such compensation was agreed at the conference on climate change in Bali in 2007. In 2008 the Brazilian government established the Fund for the Amazon (with an initial $100 million from Norway) to support conservation, research and sustainable development projects. It is hoped to increase this fund massively, to compensate forest custodians without infringing Brazilian sovereignty.

Amazon rain forests are remote, and great expanses of them are still intact. So does the threat to them matter? The answer is a resounding 'yes'. There is mounting fear that their destruction could harm all mankind. The three areas of concern are: greenhouse gases and global warming, change in rainfall and weather, and loss of biodiversity.

Amazonia's gigantic biomass is often called 'the lungs of the world'. Some scientists were, however, unsure whether it really was a 'carbon sink': they thought that mature rain forests might emit as much carbon as they capture. So, in the new millennium, Brazil led the Large-Scale Biosphere-Atmosphere Experiment in Amazonia (LBA) to resolve this critically important issue. The LBA's observation tower north of Manaus and monitoring stations all over the region studied how the system works and how it would react to continued deforestation. They measured carbon content of the atmosphere above forests, and gathered data in the physical, chemical, biological and human sciences. They wanted to understand the climate, ecology and hydrology of Amazonia – and how it affects the Earth as a whole. Their findings showed that this great mass of rain forests is extremely important, in more ways than were previously imagined; and its destruction could be devastating.

LBA researchers proved that in a year of normal weather these forests capture *560 million tonnes* of carbon. If cut down, they would not only cease to perform this essential sequestration but, instead, would *add* hugely to greenhouse gases. Philip Fearnside, of the Amazon Research Institute INPA, calculated that if all those forests were burned or felled and left to decay they could release an unimaginable 77 thousand million tonnes of carbon into the atmosphere. Put another way: during the 1980s, in the Brazilian Amazon alone, change from forest to other uses released over 550 million tonnes of carbon a year – that was nine per cent of all emissions from fossil fuels burned across the planet. (By this calculation, inhabitants of countries like Brazil were per capita among the world's worst polluters.) Growing other vegetation in place of forests is not the answer. Cattle pastures, soya plantations, or weedy scrublands absorb only seven per cent of the carbon previously sequestered by the vanished forest. Destroying tropical forests also contributes to global warming in another way. The billions of termites that so efficiently devour rotting logs and grazing cattle on cleared ranches emit another potent greenhouse gas, methane (as do rice paddies and some growing trees).

Then there is rain. Climatologists link deforestation to changes in the region's weather. The Brazilian physicist Eneas Salati in the 1980s proved the essential role of evapo-transpiration from forest trees in recycling rainwater. The quantity of water involved in this process is prodigious, as is the amount of the sun's energy and heat consumed in making moisture evaporate from the canopy.

This of course mitigates global warming (and it is why someone sleeping in a forest hammock is cold even at the height of the dry season).

Research twenty years later revealed that, surprisingly, rain clouds blowing from east to west across the Amazon basin deposit only about a third of their rain there. Some cross the Andes and reach the Pacific Ocean, but most sweep either southwards to water the fertile farmlands of southern Brazil and northern Argentina or northwards to Colombia and the Caribbean. The scientific commentator Fred Pearce wrote: 'The forest is a vital rain-making machine for most of South America.' The rain also fills the rivers whose hydroelectric dams supply two-thirds of Brazil's electricity. Reduction in this rainfall would have a disastrous effect on the breadbasket's agriculture – causing losses greater than the profits from Amazonian timber, cattle and soya. If this shortage of rain continues and is clearly linked to deforestation, it would be a compelling argument for saving rain forests.

There was serious drying in western Amazonia in 2005–2006. The great river fell by up to 12 metres (40 feet), to its lowest level in recorded history. There were harrowing pictures of millions of dead fish, beds of rivers were exposed for the first time, and hundreds of communities were stranded. 2005 was also a year of extreme weather in the Caribbean. All this may have been caused by a massive north-south sea-surface temperature (SST) anomaly in the Atlantic Ocean (like the devastating east-west El Niños in the Pacific). The drought was exacerbated by deforestation. Farmers burn pasture and brushwood in an annual *coivara*, and their fires often spread to cause raging forest fires. The Indianist and explorer Sydney Possuelo told me that during thirty years of expeditions he had never seen burning as bad as in 2006. He was shattered by the sight of seemingly endless fires, smoke and destruction. Astronauts report that the annual conflagration is visible from space.

As part of the LBA research programme, the distinguished American ecologist Dan Nepstad conducted an experiment that yielded a nightmarish result. He covered a patch of rain forest (in the Tapajós National Forest south of Santarém) with plastic sheeting that admitted solar heat but deflected rainfall. Trees in this experiment survived the first year of artificial drought by capturing ground water. In the second year they struggled. And in the third year they started to die: beginning with the tallest they crashed down, bringing other vegetation with them and exposing the fragile soil. The conclusion was that if Amazonia suffered three or four consecutive years of drought – as parts of Africa do – it would lose not just several thousand square kilometres of trees, but all of them.

SST anomalies lead to episodic droughts, which cause trees to die, and this can produce forest fires – just when forests are more vulnerable because of selective logging and clearance for the tropical agriculture 'revolution'. This will soon result in large-scale replacement of Amazon forests by fire-prone scrub vegetation – even more quickly than the same result from change in rainfall patterns. Dan Nepstad therefore calls urgently for a system of payments to the tropical nations that lower greenhouse-gas emissions from deforestation. Those countries must, however, improve planning to integrate economic activities and conservation areas, since the two are not necessarily incompatible.

Scientists try to predict how all these factors will affect the Amazon forests and *cerrado* as a whole. It is urgent research, because the world's greatest expanse of rain forests is so important to our planet, and because the threats from global warming and deforestation are so serious and accelerating. The data creates models that show when 'tipping points' might take forest dieback beyond a point of no return. This work is led by Carlos Nobre of the Brazilian space-research institute INPE, Yadvinder Malhi of Oxford's Environmental Change Institute, the famous Hadley Centre for Climate Change of the British Met Office, and scientists in other centres and universities. It is crucially important that their models are right, and that they are heeded.

Environmental threats have to relate directly to the well-being of selfish *Homo sapiens* before we take them seriously. The role of tropical forests in mitigating global warming and in delivering rain is increasingly appreciated. So, what about their also being the world's greatest repository of biodiversity? Some people feel that we should preserve forests because they might contain undiscovered pharmaceuticals or a cancer cure. Few worry about the greater moral argument: that our one profligate species has no right to destroy the habitats and existence of millions of other species with which we share this planet. All the great religions marvel at the glory of creation and feel that mankind, as the dominant species, has a duty to preserve it. Tropical forests contain half the world's described species, and probably a greater proportion of undescribed flora and fauna. Chainsaws and burning are immediate threats, and in the longer term these fellow-creatures are also vulnerable to climate change and droughts caused by human pollution and exacerbated by deforestation. The future is therefore precarious for the world's richest ecosystem. The vegetation and rivers that sustainably fed generations of indigenous peoples, that are home to millions of species, and that are so important to the survival of life on our planet, may be mortally damaged without determined action to save them and compensate those who preserve them.

CHAPTER ELEVEN

The Largest River in the Largest Forest

'The largest river in the world runs through the largest forest ... a forest which is practically unlimited – near three millions of square miles clad with trees.' RICHARD SPRUCE, 1851

Human beings are overawed by the Amazon. We are humbled by the scale of everything – the volume of the rivers, the extent of the forests, the exuberance of nature in the world's most diverse ecosystem. I am one of many who love Amazonia. Those who learn how to adapt to the forest and rivers revel in their bounty and the benign climate. Scientists have a treasure house of natural history to discover. And anyone who comes to terms with this environment is dazzled by its beauty. Others hate the hardships of these jungles, where temperate farming is impossibly difficult, movement through dense vegetation or on rapid-infested rivers seems so daunting, rains can be relentless, and none escape the mass of insects or, often, the diseases they transmit.

Look at the Amazon River on a satellite image and it resembles a gigantic tree. Twigs join branches that thicken as they move down towards a massive central trunk, which in turn broadens at its bole. The trunk is of course the main river Amazon. It flows eastwards across South America, from the Andes to the Atlantic, roughly along the Equator. The branches are the mighty tributaries, a dozen of which are larger than any river in Europe; and the twigs are the hundreds of thousands of kilometres of streams, the capillaries feeding the system.

As in a tree, the most exciting parts are often at the ends of the tributaries/branches – remote places that boats cannot reach because of barriers of rapids, where rivers cascade out of forested ravines in Wagnerian waterfalls, where the highest rainfall produces the most exuberant flora and fauna, and where some indigenous peoples have taken refuge and survive. This author has looked down into the Amazon basin in many parts of South America. In the south, I saw rivers rise in *campo* savannahs on the central Brazilian plateau. These are open grassy plains with lines of *buriti* and other palms along watercourses. They are dotted with peculiar trees that look like gnarled temperate fruit-trees, but are evergreen with shiny, waxy leaves to resist the heat of the dry season. As the plains go deeper into the Amazon basin, low, dry forests start to grip the land and continue unbroken towards the great river.

Moving westwards, clockwise around the perimeter of the Amazon basin, there is an expanse of swampy wilderness at the source of the Guaporé-Madeira on the Bolivian-Brazilian border. This tangle of moss-laden primeval trees and mysterious, scarcely explored lakes rests on extremely old Precambrian rocks. To the south of that tributary are the Bolivian Mamoré, Grande and Beni rivers, the southernmost sources of the Madeira and thus of the Amazon. They flow from the Andes across the *llanos* of the Mojos, broad plains of cattle country and low forests. Further northwest is the deeply forested Madre de Dios (another source of the Madeira) and a succession of headwaters of the Purus and Juruá that rise in the wild hills between Brazilian Acre and Peru. One range is now a national park called the Serra do Divisor – the Watershed Hills – that is home to uncontacted indigenous peoples.

The scenery in the Andes is utterly different. Below snow-capped peaks are high-altitude heaths called *puna*, a windswept land of tough, pale green *ichu* grass and swampy bogs, home to herds of llama, alpaca and vicuña. The rivers then drop into the pretty homelands of the descendants of the Incas. There are fields of potatoes, russet-coloured quinua and, in warmer valleys, maize. Some farms are terraced, others cling to impossibly steep hillsides like damp rags. These lands are ploughed and sown communally, with tractors, or oxen, or occasionally lines of men and women turning the sod with ancient digging sticks. There are trees from Inca times, including the sacred *molle*, but more common are imported eucalyptus that thrive at high altitude; and there are clusters of cactus-like prickly pears amid all the indigenous shrubs and wild flowers. The upper Marañón, once thought to be the main source of the Amazon, flows in a great ravine whose open flanks give a rider breathtaking views; and there is equally spectacular scenery along the forested canyon of the Apurímac source, with line after line of hills disappearing into the distance. The rivers soon cascade down into the cloud- and mist-forests of the delightfully named *ceja de montaña* – 'eyebrow of the jungle'. This is hot land that the Incas knew as the *yungas*, from which they got their coca and tropical fruits.

The rain forests along the eastern slopes of the Andes have the world's richest biodiversity – the greatest concentration of flora and fauna – because so many clouds that are blown westwards across the Amazon basin hit the mountains and discharge their rain there. The Peruvian national parks of Tambopata and Manú are good places to see giant otters, jaguars, and *collpa* licks (see pp. 10 and 338) covered in a riot of red and blue macaws and brilliant green parrots. At the base of the Andes in Ecuador are volcanoes, such as Sangay and Sumaco, whose lava-ridged slopes are covered in impenetrable gorse-like vegetation and are bombarded during the rainy season with constant lightning strikes.

In Colombia, great rivers rise in the northwestern corner of the Amazon basin. But only one of these, the Putumayo, is navigable – all its neighbours are blocked by magnificent waterfalls, rapids or turbulent races. As in Peru, the rivers rush down from the Andes. Once in the lowland forests, their meanders are occasionally broken by spectacular sugarloaf outcrops of quartz and granite. This complex geology, the altitudinal zonation, and high rainfall give Colombia's Amazonas opulent and diverse vegetation. The Putumayo has a headwater called Sibundoy that is a mecca to botanists. It was the scene of great discoveries by Richard Evans Schultes, the Harvard-based father of the discipline of ethnobotany. One of his disciples, Wade Davis, described Sibundoy as a valley that hangs in a high basin, an ancient lake bed surrounded on all sides by mountains. This Garden of Eden has the highest concentration of hallucinogenic plants on earth. Few outsiders have settled in the Colombian Amazon, so that (apart from horrors during the rubber boom) its indigenous peoples are little disturbed. Schultes wrote in the late twentieth century that it 'remains one of the vegetatively least disturbed and anthropologically most traditionally intact parts of the entire basin'.

Moving eastwards, the Amazon basin's northern boundary is the Guiana Shield, a long line of *tepui* table-mountains that include Roraima – whose sheer cliffs could have inspired the 'Lost World' of Arthur Conan Doyle. These sandstone outcrops were formed in the Precambrian, the most ancient of all the Earth's geological eras. The formation continues in West Africa, but it was divided tens of millions of years ago when plate tectonics, or continental drift, caused South America and Africa to move apart. I have been on the Pico de la Neblina (Mist Peak) that forms the border between Brazil and Venezuela. The top of a tepui is a strange place. It really is a lost world – not of dinosaurs, but of animals and plants totally distinct from the forests at the base of the cliffs. The closest biological relatives of some species are still in Africa. There are insects and amphibians that have evolved to be relatively gigantic. Plants that are no longer predated by big animals look like their African counterparts, but over millions of years have changed their cellular structure and become flabby.

East of Neblina the northern edge of the Amazon basin is defined by ranges of low hills – Parima, Pacaraima, Acaraí, Tumucumaque. These are densely forested, and because their rivers are full of rapids they are hardly explored and have not attracted frontier settlers. This is home to the Yanomami, the largest indigenous nation that has undergone little change. The hills towards the Atlantic Ocean contain mostly Carib-speaking tribes such as the Tiriyó. Brazilian Guiana, north of the lower Amazon, has great tracts of unspoiled, roadless rain forest.

There are exceptions to this blanket of tropical rain forests. In what is now Brazil's State of Roraima there is an expanse of natural savannahs that stretch north towards the fabled Mount Roraima. These great grasslands are similar to those south of the main river. They extend to the horizons, broken only by stands of *buriti* palms, ribbons of trees along watercourses, termite mounds, or occasional gnarled campo trees – typically *Curatela americana*, whose hard leaves are full of silica and can be used as sandpaper, and *Byrsonima crassifolia* with its edible yellow fruit. Such trees can resist both the dry months without moisture and waterlogging during the rains. This is good cattle country. The first European bovines were introduced in the late eighteenth century, and they multiplied into great herds. Now replaced by humped South Asian breeds (zebu and guzerat) which are better able to withstand tropical heat and ticks, hundreds of thousands of cattle graze on Roraima's ranches, some of which are within the Indians' traditional territory. There are struggles between cowboys and Indians on this frontier.

The Amazon is by every measure the world's largest river system. So let us tick off the superlatives. This one river discharges a *fifth* of the water that flows into the oceans from all the rivers on our planet. Put another way, its volume exceeds the combined flow of the next eight largest rivers: it is four times that of the Congo, ten times the Mississippi, and sixty times that of its only rival in length, the Nile.

There is still debate about the length of this mighty river. It used to be thought that it was shorter than the Nile's 6,695 kilometres (4,160 miles). But a Polish expedition found a stream high in the Andes that feeds a twisting headwater and would give the Amazon a length of 7,483 kilometres (4,650 miles), thus easily overtaking its African rival. The National Geographic Society in 2001 formally accepted this new source. It is in once-glaciated grassy heathland at some 5,250 metres (17,220 feet), on the slopes of Mount Mismi in a remote region north of Peru's second city Arequipa. In 2007 a team of Brazilian scientists claimed to have found another source on a snow-capped mountain in southern Peru that gives a length of 6,800 kilometres (4,225 miles), which also surpasses the Nile. The streams from both sources drain into the Apurímac river which, after some name changes, becomes the Ucayali. And the Ucayali has the greater flow of water when it joins the Marañón to form the Amazon. So it *is* the main river, in both length and volume of water.

Whichever its source, the Amazon loses no time in tumbling off the Andes mountains. After only a few hundred kilometres it forms broad lowland rivers flanked by interminable lines of unbroken rain forests. Thus for most of their length the majestic river and its mighty tributaries are at under a hundred metres (330 feet) above sea level. By the time it reaches the Atlantic Ocean, the main channel of the Amazon is gigantic – roughly five times wider than the Mississippi, and also five times as deep. Over 22,000 kilometres (14,000 miles) of this river system is navigable by ocean-going ships: they can sail for 3,700 kilometres (2,300 miles) right across Brazil to Iquitos deep inside Peru.

The Amazon *basin* is also by far the world's largest, at over 6,900,000 square kilometres (almost 2.7 million square miles), which is three-quarters the size of the continental United States, and one-and-a half times the next-largest basin, that of the Congo. (This is the area of the catchment or drainage basin. It therefore excludes the adjacent forests of the Orinoco or the Guianan rivers that flow northwards, but it does include the Tocantins-Araguaia drainage of central Brazil that enters the Pará or southern mouth of the Amazon.) The basin is roughly circular, like a gigantic toy balloon with its opening at the river's mouth. The northernmost edge is at Mount Roraima (at over 5° North); the southern some 1,800 kilometres (1,100 miles) away near Sucre in the Bolivian Andes (at over 20° South); and the western edge is in the Andes of northern Peru not far from the Pacific Ocean 2,300 kilometres (1,400 miles) from the Atlantic.

In the past, outsiders moved only by rivers and were amazed by their immensity. An American professor in the 1860s exclaimed that 'one must float for months upon its surface to understand how fully water has the mastery over land. Its watery labyrinth is rather a fresh-water ocean, cut up and divided by land, than a network of rivers'. However, now that you can fly over these lowlands you appreciate that the forests are dominant. They stretch to the horizons like a rich green deep-pile carpet. The tree canopy looks flat and uniform. But when you penetrate, you learn how deceptive this is: the ground is anything but flat and the vegetation is constantly changing. This is the world's largest mass of closed-canopy forest: at 5,300,000 square kilometres (over 2,000,000 square miles) it is the size of Western Europe.

Scientists have tried dividing the Amazon forests by different criteria. Zoologists identified three regions by animal types, seven units based on richness and endemism of amphibians, five by fish fauna, and nineteen by bird types. Botanists classified it by vegetation, with Adolpho Ducke proposing ten regions, as did Carlos T. Rizzini (although his were different), with Kurt Hueck giving fourteen, and Ghillean Prance seven based on the distribution of five families of forest trees.

The simplest division of the Amazon is into three river-water types: white, black and clear. White-water rivers are those that drain the geologically young and unstable Andes. They are full of sediment, which actually gives them a milky-brown colour. These white-water rivers occupy the western segment of Amazonia between the Madeira and Napo rivers, which includes all the upper part of the main Amazon river. Although they drain only 12 per cent of the basin, they carry the majority of its suspended solids and dissolved salts.

Black-water rivers rise in the Guiana Shield and flow into the Amazon from the north. Their blackness is because the very ancient Precambrian sandstones at their sources – five hundred million years old – have long ago ceased to erode, so the waters carry almost no sediment or soluble nutrient and few minerals. They are blackened by tannin and humic acids from leaf litter. Few mosquitoes breed in them. Swimming in black-water rivers, your arms are hardly visible in the tea-coloured liquid, and the acid stings your eyes. The largest black-water river is the eponymous Rio Negro ('Black River'). Their blackness makes these rivers a perfect mirror for baroque banks of clouds or dazzling sunsets.

Clear-water rivers drain the Brazilian Shield, which is also one of the most ancient geological formations on Earth. The great southern tributaries – Tocantins-Araguaia, Xingu and Tapajós – have clear waters, as does the Trombetas which enters the lower Amazon from the north. Like the black-water rivers, these carry no silt. The great soil scientist Harald Sioli said that these streams are almost as pure as distilled water. They are not black from leaf-litter tannin because their headwaters are in savannahs, and the absence of sediment is because their beds are flanked by broad sandy beaches and stable banks. These are beautiful rivers, which reflect the deep blue of the sky and in the dry season are framed by creamy, rippled sand banks.

When the earth was very young, South America was linked to Africa, Antarctica and Australia in a great southern land mass we call Gondwanaland. At that ancient time, the Amazon probably flowed westwards across granitic plains. Then came continental drift. Gondwanaland fragmented and the South American continent was gradually pushed westwards by eruptions of what is now the mid-Atlantic ridge. This vast plate ground against the Pacific plate and, some ninety million years ago, the resulting clash raised the Andes mountains. For millions of years, the Amazon continued to flow towards the Pacific. Perhaps thirty million years ago, the Andes finally blocked that exit, there was a series of freshwater lakes between the Brazilian and Guiana shields, and for a time the river may have drained north down what is now Colombia's Magdalena river (which shares ancient fish species with the Amazon). Some eight million years ago, rifts in the earth's crust helped the lakes to break through the Precambrian rocks to the east – at the Óbidos narrows 750 kilometres (465 miles) from the modern mouth. Since then, the Amazon has flowed eastwards. Erosion from the Andes produced the silt that created Marajó and the other islands of the great river's new Atlantic estuary.

Amazonia's mass of freshwater rivers contains a dazzling variety of fish, the world's richest repository of freshwater fauna. Some three thousand species have been described, which is almost 30 per cent of the world total; but it is estimated that there could be as many as nine thousand species. The majority belong to the families characins and siluroids (catfish). The former include the many species of piranha (*piraña* in Spanish) – which are not as bloodthirsty or dangerous as in some explorers' hyperbole. I have swum in rivers thick with piranha, knowing that they attack animals only if there is flowing blood or much agitated movement. They are most dangerous when trapped in drying lagoons and ravenously hungry. Their usual food is small fish or tree nuts: they use their famous teeth to crack nut-shells so that they can swallow only the edible insides. Because they are aggressive and greedy, piranha are easy to catch with strong hooks and line. They are edible, despite many bones, but the related *pacu* and *tambaqui* make better eating. The *tambaqui* (*Colossoma macropomum*) is another fish that enters seasonally flooded forests and eats fruit that trees drop into the water to disperse their seeds. One of their favourites is seed of the rubber tree: *tambaqui* have been found with half a kilo of these in their stomachs. Their average weight is 15 kilos (33 pounds) and they are the main food-fish species of the middle Amazon. Far larger are the prized *pirarucú* (*Arapaima gigas*), which average six times that weight and a length of

2.4 metres (8 feet). *Pirarucú* sometimes jump clean out of the water (for unknown reasons) and fishermen try to harpoon them at that instant, or by following a trail of bubbles after the great fish has dived.

The fish markets of Amazon cities are full of catfish, with pairs of long 'whiskers' trailing below their mouths. Some are huge, notably the *jaú* (*Paulicea lütkeni*) which takes two strong men to lift, *sorubim* (*Pseudoplatystoma corruscans*) and *piraíba* (*Brachyplatystoma filamentosum*). Catfish can make amazing migrations, from the mouth of the Amazon to spawn in the foothills of the Andes and then back downriver – a round trip of 10,000 kilometres (over 6,000 miles).

The Amazon's most glamorous fish – actually aquatic mammals – are its freshwater dolphins. It is always thrilling to see huge pink dolphins jump clear out of the river in a graceful arc. Each can weigh 160 kilos (350 pounds). These are *boto* in Portuguese, *uiara* in indigenous Tupi, and *Inia geoffrensis* to science. Being small whales, they breathe through a blow-hole on their backs, and emit a short, explosive snort. Legends are woven about these elegant creatures – not least that they can impregnate unwary virgins. Smaller river dolphins, grey buffeo or *tucuxi* (*Sotalia fluvitialis*), are less than 1.2 metres (4 feet) long, and swim far up the Amazon into Peru. Very fast and armed with sharp teeth, dolphins catch huge quantities of fish – a third of their body-weight each day. But the two species do not compete: the *tucuxi* attack fast fish near the surface, whereas pink *boto* hunt in deeper water. Because of their mythical aura dolphins are not deliberately fished or eaten by man. But if they are cut open, fish are packed into their stomachs like sardines in a tin.

More dangerous than piranha are freshwater sting-rays (*Potamotrygonidae*). It is all too easy to step out of a canoe onto a sting-ray, invisible with its mottled camouflage and half-buried in a creek's sandy bed. The ray's tail flicks up with a poisoned barb, causing its victim acute pain, perhaps delirium, and sometimes death. Wading in shallow water, you have to shuffle your feet rather than step, so that hidden rays rise ahead of you. At the other end of the size scale, Amazon waters teem with colourful tiny fish like the cardinal (*Cheirodon axelrodi*) that are prized as ornaments for aquaria. Such is the demand, that some of these pretty species are becoming endangered.

Some Amazon waters are full of caymans, but these are all too easy to hunt (by night using lights to catch their eyes) and they have saleable skins and edible meat, so they are rare on exposed rivers. Most caymans are too small and shy to threaten man. But the endemic Black Cayman (*Melanosuchus niger*) is one of the world's largest reptiles, growing to 7–8 metres (over 25 feet). It used to terrify travellers, but is now endangered and rarely seen. Actually, Black Caymans are harmless to humans – except when a mother feels that her young are threatened, in which case she can charge a passing canoe.

As well as being by far the world's largest river system and basin, the word Amazon is also synonymous with jungle. Its forests, with those of the adjacent Orinoco and Guianas, contain over half the world's surviving tropical rain forests. Even after recent decades of destruction, these still cover 4.9 million square kilometres, or nearly 2 million square miles (an area as large as South Asia – India, Pakistan, Bangladesh and Sri Lanka combined). They thrive because they enjoy an abundance of the two great growing agents: sun and rain. The tropical heat of course comes from the Amazon's lying on the Equator. Rainfall averages 2,300 mm (7.5 feet) a year (which surpasses the 2,000 mm to qualify as rain forest); and where the rain clouds are swept onto the eastern slopes of the Andes this annual discharge can rise to an amazing 8,000 mm (26 feet). All rain forests lie around the Equator. Their high rainfall may possibly be generated by the centrifugal force of the earth's spin here, of 40,000 kilometres (25,000 miles) a day or 1.3 times the speed of sound.

The Amazon's rain forests are the world's richest ecosystem. The number of species of plants, animals, fish and birds is prodigious, and a great many are endemic. We can only guess at the millions of species of insects and micro-organisms. The system is evergreen and constantly in motion. The rate of growth is also exuberant, five times that of a temperate forest and with no slowing down in winter. So Amazonia alone accounts for a tenth of the world's metabolism (primary production of living matter on land) and perhaps a quarter of its species.

South America has none of the big game animals of Africa. Its largest predator is the jaguar, often heard grunting or roaring but rarely glimpsed in the depths of the forests. There are plenty of smaller felines but they are even more elusive, hidden in the trees or hunting nocturnally. Human beings are one of the few animals that cannot climb. We are condemned to wander at ground level among the tree roots, with pig-like peccaries, a few brocket deer, and gentle tapirs or *anta* (*Tapirus terrestris*) hoofed ungulates as big as heifers. These large animals are becoming rarer because their meat is so tempting to hunters. (I must confess to having eaten peccary, tapir, deer and even jaguar – but at a time when we were in unexplored forest full of game, and were very hungry.)

Unfortunately for them, peccaries are as tasty to eat as any other pork. Thus, it is now only in remote forests that you run into peccary, first hearing their clacking jaws and low grumbly grunting, then smelling strong piggy scent. In the

Amazon, they come in two species: larger 'white-lippped' queixadas (*Tayassu pecari*), named after a stripe of white hair along their jaw line, and smaller 'collared' peccaries (*Tayassu tajacu*), so called because of a band of paler hair around their necks. They rummage greedily on the forest floor and are essential agents in seed dispersal. Collared peccary, or *javelina*, are only about 45 centimetres (18 inches) high and less than a metre (3 feet) long. They roam in bands of thirty or more, scurrying along and, if disturbed, rush off at speed in a pack. All peccary cover large distances and, being fine swimmers, can easily cross rivers. (Peccaries moved into the Americas millions of years ago and have evolved differently to Old World pigs. The most obvious difference is a scent gland on top of their backs, which can emit a strong smell for defence, sexual aggression and social bonding.)

Big white-lipped queixadas can live in huge herds of up to four hundred. Heavy and with precisely matching molars, they can crush very tough palm fruits that are their favourite food. They rely on agoutis to gather these nuts and bury them so that their shells rot and soften, so they rummage near outcrops or obstacles that agouti use as markers, like pirates burying treasure. Queixadas sometimes plough the forest floor in a phalanx, making a tremendous noise as they scrape the litter, crack nuts, and bark and grunt. Smaller collared peccary eat easier palm fruits, and with their more pointed snouts they can dig deeper for roots and grubs. They also venture out of the forest and rummage in human plantations, happily for them but not the farmers.

Peccaries – particularly queixadas – can be bad-tempered and aggressive. They are dangerous for three reasons: being gregarious creatures they stick together and if one is wounded the others fearlessly defend it to the death; they have scissor-like canines that can slice any flesh; and they know how to cripple men, horses and even jaguars by severing their Achilles tendons. If their boars decide to attack someone, he has to try to climb out of reach – almost impossible in a mature forest where the lowest branches start at 10 metres (30 feet). Once safely above them, a victim of peccary may have to wait for hours or days before they decide to leave. The bang of a gun does not shift them, but a burning torch will.

Apart from these few non-climbers, the action in a forest is 30 metres (100 feet) above our heads in the canopy. Almost all the Amazon's 427 mammal species (173 of which are endemic) can clamber or fly up to the sunlight and rainfall. There are 158 species of bat – far more than anywhere else on earth. The smallest bats, *Rhynoconycteris naso*, live under river rocks and weigh only a few grams – minuscule mammals as small as moths. These delighted Peter Fleming as 'the smallest and flimsiest creatures imaginable, so grey, so silent, so altogether negative ... who flit urgently in a little grey cloud with no more substance to it than a puff of vapour'. At the other end of the size scale are big fishing bats (*Noctilio leporinus*) that skim across rivers at nightfall, sense the slightest ripple under the surface, and gaff up their prey with clawed feet. Some bats are specialized fruit-eaters, and vampires take blood, but most of them devour insects. They hunt by night, navigating in darkness and catching insects on the wing with their famous sonar echo-location, by pulsed emissions of high-frequency sounds that their sensitive ears interpret instantly. The tonnage of insects eaten by bats beggars the imagination.

There are 110 species of rodent, headed by the massive metre-long (over 3 feet) riverbank capybara (*Hydrochaeris*), shy, stupid creatures that look like big beavers. There are equally shy agoutis or *cutia* (*Dasyprocta*) with powerful jaws (delicious Brazil nuts are one of Amazonia's richest commercial crops, but their tree, *Bertholletia excelsa*, relies on agoutis to crack its seed case – something that a man can do only with a heavy axe – then bury the nuts for future consumption, and forget where some of them were hidden). Paca (*Agouti paca*) are slightly smaller; there are also a variety of squirrels, and masses of small rodents on the forest floor.

A stranger entering the forest sees none of this profusion of fauna. Everything is too well camouflaged, or far overhead, or nocturnal, or shy, or fast-moving. The only easily visible species are some monkeys who stare down curiously, and bad-tempered squirrel monkeys who might pelt an intruder with nuts or urine. Brazil's 75 species of primate is twice the number of any other country's. They are densest in the forests of western Amazonia. According to the monkey expert Russell Mittermeier, 'This region has the greatest concentration of primate diversity anywhere on Earth, with no less than 15 genera, 81 species, and 134 taxa. Of these, one entire family (Pitheciidae), three genera (20 per cent of the world total), 69 species (85 per cent) and 122 taxa (91 per cent) are endemic.'

There are bands of about a dozen heavy, dignified, reddish-brown howler monkeys swinging through the branches – either *bugio* (*Allouata caraya*) or *guariba* (*A. belzebul*). At dawn and dusk they chant their lugubrious howling. After grunts and barks by the dominant males 'all hell breaks loose: an unearthly cacophony of thirty or forty voices, each amplified by a larynx the size of a fist'. To the ecologist David Campbell this deafening row is 'the sound of a demonic wind screaming through the rigging of a ship'. To me, it swells and falls like the roar of a football crowd. Howler monkeys eat only leaves, so they are always migrating to find the toxin-free youngest ones. Their howling may be a way of marking a terrain against rivals. Howlers look quite like tan-coloured woolly monkeys (*Lagothrix lagotricha*), which can weigh over ten kilos (22 pounds). More common are athletic black *coatá* spider monkeys (*Ateles*), capuchins with monk-like hoods (*Cebus*), playful little grey squirrel monkeys (*Saimiri sciureus*), and *macaco-da-noite* 'night monkeys' (*Aotus*) who sleep and hide during the day and forage by night. Many trees produce sweet and pulpy fruit to attract monkeys so that they will spread their seeds. Such fruits also appeal to us human primates – notably cacao (*Theobroma*), the source of chocolate and related *cupuaçu* that flavours my favourite ice cream.

The three genera of Pitheciidae are all delicate creatures: little *uacari* (*Cacajao*) with bright-red faces framed by a mane of silvery hair (like sunburned old men), but which die in captivity and are thus rare in zoos; secretive sakis (*Pithecia*) with fluffy fur and long bushy tails (that are used as dusters by local people); and leaf- and fruit-eating *cuxiú* (*Chiropotes*), with manes like Russian fur hats. Equally small are the many species of tamarins or *sagüi* (scientific *Saguinus* and *Callithrix*), and marmosets (*Cebuella*) who make charming pets. Tamarins come in a dazzling variety of fur colours and patterns. Some have a startled look from oddly shaped moustaches, tufts sprouting from ears or heads, and in some species bare faces. The Emperor tamarin (*Saguinus imperator*) is so called because its bushy white handlebar moustache is like that of the Austrian Emperor Franz Joseph.

Amazon forests have a fearsome reputation for being full of snakes, and there are indeed 196 species (of which 82 are endemic). But most of these are up in the canopy or nocturnal. Few snakes are poisonous, and even those that are strike humans only when threatened or trodden on. (Crossing a log, you should climb onto it and glance beyond before stepping down). The most formidable are the big *surucucú* (*Lachesis mutus*) that can grow to 3 metres (10 feet), the lance-head viper *jararaca* (*Bothrops jararaca*), and rattlesnakes (*Crotalus terrificus*). All of these have camouflaged brown skins that merge into the leaf litter of the forest floor. When they hunt at night, they are guided by the warmth of their prey, from heat-sensing crypts around their lips. This is why the third or fourth man of a column moving along a trail at night may be hit. Bites from any of these vipers can be fatal, but there are serums that save lives if applied quickly. There is no such antidote for bites of coral snakes. However, corals are quite visible, with bright bands of red, grey and black, and although their venom is lethal their teeth and delivery systems are small. Travellers used to boast of wrestling with the world's heaviest snake, 9-metre (30-foot) anacondas or *sucuri* (*Eunectes murinus*), but it is rare for an adult human to be killed by one of these enormous river-bank constrictors. Half their size, but still very big, are inoffensive boas or *giboia* (*Constrictor constrictor*). The hundreds of other snake species present no threat to humans.

These forests are also home to 138 species of lizard, of which a remarkable 111 are endemic. There is a bewildering array of anolis lizards, and monitor-like cayman lizards (*Teiidae*). Iguana are known in Brazil as *cameleão* or chameleon even though few can change colour, and they are hunted for their meat and eggs. Amphibians are dominated by frogs and toads: at latest count 406 species, of which 348 (85 per cent) are endemic. Most of the cacophony in the forest at dawn and nightfall is caused by frogs, some of whose calls sound like shrieks or grunts of far larger animals. Mittermeier wrote that Amazonia's prodigious variety of amphibians includes 'a staggering 968 species, or approximately 20% of all [the world's] known species, *as endemics*'. One frog is the poisonous little *Dendrobates leucomelas* that proclaims its danger by flaunting a garish livery of undulating lemon yellow or blue and black. Indians use its venom as curare on arrows or blow-gun darts.

Walking in the forest you often hear birds call, but you rarely see any. The most familiar cry is a piercing wolf-whistle, *wheet-wee-ooh*, repeated again and again, and strangely reassuring. It comes from an inconspicuous grey cotinga hidden high in the canopy, known as Screaming piha (*Lipaugus vociferans*) or to locals *seringueiro* (rubber-tapper). Another cotinga, the *Araponga*, is called *ferreiro* (ironsmith) because its metallic call perfectly imitates a man filing his blade and then hammering on a forge. David Campbell described the noises of a forest awakening at dawn. 'In the ucuüba above, a toucan is yipping: it sounds like an abandoned puppy, lonely and forlorn. The low-frequency murmur of a curassow [wild turkey], almost too low to be heard, like bones rubbing. The rusty-hinge squeal of a flock of mealy parrots. Somewhere a woodpecker extracting a [shade-loving] beetle larva from the safety of cellulose and lignin. Now the ululating gibber of a family of dusky titi monkeys.... After a few minutes, when the sunlight has leaked onto the low mist, the kiskadees [tyrant birds] cry '*Bem te ví*' ['I can see you'].... And then comes the hysterical, raucous call of a flock of *aracuãs* [cuckoos].' The dawn chorus would be exuberantly different in any other patch of forest. The early morning is a moment of breathtaking beauty on any Amazonian stream. After the cool night, a blanket of condensation gently covers the landscape. The sun tries to break through the thick curtain of haze, and the river surface appears placid in this ethereal, ghostly scene.

Out on open rivers, there are times when you seem to be gliding through an enchanted aviary. Some 1,300 species of bird occur regularly in Amazonia. Many of these are migrants who fly to North America, but for whom the real home is in tropical forests. Roughly a fifth, 260 species, are endemic. The main families are flycatchers (172 species, of which 25 endemic), antbirds (122 species, 53 endemic), tinamous (87 species, 20 endemic), and tanagers (71 species, 12 endemic).

The most striking of each type of animal are known as 'flagship species'. Among Amazon birds, the most attractive flagships are the macaws, parrots and parakeets. The remoter you are from inhabited places the more you see macaws flying overhead, usually in pairs since they are endearingly monogamous. The vernacular name for these large and gorgeous birds is *arara*, onomatopoeic from their raucous cry. The most common are rich red and blue *arara-canga* (*Ara macao*) and pale blue and yellow *canindé* (*Ara ararauna*). Occasionally, particularly near the Manú and Tambopata rivers in the Peruvian forests, are one of Amazonia's most dazzling sights: *collpa* mineral-licks on riverbank bluffs. Visitors watch from hides on rafts moored in the stream. Every morning, parakeets, parrots and then macaws fly in to peck at this exposed soil. They come in strict sequence by species, a literal pecking-order starting with the smallest. By late morning the cliff is swarming with a kaleidoscope of red and blue macaws. Scientists are baffled by *collpas*. One theory is that parrots are greedy eaters who often crunch poisonous kernels: they may find an antidote or digestive aid in *collpa* earth, but no-one has managed to identify this attractive chemical. It has also been noted that far more macaws visit collpas during months when their young are nesting, so the earth may be important to growing fledglings.

Nearby in the Peruvian cloud-forest a cotinga, the orange-red cock-of-the-rock (*Rupicola*), also provides a superb spectacle. Just before dawn every morning, always in the same tree-tops, males of this bird perform acrobatic mating dances to entice bored-looking and dull-coloured females. Far away in clearings of lowland forest, piprid *tangará* (*Chiroxiphia caudata*) are called *dansarinhos* ('little dancers') because they execute even more elegant ballets. The males are blue, with scarlet crowns and black faces and wings. Poets have described the graceful dances of these lovely little birds as one of the most enchanting idylls of Brazilian nature.

Equally beautiful are tiny hummingbirds with their iridescent feathers. There are 71 species of hummingbird in the Amazon. You rarely see them in the rain forest because they are pollinating blossoms high in the canopy, but you sometimes feel your face fanned by their whirring wings. Their charming name in Portuguese is *beija-flor* ('flower kisser') and in Spanish *colibrí*.

Birds of prey are headed by eagles, notably harpy eagles or *gavião real* (*Harpia harpyja*), beloved of Indians who often keep one in a wooden cage in the midst of their village and adorn headdresses with its feathers. The largest scavenger is the magisterial King vulture *urubu-rei* (*Sarcoramphus papa*): smaller black vultures give way when he arrives at carrion. There are plenty of edible game birds, of which the most sought-after is the big black curassow turkey *mutum* (*Crax sclateri*). Hunters also enjoy guan or *jacú* (with the amusing scientific name *Penelope superciliaris*) and partridge-like *jaó* tinamou (*Srypturus noctivagus*). Masses of aquatic birds include the family of Ardeidae: herons *garças* (*Ardea socoi*), great flights of snowy-white egrets, and many varieties of bittern. Pairs of dignified big *Jabiru* storks, with black heads and white bodies, stride along riverbanks or stand sentinel on their huge nests. There are cormorants or *biguá* (*Plotus anhinga*), and similar snake-birds who swim with their bodies submerged and only thin snake-like necks above water. There is a profusion of waders, small gulls and terns that skim river surfaces, beautiful kingfishers ('fishing martins' in Portuguese) that swoop on fish with deadly accuracy, waders (some with claws so long and delicate that they can walk on floating lilies), and duck and other waterfowl.

Delightful toucans have beaks that are as long as the rest of their bodies but porous and light. Strange hoatzin (*Opisthocomus hoazin*) are called *cigana* (gypsy) because of their gaudy blue, chestnut and red feathers, with a spiky crest like a punk haircut. Hoatzin seem to be a throwback to dinosaurs, with claws on their wings when young. They live and feed only on *aninga* arums (*Montrichardia arborescens*) that grow between rivers and the gallery forest that flanks them. These are just a few of the hundreds of species of birds in this richest of all habitats.

Trees of the Amazon forests grow in an evergreen battleground, with billions of seedlings trying to thrust upwards to a place in the sun. Because there are so many predatory and foraging insects and animals, and with fungi, blights and diseases targetted to individual species, every tree goes to great lengths to scatter its offspring. These plants expend much energy to tempt seed-dispersers or pollinators, and on defences against enemies. Each tree depends on different pollinating and dispersal strategies and agents, so each needs distinct animals and insects for its survival. Walking through a forest, you are therefore among the roots of sixty to a hundred different tree *species*. There are places where the tree inventory reaches 300 species per hectare, and the total of tree species throughout Amazonia might be as high as 30,000. You are in the midst of a biological engine of unimaginable intricacy.

All those hungry trees capture every scrap of nutrient that reaches the forest floor. Most of their roots are horizontal, lurking near the surface in an intertwined tangle to get at the leaf and other litter. They are helped in this by fungi called mycorrhizae – thin white veins that grow on tree roots and suck nutrient into them from leaf litter, like nature's drinking straws. Almost nothing escapes: minerals and nutrients are constantly recycled into the growing biomass. There is no fall or autumn when deciduous trees drop their leaves simultaneously; nor is there a winter when the forces of decomposition slow down and humus can accumulate. The plant biomass in a tropical forest is roughly five times that of a temperate forest, and so is the rate of growth. So most soils under tropical rain forests are impoverished – there isn't time for humus or topsoil to accumulate. Also, with their shallow roots, trees are pathetically easy to topple. These are the reasons why it is so difficult, almost impossible, for a rain forest to regenerate once it has been wantonly felled. Farming of imported crops and livestock beneath destroyed forest is precarious. Betty Meggers of the Smithsonian Institution explained why: 'We are so accustomed to dealing with hardy temperate-zone environments, able to withstand gross mistreatment, this it is difficult for us to appreciate the delicate ecological balance that exists in Amazonia.'

The region's biogeography is extremely complex. As we have seen, biologists sought to divide the region by the predominant tree or animal species – coming up with anything from three to ten sectors, in their different breakdowns. Within these sectors there are also names for general types of forest. Seasonally flooded forest on white-water rivers is *várzea*. During the rainy months you can glide for hundreds of kilometres amid the canopies of trees standing in deep water – an enchanted world of blossoms, epiphytes and birds. When the rivers subside, the *várzea* can have fertile clayey soil on which riverbank farmers grow local foods in abundance. The houses of these *ribeirinhos* are either high on stilts, or floating with domestic animals and kitchen gardens on tethered rafts. Many keep water buffalo, who wallow happily by day and are herded onto platform corrals at night. All are of course skilled fishermen, on rivers or beautiful lakes amid the forests. When the waters recede they trap quantities of fish as they swim back to larger rivers. Here and there are patches of lush vegetation called *restingas*, where river sediments hold pockets of water for a few more weeks. On the lower Amazon, where the main river is wider and there is less flooding, the *várzea* is called *canarana*, with tall grasses and marshes interspersed with forest only along river channels. A few trees grow in these waterlogged grasslands – Cecropia, 'Mulatto wood' (*Calycophyllum spruceanum*) or *açacu* (*Hura crepitans*). At the river's mouth and on Marajó island, the *várzea*'s flooding is tidal as well as from rains, and only a few species of palms survive in the salty water.

Forest flooded by nutrient-poor black or clear water is *igapó*. The trees here are scrubby, lower and of fewer species, and they grow wider apart so that there is plenty of sunlight for epiphyte perching plants. Saplings and mature trees have evolved to be submerged for half the year or more, at which time their growth ceases, only to accelerate again during the dry months. Black-water rivers in the north of the Amazon basin also have a curious vegetation peculiar to that region – *caatinga*, a low dense forest that grows on white-sandy soils lying on granite. There is almost no groundwater table, so plants depend on very high rainfall – and the northwest of Amazonia does have the most rain. Within *caatinga*, the vegetation is either *campina*, with low trees and ground covered in mosses, lichens and ferns, or *campinarana* whose tall, slender trees have tough, rigid leaves and thick bark-like savannah species even though they are in a rain forest.

Forests grow best on the slightly higher ground away from rivers known as *terra firme*; Alexander von Humboldt coined the term Hylean (from the Greek for virgin) for these tall, majestic forests that cover so much of Amazonia. He was also the first to call it a 'rain forest'. There are areas where bamboos dominate (mostly on the southern edges of the basin, in Rondônia and Acre), others are full of palms, or rich in tangles of lianas but poor in epiphyte perching plants (notably in northern Roraima and far to the south on the upper Xingu and Tapajós). You can also find forests where one tree species predominates, contrary to the normal scattering effect.

Western Amazonia has some of the world's highest biodiversity. These slopes of the Andes are not only spectacularly beautiful, with waterfalls cascading into layers of lush vegetation, they are also a treasure-house for every natural scientist. A principal cause of this is the high rainfall: rain clouds race across the flat expanse of Amazon forests and discharge their cargo when they slam into the mountains. Rainfall in the Peruvian *montaña* is some 3,500 mm (11.5 feet) a year, compared to 2,000 mm (6.5 feet) at the river's mouth. Soils on the slopes of the eroding Andes are also the best in Amazonia. So this equatorial region has the great growing agents – water, soils and sunshine.

There may be other reasons for the fertility of the Andes-Amazon interface. Natural gaps contribute to biodiversity. A huge tree falls, suddenly bringing sunlight down to ground level, and opportunist plants rush to fill the void. New species evolve. It is now thought that these gaps may be self-perpetuating: trees around them lean towards the light, so they, too, are prone to collapse. Before Europeans brought metal tools, when felling trees was horribly laborious, indigenous people relied on natural gaps for their *roça* forest gardens. The higher rainfall and hillier ground in western Amazonia makes soils more slippery, thus causing more treefalls. Another factor may be cold squalls called *friagems* or *surucus*. Three or four times each year, a fierce, icy wind whips up from Antarctica and is at its most violent as it roars off the mountains. Travellers from the early chroniclers onwards described this phenomenon. The nineteenth-century naturalist Henry Walter Bates was amazed that 'the temperature is so much lowered, that fishes die in the river ... and are cast in considerable quantities on its shores.... The inhabitants all suffer much from the cold, many of them wrapping themselves up in the warmest clothing they can get (blankets are here unknown) and shutting themselves in-doors with a charcoal fire lighted.' The eccentric explorer Colonel Fawcett noted that 'the air grew bitterly cold; the river was lashed by the wind into fine spindrift till it looked like the ocean in a squall. Forest life lay low, and a sense of gloomy desolation oppressed us.' These strong gusts cause branches to snap and trees to fall – hence more clearings, more diversity.

Amazonia has areas where endemic plant and animal species congregate. These 'refuges' or 'refugia' probably remained humid in geological eras when the climate was cooler or drier. Ice ages occurred at roughly 100,000-year intervals during the past 2.5 million years, and each locked huge quantities of water in ice sheets. Savannah then invaded rain forests, and refugia are the forest fragments that survived. Distinct fauna and flora evolved in such centres of endemism. Recent research on soils and fossil pollen has confirmed this theory.

Another common feature of Amazon rain forests is that their plants congregate in groups that have similar ecological requirements. Such interacting plant clusters are called synusia, from the Greek for a group. These are stratified in the different layers of the forest's 'architecture' – the canopy, under-storey, middle and lower stratum, shrub layer, and root-and-litter mat.

Botanists can talk endlessly about their plants, telling anecdotes about each tree, shrub and flower. We saw some of this wonder at nature's prodigality when the first biologists discovered Amazonia in the nineteenth century. Suffice it to say that this river basin has the world's richest plant diversity. Three-quarters of its estimated 40,000 species of vasculars ('higher' plants with conducting tissues) are considered as endemic. The legendary American botanist Alwyn Gentry (with whom I once jumped from a hovering helicopter onto Neblina table-mountain on the Venezuelan-Brazilian frontier, and who was later sadly killed in a plane crash) analyzed the distributions of over eight thousand plant species. He concluded that four-fifths of trees and lianas in the Amazonian canopy are endemic to the region.

It would take a book to talk about all the flowers, particularly the panoply of orchids. But the most famous Amazon flower is a gigantic water lily, *Victoria amazonica* or more often *Victoria regia*, named for that queen shortly after she ascended the throne. These lilies love tranquil, secluded lagoons, where their leaves can grow to 2 metres (over 6 feet) in diameter and cover the surface in a carpet of great green discs. Their fragrant flowers burst open with fifty or more white petals in the cool of each afternoon, and close again next morning by which time they have turned dark pink.

Some trees develop symbiotic relationships with insects. There are many species of myrmecophiles (Greek for 'ant-lovers'), notably the widespread Cecropia or *embaúba* (Tupi-Guarani for 'canoe-wood'). These trees have hollow twigs, full of tempting nectar, that make perfect homes for aggressive *Azteca* ants. In return the ants protect their hosts against all intruders: you never see cecropia leaves chewed by caterpillars. The leaves that the ants protect are lobed, the size of dinner plates, and of a lovely pale green on top and silver below. Seasoned Amazonian explorers call the cecropia 'novice's tree' because an inexperienced companion slings his hammock on its tempting smooth trunk but wakes in the night thrashing from biting ants, to the old-timers' glee. Cecropias like light, and you see them on riverbanks and in forest clearings. They do not live for long, so they grow very fast and can exploit a tree-fall gap before the canopy closes above it. Their catkins produce quantities of sweet and sticky seeds, which bats adore and carry from one clearing to a new one.

Most rainforest trees are quite slender, with trunks rarely over 100 cm (40 inches) in diameter, and most are not very tall, averaging 30 to 40 metres (100–130 feet) in height. An exception is the kapok or *sumaúma* (*Ceiba pentandra*) whose mighty trunk can reach 350 cm (over 11 feet) in diameter, its flat buttress roots as huge as the fins of moon rockets. A kapok is an 'emergent': it towers up to 60 metres (200 feet) and dwarfs other trees in the canopy. These giant trees are often hollow, their heartwood eaten by fungi and beetle larvae. The cavities are home to hundreds of dogfaced bats, who in turn produce a layer of rich guano. David Campbell wondered whether the hollows are a deliberate strategy. 'Are the minerals and ammoniac nitrogen [of the bat guano] the edge that the sumaúma requires to spread its arms above all its neighbours and possess the sky? Is a hollow heart ... the price this tree will pay for its moment in the sun?' Equally tall are *Dinizia excelsa* and Brazil-nut trees (*Bertholletia excelsa*), and *pequi* (*Caryocar villosum*) whose fruit is a favourite of indigenous people and whose bright yellow blossoms stand out amid the surrounding greens. Because soils under rain forests tend to be impoverished, tree roots spread horizontally near the surface rather than deep into the earth, and some trees have to be supported by triangular buttress roots.

Entomologists are awed by the profusion of insects. Although they are so tiny and individually weigh so little, insects come in so many billions that they account for *nine-tenths* of the biomass of Amazonian animals. Every year scientists discover thousands of new species of invertebrates ('no backbone') or arthropods ('jointed legs'), but they can only guess at the wealth of species as yet unknown. About a thousand species of spider have been described in Amazonia, but the total could be four times that number. On the Maracá Rainforest Project, Arno Lise found 26 species new to science, and Bill Overal of Pará's Goeldi Museum counted 472 species in the Ducke Reserve north of Manaus. Spiders' webs come in a dazzling profusion of designs. Photographers such as Lise publish art-books celebrating the beauty of these webs. They range in size from 10-metre-high (over 30 foot) metropolises for thousands of colonial spiders that smother expanses of riverside gallery forest, to tiny creations of a single spider. The region's two thousand species of butterfly are about a quarter of the world's total, and some three thousand bee species are about 10 per cent of the global number.

When someone asked the biologist Thomas Huxley (Charles Darwin's contemporary and supporter) whether he believed in God, Huxley said that he did not know, but that if there was a God he was inordinately fond of beetles. The American coleopterist Thomas Erwin made a survey of beetles in the canopy of four types of forest near Manaus. He recorded 1,080 species, and the vast majority of these occurred in only one of his sites. When Erwin worked in the Tambopata reserve in Peru, he found that only 2.6 per cent of its beetles were the same as those in Brazil. And when he compared beetles in two of his Tambopata survey plots, a mere 50 metres (160 feet) apart, he was amazed that fewer than 10 per cent of species were in both.

Scientists collect insects with a range of nets and traps, often using lights or other lures; or they can 'fog' a tree with poison and collect everything that falls onto collecting mats. A team found that a single *goupia* tree in the central Amazon yielded 95 species of ant – almost as many as the whole of Germany. Record numbers of every type of insect tumble out, particularly the myriad flies, but also ticks and fleas, grasshoppers, dragonflies (Odonata), moths, wasps, mosquitoes, black fly (Simuliidae) and many others.

Termites are the great waste-disposers and recyclers of the Amazon forests. These soft-bodied insects seem able to multiply in proportion to the available dead matter. There are so many billions of termites that they comprise a *third* of the forest's entire animal biomass. They combine with bacteria and protozoa to break down and consume the cellulose in dead wood, so that they recycle vast quantities of nutrients into the food chains of which they form the base. Because they dislike light and wish to hide from predators, you see termite nests everywhere. These can be round structures of wooden 'cardboard' above ground level, or narrow tunnels that they build up tree trunks, or in savannah clearings, termite hills of rocklike hardness. Many animals and some indigenous peoples, like the Yanomami, feed on nutritious termites, and birds, caymans and tortoises use their mounds for nesting. The only drawback about these essential workers is that, like cattle and other ruminants, they emit the potent greenhouse gas methane. And, because they consume all dead wood, they leave archaeologists with almost no records of early man.

In one sense, ants rule the rain forests. Their biomass is greater than that of all mammals, or birds, or reptiles, even of beetles. Forests are full of fragrant smells, but these are drowned by the smell of rotting vegetation and the acrid reek of formic acid. During the rains, the ants' pungent smell is ever-present. We have seen how the first scientists in Amazonia marvelled at ants or suffered agonies from their bites.

For all the superlatives about size and biodiversity, the Amazon's overwhelming impression on visitors is its beauty. The fauna may be invisible, but the vegetation is the most magnificent on earth. In tall, undisturbed forest I find the cathedral-like gloom protective and comforting. There are always surprises, in baroque tangles of creepers, powerful buttress roots, fallen trees like sarcophagi, stands of palms, patches of thick undergrowth, or mysterious and silent streams. You gaze up great tree-trunks to massive branches with sunlight glittering on the leaves of the canopy. On rivers, every hour of the day brings different beauty. At dawn and sunset there is a brief pyrotechnic display of gold, crimson and silver; in the early morning, lovely mists rise from the water; and the reflections of vegetation and clouds are always sublime.

References

Unless otherwise noted, all translations are the present author's own.

Chapter 1 Arrival of Strangers

p. 13 *lives'*, Francisco López de Gómara, *Hispania Victrix: La Historia General de las Indias y Conquista de México* (Zaragosa, 1552), ch. 36 (2 vols, Madrid, 1922, vol. 1, 83).

p. 13 *Germans'*, Antonio de Herrera y Tordesillas, *Historia General de los Hechos de los Castellanos en las Islas y Tierrafirme del Mar Océano* (Madrid, 1610–15), Decada 1, bk 4, ch. 6.

p. 14 *two sticks'*, Pero Vaz de Caminha, letter to King Manoel I, Porto Seguro, 1 May 1500, *A carta de Pero Vaz de Caminha*, ed. Jaime Cortesão (Rio de Janeiro, 1943), trans. William Brooks Greenlee, in *The Voyages of Pedro Álvares Cabral to Brazil and India* (Hakluyt Society, London, 2 ser., vol. 81, 1937, 3–33), 26.

p. 15 *contain them'*, Afonso Braz, letter from Espírito Santo, Brazil, 1551, *Revista do Instituto Histórico e Geográphico Brasiliero* (Rio de Janeiro, 1839–), vol. 6, 1844, 442.

pp. 15–16 *the body', anything else'*, Pierre Clastres, *Chronique des Indiens Guayaki* (Paris, 1972); trans. Paul Auster, in *Chronicle of the Guayaki Indians* (London: Faber and Faber, 1998); John Hemming, *Die If You Must* (London: Macmillan, 2004), 314–15.

p. 17 *good men', more so'*, Pero Vaz de Caminha, letter to King Manoel I, Porto Seguro, 1 May 1500, trans. Greenlee, *The Voyages of Pedro Álvares Cabral*, op. cit., 23; John Hemming, *Red Gold* (London: Papermac, 1995), 4.

pp. 17–18 *paradise', property'*, Amerigo Vespucci to Pier Francesco de' Medici, Sept. or Oct. 1502 (known as the Bartolozzi Letter), trans. Samuel Eliot Morison, *The European Discovery of America: The Southern Voyages, 1492–1616* (New York, 1974), 285.

p. 19 *ambition'*, Jean de Parmentier, the 'Capitano francese', in Giovanni Batista Ramusio, *Navigazioni et Viaggi* (3 vols, Venice, 1550–56), vol. 3, 352, quoted in Paul Gaffarel, *Histoire du Brésil français au seizième siècle* (Paris, 1878), 85–6.

p. 20 *artist', Peru'*, Gonzalo Fernández de Oviedo y Valdés, *La Historia General y Natural de las Indias* (Salamanca, 1547; Valladolid, 1557), bk 49 (or pt 3, bk. 11), ch. 2.

p. 22 *hear', devoured them'*, Pedro de Cieza de León, *La Crónica del Perú*, Pt 4, *La Guerra de Chupas* (Seville, 1555), ch. 19, trans. Clements Markham, *The War of Chupas* (Hakluyt Society, London, 2 ser., vol. 42, 1918, 60).

p. 22 *died'*, Gonzalo Pizarro, letter to King Charles, 3 Sept. 1542, in H. C. Heaton, ed., and Bertram T. Lee, trans., Gaspar de Carvajal, *The Discovery of the Amazon* (New York: Cortes Society, 1934), 246.

p. 23 *this expedition'*, Cieza de León, *The War of Chupas*, op. cit., ch. 18, 55–6.

p. 23 *that expedition'*, Hernán Pérez de Quesada to King Charles, Cali, 16 May 1543, in Juan Friede, ed., *Documentos Inéditos para la Historia de Colombia* (10 vols, Bogotá, 1955–60), vol. 7, 13.

p. 23 *returning'*, Probanza against Gonzalo Jiménez de Quesada and Hernán Pérez de Quesada, Santafé (Bogotá), 28 June 1543, in Friede, ed., *Documentos*, idem, 25–6.

p. 23 *throughout them'*, Lucas Fernández Piedrahita, *Historia General de las Conquistas del Nuevo Reyno de Granada* (Antwerp, 1688), pt 1, bk 9, ch. 3, 359; John Hemming, *The Search for El Dorado* (London and New York, 1978), 130.

p. 24 *Lord'*, Cieza de León, *The War of Chupas*, op. cit., ch. 20, 64.

p. 24 *built', sense'*, Gaspar de Carvajal, *Descubrimiento del río de las Amazonas* (1542), trans. in Heaton and Lee, *The Discovery of the Amazon*, op. cit.

p. 24 *powerful'*, Question 17 of *Probanza* [proof of merits] of the expedition member Cristóbal de Segovia, Margarita Island, October 1542, in Heaton and Lee, *The Discovery of the Amazon*, idem, 269.

p. 25 *King', ceased'*, Cieza de León, *The War of Chupas*, op. cit., ch. 20, 64, 66.

p. 25 *expedition'*, Gonzalo Pizarro to King Charles, 3 Sept. 1542, in Heaton and Lee, *The Discovery of the Amazon*, op. cit.

pp. 27–33 *river'* and subsequent quotations, Carvajal, *Descubrimiento del río*, trans. in Heaton and Lee, *The Discovery of the Amazon*, idem, 200–216.

p. 32 *Amazons'*, López de Gómara, *Hispania Victrix*, trans. in Heaton and Lee, *The Discovery of the Amazon*, idem, 26.

p. 33 *designs'*, William Curtis Farabee, *The Central Caribs* (Philadelphia: University of Pennsylvania Museum, 1924), 166.

p. 34 *event'*, Gonzalo Fernández de Oviedo y Valdés, *La Historia General y Natural de las Indias*, bk. 50 (or pt 3, bk 11), ch. 24, trans. in Heaton and Lee, *The Discovery of the Amazon*, op. cit., 405.

p. 35 *journey', Omagua'*, Marquis of Montesclaros, Viceroy of Peru, to King Charles, Callao, 12 April 1613, in Marcos Jiménez de la Espada, 'Relaciones Geográficas de Indias', vol. 4, in M. Menéndez Pelayo, ed., *Biblioteca de Autores Españoles … (Continuación)*, vol. 133, Madrid 1965, 233.

pp. 38–39 *heads', die for him'*, Toribio de Ortiguera, *Jornada del Río Marañón* (early 1580s), ch. 33, in Menéndez Pelayo, ed., *Biblioteca de Autores Españoles*, op. cit., vol. 216 (Madrid 1968), 280, 281. Ortiguera's account draws heavily on Bachiller [university graduate] Francisco López Vázquez, *Relación verdadera de todo lo que sucedió en la jornada de Omagua y Dorado*, published in M. Serrano y Sanz, ed., *Colección de Libros y Documentos Referentes a la Historia de América* (21 vols, Madrid, 1904–29), vol. 15, 1909.

p. 38 *Chile'*, Election of Hernando de Guzmán as Prince of Peru, Machifaro, 23 March 1561, in Emiliano Jos, *La Expedición de Ursúa al Dorado, la Rebelión de Lope de Aguirre y el Itinerario de los 'Marañones'* (Huesca, 1927), 77.

p. 39 *knew her'*, Custodio Hernández, *Relación de todo lo que acaeció en la entrada de Pedro de Orsúa … y de la Rebelión de don Hernando de Guzmán* (ms. in Biblioteca Nacional, Madrid), in Jos, *La Expedición*, op. cit., 87.

p. 39 *title'*, Ortiguera, *Jornada*, op. cit., ch. 37, 291.

p. 40 *his death'*, Lopez Vaz[quez], *A Discourse of the West Indies and South*.

p. 40 *Spain'*, Lope de Aguirre to King Philip II, Barquisimeto, October 1561, in Jos, *La Expedición*, op. cit., 200.

p. 42 *tribulations'*, Antonio Vázquez de Espinosa, *Compendio y descripción de las Indias Ocidentales* (1628), trans. Charles Upson Clark, Smithsonian Institution Miscellaneous Collections: Washington, D.C., vol. 102, 1942, 381–93.

pp. 42–43 *life there', horses'*, Martín de Murúa, *Historia general del Perú, Orígen y descendencia de los Incas* (1590–1611), ed. Manuel Ballesteros-Gaibrois (2 vols, Madrid, 1962; 1964), vol. 1, 260.

p. 43 *for them'*, Martín Hurtado de Arbieto, report to Viceroy Francisco de Toledo, Vilcabamba, 27 June 1572, in Roberto Levillier, *Don Francisco de Toledo, Supremo Organizador del Perú* (3 vols, Madrid and Buenos Aires, 1935–1942), vol. 1, 330.

p. 43 *rattlesnakes', pesos de oro]'*, Murúa, *Historia general*, op. cit., vol. 1, 259, 260–61.

p. 44 *rapids', foundered'*, Martín García de Loyola, *Probanza de servicios*, 3 Oct. 1572, in Victor M. Maúrtua, ed., *Juicio de límites entre el Perú y Bolivia: Prueba peruana* (12 vols, Barcelona, 1906), vol. 7, 4.

p. 44 *refused]'*, in Rómulo Cúneo-Vidal, *Historia de las guerras de los últimos Incas peruanos* (Barcelona, 1925), 264–65.

p. 44 *advice', river'*, García de Loyola, *Probanza*, op. cit., 5.

p. 44 *baptised'*, Gabriel de Oviedo, *Relación de lo que subcedio en la ciudad del Cuzco … con el Ynca Titu Cuxi Yopanqui* (1573), trans. Clements Markham, supplement to Hakluyt Society, 2 ser., vol. 22, 1908, 406.

p. 45 tributes', Baltasar Ramírez, *Descripción del Reyno del Perú* (1597), ed. Hermann Trimborn, 'Quellen zur Kulturgeschichte des präkolumbischen Amerika', *Studien zur Kulturkunde*, vol. 3 (Stuttgart, 1936, 10–68), 26.

p. 46 see them', Bartolomé de Vega, *Memorial ... sobre los agravios que reciben los indios del Perú* (1562), in Francisco de Zabálburu and José Sancho Rayón, eds, *Nueva Colección de Libros y Documentos Referentes a la Historia de España y de sus Indias*, vol. 6 (Madrid, 1896), 112; John Hemming, *The Conquest of the Incas* (London: Papermac, 1995), 340.

p. 47 loads', alive', Toribio de Ortiguera, *Jornada del Río Marañón* (*c.* 1581), ch. 57, in Meléndez Pelayo, ed., *Biblioteca de Autores Españoles*, op. cit., vol. 216 (Madrid, 1968), 347, 348–49.

Chapter 2 Anarchy on the Amazon

p. 48 temples', Sir Walter Ralegh, *The Discoverie ... of Guiana* (London, 1586), in D. B. Quinn, *Raleigh and the British Empire* (Harmondsworth: Penguin, 1973), 149–50.

p. 49 siege', Agostinho de Santa Maria, *Santuario Mariano* (Lisbon, 1772), vol. 9, 377, in João Capistrano de Abreu, ed. Vicente do Salvador, *História do Brasil* (1627) (São Paulo/Rio de Janeiro, 1931), 618.

p. 49 opposition', Bernardo Pereira de Berredo, *Annaes Históricos do Estado do Maranhão* (Lisbon, 1749), bk 5, 188; John Hemming, *Red Gold* (London: Papermac, 1995), 215.

p. 49 campaign', souls', Captain Simão Estácio da Silveira, *Relação Sumária das Cousas do Maranhão* (Lisbon, 1624), in Nelson Papavero, Dante Martins Teixeira, William Leslie Overal, José Roberto Pujol-Luz, eds, *O Novo Éden* (Belém, Pará: Museu Goeldi, 2002), 129.

p. 49 subjected them', Bishop of Lisbon to King Philip, 1617, in Arquivo Histórico Ultramarino, Lisbon, quoted in Maria Luiza Marcílio, 'The population of colonial Brazil', in Leslie Bethell, ed., *The Cambridge History of Latin America* (Cambridge, 1984), vol. 2, 42.

Maurício de Heriarte, writing in 1662, said that 222 Portuguese were killed, and that there had been over 600 indigenous villages around Pará before they were destroyed (Heriarte, *Descriçam do Estado do Maranham, Pará, Corupá, Rio das Amazonas*, in Papavero et al., eds, *O Novo Éden*, idem, 245–69), 251.

p. 49 white people', Petition by Bernard O'Brien 'del Carpio' to King Philip of Spain (*c.* 1637), ms. in the Archivo de Indias, Seville; first published by T. G. Mathews, *Caribbean Studies*, 1970, vol. 10, 89–106; and in Joyce Lorimer, ed., *English and Irish Settlement on the River Amazon, 1550–1646* (Hakluyt Society, 2 ser., vol. 171, 1989), 264.

p. 50 so happy', John Smith, *True Travels, Adventures and Observations* (1630), in Edward Arber and A. G. Bradley, eds (2 vols, Edinburgh, 1910), vol. 2, 894–95; Hemming, *Red Gold*, op. cit., 225; Lorimer, *English and Irish*, op. cit., 237.

p. 50 importeth', Smith, *True Travels*, idem, vol. 2, 894–95; P. Barbour, ed., *The works of Captain John Smith* (3 vols, London, 1968), vol. 3, 228; Lorimer, *English and Irish*, idem, 239.

pp. 50–53 small things' and subsequent quotations, Bernard O'Brien, Petition to the King of Spain, in Lorimer, *English and Irish*, idem, 264–66, 302–304; Hemming, *Red Gold*, idem, 227–79.

pp. 53–54 canoes', land', Portuguese', Luis de Figueira, SJ, *Memorial*, 10 August 1637, *Revista do Instituto Histórico e Geográphico Brasileiro* (Rio de Janeiro, 1839–), vol. 94, 148, 430, 1923.

p. 55 half way', exertions', Berredo, *Annaes*, op. cit., bk 9, 207.

pp. 56–57 tresses' and subsequent quotations, Cristóbal de Acuña, *Nuevo descubrimiento del gran río de las Amazonas* (Madrid, 1641, but rapidly suppressed), ch. 51, ch. 23, ch. 37, in Clements Markham, trans. *Expeditions into the Valley of the Amazons* (Hakluyt Society, London, 1859, vol. 24, 41–134), 96, 86, 81.

p. 57 digest,' Mexicans', Acuña, *Nuevo descubrimiento*, ch. 26, ch. 37, trans. in Markham, *Expeditions*, idem, 70, 81.

p. 57 *as such', their dead', humility',* Heriarte, *Descriçam,* op. cit., 261–62.

p. 58 *evil acts', contain them', damage',* Acuña, *Nuevo descubrimiento,* ch. 43, ch. 36, trans. Markham, *Expeditions,* op. cit., 86, 80.

p. 60 *colonists]'* and subsequent quotations, Berredo, *Annaes,* op. cit., bk 7, 247, 252, 253.

p. 60 *villages',* Francisco Teixeira de Moraes, *Relação histórica e política dos tumultos que succederam na cidade de S. Luiz do Maranhão...* (1692), *Revista do Instituto Histórico e Geográphico Brasileiro,* vol. 40, pt 1, 1877, 92.

p. 60 *victors',* João Felippe Betendorf, SJ, *Chronica da missão dos Padres da Companhia de Jesus no Estado do Maranhão* (1699), ch. 4, *Revista do Instituto Histórico e Geográphico Brasileiro,* vol. 72, pt 1, 1901, 97.

p. 61 *cruelty',* Frei Cristóvão de Lisboa quoted by António Vieira, *Resposta aos capitulos que deu contra os religiosos da Companhia o Procurador do Maranhã, o Jorge de Sampaio* (1662), reply to ch. 24, in António Sérgio and Hernâni Cidade, eds, *Padre António Vieira: Obras escolhidas* (12 vols, Lisbon, 1951–54), vol. 5, 280.

p. 61 *peace', beheld them',* Acuña, *Nuevo descubrimiento,* ch. 75, trans. in Markham, *Expeditions,* op. cit., 125, 126. Heriarte, who was with Teixeira, said that the Tapajó were still formidable, with 600,000 warriors, big and powerful men who were greatly feared by other tribes (partly because of the poison on their arrows), and with chiefs and a paramount chief, and elaborate funerary ceremonies for their elite (*Descriçam,* in Papavero et al., eds, *O Novo Éden,* op. cit., 255).

p. 62 *more or less', traffic',* Friar Laureano Montes de Oca de la Cruz, OFM, *Nuevo descubrimiento del río de Marañón llamado de las Amazonas ... año de 1651* (in Papavero et al., eds, *O Novo Éden,* idem, 207–236), 232.

p. 62 *natives',* Acuña, *Nuevo descubrimiento,* ch. 80, trans. in Markham, *Expeditions,* op. cit., 131.

p. 62 *forest',* Cristóvão de Lisboa, *Informação sobre o Maranhão* (1647), in Venâncio Willeke, 'Frei Cristóvão de Lisboa, OFM, 1o. naturalista do

Brasil', *Revista do Instituto Histórico e Geográphico Brasileiro* (Rio de Janeiro, 1839–), vol. 289 (Oct.–Dec. 1970, 112–36), 133–34.

p. 62 *unjust wars',* Vieira, *Resposta aos capitulos,* in Sérgio and Cidade, eds, *Padre António Vieira: Obras,* op. cit., vol. 5, 280.

p. 62 *remedy',* Figueira, *Memorial,* op. cit., 431.

p. 62 *Indians', province!',* Antonio Vieira sermon, Maranhão, Lent 1653, trans. in E. Bradford Burns, *A Documentary History of Brazil* (New York, 1966), 88.

p. 63 *souls',* Laureano de la Cruz, *Nuevo descubrimiento,* op. cit., 226–27.

pp. 63–64 *off them'* and subsequent quotations, João Felippe Betendorf, SJ, *Chronica,* op. cit., bk 4, chs 11 and 12, 203, 212–13, 215–16.

p. 64 *badly acquired',* João de Moura, *Descripção histórica e relação política do grande Estado do Maranhão,* unpublished manuscript in Biblioteca Nacional in Lisbon, in David G. Sweet, *A Rich Realm of Nature Destroyed: The Middle Amazon Valley, 1640–1750* (doctoral dissertation, University of Wisconsin, Madison, 1974), 57.

p. 64 *ransom Indians',* Jacintho de Carvalho, SJ, to the Jesuit Procurator in Belém, 16 December 1729, in Alexandre J. de Mello Moraes, *Corografia histórica, cronográfica, genealógica, nobiliária e política do Império do Brasil* (4 vols, Rio de Janeiro, 1872), vol. 4, 329.

pp. 64–65 *paddlers', Indians',* Vieira, *Resposta aos capítulos,* in Sérgio and Cidade, eds, *Padre António Vieira: Obras,* op. cit., vol. 5, 269, 298.

p. 65 *salt and die',* Father João Felippe Betendorf, letter of 20 July 1673, trans. in C. R. Boxer, *The Golden Age of Brazil, 1695–1750* (Berkeley/Los Angeles, 1969), 278.

p. 65 *ten children',* Moura, *Descripção,* in Sweet, *A Rich Realm,* op. cit., 117.

p. 66 *France',* Thomas Maynard report of 1666, in the Public Record Office, Kew, quoted in C. R. Boxer, *A Great Luso-Brazilian Figure, Padre António Vieira, SJ, 1608–1697* (London, 1957), 4.

pp. 66–67 *yes''', homes',* Vieira sermon, Maranhão, Lent 1653, trans. in Burns, *A Documentary History,* op. cit., 88. It was Friar Laureano de la Cruz who wrote that Belém had 300 European inhabitants in 1651, and Maurício de Heriarte a decade later said 400 but that many of them were off in their farms and plantations.

p. 67 *derisory]'*, Vieira to King Afonso VI, Maranhão, 4 April 1654, in João Lúcio de Azevedo, ed., *Cartas do Padre António Vieira* (3 vols, Coimbra, 1925–1928), 1418.

pp. 67–68 *150,000 souls', disfavour', up to now!'*, António Vieira to Jesuit Provincial in Brazil, *c*. Jan. 1654, in Alfred do Vale Cabral, ed., *Cartas Jesuíticas* (3 vols, Rio de Janeiro, 1931), vol. 1, 411; Jaime Cortesão, 'A maior bandeira do maior bandeirante', *Revista Histórica*, São Paulo, vol. 22:45, Jan.–March 1961, 3–27, trans. in Richard M. Morse, *The Bandeirantes* (New York, 1965), 100–113.

p. 68 *complained', multitude'*, André de Barros, *Vida do apostólico Padre António Vieyra* (Lisbon, 1745), 191–92, 197.

p. 68 *Your Majesty'*, Vieira to King Afonso VI, São Luis do Maranhão, 20 April 1657, in Azevedo, ed., *Cartas*, op. cit., vol. 1, 462.

p. 69 *transmigration'* and subsequent quotations, Vieira to King Afonso VI, Maranhão, 28 November 1659, in Azevedo, ed., *Cartas*, op. cit., vol. 1, 555.

p. 70 *Out!'*, Betendorf, *Chronica*, op. cit., bk 4, ch. 4, 177.

p. 70 *that state'*, Vieira opinion to the Prince Regent, 1669, in *Obras escolhidas*, vol. 5, 316–17, trans. in Boxer, *A Great Luso-Brazilian*, 22.

p. 71 *necks'* and subsequent quotations, João Daniel, SJ, *Thesouro descoberto no máximo rio Amazonas*, *Revista do Instituto Histórico e Geographico Brasileiro*, Rio de Janeiro, vol. 1:2, 1840, 328–47 and 447–500; vol. 1:3, 1841, 39–52, 158–83, 282–97, 422–41; pt 2, ch. 11, ch. 5, vol. 1:2, 490; pt 2, ch. 11, ch. 5, vol. 1:2, 459; pt 2, ch. 14, vol. 1:3, 48; pt 2, ch. 1, 340; pt 2, ch. 1, 363; pt 2, ch. 5, 458–59. Daniel is also in *Anais da Biblioteca Nacional*, vol. 95, 1976.

p. 72 *Indians]'*, Daniel, *Thesouro*, idem, pt 2, ch. 14, vol. 1:3, 46–7.

Chapter 3 The Empty River

p. 73 *far away', transplanted', defects'*, Charles-Marie de La Condamine, *Relation abrégée d'un voyage fait dans l'intérieur de l'Amérique Méridionale* (Paris, 1745), 52–3, 94.

p. 74 *two years'*, Friar Diogo da Trinidade, Lisbon, 16 July 1729, in Alexandre J. de Mello Moraes, *Corografia histórica, cronográfica, genealógica, nobiliaria e política do Império do Brasil* (4 vols, Rio de Janeiro, 1872), vol. 4, 282.

p. 74 *lost'*, Fr. Bartholomeu Rodrigues, Tupinambarana mission, 2 May 1714, in Mello Moraes, *Corografia*, idem, vol. 4, 365–66.

p. 74 *guns', people'*, João Felippe Betendorf, SJ, *Chronica da missão dos Padres da Companhia de Jesus no Estado do Maranhão* (1699), *Revista do Instituto Histórico e Geographico Brasileiro*, vol. 72, pt 1, 1901, 206.

p. 75 *victory'*, Bernardo Pereira de Berredo, *Annaes Históricos do Estado do Maranhão* (Lisbon, 1749), bk 16, 537.

pp. 76–77 *burnings'* and subsequent quotations, Samuel Fritz, SJ, *Mission de los Omaguas, Jurimaguas, Aysuares, Ibanomas, y otras naciones desde Napo hasta el Rio Negro*, trans. George Edmundson, *Journal of the Travels and Labours of Father Samuel Fritz in the River of the Amazons* (Hakluyt Society, 2 ser., vol. 51, 1892), 60, 65, 73.

p. 78 *other Indians'*, Fr. Manoel de Seixas to King João V, Pará, 13 June 1719, in David Sweet, *A Rich Realm of Nature Destroyed: The Middle Amazon Valley, 1640–1750* (doctoral dissertation, University of Wisconsin, Madison, 1974), 499.

p. 79 *Custodia'*, Record of a ransom troop, Camp of São José e Santa Anna on the Rio Negro, 28 July 1726, in João Francisco de Lisboa, *Obras* (4 vols, São Luis, Maranhão, 1864–1865), vol. 4, 729; Sweet, *A Rich Realm*, idem, 589.

p. 79 *in vain'*, Francisco da Gama Pinto to King João V, Pará, 21 Aug. 1722, in Sweet, *A Rich Realm*, idem, 482.

p. 79 *hostilities', extinct'*, José Gonçalves da Fonseca, *Primeira exploração dos rios Madeira e Guaporé em 1749*, in Cândido Mendes de Almeida, *Memorias para a história do extincto estado do Maranhão* (2 vols, Rio de Janeiro, 1820), vol. 2, 304.

p. 80 *Dutch'*, King João V to Capitão-Mór of Pará, 4 July 1716, in Artur César Ferreira Reis, ed., *Livro Grosso do Maranhão* (2 vols, Anais da Biblioteca Nacional do Rio de Janeiro, 66–67, 1948), vol. 2, 137.

p. 80 *killings', suggestion'*, King João V to Governor Maia da Gama, 17 Feb. 1724, in Joaquim Nabuco, ed., *Limites entre le Brésil et la Guyane Anglaise: Annexes du premier mémoire du Brésil* (Rio de Janeiro, 1903), vol. 1, 34, 35.

p. 80 *Indians'*, Francisco Xavier Ribeiro de Sampaio, *Relação geographica historica do Rio Branco da America Portugueza*, quoted in Hakluyt Society's edition of Samuel Fritz, *Journal*, 42–3.

p. 81 *soldiers', dead'*, Francisco Xavier Ribeiro de Sampaio, *Diário da viagem que em visita e correição das povoações da Capitania de S. Jorge do Rio Negro fez o Ouvidor e Tenente-geral da mesma...* (1775) (Rio de Janeiro, 1903), ch. 376, 81.

p. 81 *alive'*, Maia da Gama to King João V, Belém, 26 Sept. 1727, in Nabuco, ed., *Limites*, op. cit., 37.

p. 82 *city', assessment'*, Anon, *Notícia Verdadeira do Terryvel Contagio...* (Lisbon, 1749), in Carlos de Araujo Moreira Neto, *Os Índios e a Ordem Imperial* (Brasília: CODOC Funai, 2005), 37.

p. 82 *rigour'*, Alexandre Rodrigues Ferreira, *Diário da viagem philosophica pela Capitania de São-José do Rio Negro* (1786), *Revista do Instituto Histórico e Geographico Brasileiro* (vol. 48:1, 1885, 1–234), 30.

p. 83 *rocks'* and subsequent quotations, Charles-Marie de La Condamine, *Relation abrégée d'un voyage fait dans l'intérieur de l'Amérique méridionale* (Maestricht: J. E. Dufour and P. Roux, 1778), trans. John Pinkerton, *A General Collection of the Best and Most Interesting Voyages and Travels in All Parts of the World* (London, 1813), vol. 14, 219.

p. 93 *thirst', dead children]'*, Letter by Jean Godin des Odonnais to La Condamine, 1773 (first published in La Condamine's *Relation abrégée*, and the Pinkerton translation); Robert Whitaker, *The Mapmaker's Wife* (New York: Basic Books, 2004), 262, 281.

p. 95 *time'*, *Tratado de Madrid* (1750), trans. E. Bradford Burns, *A Documentary History of Brazil* (New York: Alfred A. Knopf, 1966), 126.

Chapter 4 Directorate to Cabanagem

p. 97 *churches'*, Charles-Marie de La Condamine, *Relation abrégée d'un voyage fait dans l'intérieur de l'Amérique Méridionale* (Paris, 1745), 95.

p. 99 *them'*, Mendonça Furtado to Pombal, 18 Feb. 1754, in Marcos Carneiro Mendonça, ed., *Amazônia na era Pombalina* (3 vols, São Paulo, 1963), vol. 2, 503.

p. 100 *hitherto'*, King José I's instructions to Governor Mendonça Furtado, 31 May 1751, idem, vol. 1, 28.

p. 100 *commerce'*, Law of 6 June 1755, in L. Humberto de Oliveira, *Coletânea de leis, atos e memorias referentes ao indígena brasileiro* (Rio de Janeiro, 1952), 63–4.

p. 100 *dignity'*, Álvara (Edict) of 4 April 1755. Agostinho M. Perdigão Malheiro, *A escravidão no Brasil* (2 vols, Rio de Janeiro, 1867), vol. 2, 99.

p. 101 *director', duty'*, Mendonça Furtado to King José I, 21 May 1757, in João Capistrano de Abreu, *Capítulos de história colonial* (1907; 5th edn. Brasília, 1963), 185.

p. 101 *themselves!'*, Regimento of the Diretório, 3 May 1757, in Perdigão Malheiro, *A escravidão*, op. cit., 110.

p. 102 *return'*, Law of 3 September 1759, in Marcos Carneiro de Mendonça, *O Marquês de Pombal e o Brasil* (Brasiliana, vol. 299, Editóra Nacional, São Paulo, 1960), 62; also in Magnus Mörner, *Expulsion of the Jesuits from Latin America* (New York: Alfred Knopf, 1965), 127.

p. 102 *asleep', military'*, António José Pestana da Silva report, *Meios de dirigir o governo temporal dos índios* (1788), in Alexandre J. de Mello Moraes, *Corografia histórica, cronográfica, genealógica nobiliária e política do Império do Brasil* (4 vols, Rio de Janeiro, 1872), vol. 4, 150.

p. 102 *military', tigers!'*, Francisco de Sousa Coutinho, *Plano para a civilização dos índios da Capitania do Pará*, (1797), in Colin MacLachlan, 'The Indian labor structure in the Portuguese Amazon, 1700–1800', in Dauril Alden, ed., *Colonial Roots of Modern Brazil* (Berkeley: University of California Press, 1973), 370.

p. 102 *greed'*, Pestana da Silva, *Meios de dirigir*, op. cit., 141.

p. 102 *work'*, Francisco Xavier Ribeiro de Sampaio, *Diario da viagem ... que fez ... [a] Capitania de S. Jozé do Rio Negro ... no anno de 1774 e 1775* (Lisbon, 1856 edn.), 101.

p. 103 *private ends'*, Johann Baptist von Spix and Carl Friedrich Philip von Martius, *Reise in Brasilien in den Jahren 1817 bis 1820* (3 vols, Munich, 1823–1831), vol. 3, 930–31.

p. 103 *innocence', sheep'*, João de São José Queiroz, *Viagem e visita do sertão em o Bispado do Gram-Pará em 1762 e 1763*, *Revista do Instituto Histórico e Geográphico Brasileiro*, vol. 9, 1847 (repeated 1869), 185–86.

p. 104 *class'*, Lt-Col. Theodozio Constantino de Chermont, *Memoria dos mais terríveis contagios de bexigas e sarampo d'este Estado desde o anno de 1720 por diante* (c. 1780), in Alexandre Rodrigues Ferreira, 'Participação segunda: de Moreira a Tomar', *Viagem Filosófica*, 1974 edn., 78.

p. 104 *labourers]'*, Alexandre Rodrigues Ferreira, *Diário da viagem philosophica pela Capitania de São-José do Rio Negro* (1786), 82.

p. 105 *whites'*, Mendonça Furtado to the Secretary of State (his brother Pombal), Barcellos, 4 July 1758, British Foreign Office, *Question de la Frontière entre La Guyane Britannique et le Brésil* (4 vols, London, 1930), vol. 1, 67.

p. 105 *greed'*, Sousa Coutinho, *Plano para a civilização*, op. cit., 30; and Robin A. Anderson, *Following Curupira: Colonization and Migration in Pará, 1758 to 1930* (doctoral dissertation, University of California at Davis, 1976), 139.

p. 105 *must be'*, Joseph Banks, in J. C. Beaglehole, ed., *The Endeavour Journal of Joseph Banks, 1768–1771* (Sydney, 1963), vol. 1, 191.

p. 106 *patient'*, Report by Francisco Requena y Herrera to the Minister of the Indies, José de Gálvez, Marqués de la Sonora, in J. M. Quijano Otero, ed., *Límites de la República de los Estados-Unidos de Colombia* (Sevilla, 1881), 195.

p. 107 *tree', difficult'*, Report by Captain Ricardo Franco de Almeida Serra and Dr Antonio Pires da Silva Pontes, Barcellos, 19 July 1781, in [British] Foreign Office, *Question de la Frontière*, op. cit., vol. 1, 140.

p. 107 *disintegrated', rapids'*, Col. Manuel da Gama Lobo d'Almada to Governor-General João Pereira Caldas, 1 April 1787, in British Foreign Office, *Question de la Frontière*, idem, vol. 1, 175, 177.

p. 108 *turn'*, Alexandre Rodrigues Ferreira to the Minister of Marine and Overseas, Martinho de Mello e Castro, Belém, October 1783, Americo Pires de Lima, *O Doutor Alexandre Rodrigues Ferreira: Documentos coligidos* (Lisbon: Agência Geral do Ultramar, 1953), 114.

p. 108 *caraná, etc.'*, Alexandre Rodrigues Ferreira, *Viagem Filosófica ao Rio Negro*, ed. Carlos de Araújo Moreira Neto (Belém: Museu Paraense Emílio Goeldi, 1983), 255.

p. 109 *work on them'*, Etienne Geoffroy de Saint-Hilaire, quoted in William Joel Simon, *Scientific Expeditions in the Portuguese Territories* (Lisbon: Instituto de Investigação Científica Tropical, 1983).

p. 109 *reason'*, João Daniel, *Thesouro descoberto no maximo rio Amazonas*, pt. 2, ch. 17, *Revista do Instituto Histórico e Geográphico Brasileiro* (Rio de Janeiro, 1839–), *Revista do Instituto Histórico e Geográphico Brasileiro*, vol. 3, 166, 1841.

p. 110 *losses upon them'*, Robert Southey, *History of Brazil* (3 vols, London, 1810–1819), vol. 3, ch. 44, 724.

p. 110 *speed', animosity'*, Anon, *Illustração necessaria, e interessante, relativa ao gentio da nação Mura* (ms. of 1780s) in André Fernandes de Sousa, *Notícias geographicas da Capitania do Rio Negro* (c. 1820) (*Revista do Instituto Histórico e Geográphico Brasileiro*, vol. 10, 1848, 411–504), 431.

p. 110 *settling there'*, Southey, *History*, op. cit., ch. 44, vol. 3, 725.

p. 110 *sex nor age'*, A. C. do Amaral, *Memorias para a historia da vida do veneravel Arcebispo de Braga D. Fr. Caetano Brandão* (2 vols, Lisbon, 1818), vol. 1, 378.

p. 111 *His Majesty's subjects'*, Alexandre Rodrigues Ferreira, 'Participação quarta: De Carvoeiro a

Moura', Barcellos, 11 May 1787, *Viagem Filosófica*, ed. Moreira Neto, op. cit., 540.

p. 111 *"Comrade Mathias"'*, Lourenço da Silva Araújo e Amazonas, *Diccionario Topographico, Historico, Descriptivo da Comarca do Alto-Amazonas* (Recife, 1852), 256.

p. 111 *settlements', reduction'*, Rodrigues Ferreira, *Viagem Filosófica*, op. cit., 541.

p. 112 *Madeira river'* and subsequent quotations, Henrique João Wilkens, *A Muhraida, Senhor ou A conversão, e reconciliação do Gentio Muhra* (1785, first published Lisbon, 1819), in David Treece, *Exiles, Allies, Rebels* (Westport, Connecticut: Greenwood Press, 2000), 70.

p. 112 *given them'*. An aged Mundurukú recounting to the American anthropologist Robert F. Murphy what his grandfathers had told him, in Murphy's *Headhunter's Heritage* (Berkeley and Los Angeles: University of California Press, 1960), 27.

p. 113 *to react'*, João Lúcio de Azevedo, *Os Jesuítas no Grão-Pará: suas missões e a colonização* (Coimbra, 1930), trans. in Mörner, ed., *The Expulsion of the Jesuits*, op. cit., 188.

p. 114 *in name only'*, Araújo e Amazonas, *Diccionario*, op. cit., 153–54.

p. 114 *What inhumanity!'*, André Fernandes de Sousa, *Noticias geographicas da Capitania do Rio Negro no grande Rio Amazonas* (c. 1820), *Revista do Instituto Histórico e Geográphico Brasileiro*, 1848, vol. 10, 474.

p. 114 *cloth mills, etc.'*, Araújo e Amazonas, *Diccionario*, op. cit., 264.

pp. 114–15 *avaricious'* and subsequent quotations, Fernandes de Sousa, *Noticias geographicas*, op. cit., 478–79, 489–90, 501–503.

p. 116 *Rio de Janeiro'*, Henry Lister Maw, *Journey of a Passage from the Pacific to the Atlantic* (London, 1829), 319, 434.

p. 116 *charges', buy them', other Indians'*, Spix and Martius, *Reise in Brasilien*, op. cit., bk 9, ch. 4, vol. 3, 1219–20, 1230, 1242.

p. 118 *one another'*, Prince Adalbert of Prussia, *Aus meinem Reisetagbuch, 1842–43* (Berlin, 1847), trans.

Sir Robert H. Schomburgk and John Edward Taylor, *Travels of His Royal Highness Prince Adalbert of Prussia … in Brazil, with a voyage up the Amazon and Xingu, now first explored* (2 vols, London, 1849), vol. 2, 153.

p. 119 *revolts!'*, Bernardo Lobo de Souza, President of Pará, to the Ministro do Império, Belém, 13 May 1834, in Carlos Moreira Neto, 'A política indigenista brasileira durante o século XIX' (doctoral dissertation, Rio Claro University, São Paulo, 1971), 16.

p. 120 *lost their lives'*, Charles Jenks Smith, letter, 20 Jan. 1835, quoted in Willliam Lewis Herndon and Lardner Gibbon, *Exploration of the Valley of the Amazon* (2 vols, Washington, D.C., 1854), vol. 1, 341.

p. 120 *coloured people'*, Captain Isidoro Guimarães, *Memória sobre os sucesos do Pará em 1835*, in Domingos Antonio Raiol, *Motins políticos ou História dos principais acontecimentos políticos da Província do Pará* (5 vols, Rio de Janeiro, São Luiz do Maranhão, Belém, 1865–1891), 1020.

p. 120 *soldiers'*, Letter from an Englishman 'C' to his brother 'M', Pará, 12 May 1835, in National Archive, Kew, in David Cleary, ed., *Cabanagem: Documentos Ingleses* (Belém: Secult/IOE, 2002), 57.

p. 121 *streets', escape'*, Henry Walter Bates, *The Naturalist on the River Amazons* (2 vols, London: John Murray, 1863), vol. 1, 40.

p. 121 *rice'*, Captain Sir James Everard Home, on HMS *Racehorse*, to Vice Admiral Sir George Cockburn, 20 Dec. 1835, in Cleary, ed., *Cabanagem*, op. cit., 69.

p. 121 *passing ships'*, Eduard Poeppig, *Reise in Chile, Peru und auf dem Amazonenstrome, während der Jahre 1827–1832* (2 vols, Leipzig, 1835–1836), vol. 2, 439.

pp. 121–22 *Europeans', Portuguese'*, William Smyth and Frederick Lowe, *Narrative of a Journey from Lima to Pará across the Andes and down the Amazon* (London, 1836), 300.

p. 122 *own faces'*, Richard Spruce, *Notes of a Botanist on the Amazon and Andes*, ed. A. R. Wallace (2 vols, London: Macmillan & Co., 1908), vol. 1, 61.

p. 122 *the day'*, Rev. Daniel P. Kidder, *Sketches of Residence and Travels in Brazil* (2 vols, Philadelphia, 1845), vol. 2, 318.

p. 122 *suffered from it'*, Bernardino de Souza, *Lembranças e curiosidades do Valle do Amazonas* (Pará, 1873), 113–14.

p. 122 *in cruelty'*, Herbert Huntington Smith, *Brazil: The Amazons and the Coast* (New York, 1878; London, 1880), 75–6.

p. 122 *anarchy', more than here'*, Prince Adalbert of Prussia, *Aus meinem Reisetagebuch, 1842–43*, trans. Schomburgk and Taylor, op. cit., 154–55.

p. 123 *attempt'*, Captain Sir Richard Warren on HMS *Snake* to Capt. Charles Strong on HMS *Belvidera* in Barbados, 27 July 1836, in Cleary, *Cabanagem*, op. cit., 116.

p. 123 *gulp', alive'*, President Francisco José de Sousa Soares de Andrea, *Falla dirigida … à Assembleia Provincial*, Belém, 2 March 1838, 4.

p. 123 *relatives'*, Andrea letter, quoted in Arthur Cézar Ferreira Reis, 'Cabanagem', *Revista do Instituto Histórico e Geográphico Brasileiro*, vol. 347, April–June 1985, 27.

p. 123 *everything'*, Despatch from the President of Pará to the Minister of the Empire, 8 Nov. 1836, in Carlos de Araujo Moreira Neto, *Os Índios e a Ordem Imperial* (Brasília: Funai, 2005), 45.

p. 123 *they take'*, Captain Sir James Everard Home, HMS *Racehorse*, to Captain Sir Charles Strong on HMS *Belvidera*, Pará, 12 July 1836, in Cleary, *Cabanagem*, op. cit., 115.

p. 123 *liberty'*, Andrea, *Falla*, 5.

pp. 123–24 *noble sentiments'* and other quotations, President Soares de Andrea to his successor Bernardo de Sousa Franco, Belém, 8 April 1839, in Moreira Neto, *Política indigenista*, op. cit., 22, 25.

p. 123 *needs him'*, Andrea to his successor Bernardo de Souza Franco, Belém, 8 April 1839, paras 5 and 6, in Moreira Neto, 'A política', op. cit., 25.

p. 124 *hospital'*, Andrea, *Falla*, in Henrique Jorge Hurley, 'Traços cabanos', *Revista do Instituto Histórico e Geográfico do Pará* (Belém, 1936), vol. 10, 176.

p. 124 *apologies', Indians'*, Kidder, *Sketches*, op. cit., vol. 2, 318–19.

p. 124 *instincts'*, Bento de Figueiredo Tenreiro de Aranha, *Archivo do Amazonas* (3 vols, Manaus, 1906–1908), vol. 1, 20.

p. 124 *victim'*, President Soares de Andrea to Minister of War, Belém, 23 Oct. 1838, in Moreira Neto, 'A política', op. cit., 21.

p. 125 *legalists'* and subsequent quotations, Raiol, *Motins políticos*, op. cit., 999–1000.

p. 125 *terror'* and subsequent quotations, Bernardo de Souza Franco, *Ofício*, 25 Dec. 1839, in Raiol, *Motins políticos*, op. cit., 27.

p. 125 *suffered'*, Report by President Bernardo de Souza Franco to the Provincial Assembly of Pará, 15 Aug. 1839, 52–3, in Moreira Neto, *Os Índios*, op. cit., 52.

p. 126 *authorities'*, William Edwards, *A Voyage Up the River Amazon, with a Residency at Pará* (New York, 1847), 81.

p. 126 *Laborers''', individuals'*, William Lewis Herndon and Lardner Gibbon, *Exploration of the Valley of the Amazon made under Direction of the Navy Department* (2 vols, Washington, D.C.: Robert Armstrong Public Printer, 1854), vol. 1, 256.

p. 126 *servants'*, Bates, *The Naturalist*, op. cit., 84.

p. 127 *together'*, Edward Mathews, *Up the Amazon and Madeira Rivers* (London: S. Low, Marston, Searle & Rivington, 1879), in Nigel J. H. Smith, 'Destructive exploitation of the South American river turtle', *Yearbook, Association of Pacific Coast Geographers* (Corvallis, Oregon, vol. 36, 1974, 85–102), 93–94.

p. 127 *Plate!'*, Spix and Martius, *Reise in Brasilien*, op. cit., vol. 3, bk 9, ch. 6, 1363.

p. 127 *recognisable'*, Henry Lister Maw, *Journal of a Passage from the Pacific to the Atlantic* (London: John Murray, 1829), 45.

p. 127 *valley'*, Matthew F. Maury, 'On extending the commerce of the South and West by sea' (*De Bow's Southern and Western Review*, 1852, vol. 12, 381–99), 393.

p. 127 *hidden there'*, Matthew Maury, letter to William Herndon, Washington, 20 April 1850, in D. M. Dozer, 'Matthew Fontaine Maury's letter of instruction to William Lewis Herndon', *Hispanic American Historical Review* (28, 1948, 212–28), 217.

p. 128 *La Plata'*, Herndon and Gibbon, *Exploration of the Valley*, quoted in Frédérique Joseph, Baron de Santa-Anna Néry, *Le pays des Amazones* (Paris, 1885), trans. George Humphrey, *The Land of the Amazons*, London, 1901, 293–94.

p. 128 *fortune'*, Mark Twain (ed. A. B. Paine), *Mark Twain's Autobiography* (2 vols, New York: P. F. Collier, 1924), vol. 2, 289.

p. 128 *produce'*, Alfred Russel Wallace, *A Narrative of Travels on the Amazon and Rio Negro* (London: Reeve & Co., 1853), 232.

p. 128 *domain'*, Bates, *The Naturalist*, op. cit., 406.

p. 128 *if we must'*, Lieut. Matthew Maury, *Letters on the Amazon and Atlantic Slopes of South America* (Washington, D.C.: F. Taylor, 1853), in John Hemming, *Amazon Frontier* (London: Pan, 2004), 234.

Chapter 5 A Naturalist's Paradise

p. 131 *man', insects', states'*, Alexander von Humboldt, *Relation historique du voyage aux régions équinoxiales du Nouveau Continent* (3 vols, Paris, 1814–1825), trans. Thomasina Ross, *Personal Narrative of a Journey to the Equinoctial Regions of the New Continent* (3 vols, London, 1852), vol. 1, 371, 422, 391–92.

p. 132 *deal with'*, Douglas Botting, *Humboldt and the Cosmos* (New York: Harper and Row, 1973), 125.

pp. 133–35 *fruits'* and subsequent quotations, Charles Waterton, *Wanderings in South America ... in the years 1812, 1816, 1820 and 1824* (London: John Murray, 1825), ed. L. Harrison Matthews (Oxford: Oxford University Press, 1973), 2–3, 4, 28, 79, 80, 133–34.

p. 135 *Mulatresses!'*, Charles Darwin to Charles Lyell, 1845, *Darwin Life and Letters*, vol. 1, 343–44; Julia Blackburn, *Charles Waterton, Traveller and Conservationist* (London: Bodley Head, 1989), 178.

p. 136 *self-esteem'*, Langsdorff's Journal, entry for 11 April 1828, in Noemi G. Shprintsin, 'The Apiacá Indians', *Kratkiye Soobschcheniya Instituta Etnografi*, An. SSSR, vol. 10, 1959, 89; also Roderick J. Barman, 'The forgotten journey: George Heinrich Langsdorff and the Russian Imperial Scientific Expedition to Brazil, 1821–1829', *Terrae Incognitae* (Amsterdam, 1971), vol. 3, 367–96.

p. 136 *fury'*, Alfredo d'Escragnolle Taunay, 'A cidade de Mato Grosso (antiga Villa Bella) o rio Guaporé e a sua mais illustre victima', *Revista do Instituto Histórico e Geográphico Brasileiro* (Rio de Janeiro, 1839–) supplement to 51:2, 1891, 14–15.

p. 136 *civilised men', infected them'*, Hércules Florence, *Esboço da viagem feito pelo Sr. de Langsdorff no interior do Brasil*, trans. from French by Alfredo d'Escragnolle Taunay, *Revista do Instituto Histórico e Geographico Brasileiro*, vol. 38:2, 1876, 281–82.

p. 137 *delirium', place', alive'*, Langsdorff journal, in Shprintsin, 'The Apiacá', op. cit., 188, 188, 95–96.

p. 137 *forms'*, Alfred Russel Wallace, *A Narrative of Travels on the Amazon and Rio Negro* (London: Reeve & Co., 1853), 2–3.

p. 138 *Andes'*, Henry Walter Bates, *A Naturalist on the River Amazons* (2 vols, London: John Murray, 1863), vol. 1, 2.

p. 138 *parasites, &c.'*, Bates to Frederick Bates, Ega (on the Solimões), 30 May 1856, 'Extracts from the Correspondence of Mr. H. W. Bates, now forming entomological collections in South America' (*Zoologist* nos. 8–15, 1849–56), no. 15, 1856, 5658–9; Hugh Raffles, *In Amazonia, A Natural History* (Princeton and Oxford: Princeton University Press, 2002), 123.

p. 138 *none of them'*, Bates to Edwin Brown, Pará, 17 June 1848, *Zoologist*, no. 8, 1849, 2837.

p. 138 *forests', together'*, Bates, *A Naturalist*, op. cit., vol. 2, 415–17.

p. 140 *cable', undergrowth'*, Richard Spruce, *Notes of a Botanist on the Amazon and Andes*, ed. A. R. Wallace (2 vols, London: Macmillan & Co., 1908), vol. 1, 17.

p. 141 *Alders', flowers',* Spruce to Matthew Slater, Barra (Manaus), Oct. 1851, *Notes of a Botanist*, vol. 1, 256.

p. 141 *at the place',* Bates, *A Naturalist*, op. cit., vol. 1, 29.

pp. 141–42 *birds (ant-thrushes)', pupae',* Bates, idem, vol. 2, 96.

p. 142 *forest',* Wallace, *A Narrative*, op. cit., 95.

pp. 142–43 *Cedros', friend',* Spruce, *Notes of a Botanist*, op. cit., vol. 1, 105, 62–3.

p. 143 *great expense',* Bates to Darwin, 17 Oct. 1862, in Robert M. Stecher, 'The Darwin-Bates letters: correspondence between two nineteenth-century travellers and naturalists' (*Annals of Science*, vol. 25:1, 1969, 1–47), 35; Raffles, *In Amazonia*, op. cit., 30.

p. 143 *species grubbers',* Bates to Darwin, 2 May 1863, in Stecher, 'The Darwin-Bates letters', idem, 45.

p. 143 *colonists of long standing',* Spruce, *Notes of a Botanist*, op. cit.

pp. 143–44 *South America', new',* Samuel Stevens, *Zoologist*, no. 8, 1849, 2663–4.

p. 144 *12 feet long',* Bates to Stevens, Santarém, 8 Jan. 1852, *Zoologist*, no. 10, 1852, 3450.

pp. 144–45 *alternative'* and subsequent quotations, Spruce to Bentham, Barra (Manaus), 7 Nov. 1851, *Zoologist*, no. 1, 227, 293, 227. Richard Evans Schultes, 'Some impacts of Spruce's Amazon explorations on modern phytochemical research' (*Rhodora*, 70:783, 313–39), 336–37.

pp. 145–46 *hammock', sticks',* Wallace, *A Narrative*, op. cit., 340.

p. 146 *continued fever'* and subsequent quotations, Spruce, *Notes of a Botanist*, op. cit., vol. 1, 464–5.

pp. 146–48 *fever'* and subsequent quotations, Bates, *The Naturalist*, op. cit., vol. 2, 263, 265, 278, 279, 338, 344, 409–10.

pp. 148–50 *ferocity'* and subsequent quotations, Spruce, *Notes of a Botanist*, op. cit., vol. 2 69, vol. 1 364, 94–5, 271, 125, 249–50.

p. 150 *help to me',* Bates to Stevens, Belém, 30 Aug. 1849, *Zoologist*, no. 8, 1849, 2665.

p. 150 *on earth', heard him',* Grant Allen, 'Bates of the Amazons' (*The Fortnightly Review*, no. 58, 1892, 798–809), 802–803; Raffles, *In Amazonia*, op. cit., 148.

pp. 150–51 *leaf', appearances', describe them',* Bates, *The Naturalist*, op. cit., vol. 1 299, vol. 1 v.

p. 151 *after them', best things',* Bates to Stevens, Pará (Belém), 3 June 1851, *Zoologist*, no. 9, 1852, 3321; Raffles, *In Amazonia*, op. cit., 141.

p. 151 *reflection',* Bates, *The Naturalist*, op. cit., vol. 2, 305–306.

p. 152 *species',* Wallace, *Essay on the Law which has Regulated the Introduction of New Species* (1855).

p. 153 *sounds',* Spruce to John Teasdale, Tarapoto, Peru, July 1855, *Notes of a Botanist*, op. cit., vol. 2, 27.

p. 153 *wanderings',* Spruce to George Bentham, Tarapoto, 25 Dec. 1855, *Notes of a Botanist*, idem, vol. 2, 49.

p. 153 *groups',* Wallace note, *Notes of a Botanist*, idem, 101.

p. 153 *tree-ferns',* Spruce, 'Précis d'un voyage dans l'Amérique équitoriale pendant les années 1849–64' (*Revue Bryologique*, 1886, 61–79), *Notes of a Botanist*, idem, 99.

p. 154 *suffered'* and subsequent quotations, Spruce, *Notes of a Botanist*, vol. 2, 104, 109, 121–22.

p. 155 *Red Bark tree',* Spruce, 'Report on the Expedition to procure seeds and plants of the *Cinchona succirubra* or Red Bark tree', part of a Government Blue Book on the transfer of the trees to India, *Notes of a Botanist*, 261.

p. 155 *genus',* Clements Markham, *Travels in Peru and India, while Superintending the Collection of Chinchona Plants and Seeds in South America and their Introduction into India* (London: John Murray, 1862); Fiametta Rocco, *The Miraculous Fever-Tree* (London: HarperCollins, 2003), 219.

p. 155 *pain',* Spruce, *Notes of a Botanist*, op. cit., vol. 2, 157.

p. 156 *dose',* Spruce to George Bentham, São Gabriel, Rio Negro, 18 Aug. 1852, *Notes of a Botanist*, idem, vol. 1, 315 (describing a *dabicuí* festival of Baré Indians); also vol. 1, 217. Spruce wrote an article 'On some remarkable narcotics of the Amazon valley and Orinoco', *Geographical Magazine*, 1870, in *Notes of a Botanist*, idem, vol. 2, 413–55.

p. 156 *caapi'*, Richard Spruce's field notebook, Royal Botanic Gardens, Kew, quoted by Richard Evans Schultes, 'Some impacts of Spruce's Amazon explorations on modern phytochemical research' (*Rhodora*, 79:783, 1968, 313–39), 326.

p. 165 *ground'*, Spruce, *Notes of a Botanist*, op. cit., vol. 2, 424.

p. 165 *sun'*, Wade Davis, *One River: Explorations and Discoveries in the Amazon Rain Forests* (New York: Simon and Schuster, 1996), 216.

p. 166 *no tired!'*, Spruce's comment to Sir William Hooker, with a specimen of caapi sent on 25 June 1864, Royal Botanic Gardens, Kew, Museum: R. Spruce 177, Kew Cat. no. 59120.

pp. 166–67 *duration', timbers'*, Schultes, 'Some impacts', op. cit., 316; also in his 'Richard Spruce, the man', M. R. D. Seaward and S. M. D. FitzGerald, eds, *Richard Spruce (1817–1893) Botanist and Explorer* (Kew: Royal Botanic Gardens, 1996), 16–25.

p. 167 *interest for me', existence?'*, Spruce, letter to Daniel Hanbury, 1873, in Wallace's introduction to Spruce, *Notes of a Botanist*, op. cit., xxxviii.

p. 167 *conscious"'*, Davis, *One River*, op. cit., 373–74.

pp. 167–68 *companion', pleasure'*, Wallace's Obituary of Spruce, *Nature*, 1 Feb. 1894; *Notes of a Botanist*, op. cit., vol. 1, xliii.

p. 168 *fish'*, William James papers, Houghton Library, Harvard University, quoted in Nancy Leys Stepan, *Picturing Tropical Nature* (London: Reaktion Books, 2001), 34.

p. 168 *worth'*, William James quoted in Howard M. Feinstein, *Becoming William James* (Ithaca and London: Cornell University Press, 1984), 174; Stepan, *Picturing Tropical Nature*, idem, 91.

p. 169 *Indian'*, Professor and Mrs Louis Agassiz, *A Journey in Brazil* (Boston, 1868), 293; Stepan, *Picturing Tropical Nature*, idem, 109.

p. 171 *relief!'*, Karl von den Steinen, *Durch Central-Brasilien* (Leipzig, 1886), 159; John Hemming, *Amazon Frontier* (London: Pan, 2004), 402.

p. 172 *overland'*, Steinen, *Unter den Naturvölkern Zentral-Brasiliens* (Berlin, 1894), 69–70.

p. 173 *animation'*, Steinen, *Durch Central-Brasilien*, op. cit., 181.

p. 173 *cause it', decay', indecent'*, Steinen, *Unter den Naturvölkern*, op. cit., 58, 190.

pp. 173-74 *far bank'* and subsequent quotations, Steinen, *Durch Central-Brasilien*, op. cit., 192, 201, 204.

Chapter 6 The Rubber Boom

p. 175 *quantity'*, Spruce, *Notes of a Botanist on the Amazon and Andes*, ed. A. R. Wallace (2 vols, London: Macmillan & Co., 1908), vol. 1, 507.

p. 175 *air'*, Charles-Marie de La Condamine, *Relation abrégée d'un voyage fait dans l'intérieur de l'Amérique Meridionale* (Paris, 1745), 79.

p. 177 *materials'*, Advertisement by Dr Francisco Xavier d'Oliveira in *Gazeta de Lisboa*, March 1800, in Manoel Barata, 'Apontamentos para as Ephemérides Paraenses', *Revista do Instituto Histórico e Geográphico Brasileiro*, 99, 52–3, 1924; John Hemming, *Amazon Frontier* (London: Pan, 2004), 262.

p. 177 *decent'*, Johann Baptist von Spix and Carl Friedrich Philip von Martius, *Reise in Brasilien in den Jahren 1817 bis 1820* (Portuguese trans., 4 vols, Rio de Janeiro, 1938), vol. 3, 30–31.

p. 179 *beauty'*, Franz Keller, *The Amazon and Madeira Rivers* (London, 1874), 34.

p. 180 *city'*, *Mensagem do Governador Eduardo Ribeiro, em 10. de março de 1896* (Manaus, 1897), quoted in Frederico José Barão de Santa-Anna Nery, *Le Pays des Amazones* (Paris, 1899 ed.).

p. 180 *Rio Negro!'*, Auguste Plane, *Le Pérou* (Paris: Plon, 1903), in Márcio Souza, *Breve História da Amazônia* (São Paulo: Marco Zero, 1994), 141.

p. 181 *bookshops'*, Richard Collier, *The River that God Forgot* (London: Collins, 1968), 19.

p. 182 *champagne'*, Robin Furneaux, *The Amazon: The Story of a Great River* (London, 1969), 153.

p. 182 *included'*, Tony Morrison, Ann Brown and Anne Rose, *Lizzie: A Victorian Lady's Amazon Adventure* (London: British Broadcasting Corporation, 1985), 39.

p. 182 *champagne', drinks',* Anibal Amorim, *Viagens pelo Brasil* (Rio de Janeiro: Livraria Garnier, 1917), 157–58.

p. 183 *Apiaká',* Henri Coudreau, *Voyage au Tapajóz* (Paris: A. Lahure, 1897), 60–61.

p. 184 *treachery',* Henry Pearson, *The Rubber Country of the Amazon* (New York, 1911), 148–49.

p. 185 *upset',* Lizzie Hessel, letter to her family from Mishagua, Urubamba, 20 July 1897, in Morrison et al., *Lizzie,* op. cit., 67.

p. 186 *road',* Petition in Chancery by the Public Works and Construction Company, London, 1873, in Neville B. Craig, *Recollections of an Ill-fated Expedition to the Headwaters of the Madeira River in Brazil* (Philadelphia and London, 1907), 57.

pp. 192–93 *seeds'* and subsequent quotations, H. A. Wickham, *On the Plantation, Cultivation, and Curing of Pará Indian Rubber (Hevea Brasiliensis)* (London: Kegan Paul, Trench, Trübner & Co., 1908), 47–54.

p. 193 *planter-hero',* Warren Dean, *Brazil and the Struggle for Rubber* (Cambridge, New York, etc.: Cambridge University Press, 1987), 21.

p. 194 *trees',* Clements R. Markham, 'The cultivation of caoutchouc-yielding trees in British India' (*Journal of the Royal Society of Arts,* vol. 24, 7 April 1876, 475–81), in Dean, *Brazil,* idem, 12.

p. 194 *70,000 seeds',* O. Labroy and V. Cayla, *A Borracha no Brasil* (Rio de Janeiro: Ministério da Agricultura, Indústria e Commércio, 1913), 42.

p. 195 *odd of them',* Wickham, *On the Plantation,* op. cit., 55.

p. 196 *Malaysia',* Wilfred Blunt, *Of Flowers and a Village,* quoted in Anthony Smith, *Explorers of the Amazon* (London and New York: Viking, 1990), 285.

p. 197 *half- price',* Collier, *The River,* op. cit., 279 .

Chapter 7 The Black Side of Rubber

p. 198 *returns',* James Drummond Hay, 'Report on the industrial classes in the Provinces of Pará and Amazonas, Brazil', in Henry Alexander Wickham, *Rough Notes of a Journey through the Wilderness* (London, 1872), 292.

p. 199 *following day',* President Sebastião do Rego Barros, *Relatório,* Belém, 15 Aug. 1854, in John Hemming, *Amazon Frontier* (London: Pan, 2004), 280.

p. 199 *constitution!',* Kenneth Grubb, *Amazon and Andes* (London: Methuen, 1930), 12.

p. 200 *devastation!',* Esther de Viveiros, *Rondon conta sua Vida* (Rio de Janeiro: Livraria São José, 1970), 331–32.

p. 200 *extinguished',* Joseph F. Woodroffe and Harold Hamel Smith, *The Rubber Industry of the Amazon* (London: John Bale, Sons & Danielsson, Ltd., 1915), 28.

p. 200 *class',* President Francisco de Araújo Brusque, *Relatório,* Belém, 1 Sept. 1862; Hemming, *Amazon Frontier,* op. cit., 280.

p. 200 *Indians',* Neville B. Craig, *Recollections of an Ill-fated Expedition to the Headwaters of the Madeira River in Brazil* (Philadelphia and London: J. B. Lippincott & Co., 1907), 257.

pp. 200–201 *ferocious man', appearance',* Antonio Manuel Gonçalves Tocantins, 'Estudos sobre a tribo Mundurucu' (*Revista do Instituto Histórico e Geographico Brasiliensis,* 40:2, 1877, 73–162), 158.

p. 201 *vice',* Frei Pelino de Castrovalva to President of Pará, 20 Jan. 1876, in Tocantins, 'Estudos', idem, 137–38.

p. 201 *onwards',* Curt Nimuendajú, 'Os índios Parintintin do Rio Madeira', *Journal de la Société des Américanistes de Paris,* no. 16, 1924 (201–278), 230; John Hemming, *Die If You Must* (London: Macmillan, 2003), 63–4.

pp. 201–202 *launch', nothing more',* Euclides da Cunha, *À margem da história* (Pôrto, 1941), 23; Arthur Cézar Ferreira Reis, *O seringal e o seringueiro* (Rio de Janeiro: Ministério da Agricultura, 1953), 95.

p. 202 *soot',* Woodroffe and Smith, *The Rubber Industry,* op. cit., 45.

p. 202 *occupation',* Grubb, *Amazon and Andes,* op. cit., 7.

p. 202 *surrounds them',* Woodroffe and Smith, *The Rubber Industry,* op. cit., 45.

p. 203 *wrongs',* Kenneth Grubb, *From Pacific to Atlantic: South American Studies* (London: Methuen, 1933), 104.

p. 203 *region', hunger',* Dr Oswaldo Cruz, *Considerações gerais sobre as condições sanitárias do Rio Madeira* (Rio de Janeiro, 1910), 11.

p. 203 *lust',* Grubb, *From Pacific to Atlantic,* op. cit., 104.

p. 204 *perish',* José Eustacio Rivera, *La Vorágine, novela de la violencia* (Santiago, 1957), 287.

p. 204 *selfishness',* Cunha, *À margem da história,* op. cit., 24.

p. 205 *advances',* Julio César Arana deposition, *Report and Special Report from the Select Committee on Putumayo, Proceedings, Minutes of Evidence,* Appendix 3, 1913 (House of Commons Paper 148), in Roger Sawyer, *Casement: The Flawed Hero* (London: Routledge & Kegan Paul, 1984), 79.

pp. 206–209 *outraged'* and subsequent quotations, Walter Hardenburg, *The Putumayo: The Devil's Paradise* (London: T. Fisher Unwin, 1912), 148, 173, 175, 176, 152, 153, 159.

p. 210 *shoulders',* Thomas Whiffen, *The North-West Amazons: Notes of Some Months Spent Among Cannibal Tribes* (London: Constable, 1915), 64.

pp. 210–11 *labour!'* and subsequent quotations, Hardenburg, *The Putumayo,* op. cit., 214, 180, 214, 195.

p. 212 *children', La Felpa,* Iquitos, 29 Dec. 1907, trans. in Hardenburg, *The Putumayo,* idem, 217.

p. 212 *hidden', house', company',* testimony of Julio F. Muriedas, *La Sanción,* Iquitos, 22 Aug. 1907, trans. in idem, 225–26, 227, 227.

p. 212 *fifteen', killed',* testimony of Anacleto Portocarrero, sworn before Federico M. Pizarro, Notary Public, *La Sanción,* 29 August 1907, trans. in idem, 229, 229–30.

p. 212 *flogging', region',* testimony of Carlos Soplín, sworn before Pizarro, *La Sanción,* 10 Oct. 1907, trans. in idem, 230, 231–32.

p. 213 *Indians',* Anonymous witness, *La Felpa,* 5 Jan. 1908, trans. in idem, 234, 236.

p. 213 *shrieks'* and subsequent quotations, testimony of Brazilian João Batista Braga, before Lt José Rosa Brazil, commandant of Constantópolis, Brazil, 6 Oct. 1908, trans. in idem, 237, 238, 239.

pp. 213–14 *revolver', skeletons', eyes',* Juan Rosas, witnessed letter to Hardenburg, Iquitos, 6 June 1908, trans. in idem, 241, 242, 243.

p. 214 *years'* and subsequent quotations, Celestino López, notarized letter to Hardenburg, Iquitos, 15 May 1909, idem, 244, 244/249, 245–46, 248, 249–50, 250.

pp. 214–15 *blood'* and subsequent quotations, Genaro Caporo, notarized letter to Hardenburg, Iquitos, 17 May 1909, idem, 251–55.

p. 215 *today'* and subsequent quotations, testimony of Daniel Collantes, idem, 204–208.

p. 216 *itself', distant',* testimony of López, idem, 180, 181.

p. 216 *white rubber-gatherers',* Whiffen, *The North-West Amazons,* op. cit., 64.

p. 216 *blow',* Roger Casement, *Journal for 1910,* entry for 31 Oct. at La Chorrera, after interviewing Evelyn Batson, in Angus Mitchell, ed., *The Amazon Journal of Roger Casement* (London: Anaconda Editions, 1997), 337.

p. 218 *machetes', Truth,* 22 September 1909, quoting *La Sanción,* Iquitos.

p. 220 *humane', depopulation',* Roger Casement to Sir Edward Grey, March 1911, in Hardenburg, *The Putumayo,* op. cit., 283.

p. 220 *death', short"',* Casement 'white diary', La Chorrera, 23 Sept. 1910, in Roger Sawyer, ed., *Roger Casement's Diaries. 1910: The Black & The White* (London: Pimlico, 1997), 139. Also 'Black' diary for the same day, idem, 85. Also in Mitchell, ed., *The Amazon Journal,* op. cit., 122–23.

p. 221 *screamed out"',* Casement report to Foreign Secretary, 1911, in Robin Furneaux, *The Amazon: The Story of a Great River* (London, 1969), 180.

p. 221 *night',* Casement to Spicer, Sept. 1910, in Furneaux, *The Amazon,* idem, 175.

p. 221 *tricks',* Casement, diary La Chorrera, 23 Sept., Sawyer, ed., *Roger Casement's Diaries,* op. cit., 137; Mitchell, ed., *The Amazon Journal,* op. cit., 121.

p. 221 *hawk-like'* and subsequent quotations, Casement diary for 12 Oct., 1 Nov. and 6 Nov.;

Mitchell, ed., *The Amazon Journal*, idem, 230, 344, 344, 360.

p. 222 *larger number'*, Casement report to Grey, in Hardenburg, *The Putumayo*, op. cit., 306.

p. 222 *place'*, Casement journal, 29 Sept., Occidente, 30 Oct., La Chorrera; Mitchell, ed., *The Amazon Journal*, op. cit., 144.

p. 222 *amity with him'*, Whiffen, *The North-West Amazons*, op. cit., 190.

p. 222 *head'*, Casement, diary for 29 Sept., Occidente, in Sawyer, ed., *Roger Casement's Diaries*, op. cit., 146; Mitchell, ed., *The Amazon Journal*, op. cit., 144.

p. 223 *free life', good', blood'*, Casement, diary for 18 Oct., Matanzas, and 30 Oct., La Chorrera; Mitchell, ed., *The Amazon Journal*, idem, 264, 335, 335.

p. 223 *pieces'*, Casement report to Sir Edward Grey, 1911, in Hardenburg, *The Putumayo*, op. cit., 306.

p. 224 *horrible'*, Sir Edward Grey, in Anthony Smith, *Explorers of the Amazon* (London and New York: Viking, 1990), 318.

p. 225 *forests'*, Casement's 1912 report, in Hardenburg, *The Putumayo*, op. cit., 334.

p. 225 *tribes'*, Report by Dr Rómulo Paredes, Comisario del Putumayo, quoted in Furneaux, *The Amazon*, op. cit., 189.

p. 225 *indefatigable'*, Report by His Majesty's Consul at Iquitos (George Michell) on his Tour in the Putumayo District, Foreign Office papers, Miscellaneous No. 6, 1913 (Cd 6678) in National Archive (PRO); Furneaux, *The Amazon*, idem, 192; Sawyer, ed., *Roger Casement's Diaries*, op. cit., 98.

p. 226 *forced labour'*, Sir Edward Grey to Ambassador Sir James Bryce in Washington, 17 June 1912, in Collier, *The River that God Forgot* (London: Collins, 1968), 236.

p. 226 *confidently'*, *The Daily Mirror*, 9 April 1913, quoted in Collier, *The River*, idem, 272.

p. 226 *determination'* and subsequent quotations, *Report and Special Report from the Select Committee on Putumayo, Proceedings, Minutes of Evidence* (House of Commons Paper 148, 1913), in Collier, *The River*, idem, 268 ff.

p. 228 *rot'*, *El Oriente*, Iquitos, 1912, in Furneaux, *The Amazon*, op. cit., 191.

p. 229 *thin', room'* and other diary entries, Sawyer, ed., *Roger Casement's Diaries*, op. cit., 65–7.

p. 229 *yourself'*, Telegram from Arana to Casement, Manaus, 14 June 1916, a document discovered by Robin Furneaux in the Public Record Office (National Archive) and published in his *The Amazon*, op. cit., 198.

p. 230 *rubber'*, Father Leo Sandbrook, OFM, to the acting British Consul in Iquitos, 20 Sept. 1916, in Furneaux, *The Amazon*, idem, 198–99.

p. 231 *cultivation'*, Colonel G[eorge] E. Church, *The Aborigines of South America* (London: Chapman and Hall, 1912), 13; Woodroffe and Smith, *The Rubber Industry*, op. cit., 22.

Chapter 8 Explorers and Indians

p. 233 *cheese', inhabitants'*, Roy Nash, *The Conquest of Brazil* (London: Jonathan Cape, 1926), 387–88.

pp. 233–36 *high'* and subsequent quotations, Hiram Bingham, *Lost City of the Incas: The Story of Machu Picchu and its Builders* (New York, 1948; Phoenix House, London, 1951; Folio Society, London, 2004), ch. 7, 162–63.

p. 237 *distance'''*, Esther de Viveiros, *Rondon conta sua vida* (Rio de Janeiro: Livraria São José, 1958), 78.

p. 239 *shame', bowstrings', arrows'*, Cândido Mariano da Silva Rondon, *Conferências Realizadas em 1910 no Rio de Janeiro e em São Paulo* (2nd edn. Rio de Janeiro: Conselho Nacional de Proteção aos Índios, vol. 68, 1946), 88–9, 23.

p. 241 *companion'* and subsequent quotations, Theodore Roosevelt, *Through the Brazilian Wilderness* (London: John Murray, 1914), 48, 72.

p. 241 *gradually'*, Viveiros, *Rondon conta*, op. cit., 410.

pp. 241–44 *manners'* and subsequent quotations, Roosevelt, *Wilderness*, idem, 186, 186, 186, 208–9, 209–10, 234, 244, 361, 259, 268, 279, 285, 255, 285, 307. The letter to the Foreign Minister, General Lauro Müller, was written from Manaus on 1 May 1914.

p. 244 *without me!', agony'*, Viveiros, *Rondon conta*, 418.

p. 244 *undiminished'*, Leo E. Miller, *In the Wilds of South America* (London: T. Fisher Unwin, 1919), 264.

p. 253 *importance'*, Roosevelt, *Wilderness*, op. cit., 322–23.

p. 253 *charms'*, Max Schmidt, *Indianerstudien in Zentralbrasilien* (Berlin, 1905), 108.

p. 256 *oppressions'*, Egon Schaden, 'Notas sôbre a vida e a obra de Curt Nimuendajú' (*Revista do Instituto de Estudos Brasileiros*, Universidade de São Paulo, vol. 3, 1968, 7–19), 1

p. 256 *people'*, Curt Nimuendajú, 'Nimongarai', *Deutsche Zeitung*, São Paulo, 6:3, 15 July 1910, in Schaden, 'Notas', idem, 18.

pp. 256–57 *voice', pick them up', hours!'*, Curt Nimuendajú, 'Os índios Parintintin do Rio Madeira' (*Journal de la Société des Américanistes de Paris*, vol. 16, 1924, 201–278), 215–16.

p. 257 *lands'*, Herbert Baldus, 'Curt Nimuendajú' (*Boletim Bibliográfico*, vol. 2[3], 1945, 91–9), 92.

p. 258 *fall!'*, Curt Nimuendajú, 'Reconhecimento do rios Içana, Ayarí e Uaupés. Relatório apresentado ao Serviço de Proteção aos Índios do Amazonas e Acre, 1927' (*Journal de la Société des Américanistes de Paris*, vol. 39, 1950, 125–82).

p. 259 *ethnology'*, Darcy Ribeiro, 'Por uma antropologia melhor e mais nossa', *Ensaios insólitos* (Porto Alegre: L & P M Editora, 1979), 210.

pp. 259–62 *people's'* and subsequent quotations, P. H. Fawcett, *Exploration Fawcett* (London: Hutchinson, 1953), 57, 59, 95, 201–202, 251, 269, 271, 269, 285, 14–15. This book was published in New York in the same year as *Lost Trails, Lost Cities*.

p. 263 *Xingu'*, Opinion by the Director of the SPI (Capitão Vasconcellos) to the Council for Approving Artistic and Scientific Expeditions, 1938, in Luis Donisete Benzi Grupioni, *Coleções e Expedições Vigiadas* (São Paulo: Editora Hucitec, 1998), 99.

p. 264 *in him'*, Orlando and Cláudio Villas Boas, *A Marcha para o Oeste: A Epopéia da Expedição Roncador-Xingu* (São Paulo: Editôra Globo, 1994), 167.

pp. 265–66 *swindle', site'*, Warren Dean, *Brazil and the Struggle for Rubber* (Cambridge: Cambridge University Press, 1987), 71, 72.

p. 267 *altogether'*, Weir to R. I. Roberge, Departmental communication, 24 May 1935, in Dean, *Brazil*, idem, 77.

Chapter 9 Archaeologists Find Early Man

p. 271 *generations', unknown'*, Alexander von Humboldt, *Relation historique du voyage aux régions équinoxiales du Nouveau Continent* (3 vols, Paris, 1814–1825), trans. Thomasina Ross, *Personal Narrative of a Journey to the Equinoctial Regions of the New Continent* (3 vols, London, 1852), vol. 1, 371.

p. 271 *China'*, Toribio de Ortiguera, *Jornada del Río Marañón* (c. 1585), in M. Meléndez Pelayo, ed., *Biblioteca de Autores Españoles... (Continuación)* (Madrid, 1905–), vol. 15, 1909, 317.

p. 274 *explanations'*, Theodor Koch-Grünberg, *Südamerikanische Felszeichnungen*, Berlin, 1907.

p. 274 *experiences'*, Gerardo Reichel-Dolmatoff, *Beyond the Milky Way: Hallucinatory Imagery of the Tukano Indians* (1978), in Richard Evans Schultes, *Where the Gods Reign: Plants and Peoples of the Colombian Amazon* (Oracle, Arizona and London: Synergetic Press, 1988), 80.

p. 275 *occupies'*, Betty J. Meggers, *Amazonia: Man and Culture in a Counterfeit Paradise* (Washington, D.C.: Smithsonian Institution, 1971).

p. 276 *latter'*, Betty J. Meggers, 'Sustainable intensive exploitation of Amazonia: cultural, environmental, and geopolitical perspectives', in Alf Hornborg and Carole Crumley, eds, *The World System and the Earth System* (Walnut Creek, CA: Left Coast Press, 2006, 191–205), 192.

p. 276 *years?'*, Robert L. Carneiro, 'Forest clearance among the Yanomamö: Observations and implications', *Anthropologica*, no. 42, 1979, 39–76.

p. 276 *myth'*, William M. Denevan, 'The aboriginal population of Amazonia', in W. M. Denevan, ed., *The Native Population of the Americas in 1492* (Madison: University of Wisconsin Press, 1976, 205–233).

p. 277 *environment'*, Anna C. Roosevelt, 'Ancient and modern hunter-gatherers of lowland South America: an evolutionary problem', in William Ballée, ed., *Advances in Historical Ecology* (New York: Columbia University Press, 1998, 190–212), 191.

p. 279 *tally'*, Anna C. Roosevelt, 'Paleoindian cave dwellers in the Amazon: the peopling of the Americas', *Science* 272, 1996, 373–84.

p. 280 *diet'*, Peter Silverwood-Cope, 'Maku – In the heart of the forest' (*Survival International News*, no. 39, 1998, 8–11), 10.

p. 280 *economies'*, Schultes, *Where the Gods Reign*, op. cit., 100.

p. 282 *New World'*, Anna Roosevelt, *Moundbuilders of the Amazon: Geophysical Archaeology on Marajó Island, Brazil* (San Diego, CA: Academic Press, 1991).

p. 282 *societies of Amazonia'*, Roosevelt, *Moundbuilders of the Amazon*, idem, 436.

p. 282 *degradation'*, Betty Meggers in *Latin American Antiquity*, 2001, in Marion Lloyd, 'Earth movers', *Chronicle of Higher Education*, 51:15, Dec. 2004.

p. 282 *CIA'*, Charles C. Mann, *1491: New Revelations of the Americas before Columbus* (New York: Vintage Books, 2006), 333.

pp. 282–83 *lakes'* and subsequent quotations, Mark B. Bush et al., 'Holocene fire and occupation in Amazonia: records from two lake districts' (*Philosophical Transactions of The Royal Society, B*, vol. 362, 2007, 209–218), 215, 209, and author's comments about it. Also cites William M. Denevan, 'A bluff model of riverine settlement in prehistoric Amazonia', *Annals of the Association of American Geographers*, 86, 1996, 654–81, and Nigel J. H. Smith, 'Anthrosols and human carrying capacity in Amazonia', *Annals of the Association of American Geographers*, vol. 50, 1980, 553–66.

p. 283 *the Amazons'*, Herbert H. Smith, *Brazil, the Amazons and the Coast* (New York, 1879).

p. 284 *the secret'*, William I. Woods and J. M. McCann, 'The anthropogenic origin and persistence of Amazonian dark earths' (*Yearbook, Conference of Latin American Geographers*, 1999, vol. 25, 2000, 7–14), 10.

p. 284 *amazing'*, Betty J. Meggers, 'Aboriginal adaptation to Amazonia', in Ghillean T. Prance and Thomas E. Lovejoy, eds, *Key Environments: Amazonia* (Oxford, etc.: Pergamon Press, 1985, 307–327), 323.

p. 284 *4900 BC'*, James B. Petersen, Eduardo Neves and Michael J. Heckenberger, '*Terra Preta* and prehistoric Amerindian occupation in Amazonia', in Colin McEwan, Cristiana Barreto and Eduardo Neves, eds, *Unknown Amazon* (London: British Museum Press, 2001, 86–105), 97.

p. 285 *Paradise'*, Antonio Vázquez de Espinosa, *Compendio, y Descripción de las Indias Occidentales*, trans. Charles Upson Clark (Washington, D.C.: Smithsonian Institution Press [Miscellaneous Collections 102], 1968), para. 1689, p. 645.

p. 286 *ditches'*, Alf Hornborg, 'Ethnogenesis, regional integration, and ecology in prehistoric Amazonia' (*Current Anthropology*, 46:4, Aug.–Oct. 2005, 589–619), 603.

p. 286 *built environment'*, Michael J. Heckenberger, 'Amazonia 1492: pristine forest or cultural parkland?', *Science*, no. 30, 2003, 1710–14.

p. 287 *charcoal'*, C. Uhl, D. Nepstad, R. Buschbacher, K. Clark, B. Kauffman and S. Subler, 'Studies of ecosystem response to natural and anthropogenic disturbances ... in Amazonia', in Anthony B. Anderson, ed., *Alternatives to Deforestation* (New York: Columbia University Press, 1990, 24–42); William M. Denevan, 'The pristine myth: the landscape of the Americas in 1492' (*Annals of the Association of American Geographers*, vol. 82:3, 1992, 369–85), 373.

Chapter 10 Planes, Chainsaws and Bulldozers

p. 296 *Indians'*, Tuira Kayapó quoted in Nicholas Hildyard, 'Adios Amazonia?' (*Ecologist*, no. 19:2, 1989, 53–62), 53; John Hemming, *Die If You Must* (London: Macmillan, 2003), 377.

p. 307 *projects'*, *Veja*, 5 July 1989, 86.

p. 309 *species'*, Gregory P. Asnner et al., 'Selective logging in the Brazilian Amazon', *Science*, no. 310, 21 Oct. 2005, 480.

p. 311 *mining'*, *The Guardian*, 18 Jan. 2005, quoted in Greenpeace, *Eating up the Amazon* (Amsterdam: Greenpeace, 2006), 11.

p. 311 *moment'*, Kory Melby in *USDA agricultural baseline projections to 2014* (US Department of Agriculture website, 2005), in Greenpeace, idem, 12.

p. 311 *forest'*, Fr Edilberto Sena in Daniel Howden, 'Moratorium on new soya crops wins reprieve for rainforest', *The Independent*, 26 July 2006.

p. 311 *watershed', economic'*, Scott Wallace, 'Last of the Amazon', *National Geographic*, Jan. 2007, 65, 68

p. 314 *production'*, President Fernando Henrique Cardoso, quoted in R. de Cassia, 'BR-174: FHC anuncia abertura de nova fronteira agrícola no Norte', *Amazonas em Tempo*, Manaus, 25 June 1997.

p. 315 *major road', process'*, Kathryn R. Kirby et al, 'The future of deforestation in the Brazilian Amazon', (*Futures*, vol. 38, 2006, 432–53), 442, 445.

p. 316 *deforestation ends'*, Stephan Schwartzman quoted in Wallace, 'Last of the Amazon', op. cit., 68.

p. 323 *Amazon'*, Fred Pearce, *The Last Generation* (London: Transworld Publishers, 2006), 95.

Chapter 11 The Largest River in the Largest Forest

p. 325 *clad with trees'*, Richard Spruce to Matthew Slater, Barra (Manaus), Oct. 1851, in Richard Spruce, *Notes of a Botanist on the Amazon and Andes*, ed. A. R. Wallace (2 vols, London: Macmillan & Co., 1908), vol. 1, 256.

p. 327 *basin'*, Richard Evans Schultes, *Where the Gods Reign: Plants and Peoples of the Colombian Amazon* (Oracle, Arizona and London: Synergetic Press, 1988), 14.

p. 329 *network of rivers'*, Professor and Mrs Louis Agassiz, *A Journey in Brazil* (Boston, 1879), 383.

p. 335 *vapour'*, Peter Fleming, *Brazilian Adventure* (London: Jonathan Cape, 1933), 139.

p. 335 *endemic'*, Russell A. Mittermeier, Norman Myers et al., *Hotspots: Earth's Biologically Richest and Most Endangered Biological Terrestrial Ecoregions* (Mexico: Cemex, 1999); Mittermeier et al. (Patricio Robles Gil, ed.), *Wilderness, Earth's Last Wild Places* (Mexico: Cemex, 2002), 73.

p. 335 *fist', ship'*, David G. Campbell, *A Land of Ghosts* (London: Jonathan Cape, 2004), 125.

p. 337 *endemics'*, Mittermeier et al., *Wilderness*, op. cit., 68.

p. 337 *cuckoos]'*, Campbell, *A Land*, op. cit., 90.

p. 340 *Amazonia'*, Betty J. Meggers, 'Environment and culture in Amazonia', in Charles Wagley, ed., *Man in the Amazon* (Gainesville: University of Florida, 1973, 91–110), 108.

p. 342 *lighted'*, Henry Walter Bates, *The Naturalist on the River Amazons* (2 vols, London: John Murray, 1863), vol. 2, 224.

p. 342 *oppressed us'*, P. H. Fawcett, *Exploration Fawcett* (London: Hutchinson, 1953), 102.

p. 343 *in the sun?'*, Campbell, *A Land*, op. cit., 130.

Picture Credits

a = above, b = below, c = centre, l = left and r = right

2–3, 4–5, 6–7, 9a, 11bl, 12a, 12bl, 12br, 85a, 85b, 249a, 252a, 319b, 320a Photos John Hemming
9b Photo Dudu Tresca
10a Photo Michael & Patricia Fogden/Corbis
10cl Photo James Ratter
10cr Photo William Milliken
10b Photo Martin Wendler/NHPA/Photoshot
11a Photo Mason Fischer/Still Pictures
11br Photo Haroldo Palo
86a From Hans Staden, *Die wahrhaftige Historie der wilden, nackten, grimmigen Menschenfresser-Leute*, Marburg, 1557
86b From Theodor de Bry, *Historia Americae sive Novi Orbis*, Frankfurt, 1634, vol. XIII
87a From Felipe Guaman Poma de Ayala, *Nueva Corónica y buen gobierno*, Peru, c. 1610
87b From Jean de Léry, *Histoire d'un voyage fait en la terre du Brésil*, La Rochelle, 1578
88a, 88b From André de Barros, *Vida do Apostólico Padre Antonio Vieyra*, Lisbon, 1745
88–89, 90 From Jean-Baptiste Debret, *Voyage Pittoresque et Historique au Brésil*, Paris, 1834–39
91a Photo Roger-Viollet
91b Engraving by Johann Moritz Rugendas, *Voyage Pittoresque dans le Brésil*, Paris, 1835
92 Moritz Richard Schomburgk, *Reisen in Britisch-Guiana in den Jahren 1840–44*, Leipzig, 1847–48
157 Francisco Requena y Herrera, *Vista del Pueblo de San Joaquin de Omaguas, Provincia de Mainas en el Río Marañón*, c. 1780. The Catholic University of America, Oliveira Lima Library, Washington, D.C.
158a, 158b From Johann Baptist von Spix and Carl Friedrich Philip von Martius, *Atlas zur Reise in Brasilien*, Munich, 1831
159b From Richard Spruce, *Notes of a Botanist on the Amazon and Andes*, Macmillan & Co., London, 1908, vol. 2, p. 41

160 From Henry Walter Bates, *The Naturalist on the River Amazons*, John Murray, London, 1863, vol. 1
162 From Franz Keller-Leuzinger, *Vom Amazonas und Madeira*, Stuttgart, 1874
163a, 164a From Carl [sic] von den Steinen, *Durch Central-Brasilien*, Leipzig, 1886, plates 250 and 173
163b Engraving by Robert Schomburgk
164b, 250br, 251a From Wade Davis, *The Lost Amazon*, p. 142, p. 20, p. 98, published by Thames & Hudson Ltd. by arrangement with Insight Editions, © 2007 the Estate of Richard Evans Schultes. All rights reserved. Used with permission
245a, 245b, 247al, 247bl, 249bl Collection Richard Collier
246b Museu Paulista of the Universidade de São Paulo, Brazil
247ar Photo Mrs Deborah Bressi
247br Photo Mansell Collection
248a From Henry C. Pearson, *The Rubber Country of the Amazon*, New York, 1911, plate 193
248b From Walter E. Hardenburg, *The Putumayo: The Devil's Paradise*, T. Fisher Unwin, London, 1912, frontispiece
249br From Richard Spruce, *Notes of a Botanist on the Amazon and Andes*, Macmillan & Co., London, 1908, vol. 1, fig. 49
250a Photo Anthony Fiala
250bl Photo by E. C. Erdis
251c National Anthropological Services, NMNH, Smithsonian Institution, Washington, D.C. Courtesy Betty J. Meggers
251b Photo Al O'Brian. Courtesy Anna C. Roosevelt
252b, 318, 319a Photos Adrian Cowell
317a Photo Janduari Simões
317b Photo Eduardo Neves
318b Photo R. F. Montgomery
320b Photo J. C. Vincent/Still Pictures

Index